INTRODUCTION

Ladbrokes

The old format of the Euro Championships was pretty much pe writes Paul Charlton. With 16 teams, it outstayed its welcome, virtually every game was a big one and stakes were high from the first whistle of the opening match. It was tense, compact and easy to follow.

So changing that format to include just under half of Europe's footballing nations at the finals could turn out to be another blow to Michel Platini's already tarnished legacy. Eight more teams inevitably dilutes the quality of the tournament and even the biggest anoraks will struggle to work out the permutations for the last 16 without a cheat sheet.

And yet. An extra 20 games – up to 51 from 31 – won't go amiss, and if qualification is any guide, there could be a few upsets along the way. In fact, the qualifying groups give real cause for optimism that this tournament could be something special.

It seemed unthinkable that Holland, third at the World Cup in Brazil, would fail to qualify, especially given the new format, but the Oranje finished behind Czech Republic, Iceland and Turkey to miss out. Iceland might be the smallest nation to qualify for a European Championship by a distance but they won't be the only supposed minnows in attendance, with Northern Ireland, Wales and Albania all joining them in France, and between them, those sides took some notable scalps along the way.

With England and Ireland through, domestic interest will be high and although a European competition there will be plenty of world-class talent on display with the likes of Cristiano Ronaldo, Zlatan Ibrahimovic, Gareth Bale, Robert Lewandowski, Mario Gotze and Andres Iniesta headlining a star-studded cast.

There's plenty to get excited about – even before you've had a bet. To that end, we've assembled a team of some of the brightest brains in betting to help give you a fighting chance of beating the bookies. Here's to a fun and profitable summer!

Edited by
Paul Charlton & Mark Langdon

Contributors
Andy Brassell, Paul Charlton, Dan Childs, Michael Cox, Mark Langdon, James Milton, John Motson, Kevin Pullein

Data
Chris Mann, David Horgan, Mark Bowers

Subeditors
Michael Brear, Alex Hilton, Dan Sait

Design
Paul Charlton

Cover design
Jay Vincent

Graphics
David Penzer, Stefan Searle

Published in 2016 by Racing Post Books
27 Kingfisher Court, Hambridge Road, Newbury RG14 5SJ

Copyright © Racing Post 2016

A catalogue record for this book is available from the British Library.

ISBN 978-1-910498-50-7

Printed and bound in Great Britain by Buxton Press

CONTENTS

Mark Langdon's team profiles & group previews

BET IN SHOP
& TRACK IN PLAY

Scan and track your shop bets only at Ladbrokes.

EURO 2016 TOURNAMENT WINNER

FRANCE	3/1	ITALY	16/1	SWITZERLAND	50/1	SLOVAKIA	100/1
GERMANY	10/3	CROATIA	25/1	UKRAINE	66/1	ROMANIA	125/1
SPAIN	5/1	AUSTRIA	33/1	CZECH REPUBLIC	80/1	REP.OF IRELAND	150/1
ENGLAND	9/1	RUSSIA	40/1	ICELAND	80/1	HUNGARY	250/1
BELGIUM	10/1	POLAND	50/1	TURKEY	80/1	ALBANIA	300/1
PORTUGAL	14/1	SWEDEN	50/1	WALES	80/1	NORTHERN IRELAND	500/1

Each-way one-half the odds a place 1, 2

Ladbrokes

WHEN THE **FUN** STOPS **STOP**™   gambleaware.co.uk

FOREWORD

Having had the privilege of covering ten World Cups and ten European Championship finals, I would venture to suggest that the Euros, as they are now called, have produced at least as many, if not more, thrilling moments as their elder brother.

The World Cup has been with us since 1930, the Euros came along 30 years later. When I first went to the finals as a commentator in 1976, there were only four teams. Even the quarter-finals had been played on a home and away basis, leaving us with West Germany, Holland, Yugoslavia (the hosts) and Czechoslovakia.

And it was the Czechs who won the trophy, thanks to the famous Panenka penalty. It was the first and only time the Germans lost a penalty shoot-out in a major tournament.

Four years later, I was in Turin for the infamous "tear gas" match when crowd trouble interrupted England's group match against Belgium. Ron Greenwood's team were eliminated at the group stage, and the Germans went on to win the final in Rome.

By now, there were eight teams in the final. But sadly, England failed to qualify in 1984. Their absence was hardly noticed as Michel Platini led the French to victory on their own soil. Remember that marvellous goal Tigana made for him against Portugal?

England were back in 1988 but Bobby Robson's team lost all three games – victims of a hat-trick by Marco Van Basten, who scored a wonder goal to help Holland win against the Russians in the final.

And 1992 was not much better. Graham Taylor's team flopped as well, summed up by the substitution of top scorer Gary Lineker against Sweden.

But along came Paul Gascoigne when the finals were held in England in 1996. Gazza's exquisite goal against Scotland at Wembley has gone down in football folklore, even though England (not for the first time or the last) stumbled in a penalty shoot-out.

Euro 2000, in my opinion the best tournament from a football point of view, was jointly staged in Holland and Belgium. The final was settled by the now extinct "Golden Goal", giving France victory over Italy, who had led with barely a minute to go in normal time.

England were penalty poopers again in Portugal in 2004, remembered surely for the arrival on the international scene of the teenage Wayne Rooney. What might have happened had he not been injured?

Absent again in 2008, England could only look on as a brilliant Spanish generation announced their arrival with a winning goal against Germany from Fernando Torres. Spain went on to win the World Cup in 2010 and retained the European crown in 2012.

By then, there were 16 teams in the finals, and this year there will be 24. The Euros have grown over their 56 years to include countries who did not exist for a great deal of that time. It has become a highly valued and widely publicised event renowned for the technical quality of the football. Let's hope we see a lot more of that this summer.

John Motson OBE

Hosts to emulate the class of '84

France were the last host nation to be crowned European champions and they can make home advantage count once again this summer, writes Dan Childs.

Three-time winners Germany have regressed since their 2014 World Cup triumph and could be eclipsed by France, who are possible semi-final opponents in what would be a showdown between two nations battling for tournament favouritism.

Les Bleus may need time to rediscover their competitive edge after two years of playing friendlies and results have been mixed. They have enjoyed wins over Portugal (2-1 and 1-0), Holland (3-2) and Germany (2-0) but also suffered the lows of a loss in Albania and at home to Belgium.

Those defeats came in June 2015 but they have won seven of their last eight friendlies and Didier Deschamps has a talented group of players to choose from. A favourable draw gives them time to grow into the tournament.

France are in the same group as Switzerland for the second successive tournament. At the 2014 World Cup they hammered the Swiss 5-2 and the gap between them has grown.

Switzerland were ranked sixth before Brazil 2014 but slipped to 12th after an unconvincing Euro 2016 qualification campaign that saw them finish nine points behind England.

France's progress is harder to judge but they looked a good side in Brazil and should be stronger with key players Hugo Lloris, Paul Pogba and Antoine Griezmann having

enhanced their reputations since. They lack a truly world-class centre-forward unless Karim Benzema returns to the fold but Anthony Martial is looking the part and this could be the moment he comes of age.

If France win their group they will go into the bottom half of the last-16 draw, along with Germany if they top Group C.

Nobody could deny Germany were worthy winners at the World Cup but it did not take long for their standards to slip.

The retirements of Philipp Lahm and Per Mertesacker left big holes to fill at the back and a new-look defence was exposed as Germany lost 4-2 at home to Argentina in their first post-World Cup friendly.

They failed to convince in European Championship qualifying, losing away to Poland (2-0) and Ireland (1-0), and they need to show improvement if they are to justify their position in the market.

Apart from losing Mertesacker and Lahm, there are doubts over the fitness of Mario Gotze, who spent much of the winter sidelined through injury, and Bastian Schweinsteiger, who has had an injury-hit first season with Manchester United.

Everything is in France's favour if they can rediscover their competitive edge

Their place at the head of the betting with some bookmakers seems to be based more on their reputation than anything else and, at the prices, they make no appeal.

England looked better value at 12-1 after qualifying with a 100 per cent record but that price was slashed after the Three Lions beat Germany 3-2 in Berlin. It was a thrilling performance but they were cut to 9-1.

Roy Hodgson's side should be too strong for Group B opponents Russia, Slovakia and Wales but they barely laid a glove on Spain during last November's 2-0 friendly defeat in Alicante and a tough quarter-final looks assured with Portugal, Italy and Belgium all possible opponents in the last eight.

Third favourites Spain recovered fairly well from their miserable World Cup but their qualifying group, featuring Ukraine, Slovakia, Belarus, Macedonia and Luxembourg, was not the most demanding.

They seem too reliant on injury-prone forward Diego Costa to lead the attack and there is the risk of a shaky start after landing in a tough group alongside Croatia, Czech Republic and Turkey.

In an open tournament there is scope for some of the less fancied teams to make an impact.

Austria look interestingly priced at 40-1, given their hugely impressive qualification (28 points from 30) but the each-way preference is for **Poland**, whose challenge is to be spearheaded by Robert Lewandowski.

Aside from Lewandowski, the Poles lack world-class talent but they are well organised and have improved since their group-stage exit as joint-hosts at Euro 2012.

There is less pressure on them this time and the draw has worked out well. Poland would seem to be in battle with Ukraine to finish as runners-up behind Germany in Group C and second place would probably set up a winnable last-16 encounter against Switzerland or Romania.

Progress beyond the last eight would be tough but Poland took a big scalp by beating Germany in Warsaw in qualifying, and they are capable of doing something similar in what looks a fascinating finals this summer.

Recommended bets

€€€€€ France to win Euro 2016

€€€€€ Poland to win Euro 2016 (each-way)

Don't bet against a surprise in the top scorer market

It often pays to look beyond the obvious when searching for a European Championship tournament top goalscorer, writes Mark Langdon. That could be the case again, despite the expansion to 24 teams allowing the better forwards to potentially play more games against weaker opponents.

Sweden's Tomas Brolin obliged at 40-1 in 1992 and favourite Jurgen Klinsmann was beaten by 12-1 shot Alan Shearer in 1996. Market leader Patrick Kluivert dead-heated for first place in 2000 alongside 50-1 poke Savo Milosevic and then Milan Baros claimed the top marksman honours at similar odds to the Yugoslav striker in 2004.

David Villa was a 20-1 shot in 2008, while the places included Hakan Yakin (150-1), Semih Senturk (150-1) and Roman Pavlyuchenko (100-1). Four years ago there was a six-way tie which led to betting confusion – remember that bookmakers don't pay out on the Golden Boot winner and if it's level then dead-heat rules will apply.

Mario Gomez (8-1), Cristiano Ronaldo (14-1), Fernando Torres (20-1) and Mario Balotelli (28-1) were among those who scored three goals but Alan Dzagoev and **Mario Mandzukic** also went in at much larger odds of 150-1 and 200-1 respectively.

Tournament football has a funny way of throwing up quirky stories.

For instance, in 2004 Jon Dahl Tomasson scored as many goals as Zinedine Zidane, while Marek Heinz matched the two-goal efforts of Ronaldo, Zlatan Ibrahimovic and Thierry Henry.

Thomas Muller is favourite but Germany's holistic approach to attacking means the goals could be shared around with any one of their attacking midfielders potentially going well.

Ronaldo's influence at Real Madrid isn't what it was so he doesn't appeal at short odds and his Real team-mate Karim Benzema is a long way from guaranteed to be involved at Euro 2016, which could open the door for French colleague Antoine Griezmann. Robert Lewandowski, meanwhile, will need Poland to go well long enough for the Bayern Munich goal machine to get involved.

It's not certain who will lead the line for England, Italy, Spain and Belgium at this stage and, such is the level of competition, the individual excellence of Ibrahimovic and Gareth Bale may still not get enough games to reward even each-way backers.

Nearer the start of the tournament could be the best time to get involved in one of those towards the top of the market but for now I prefer the chances of two big-priced outsiders in the shape of Mandzukic (40-1) and **Marc Janko** (66-1).

Mandzukic is proven at tournament finals. He scored three goals at the last European Championships, despite Croatia failing to qualify for the knockout stages after a difficult draw that saw them in with finalists Spain and Italy.

He also scored twice in two matches at the 2014 World Cup and he should benefit from a technically gifted midfield that includes the likes of Real Madrid's Luka Modric and Mateo Kovacic, Barcelona's Ivan Rakitic and Inter pair Ivan Perisic and Marcelo Brozovic.

Spain will be difficult group opponents for Croatia but Turkey are inconsistent and

Mario Mandzukic operates in front of a world-class midfield

Czech Republic are wide open at the back, which should be music to the ears of Mandzukic.

The powerful Juventus target-man doesn't have a huge amount of competition for the lone striking role and Mandzukic, having previously played for Bayern Munich and Atletico Madrid, is very much the man for the big occasion.

Austria could be a surprise package in France and their coach Marcel Koller demands his team play on the front foot so there could be goals to come in Group F if inexperienced duo Iceland and Hungary are caught cold by the big occasion.

The tall Janko benefits from the creativity behind him with David Alaba, Martin Harnik, Marko Arnautovic and Zlatko Junuzovic all capable of supplying the Basel bully, while right-back Florian Klein can deliver from wide so Koller's team can attack from all angles.

Janko looked as if he had given up when he went to join Sydney but he won the Australian Golden Boot last season and has scored plenty of goals since moving to Switzerland this term.

England's forward options are worth considering as the Three Lions have a decent group against Slovakia, Russia and Wales and, should they top the section, there is a nice path until the quarter-finals at the very least.

Wayne Rooney has a lamentable recent tournament record and has suffered a dip in fitness and form but that is reflected in a big price drift.

England's record goalscorer remains beloved by boss Roy Hodgson and the penalty-taking skipper seems to enjoy performing in the role of captain.

However, Tottenham's Harry Kane is favourite to be England's top scorer in France after a stunning rise up the rankings for club and country. What Kane lacks in experience he makes up for in confidence and is one for the shortlist.

Recommended bets

€€€€ Mario Mandzukic and Marc Janko tournament top scorer (each-way)

RISING STARS

Mark Langdon picks out the young players who could be set to shine brightest in France

BERNARDO SILVA

Country Portugal
Age (DOB) 21 (August 10, 1994)
Club Monaco
Position Midfield
Qualifying record P 2 **G** 0 ⬜ 0 ⬛ 0

Portugal manager Fernando Santos is a conservative character who relied on the old stagers during qualifying but he must be tempted to unleash this potential superstar.

The Monaco magician was named in the team of the tournament at the European Under-19 Championship in 2013 and again the Under-21 equivalent two years later with Fernando Chalana, a star at Euro 84, calling Silva a "mini-Messi."

Few players so young can combine the 21-year-old's grace around the pitch, eye for a pass and ability to dribble past opponents and it should surprise nobody that super agent Jorge Mendes has already snapped up this tremendous talent.

ELSEID HYSAJ

Country Albania
Age (DOB) 22 (February 20, 1994)
Club Napoli
Position Defender
Qualifying record P 6 G 0 ▢ 0 ▮ 0

It is often said that there are no bargains to be had in a world of inflated transfer prices but try telling that to Napoli, who paid Empoli less than £5m for Hysaj.

Hysaj marauds down the flank for Napoli but he is far from a one-trick pony – the 22-year-old can also defend having been coached expertly by Mauricio Sarri who took the right-back from Tuscany to Naples when he too made the switch last summer.

DELE ALLI

Country England
Age (DOB) 20 (April 11, 1996)
Club Tottenham
Position Midfield
Qualifying record P 2 G 0 ▢ 0 ▮ 0

The career of Alli has been on a rapid rise. In May 2015 he played against Yeovil for MK Dons in League One and in November Alli scored his first England goal with a screamer against France at Wembley following a summer move to Tottenham.

Alli has that rare blend of being as technically gifted as he is energetic and the sky's the limit for a midfielder who has been red-hot for Spurs this season.

MICHY BATSHUAYI

Country Belgium
Age (DOB) 22 (October 2, 1993)
Club Marseille
Position Forward
Qualifying record P 1 G 1 ▢ 0 ▮ 0

There is a lot of competition for the striking role for Belgium and Batshuayi has put

Left: Portugal's rising star Bernardo Silva looks set to boost his burgeoning reputation in France this summer

pressure on Romelu Lukaku and Christian Benteke after making a fine start to his international career.

The Marseille man scored on his debut against Cyprus and followed that with a goal in his second appearance against Italy, while the 22-year-old has enjoyed life in Ligue 1 since Marcelo Bielsa departed the club.

Bielsa never seemed to trust Batshuayi, who scored 21 league goals for Standard Liege in the 2013-14 Belgian championship.

MARCO VERRATTI

Country Italy
Age (DOB) 23 (November 5, 1992)
Club Paris Saint-Germain
Position Midfielder
Qualifying record P 5 G 0 ▢ 0 ▮ 0

For so long Italy's midfield revolved around Andrea Pirlo but now the new Pirlo is in town and ready to pull the strings.

Like Pirlo, Verratti started out as a number ten looking to create further up the pitch and – just like Pirlo – he reverted to a player who picks up the ball from the defence to orchestrate attacks.

Verratti has never played in Serie A after being snapped up by Paris Saint-Germain from Pescara in 2012 from under the noses of Juventus and a host of other clubs.

He has developed fantastically in France and at 5ft 5in is proof that size doesn't matter.

HAKAN CALHANOGLU

Country Turkey
Age (DOB) 22 (February 8, 1994)
Club Bayer Leverkusen
Position Midfield
Qualifying record P 7 G 1 ▢ 0 ▮ 0

There won't be many better free-kick takers at Euro 2016 than Calhanoglu, who says he developed his style after watching David Beckham and Juninho Pernambucano.

The set-piece specialist has had to be patient to wait for his international chances but he started five games in qualifying for Turkey and Fatih Terim's team had a record of four wins and one draw when Calhanoglu played.

LEROY SANE
Country Germany
Age (DOB) 20 (January 11, 1996)
Club Schalke
Position Winger
Qualifying record P - **G** - ☐ - ■ -

It won't be easy for the Schalke speedster to force his way into the German squad, although Joachim Low must be tempted to chuck him in as a wildcard.

Sane served notice of his quality with a stunning goal at Real Madrid in last season's Champions League and has carried on those displays in the Bundesliga.

MATEO KOVACIC
Country Croatia
Age (DOB) 22 (6 May, 1994)
Club Real Madrid
Position Midfield
Qualifying record P 8 **G** 0 ☐ 3 ■ 0

Perhaps it is best to let former Real Madrid manager Rafael Benitez describe Kovacic's talents seeing as he worked with him on a daily basis before getting the Bernabeu boot.

Benitez said: "He is not a typical, defensive midfielder – he offers quality. He joins the attack, he's dynamic, passes the ball well and has a decent shot. He doesn't shy away from his responsibilities and that will make him a great player for Real Madrid."

ANTHONY MARTIAL
Country France
Age (DOB) 20 (December 5, 1995)
Club Manchester United
Position Forward
Qualifying record P - **G** - ☐ - ■ -

Plenty of eyebrows were raised when Manchester United paid a world-record fee for a teenager, although Martial's superb solo goal on his debut against Liverpool quietened the doubters.

Martial is a lightning-quick forward who can play on the left or through the middle and has been likened to former French international Thierry Henry.

ALVARO MORATA
Country Spain
Age (DOB) 23 (October 23, 1992)
Club Juventus
Position Forward
Qualifying record P 4 **G** 1 ☐ 1 ■ 0

If Spain are to win the European Championship they may need one of their forwards to step up and Morata certainly showed his pedigree in youth football.

Morata bagged six goals in the European Under-19 Championship in 2011 as Spain won the tournament and then collected the Under-21 Golden Boot in 2013 as he grabbed four goals in another Spanish success.

It was a big call to leave Real Madrid in 2014 but he helped Juventus to reach the Champions League final in 2015 and returned to the Bernabeu to break Real's hearts with a decisive goal in the semi-finals.

Morata has few weaknesses and could play a major role for Spain this summer.

Anthony Martial

FLIGHTS OF FANTASY

Mark Langdon highlights a few gems for Fantasy Football managers

The scoring systems vary, but generally speaking, Euro 2016 pretend gaffers will be looking for goalkeepers who keep clean sheets, defenders who chip in with goals and shutouts, midfielders that assist and forwards who bang in the goals.

GOALKEEPERS

Ciprian Tatarusanu (Romania)

A clean-sheet machine in qualifying, conceding just twice in nine matches and has proven his shot-stopping prowess in Serie A with Fiorentina.

Hannes Halldorsson (Iceland)

Six shutouts as Iceland stunned Europe's finest and his two clean sheets against Holland bodes well for matches at this level.

DEFENDERS

Pavel Kaderabek (Czech Rep)

Hoffenheim's attacking right-back scored a beauty in the European Under-21 Championship last summer and weighed in with a couple of goals in qualifying against Iceland and Holland.

Sergio Ramos (Spain)

The Real Madrid superstar isn't exactly flying under the radar but it's worth pointing out he scored a Panenka penalty against Macedonia.

MIDFIELDERS

David Alaba (Austria)

Bayern Munich's brilliant utility man is a midfield dynamo for his country and also takes penalties. Will be a bargain for anyone and so too will international team-mate Zlatko Junuzovic, who is a set-piece master.

Selcuk Inan (Turkey)

His Beckham-esque last-gasp free-kick against Iceland saw Turkey qualify automatically. Inan's three qualifying goals also included a penalty.

Vladimir Weiss (Slovakia)

Nobody made more assists than the little winger in qualifying and that tally of six was achieved in only 583 minutes.

FORWARDS

Artem Dzyuba (Russia)

He'd lose in a sprint against a tortoise but the 6ft 4in hitman came alive towards the end of qualifying. The Zenit striker scored eight times in total with six of those coming in the final four fixtures.

Marc Janko (Austria)

Giant striker who stands at 6ft 4in tall and can't fail to reach decent goalscoring heights playing as the main target in Austria's gung-ho side. Won the A-League Golden Boot in Australia last season at Sydney but has since moved to Basel.

A LACK OF TOP STRIKERS LEAVES EUROS WIDE OPEN

Zonal Marking editor Michael Cox on tournament tactics

"The strikers are South American today," said Arsene Wenger last year, "Europe doesn't produce strikers any more."

Perhaps Wenger was simply making excuses for failing to sign a genuinely world-class centre-forward, but the calibre of strikers set to start at Euro 2016 rather proves his point.

There will be arguably only two genuinely world-class centre-forwards at Euro 2016 – Poland's Robert Lewandowski and Zlatan Ibrahimovic of Sweden. If Portugal decide to deploy Cristiano Ronaldo upfront, that becomes three. And if you were being particularly charitable, you could perhaps include Mario Mandzukic, not a prolific striker but an excellent team player.

What's particularly interesting is that none of these four strikers plays for the serious favourites – indeed, the three major

tournament favourites are all struggling for genuine centre-forwards.

The holders, Spain, have continually handed opportunities to Diego Costa but he's underperformed at international level. Valencia's Paco Alcacer top-scored in qualification but, at 22, is he mature enough to lead the line at a major tournament?

For two decades they could count upon the likes of Raul, David Villa and Fernando Torres, the three top scorers in their history. Now, there's not much to get excited about.

Germany can call upon the prolific Thomas Muller but they've looked much more comfortable fielding him on the right, with Mario Gotze upfront as a false nine. Miroslav Klose broke into the side during their World Cup win two years ago, but has now retired from international football with no obvious replacement.

HODGSON SHOULD LOOK TO MAKE CLUB TIES WORK FOR ENGLAND

Roy Hodgson's World Cup 2014 XI was heavily influenced by the Liverpool side that nearly won the title – they accounted for half of his outfield players. Two years later, Tottenham look set to contribute a similar number.

Eric Dier is now the obvious candidate to play England's deep midfield role, and his habit of dropping into the defence suits Spurs' attack-minded full-backs Kyle Walker and Danny Rose. Dele Alli, meanwhile, boasts good partnerships with Dier and centre-forward Harry Kane, and successful international sides usually build upon harmonious club relationships.

Chris Smalling's centre-back partner is up for debate: Gary Cahill is a better defender, but John Stones provides the

Meanwhile, hosts France seem likely to depend upon Olivier Giroud, a handy link-up striker, but clearly not a top-class number nine. Anthony Martial is still very raw and Karim Benzema is out of favour for disciplinary reasons.

The second tier of sides, meanwhile, have options but seem undecided about their first-choice centre-forward. For Belgium, Christian Benteke started four qualifiers, Divock Origi and Romelu Lukaku three apiece.

Antonio Conte is counting upon a depressingly average group of Italian strikers – Graziano Pelle, Simone Zaza and Eder wouldn't have been close to the national side a decade ago.

Roy Hodgson could pick recent revelations Harry Kane and Jamie Vardy, but both lack international experience. Will Daniel Sturridge and Danny Welbeck get through the tournament unscathed? Will Wayne Rooney continue to be selected despite inconsistent form?

Even the genuine minnows generally have a clear weakness upfront. No Albanian scored more than once in qualifying, for example. Wales, Hungary and Ukraine have exciting wingers but poor centre-forwards. Slovakia, Romania and the Czech Republic also lack quality upfront.

Of the lesser sides, only Turkey's Burak Yilmaz could be considered a genuinely exciting centre-forward.

It means we're in a peculiar situation where the sides with the strongest defences and midfields are completely lacking a reliable, prolific, established centre-forward. Those who have a good striker have obvious flaws elsewhere. There are no perfect sides, which should make for an open, entertaining tournament.

But then, what are we looking for in terms of a tournament-winning centre-forward? The Spanish and German sides who have dominated international football in recent years have often played without a conventional striker.

It's often been common, too, for tournament-winning sides to field strikers concerned more about hold-up play rather than scoring goals, like Stephane Guivarc'h for France in 1998 or Luca Toni for Italy in 2006.

In that respect, perhaps Giroud – a master at one-touch link play, feeding on-rushing attacking midfielders – is the perfect tournament striker.

And considering Wenger's view about European strikers, it would be funny if an Arsenal forward led his side to Euro 2016 success.

Does Olivier Giroud's all-round game make him the perfect tournament striker?

passing quality Smalling lacks.

In midfield, Jordan Henderson is the natural choice on the right of a trio, despite rarely performing well for England.

Then there's the Rooney debate. England have looked better in a 4-3-1-2 rather than a 4-3-3 recently, which would suit the England captain. However, the ability of Raheem Sterling and Danny Welbeck to play both centrally and out wide shouldn't be ignored, and while Rooney will surely start the opening game, his place is far from guaranteed.

....

Michael Cox's ideal England team v Russia
(4-1-2-3) Hart; Walker, Stones, Smalling, Rose; Dier; Henderson, Alli; Welbeck, Kane, Sterling

MORE TEAMS SHOULD MEAN HIGHER SCORES

Racing Post football analyst
Kevin Pullein on how the expansion of
the European Championship from 16
to 24 teams is likely to affect results

There will be eight more teams in France than there were at Euro 2012. Widening participation inevitably widens the range of abilities among competitors, so there should be fewer finely balanced games at Euro 2016 and more contests between teams with disparate talents. When that happens there are usually fewer draws and more goals.

We can see for ourselves if we look at the history of the competition.

The European Championship is a four-yearly tournament. Between 1980 and 1992 there were eight qualifiers. From 1996 to 2012 there were 16. From this year there will be 24 – almost half the members of Uefa.

Between 1980 and 1992 there were 2.2 goals per game. From 1996 to 2012 there were 2.4 – an increase of almost ten per cent. Goals scored in extra time have been ignored, as they are for most bets.

Look at how scores changed during tournaments, though.

In eight-team tournaments goals per game in the group stage and in knockout ties were much the same – just over two.

It was only in larger tournaments that there was a difference. From 1996 to 2012 tournaments concluded with an eight-team knockout competition consisting of quarter-finals, semi-finals and the final. Overall the eight knockout qualifiers would have been broadly similar to the eight teams who started tournaments between 1980 and 1992. And goals per game were similar. In fact, scores in knockout rounds between 1996 and 2012 were slightly lower. There were 1.9 goals per game – just under two.

In the group stage there were 2.5 goals per game. In the group stage there was a larger pool of teams with a wider spread of skills.

Between 1980 and 1992, 31 per cent of group games were drawn. Between 1996 and 2012 only 22 per cent of group games were drawn.

But that is not the end. Patterns of play evolved during the group stage. The second round of fixtures produced more goals than the first, and the third round more than the second. There were more wins in the second round of fixtures than the first, and more in the third round than the second.

As a group stage wore on teams became increasingly desperate for points if they could still qualify for the knockout phase. In the last round of group games some teams had everything to play for – they needed to win. Other teams had nothing to play for – they could no longer get enough points to qualify. Put those two together and you tend to get positive results with plenty of goals.

The expansion of the Euros to 24 teams meant the stage got very crowded at the draw for the finals

From 1996 to 2012 the first set of group fixtures averaged 2.2 goals, the second set 2.5 and the third set 2.8. Thirty-two per cent of first games were drawn, 25 per cent of second games and ten per cent of third games.

In the knockout rounds play was again tense and tight. Often there was little difference in skill between opponents. The smaller the difference in skill, as a rule, the fewer goals there will be and the more likely it becomes that both teams will score the same number. Between 1980 and 2012, 42 per cent of knockout ties went into extra time and 30 per cent were decided by a penalty shootout. Two-thirds of ties that were level after 90 minutes were still level after 120 minutes.

The comparable part of Euro 2016 will be the quarter-finals onward. Expect few goals, lots of extra time and fairly regular penalty shootouts. In the groups and last 16, more games should be open and high scoring.

GROUP STAGE

GROUP A

France v Romania	8pm June 10th, Saint-Denis	ITV
Albania v Switzerland	2pm June 11th, Lens	BBC
Romania v Switzerland	5pm June 15th, Paris	ITV
France v Albania	8pm June 15th, Marseille	ITV
Romania v Albania	8pm June 19th, Lyon	BBC
Switzerland v France	8pm June 19th, Lille	BBC

GROUP B

Wales v Slovakia	5pm June 11th, Bordeaux	BBC
England v Russia	8pm June 11th, Marseille	ITV
Russia v Slovakia	2pm June 15th, Lille	BBC
England v Wales	2pm June 16th, Lens	BBC
Russia v Wales	8pm June 20th, Toulouse	ITV
Slovakia v England	8pm June 20th, Saint-Etienne	ITV

GROUP C

Poland v N Ireland	5pm June 12th, Nice	BBC
Germany v Ukraine	8pm June 12th, Lille	BBC
Ukraine N Ireland	5pm June 16th, Lyon	ITV
Germany v Poland	8pm June 16th, Saint-Denis	ITV
Ukraine v Poland	5pm June 21st, Marseille	BBC
N Ireland v Germany	5pm June 21st, Paris	BBC

GROUP D

Turkey v Croatia	2pm June 12th, Paris	ITV
Spain v Czech Rep	2pm June 13th, Toulouse	ITV
Czech Rep v Croatia	5pm June 17th, Saint-Etienne	BBC
Spain v Turkey	8pm June 17th, Nice	ITV
Czech Rep v Turkey	8pm June 21st, Lens	ITV
Croatia v Spain	8pm June 21st, Bordeaux	ITV

GROUP E

Ireland v Sweden	5pm June 13th, Saint-Denis	BBC
Belgium v Italy	8pm June 13th, Lyon	BBC
Italy v Sweden	2pm June 17th, Toulouse	ITV
Belgium v Ireland	2pm June 18th, Bordeaux	ITV
Italy v Ireland	8pm June 22nd, Lille	ITV
Sweden v Belgium	8pm June 22nd, Nice	ITV

GROUP F

Austria v Hungary	5pm June 14th, Bordeaux	ITV
Portugal v Iceland	8pm June 14th, Saint-Etienne	BBC
Iceland v Hungary	5pm June 18th, Marseille	BBC
Portugal v Austria	8pm June 18th, Paris	BBC
Iceland v Austria	5pm June 22nd, Saint-Denis	BBC
Hungary v Portugal	5pm June 22nd, Lyon	BBC

GROUP STAGE FORMAT AND TIE-BREAK CRITERIA

If teams are level on points after all the group-stage matches have been played, qualification is decided as follows: **1** points in matches between the teams in question **2** goal difference in those games **3** goals scored in those games. If there are still teams in a group that can't be seperated, the criteria listed above are reapplied exclusively to matches between those teams. If that fails, qualification is decided as follows: **4** goal difference in all group matches **5** goals scored in all group matches **6** fair play in the group stage **7** Uefa coefficients

If two teams are level on points, goals for and goals against and play each other in their final group game, their final positions within the group relative to each other are determined on penalties.

The four best third-placed teams are decided as follows: **1** points **2** goal difference **3** goals scored **4** fair play in the group stage **5** Uefa coefficients

The table to the right shows the possible pairings for the last 16 depending on which groups supply the third-placed qualifiers.

POSSIBLE LAST-16 TIES

Best thirds	1st A v	1st B v	1st C v	1st D v
ABCD	3rd C	3rd D	3rd A	3rd B
ABCE	3rd C	3rd A	3rd B	3rd E
ABCF	3rd C	3rd A	3rd B	3rd F
ABDE	3rd D	3rd A	3rd B	3rd E
ABDF	3rd D	3rd A	3rd B	3rd F
ABEF	3rd E	3rd A	3rd B	3rd F
ACDE	3rd C	3rd D	3rd A	3rd E
ACDF	3rd C	3rd D	3rd A	3rd F
ACEF	3rd C	3rd A	3rd F	3rd E
ADEF	3rd D	3rd A	3rd F	3rd E
BCDE	3rd C	3rd D	3rd B	3rd E
BCDF	3rd C	3rd D	3rd B	3rd F
BCEF	3rd E	3rd C	3rd B	3rd F
BDEF	3rd E	3rd D	3rd B	3rd F
CDEF	3rd C	3rd D	3rd F	3rd E

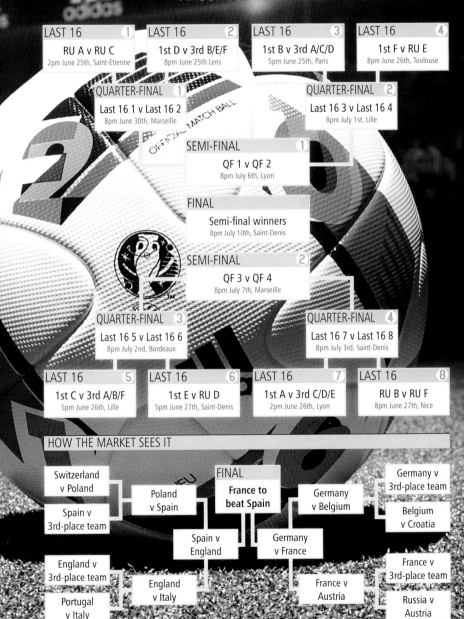

KNOCKOUT ROUNDS

LAST 16 ①
RU A v RU C
2pm June 25th, Saint-Etienne

LAST 16 ②
1st D v 3rd B/E/F
8pm June 25th Lens

LAST 16 ③
1st B v 3rd A/C/D
5pm June 25th, Paris

LAST 16 ④
1st F v RU E
8pm June 26th, Toulouse

QUARTER-FINAL ①
Last 16 1 v Last 16 2
8pm June 30th, Marseille

QUARTER-FINAL ②
Last 16 3 v Last 16 4
8pm July 1st, Lille

SEMI-FINAL ①
QF 1 v QF 2
8pm July 6th, Lyon

FINAL
Semi-final winners
8pm July 10th, Saint-Denis

SEMI-FINAL ②
QF 3 v QF 4
8pm July 7th, Marseille

QUARTER-FINAL ③
Last 16 5 v Last 16 6
8pm July 2nd, Bordeaux

QUARTER-FINAL ④
Last 16 7 v Last 16 8
8pm July 3rd, Saint-Denis

LAST 16 ⑤
1st C v 3rd A/B/F
5pm June 26th, Lille

LAST 16 ⑥
1st E v RU D
5pm June 27th, Saint-Denis

LAST 16 ⑦
1st A v 3rd C/D/E
2pm June 26th, Lyon

LAST 16 ⑧
RU B v RU F
8pm June 27th, Nice

HOW THE MARKET SEES IT

Switzerland v Poland

Poland v Spain

FINAL
France to beat Spain

Germany v Belgium

Germany v 3rd-place team

Spain v 3rd-place team

Belgium v Croatia

Spain v England

Germany v France

England v 3rd-place team

England v Italy

France v Austria

France v 3rd-place team

Portugal v Italy

Russia v Austria

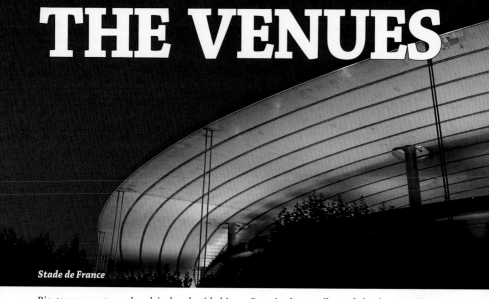

THE VENUES

Stade de France

Big tournaments go hand in hand with big building projects and France's football grounds have undergone some serious gentrification ahead of the Euros, with the bill coming in at around €1.6bn, writes Paul Charlton.

There was a similar programme of work ahead of the 1998 World Cup, with the Stade de France, newly built for that tournament, the only ground being used this summer not to have been the subject of major renovation works or built from scratch.

Lyon, Bordeaux, Marseille, Saint-Etienne, Lens and Toulouse all hosted matches in 1998 and all will do so again, with Lyon and Bordeaux – along with Lille and Nice – boasting brand new stadiums.

At 33,000 seats, the historic Stadium de Toulouse, built in its turn for the 1938 World

Cup, is the smallest of the host stadiums, while the four new grounds have an average capacity of over 46,000.

To put the scale of the work in context, only three stadiums with a capacity of more than 30,000 have been built in France since 1945 – Parc des Princes, rebuilt in 1972, La Beaujoire in Nantes, built in 1984, and Stade de France, which was completed in 1998.

Between them the ten venues offer nearly half a million seats but whether they will be filled when the tournament is over remains to be seen. In recent years, more than half the clubs in Ligue 1 have averaged attendances of fewer than 20,000 and by the end of 2015, the new grounds in Nice, Lille and Bordeaux had all had plenty of empty seats on matchdays.

EURO 2016 STADIUMS

Stadium	City	Games	Capacity	Type of work	Cost	Finished
Stade de France	Saint-Denis	7	80,000	Minor renovation		
Stade Velodrome	Marseille	6	67,000	Major renovation	€267m	Oct 2014
Stade de Lyon	Lyon	6	59,000	New build	405m	Jan 2016
Stade Pierre Mauroy	Lille	6	50,000	New build	324m	Aug 2012
Parc des Princes	Paris	5	45,000	Major renovation	75m	Aug 2015
Stade de Bordeaux	Bordeaux	5	42,000	New build	184m	May 2015
Stade Geoffroy Guichard	Saint-Etienne	4	42,000	Major renovation	75m	Jan 2015
Stade de Nice	Nice	4	35,000	New build	204m	Sept 2013
Stade Bollaert-Delelis	Lens	4	35,000	Major renovation	70m	Aug 2015
Stadium de Toulouse	Toulouse	4	33,000	Major renovation	35m	Jan 2016

Stade de France

Parc des Princes

Stadium de Toulouse

Stade Velodrome

Stade Bollaert-Delelis

Stade de Lyon

Stade de Nice

Stade Pierre Mauroy

Stade Geoffroy-Guichard

Nouveau Stade de Bordeaux

HOSTS FULL OF AMBITION

European football expert Andy Brassell takes the temperature of the host nation and finds France preparing for a party

"The aim, it's to win it." Speaking to L'Equipe in early March Noel Le Graet, the president of the Federation Francaise de Football, could not have been any clearer about France's ambitions for Euro 2016.

He has every reason to be bold – in a tournament lacking an overwhelming favourite, Les Bleus have the players to trouble the very best, even with the continuing legal troubles of Real Madrid's Karim Benzema putting the forward's participation in jeopardy. Juventus midfielder Paul Pogba is expected to take centre stage in a group bursting with exciting young talent, including Antoine Griezmann and Anthony Martial.

Even in a country which has traditionally had a love-hate relationship with its national team, optimism is high and supporters realise that they have a great deal of quality at their disposal. The measure of that is the realisation that a players with the ability of Alexandre Lacazette is likely to miss the final 23-man cut.

After a shaky first half of 2015, a clutch of wins towards its end, including victory over world champions Germany, has calmed the nerves. And that positivity is expected to spill over into the tournament, with the nation expecting their side to cruise through a group containing Switzerland, Albania and Romania. Le Graet and the federation have worked hard to mobilise support in recent times, creating an official supporters group which, despite being founded just over two years ago, already has 120,000 members and promises that France should get noisy support wherever they go.

Security has of course become a concern in the light of the November terrorist attacks on Paris – which coincided with the Germany friendly – and extensive planning continues to go towards fan safety and enjoyment.

In terms of stadia and infrastructure, l'Hexagone couldn't be better prepared. The last of the ten host venues to be completed, Lyon's 59,000-capacity Parc OL, opened its doors to some fanfare in January with president Francois Hollande in attendance and Will.I.Am DJing live on the pitch.

If France win their group as expected, they'll play their last 16 tie at Parc OL, and they will also be at Lille's Stade Pierre Mauroy and the spectacularly redeveloped Stade Velodrome in Marseille, which is perhaps the jewel in the country's Euro crown.

With coach Didier Deschamps, a key member of 1998's World Cup winners, a hard but fair presence at the helm, there promises to be less in-fighting during the squad than at recent tournaments. France is ready to be proud of its footballers again.

EURO 2016 JURY

Michael Brear
Racing Post Sport

BACK AUSTRIA

Why Austria?
It's early days in David Alaba's career but the phenomenally versatile 23-year-old has the whiff of an all-time great and can guide a surprisingly potent side to glory.

Which fancied team do you think might be vulnerable?
France, who could be unsettled and under enormous pressure.

Name a potential dark horse?
Ukraine keep it tight, have good team spirit and trickery on the wings. They unluckily lost their opener to Slovakia in qualifying and faced a battle to get back on track, but they kept their cool in the playoffs.

Who do you fancy to be top scorer?
Artem Dzyuba has been banging in the goals during qualifying and at club level for Zenit. He looks value to make a big impact for improving Russia.

What's the best bet for the group stage?
Austria-Portugal straight forecast. The resolute Austrians are capable of shutting down Cristiano Ronaldo in Group F's key head-to-head battle.

Paul Charlton
Racing Post

BACK FRANCE

Why France?
With home advantage, a kind draw and some serious talent in their squad, Les Bleus can build on a promising performance at the last World Cup.

Which fancied team do you think might be vulnerable?
The cliche says you should never write off the Germans, but they could have a very tough route to the final, with Belgium and France possible opponents in the quarters and semis, and they've thrown in a few dodgy results since the World Cup win two years ago.

Name a potential dark horse?
The extra games in the longer format might favour the fancied teams so I'm not looking too far down the list. Croatia have some real quality.

Who do you fancy to be top scorer?
Harry Kane can grab the bull by the horns – England are potential semi-finalists and he goes to France in great form.

What's the best bet for the group stage?
A Spain-Croatia dual forecast in Group D.

Dan Childs
Racing Post Sport

BACK FRANCE

Why France?
France have twice won tournaments as hosts. Hugo Lloris is among the top keepers on show and Paul Pogba one of the best midfielders.

Which fancied team do you think might be vulnerable?
Germany made hard work of qualifying, finishing one point above Poland, and have had problems with their defence since winning the World Cup.

Name a potential dark horse?
Poland are well organised and Robert Lewandowski is a world-class striker. They beat Germany 2-0 in qualifying and are capable of springing more surprises.

Who do you fancy to be top scorer?
Belgium could go well and may rely heavily on goals from Romelu Lukaku, who has had a great Premier League season for an ordinary Everton side.

What's the best bet for the group stage?
England can win Group B at the expense of Russia, Slovakia and Wales. They made short work of average opposition in qualifying and can do so again.

Steve Davies
Racing Post Sport

 **BACK GERMANY**

Why Germany?

Ignore friendly results, Joachim Low's men are the best team in the world. More potent than most in attack where they have countless options, they are also seasoned tournament performers.

Which fancied team do you think might be vulnerable?

Spain. They'll be as easy on the eye as usual but a lack of goals – as witnessed in the March friendlies – will ultimately be their undoing.

Name a potential dark horse?

Austria – a team on the up with bags of Bundesliga class and a top, top head coach in Marcel Koller.

Who do you fancy to be top scorer?

Aleksandr Kokorin. There are good grounds for thinking Russia will get five matches and they'll be looking to the Zenit St Petersburg striker (and national penalty taker) to fire for them.

What's the best bet for the group stage?

Austria to win Group F. They have little to fear from Portugal in a section that looks like a straight head-to-head.

James Milton
Racing Post Sport

BACK SPAIN

Why Spain?

They responded to their disappointing defence of the World Cup in Brazil with a ruthless qualifying campaign. The defence looks back to its miserly best – Spain won each of their last eight qualifiers to nil – and the squad is packed with creative talent.

Which fancied team do you think might be vulnerable?

France's team is just short of top-class in key areas and home advantage may not be as big a factor as the betting suggests.

Name a potential dark horse?

Italy went through qualifying unbeaten and their first XI is shaping up nicely.

Who do you fancy to be top scorer?

This market is wide open as usual, but backers of Robert Lewandowski each-way could be in a strong position by the end of the group stage.

What's the best bet for the group stage?

The Spain-Croatia dual forecast in Group D – both should outclass Turkey and Czech Republic, who have a terrible defensive record.

Dave Wright
Ladbrokes

BACK FRANCE

Why France?

The hosts not only benefit from playing on home turf but also from being in Group A, with the possibility of reaching the semi-finals without playing another group winner.

Which fancied team do you think might be vulnerable?

Spain may struggle to retain the trophy. Their group looks tough and La Roja's slow-paced passing game has become a bit predictable and easy to defend against.

Name a potential dark horse?

Austria had a great qualifying campaign and with many players hitting fine form this season they could be a tough test for any team.

Who do you fancy to be top scorer?

Thomas Muller. The German always gets goals at tournaments and with a relatively easy group he could fill his boots early on.

What's the best bet for the group stage?

Austria to win Group F. Portugal have never really convinced me and rely too much on Cristiano Ronaldo. The group is there for Austria's taking.

EURO 2016 WINNER

	bet365	BetBright	Betfair	Betfred	Betway	Boyles	Coral	Hills	Lads	Power	Sky Bet
France	10-3	16-5	10-3	3	3	3	11-4	3	3	**7-2**	10-3
Germany	3	16-5	10-3	10-3	10-3	10-3	10-3	**7-2**	10-3	**7-2**	**7-2**
Spain	5	5	**11-2**	**11-2**	**11-2**	**11-2**	**11-2**	**11-2**	5	**11-2**	**11-2**
England	8	8	8	9	9	9	9	9	9	9	9
Belgium	11	10	10	10	11	10	**12**	11	10	11	**12**
Italy	16	16	16	16	16	16	**18**	16	16	**18**	16
Portugal	**25**	16	18	20	20	16	20	16	14	14	18
Croatia	**33**	26	**33**	28	25	28	25	25	25	25	25
Austria	33	**40**	33	**40**	33	33	33	33	33	33	**40**
Poland	**66**	50	40	50	40	50	50	50	50	**66**	**66**
Switzerland	**66**	**66**	33	**66**	50	50	50	50	50	**66**	33
Russia	**66**	65	**66**	**66**	**66**	**66**	40	**66**	40	50	40
Wales	50	60	**80**	**80**	66	66	**80**	66	**80**	66	**80**
Turkey	**80**	70	66	**80**	**80**	**80**	**80**	66	**80**	**80**	**80**
Sweden	100	99	80	**100**	80	80	**100**	**100**	50	80	66
Ukraine	100	66	50	**100**	**100**	80	50	**100**	66	66	66
Czech Rep	80	70	66	**100**	**100**	80	80	80	80	80	**100**
Iceland	80	70	**150**	100	80	80	100	80	80	80	**150**
Ireland	**150**	80	66	125	125	**150**	**150**	100	**150**	125	**150**
Slovakia	**150**	100	100	**150**	125	**150**	**150**	**150**	100	**150**	**150**
Romania	**250**	100	80	125	200	125	150	150	125	100	80
Hungary	**350**	220	250	250	250	200	**350**	250	250	200	250
N Ireland	**500**	450	350	**500**	250	400	400	250	**500**	**500**	250
Albania	**500**	450	**500**	**500**	250	400	250	300	300	300	250

Win or each-way. See individual bookmakers for terms. Prices correct March 31

HOW TO READ THE DATA

Unless noted otherwise, all stats in team profiles and group pages are 90 minutes only and include competitive matches since the final of Euro 2012. Stats from Soccerbase.com & Opta. Stats correct as of March 31.

Typical starting XI The most frequent starters in qualifying in the formation most likely to be used at Euro 2016. For France that was most starts in 2015 friendlies.
Possession The percentage of game time that each team had possession of the ball, based on passes made. Only games in qualifying for Euro 2016 included.
Shots on target Any attempt on goal that goes into the net or is only prevented from going into the net by a goalkeeper's save or a defender who is the last man. Only games in qualifying for Euro 2016 are included.
Shots off target Any attempt on goal where the ball is going wide of the target, misses or hits the woodwork. Only games in qualifying for Euro 2016 included.
Corners Only corners taken are counted. Corners

awarded but not taken do not count for betting purposes. Only games in qualifying for Euro 2016 included.
Profit & loss figures Figures are based on a £1 level stake backing each outcome to best prices published in the Racing Post on the day of the match. Only games in qualifying for Euro 2016 included.
Players used in qualifying GK goalkeeper, DEF defender, MID midfielder, ATT attacker. Clubs current as of March 31. Age shows players age on the day of the opening match of Euro 2016. P matches played, G goals scored.
Correct scores The number of occurrences of each scoreline since the final of Euro 2012 in friendlies and competitive matches. Goals scored by the team being

EURO 2016 TOP SCORER

	bet365	Betfair	Betfred	Betway	Boyles	Coral	Hills	Lads	Power	Sky Bet
T Muller (GER)	7	8	7	8	7	6	7	7	7	7
C Ronaldo (POR)	7	7	9	9	7	7	7	8	7	7
K Benzema (FRA)	10	10	10	10	10	10	-	10	8	10
A Griezmann (FRA)	12	12	12	10	10	12	14	11	12	12
R Lewandowski (POL)	16	10	14	14	14	16	14	11	16	12
O Giroud (FRA)	16	14	14	16	14	16	12	14	12	16
R Lukaku (BEL)	12	18	16	16	14	16	16	16	16	16
H Kane (ENG)	16	16	20	16	20	16	16	18	20	18
D Costa (ESP)	20	12	20	20	20	16	20	20	16	20
M Gotze (GER)	25	20	25	20	25	-	25	25	20	25
Z Ibrahimovic (SWE)	33	25	25	25	25	22	25	25	25	25
P Alcacer (ESP)	20	25	25	22	25	22	25	33	22	33
A Morata (ESP)	33	33	20	25	25	16	25	33	25	28
C Benteke (BEL)	33	20	33	33	25	16	33	25	33	25
M Mandzukic (CRO)	33	33	33	33	33	25	40	33	33	33
M Janko (AUS)	66	66	66	66	66	40	66	66	50	66

Win or each-way. See individual bookmakers for terms. Others available on request. Prices correct March 31

ODDS CONVERSION

Odds-on As %	Decimal	Fractional	Odds-against Decimal	As %	Odds-on As %	Decimal	Fractional	Odds-against Decimal	As %
50.00%	2.00	Evens	2.00	50.00%	69.23%	1.44	9-4	3.25	30.77%
52.38%	1.91	11-10	2.10	47.62%	71.43%	1.40	5-2	3.50	28.57%
54.55%	1.83	6-5	2.20	45.45%	72.22%	1.38	13-5	3.60	27.78%
55.56%	1.80	5-4	2.25	44.44%	73.33%	1.36	11-4	3.75	26.67%
57.89%	1.73	11-8	2.38	42.11%	73.68%	1.36	14-5	3.80	26.32%
60.00%	1.67	6-4	2.50	40.00%	75.00%	1.33	3-1	4.00	25.00%
61.90%	1.62	13-8	2.63	38.10%	76.92%	1.30	10-3	4.33	23.08%
63.64%	1.57	7-4	2.75	36.36%	77.78%	1.29	7-2	4.50	22.22%
65.22%	1.53	15-8	2.88	34.78%	80.00%	1.25	4-1	5.00	20.00%
66.67%	1.50	2-1	3.00	33.33%	81.82%	1.22	9-2	5.50	18.18%
					83.33%	1.20	5-1	6.00	16.67%

profiled are given first, no matter where the game was played. For example, since the final of Euro 2012, France have won one and lost two competitive matches 1-0.

Half-time/full-time double results The number of occurrences of each possible combination of results at half time and full time. For example, win/win means that a team was ahead at both half time and full time. Includes stats for the related win/score by half markets.

Clean sheets Games in which the team conceded no goals.

Win to nil Games won without conceding a goal.

Fail to score Games in which the team did not score a goal. Competitive games since the final of Euro 2012.

Lose to nil Games lost without scoring.

Under & over goals Games in which the total number of match goals was smaller than or greater than 1.5, 2.5, 3.5 and 4.5, the typical betting lines.

Both teams to score Games in which both teams

scored, both teams scored and the team being profiled won, both teams scored and the team lost.

Goal times Numbers of goals scored and conceded at different points in time throughout their matches.

If... Number of games in which a team went on to win, lose or draw after scoring or conceding the first goal.

Goalscorers Total number of goals scored, first goal denotes first goal of game (own goals do not count – if an own goal is the first goal of a game, the next subsequent goal counts for betting purposes), anytime denotes any goalscoring appearance. Only games in qualifying for Euro 2016 included.

Bookings Number of yellow cards awarded and number of red cards awarded. For spread betting average make-ups, yellow cards count as 10pts, red cards 25pts, with a maximum of 35pts per player per game. Only games in qualifying for Euro 2016 included.

French are fancied to get group favourite backers off to a flyer

There were plenty of shocks in the Euro 2016 qualifying phase but normal service can be resumed at the finals. Most of the big nations should make no mistake in reaching the knockout stages with the expansion to 24 teams allowing more margin for error.

The market looks to have called most of the groups correctly and it would be no surprise if Group A finished in betting order, with **France** winning the section from Switzerland and Romania, who should battle it out for the second automatic qualifying place. Albania are odds-on for bottom spot.

From a punting point of view there seems little reason to look further than the obvious – a bet on France to top Group A. They should be bankers for accumulator bets.

France and Switzerland were drawn together in the last World Cup, finishing one and two with a 5-2 win for Les Bleus proving pivotal in the race for top spot.

Not a huge amount has changed since then and as long as France deal with the pressure of being hosts it should be a comfortable start, even if Karim Benzema's off-field issues keep him out of Didier Deschamps' 23-man squad. Antoine Griezmann and Olivier Giroud should score the goals – at least before the really serious stuff starts – and a midfield containing Paul Pogba and Blaise Matuidi is nicely balanced.

Skipper Hugo Lloris is a dependable last line of defence, although the goalkeeper is unlikely to be overworked by Romania and Albania, who scored just 18 goals between them in their 17 completed qualifiers.

The group's two outsiders are likely to concentrate on clean sheets in a bid to make the knockouts but both could be on the verge of elimination before their meeting in the final round of group games on June 19.

Switzerland struggled in qualifying before finishing second to England but this is a side who took Argentina to extra-time in the World Cup last 16 and they are superior in the final third to Romania and Albania, with Xherdan Shaqiri and Granit Xhaka – both of whom could have played for Albania – players of considerable talent.

Recommended bet

€€€€€ France to win Group A

TO WIN THE GROUP

	bet365	BetBright	Betfair	Betfred	Betway	Boyles	Coral	Hills	Lads	Power	Sky Bet
France	4-11	1-3	4-11	3-10	4-11	2-7	2-7	2-7	1-3	4-11	**2-5**
Switzerland	7-2	4	**9-2**	7-2	4	4	**9-2**	4	**9-2**	4	4
Romania	8	17-2	8	**10**	7	**10**	**10**	9	8	13-2	15-2
Albania	25	22	25	**28**	20	**28**	20	25	16	20	16

Win only. Prices correct March 31

| FRA v ROM | ALB v SWI | | ROM v SWI | FRA v ALB | | ROM v ALB | FRA v SWI |
| 8PM JUNE 10 | 2PM JUNE 11 | ▶▶▶ | 5PM JUNE 15 | 8PM JUNE 15 | ▶▶▶ | 8PM JUNE 19 | 8PM JUNE 19 |

Olivier Giroud headed the opening goal when France beat Switzerland 5-2 in the 2014 World Cup

TO QUALIFY

	bet365	BetBright	Betfair	Betfred	Betway	Boyles	Coral	Hills	Lads	Power	Sky Bet
France	1-50	1-50	1-50	1-66	1-50	1-100	1-50	1-80	1-50	**1-33**	**1-33**
Switzerland	1-4	2-9	2-7	1-4	2-7	1-4	2-9	1-4	**1-3**	2-7	2-7
Romania	4-6	3-4	4-6	4-6	8-11	8-13	4-5	**5-6**	8-11	4-9	8-13
Albania	7-4	19-10	**2**	7-4	13-8	**2**	6-4	15-8	17-10	13-8	15-8

Win only. Prices correct March 31

8PM JUNE 10 – FRANCE V ROMANIA

	bet365	Betfair	Betfred	Betway	Boyles	Coral	Hills	Lads	Power	Sky Bet
France	1-3	2-5	4-11	4-11	4-11	4-11	2-5	7-20	2-5	**4-9**
Draw	**7-2**	3	**7-2**	**7-2**	10-3	17-5	3	10-3	10-3	10-3
Romania	**10**	6	17-2	19-2	17-2	7	7	9	13-2	6

Best prices as decimal odds: France 1.44, draw 4.5, Romania 11. 101%. Prices correct March 31

2PM JUNE 11 – ALBANIA V SWITZERLAND

	bet365	Betfair	Betfred	Betway	Boyles	Coral	Hills	Lads	Power	Sky Bet
Switzerland	4-6	8-13	8-13	13-20	8-13	8-13	13-20	13-20	8-13	8-13
Draw	13-5	5-2	13-5	13-5	13-5	5-2	23-10	5-2	13-5	**11-4**
Albania	9-2	9-2	**5**	**5**	19-4	9-2	9-2	19-4	9-2	9-2

Switzerland 1.67, draw 3.75, Albania 6. 103%

5PM JUNE 15 – ROMANIA V SWITZERLAND

	Betfair	Betfred	Power
Switzerland	9-10	**10-11**	**10-11**
Draw	12-5	**5-2**	12-5
Romania	**3**	**3**	14-5

Switzerland 1.91, draw 3.5, Romania 4. 106%

8PM JUNE 15 – FRANCE V ALBANIA

	Betfair	Betfred	Power
France	2-11	**1-5**	**1-5**
Draw	5	**11-2**	5
Albania	**14**	12	11

France 1.2, draw 6.5, Albania 15. 105%

8PM JUNE 19 – SWITZERLAND V FRANCE

	Betfair	Betfred	Power
France	**10-11**	9-10	**10-11**
Draw	**23-10**	**23-10**	**23-10**
Switzerland	3	**10-3**	3

France 1.91, draw 3.3, Switzerland 4.33. 106%

8PM JUNE 19 – ROMANIA V ALBANIA

	Betfair	Betfred	Power
Romania	**10-11**	**10-11**	**10-11**
Draw	23-10	**12-5**	23-10
Albania	3	**16-5**	3

Romania 1.91, draw 3.4, Albania 4.2. 106%

Albania's Taulant Xhaka

HOW THEY PERFORMED IN QUALIFYING

			Home			Away							Home	Shots	
	Group/Pos	P	W	D	L	W	D	L	F	A	GD	Pts	Pos%	On	Off
France qualified as hosts															
Switzerland	Group E 2nd	10	4	0	1	3	0	2	24	8	+16	**21**	68.8	42	45
Romania	Group F 2nd	10	2	3	0	3	2	0	11	2	+9	**20**	58.2	25	40
Albania	Group I 2nd	7	1	1	2	2	1	0	7	5	+5	**11**	48.8	13	22

Pos% percentage of total possession, **Shots on/off** shots on and off target, **Shots On%** percentage of shots on target (accuracy), **Shots%** percentage of total match shots

If you backed them P/L figures based on a £1 level stake using best odds in the Racing Post on day of match. Percentages represent probablility of victory implied by the win odds. **75%+** matches where the best price

	France					Romania					Albania					Switzerland				
	W	D	L	F	A	W	D	L	F	A	W	D	L	F	A	W	D	L	F	A
France						1	4	0	5	3	2	0	0	5	1	2	3	0	9	4
						-	-	-	-	-	0	1	1	1	2	1	0	0	2	0
Romania	0	4	1	3	5						2	2	0	10	3	-	-	-	-	-
	-	-	-	-	-						1	0	0	1	0	1	0	0	1	0
Albania	0	0	2	1	5	0	2	2	3	10						0	1	3	4	8
	1	1	0	2	1	0	0	1	0	1						-	-	-	-	-
Switzerland	0	3	2	4	9	-	-	-	-	-	3	1	0	8	4					
	0	0	1	0	2	0	0	1	0	1	-	-	-	-	-					

Includes all European Championship and World Cup matches since the 2002 World Cup. 90-minute results only. Competitive results above friendly results (in grey).

Euro 2004 qualifying
October 12, 2002
Albania .... (0) 1-1 (1) ...... Switzerland

June 11, 2003
Switzerland .... (2) 3-2 (1) .... Albania

Friendly
August 20, 2003
Switzerland .... (0) 0-2 (1) .... France

Euro 2004 group stage
June 21, 2004
Switzerland .... (1) 1-3 (1) .... France

World Cup 2006 qualifying
March 26, 2005
France .... (0) 0-0 (0) .... Switzerland

October 8, 2005
Switzerland .... (1) 1-1 (1) .... France

World Cup 2006 group stage
June 13, 2006
France .... (0) 0-0 (0) .... Switzerland

Euro 2008 qualifying
September 6, 2006
Albania .... (0) 0-2 (0) .... Romania

November 21, 2007
Romania .... (1) 6-1 (0) .... Albania

Euro 2008 group stage
June 9, 2008
Romania .... (0) 0-0 (0) .... France

World Cup 2010 qualifying
October 11, 2008
Romania .... (2) 2-2 (1) .... France

September 5, 2009
France .... (0) 1-1 (0) .... Romania

Euro 2012 qualifying
September 3, 2010
Romania .... (0) 1-1 (0) .... Albania

October 9, 2010
France .... (0) 2-0 (0) .... Romania

September 2, 2011
Albania .... (0) 1-2 (2) .... France

September 6, 2011
Romania .... (0) 0-0 (0) .... France

October 7, 2011
France .... (2) 3-0 (0) .... Albania

October 11, 2011
Albania .... (1) 1-1 (0) .... Romania

Friendly
May 30, 2012
Switzerland .... (0) 0-1 (0) .... Romania

World Cup 2014 qualifying
September 11, 2012
Switzerland .... (1) 2-0 (0) .... Albania

October 11, 2013
Albania .... (0) 1-2 (0) .... Switzerland

Friendly
May 31, 2014
Albania .... (0) 0-1 (0) .... Romania

World Cup 2014 group stage
June 20, 2014
Switzerland .... (0) 2-5 (3) .... France

Friendly
November 14, 2014
France .... (0) 1-1 (1) .... Albania

June 13, 2015
Albania .... (1) 1-0 (0) .... France

The managers pose at the draw

Away	Shots		Shots overall		If you backed them							
Pos%	On	Off	On%	Shots%	P	75%+	P	50-75%	P	25-50%	P	<25%
66.8	31	37	47.1	70.8	4	+0.50	3	+1.48	2	-2.00	1	-1.00
50.0	18	30	38.1	62.4	2	+0.45	4	-2.40	3	-0.25	1	+3.33
37.3	10	6	45.1	38.9	0	0.00	1	+0.95	3	-0.62	4	+10.00

was 1-3 or shorter **50-75%** matches where the best price was longer than 1-3 and no bigger than Evens **75-25%** matches where the best price was longer than Evens and no bigger than 3-1 **<25%** matches where the best price was longer than 3-1

Only completed matches are included. See pages 228-254 for full qualifying results

FRANCE

France v Romania ʷ2-1

France won the last two major tournaments they hosted with triumphs at Euro 84 and the 1998 World Cup. On those occasions the mercurial talents of Michel Platini and Zinedine Zidane helped lift the nation to glory and anyone backing Les Bleus to complete a hat-trick of home successes at Euro 2016 will be hoping a new leader emerges from a potentially golden generation.

GROUP A

How they qualified

As hosts they have had a succession of friendlies since the World Cup. Things started well with wins over Spain and Portugal but threatened to turn nasty in 2015 with defeats by Brazil, Belgium and, most worryingly, Albania.

The 1-0 loss in Albania seemed to be a watershed moment for the man nicknamed the water carrier – coach Didier Deschamps – and Maxime Gonalons, Geoffrey Kondogbia and Alexandre Lacazette have not started for Les Bleus since.

"We got slapped in the face," said left-back Patrice Evra. "It is not acceptable. We got too comfortable after the World Cup. Now, we need to shut up and work harder."

Evra was right. Things have improved since then with seven wins in eight, and it would be wrong to read anything into November's friendly defeat in England, given that it took place immediately after the Paris attacks.

The manager

Deschamps, a tough disciplinarian, earned respect for guiding France to the quarter-finals at Brazil 2014 and signed a new contract in February 2015 to take him up to the 2018 World Cup finals.

As a player, Deschamps captained France to their World Cup and European Championship successes and also won the Champions League with Juventus. However, after the loss in Albania in June 2015, his win ratio with the national team stood at just 51 per cent – the worst record since Henri Michel in 1984-88 – before five straight victories eased concerns.

FACTFILE

FA founded 1919
www fff.fr
Head coach Didier Deschamps
National league Ligue 1
Date qualified As hosts

Typical starting XI (4-1-2-3) Lloris; Sagna, Varane, Koscielny, Evra; Schneiderlin; Pogba, Matuidi; Sissoko, Giroud, Griezmann

Strengths
☑ Home advantage and an easy path all the way to the semi-finals
☑ Pogba is destined for superstardom

Weaknesses
☒ Full-backs Sagna and Evra have seen better days
☒ Doubts over Benzema, France's most talented striker, are a problem

Star rating ☆☆☆☆☆

Fixtures

1 Romania, 8pm June 10, Saint-Denis

2 Albania, 8pm June 15, Marseille

3 Switzerland, 8pm June 19, Lille

Base Clairefontaine

PARIS

Paul Pogba could join the greats at Euro 2016

Match winners

Antoine Griezmann has starred for Atletico Madrid in the Champions League and La Liga but most eyes will be on the brilliant Paul Pogba.

Platini and Zidane have gone down in history as Juventus and France greats and Pogba, who turned 23 in March, has the potential to match those achievements for club and country. He could also quite easily become the first player to transfer for £100m with Real Madrid and Barcelona both desperate for his services.

Question marks

Whether Pogba is able to cope with the pressure at such a young age remains open for debate given that Platini turned 29 in 1984 and Zidane turned 26 during his World Cup heroics.

But the bigger concern is the cloud hanging over Karim Benzema, who was caught up in an alleged blackmail plot involving teammate Mathieu Valbuena. Benzema is clearly France's most talented striker and the Real Madrid man top-scored for his country at the World Cup in Brazil with three goals.

How to back them

France are going to be popular picks to win the tournament, particularly with a peach of a group-stage draw. They are around 2-1 to win all three group games, which is a fair bet, but the slightly odds-on quotes about them reaching the semi-finals look like a gimme, because the market suggests Les Bleus will meet a third-placed side in the last 16 and either Austria or Russia in the quarter-finals.

It's hard to pick out a top goalscorer until the Benzema issue is resolved, but 11 different players scored their 17 friendly goals in 2015, so punters should not be afraid to avoid those at the top of the market even though Griezmann is a class act.

FRANCE

EUROPEAN CHAMPIONSHIP RECORD

1960	P	W	D	L	GF	GA
● Fourth	2	0	0	2	4	7
Qualifying	4	3	1	0	17	6

1964	P	W	D	L	GF	GA
Did not qualify	-	-	-	-	-	-
Qualifying	6	2	1	3	11	10

1968	P	W	D	L	GF	GA
Did not qualify	-	-	-	-	-	-
Qualifying	8	4	2	2	16	12

1972	P	W	D	L	GF	GA
Did not qualify	-	-	-	-	-	-
Qualifying	6	3	1	2	10	8

1976	P	W	D	L	GF	GA
Did not qualify	-	-	-	-	-	-
Qualifying	6	1	3	2	7	6

1980	P	W	D	L	GF	GA
Did not qualify	-	-	-	-	-	-
Qualifying	6	4	1	1	13	7

1984	P	W	D	L	GF	GA
● Winners	5	5	0	0	14	4
Qualifying	-	-	-	-	-	-

1988	P	W	D	L	GF	GA
Did not qualify	-	-	-	-	-	-
Qualifying	8	1	4	3	4	7

1992	P	W	D	L	GF	GA
Group stage	3	0	2	1	2	3
Qualifying	8	8	0	0	20	6

1996	P	W	D	L	GF	GA
● Semi-finals	5	2	3	0	5	2
Qualifying	10	5	5	0	22	2

2000	P	W	D	L	GF	GA
● Winners	6	5	0	1	13	7
Qualifying	10	6	3	1	17	10

2004	P	W	D	L	GF	GA
Quarter-finals	4	2	1	1	7	5
Qualifying	8	8	0	0	29	2

2008	P	W	D	L	GF	GA
Group stage	3	0	1	2	1	6
Qualifying	12	8	2	2	25	5

2012	P	W	D	L	GF	GA
Quarter-finals	4	1	1	2	3	5
Qualifying	10	6	3	1	15	4

Totals	P	W	D	L	GF	GA
Finals	32	15	8	9	49	39
Qualifying	102	59	26	17	206	85

Results & goals include extra time

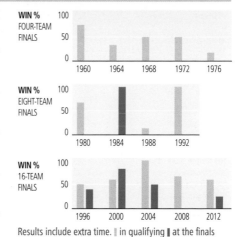

WIN % FOUR-TEAM FINALS — 1960, 1964, 1968, 1972, 1976

WIN % EIGHT-TEAM FINALS — 1980, 1984, 1988, 1992

WIN % 16-TEAM FINALS — 1996, 2000, 2004, 2008, 2012

Results include extra time. ▌ in qualifying ▌ at the finals

LEGENDARY PLAYER

His reputation is tarnished but Denmark were the only team who could match **Michel Platini**'s tally of nine goals at Euro 84. His record haul included hat-tricks against Belgium and Yugoslavia as well as France's opener in their 2-0 win over Spain in the final.

MICHEL PLATINI   LEGEND

WORLD CUP RECORD

Year	Point of exit	Year	Point of exit
1930	Group stage	1978	Group stage
1934	First round	1982	● Fourth
1938	Quarter-finals	1986	● Third
1950	Withdrew	1990	Did not qualify
1954	Group stage	1994	Did not qualify
1958	● Third	1998	● Winners
1962	Did not qualify	2002	Group stage
1966	Group stage	2006	● Runners-up
1970	Did not qualify	2010	Group stage
1974	Did not qualify	2014	Quarter-finals

DID YOU KNOW?

France's first game in the European Championship finals — a 5-4 loss to Yugoslavia in the 1960 semis — is still the tournament's highest-scoring match

HOW FRANCE PERFORMED IN CENTRALISED FRIENDLIES*

Group I	P	W	D	L	F	A	GD	Pts
France	10	7	2	1	18	6	12	23
Portugal	10	7	0	3	12	8	4	21
Albania	10	5	3	2	12	6	6	18
Denmark	10	3	3	4	9	9	0	12
Serbia	10	2	2	6	10	16	-6	5
Armenia	10	0	2	8	5	21	-16	2

Serbia deducted 3pts

*France qualified automatically as hosts but played ten friendlies against the teams from Group I within the European Championships qualifying schedule. The league table above shows how Group I would have looked had results from these centralised friendlies counted. The squad stats below and the P&L figures to the right also use these matches

Results & prices	W	D	L
Serbia ....(0) 1-1 (1) .... France	11-10	12-5	13-5
France.......(1) 2-1 (0) .... Portugal	17-20	13-5	7-2
Armenia....(0) 0-3 (1) .... France	4-9	7-2	7-1
France.......(0) 1-1 (1) ......Albania	1-4	5-1	14-1
France.......(2) 2-0 (0) ....Denmark	8-13	3-1	6-1
Albania .....(1) 1-0 (0) .... France	8-15	31-10	13-2
Portugal ...(0) 0-1 (0) .... France	7-4	23-10	7-4
France.......(2) 2-1 (1) ....Serbia	8-15	3-1	15-2
France.......(1) 4-0 (0) .... Armenia	2-7	11-2	14-1
Denmark...(0) 1-2 (2) ...... France	11-10	13-5	5-2
Profit & loss	**2.58**	**-0.60**	**-2.50**

Figures based on a £1 level stake using best odds in the Racing Post on day of match. W shows win price, whether home or away, L the price of the opposition

PLAYERS USED IN CENTRALISED FRIENDLIES   CAREER   QUALIFYING

Pos		Club	Age	P	G	P	G	🟨	🟥
GK	Hugo Lloris	Tottenham	29	75	-	6	-	-	-
GK	Steve Mandanda	Marseille	31	22	-	3	-	-	-
GK	Stephane Ruffier	St-Etienne	29	3	-	1	-	-	-
DEF	Bacary Sagna	Man City	33	55	-	7	-	-	-
DEF	Benoit Tremoulinas	Seville	30	5	-	2	-	-	-
DEF	Christophe Jallet	Lyon	32	11	1	5	-	1	-
DEF	Eliaquim Mangala	Man City	25	7	-	3	-	-	-
DEF	Kurt Zouma	Chelsea	21	2	-	2	-	-	-
DEF	Laurent Koscielny	Arsenal	30	27	-	3	-	-	-
DEF	Lucas Digne	Roma	22	12	-	3	-	-	-
DEF	Mamadou Sakho	Liverpool	26	28	2	2	-	1	-
DEF	Mathieu Debuchy	Arsenal	30	27	2	1	-	-	-
DEF	Patrice Evra	Juventus	35	71	-	4	-	-	-
DEF	Raphael Varane	Real Madrid	23	28	2	10	-	-	-
DEF	Jeremy Mathieu	Barcelona	32	5	-	2	-	-	-
DEF	Mapou Yanga-Mbiwa	Lyon	27	4	-	1	-	-	-
DEF	Layvin Kurzawa	Paris St-Germain	24	2	-	1	-	-	-
MID	Blaise Matuidi	Paris St-Germain	29	42	7	8	2	-	-
MID	Dimitri Payet	West Ham	29	17	2	5	-	-	-
MID	Geoffrey Kondogbia	Inter	23	5	-	3	-	-	-
MID	Lassana Diarra	Marseille	31	33	-	1	-	-	-
MID	Mathieu Valbuena	Lyon	31	52	8	9	1	1	-
MID	Maxime Gonalons	Lyon	27	7	-	1	-	-	-
MID	Morgan Schneiderlin	Man Utd	26	15	-	8	-	1	-
MID	Moussa Sissoko	Newcastle	26	35	1	8	-	1	-
MID	Paul Pogba	Juventus	23	29	5	7	2	1	-
MID	Yohan Cabaye	Crystal Palace	30	44	4	6	1	1	-
MID	Remy Cabella	Marseille	26	4	-	2	-	-	-
MID	Joshua Guilavogui	Wolfsburg	25	7	-	1	-	-	-
ATT	Alexandre Lacazette	Lyon	25	10	1	6	1	-	-
ATT	Anthony Martial	Man Utd	20	8	-	4	-	-	-
ATT	Antoine Griezmann	Atl Madrid	25	26	7	9	3	-	-
ATT	Karim Benzema	Real Madrid	28	81	27	7	3	-	-
ATT	Nabil Fekir	Lyon	22	5	1	3	-	-	-
ATT	Olivier Giroud	Arsenal	29	47	14	6	3	-	-
ATT	Paul Ntep	Rennes	23	2	-	1	-	-	-
ATT	Loic Remy	Chelsea	29	31	7	2	1	-	-
ATT	Andre-Pierre Gignac	Tigres	30	25	7	3	1	-	-

CORRECT SCORES

	Competitive	Friendly
1-0	1	3
2-0	1	3
2-1	-	4
3-0	3	1
3-1	2	-
3-2	-	1
4-0	-	2
4-1	-	-
4-2	1	1
4-3	-	-
0-0	2	2
1-1	1	3
2-2	-	-
3-3	-	-
4-4	-	-
0-1	2	3
0-2	1	1
1-2	-	1
0-3	-	1
1-3	-	1
2-3	-	-
0-4	-	-
1-4	-	-
2-4	-	-
3-4	-	1
Other	1	2

Since Euro 2012

HALF-TIME/FULL-TIME DOUBLE RESULTS

Win/Win	6	40%
Draw/Win	2	13%
Lose/Win	1	7%
Win/Draw	0	0%
Draw/Draw	2	13%
Lose/Draw	1	7%
Win/Lose	0	0%
Draw/Lose	2	13%
Lose/Lose	1	7%

Win 1st half	6	40%
Win 2nd half	8	53%
Win both halves	4	27%
Goal both halves	7	47%

Overall
- **Win** 60%
- **Draw** 20%
- **Lose** 20%

WIN 60%

Overall: W9, D3, L3 in 15 competitive games since Euro 2012

CLEAN SHEETS

7 (47%) **Clean sheets** 8 (53%) ✓ ✗

5 (33%) **Win to nil** 10 (67%) ✓ ✗

5 (33%) **Fail to score** 10 (67%) ✓ ✗

3 (20%) **Lose to nil** 12 (80%) ✓ ✗

UNDER & OVER GOALS

10 (67%) **Over 1.5** 5 (33%) ✓ ✗

7 (47%) **Over 2.5** 8 (53%) ✓ ✗

4 (27%) **Over 3.5** 11 (73%) ✓ ✗

2 (13%) **Over 4.5** 13 (87%) ✓ ✗

BOTH TEAMS TO SCORE

5 (33%) **Both score** 10 (67%) ✓ ✗

4 (27%) **& win** 11 (73%) ✓ ✗

0 (0%) **& lose** 15 (100%) ✓ ✗

In 15 competitive games since Euro 2012

GOAL TIMES

Total match goals by half

9 (75%) **1st half** 3 (25%)
F ▮▮▮▮▮▮ A

19 (70%) **2nd half** 8 (30%)
F ▮▮▮▮▮▮ A

Goals for & against by half

9 (32%) **For** 19 (68%)
1st ▮▮▮ ▮▮▮▮▮ 2nd

3 (27%) **Against** 8 (73%)
1st ▮▮▮ ▮▮▮▮▮ 2nd

● GOALS FOR ● GOALS AGAINST

	0-9	10-18	19-27	28-36	37-45	46-54	55-63	64-72	73-81	82-90
For	1	2	2	1	3	4	1	6	5	3
Against	0	1	1	1	0	0	3	2	1	2

In 15 competitive games since Euro 2012

IF FRANCE SCORE FIRST

They win	8	▮▮▮▮▮▮▮▮	100%
Draw	0		0%
They lose	0		0%

In 15 competitive games since Euro 2012

IF FRANCE CONCEDE FIRST

They win	1	▮▮	20%
Draw	1	▮▮	20%
They lose	3	▮▮▮▮▮	60%

GROUP A

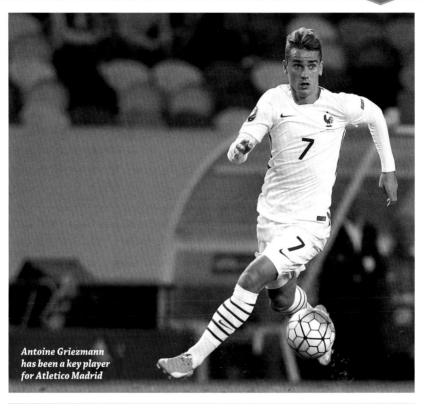

Antoine Griezmann has been a key player for Atletico Madrid

GOALSCORERS IN FRANCE'S CENTRALISED FRIENDLIES ● FIRST GOALS

	Goals		1st		Anytime		Percentage of team goals	
K Benzema	3	●●●	1	33%	2	66%	▮▮▮	17%
O Giroud	3	●●●	1	33%	2	33%	▮▮▮	17%
A Griezmann	3	●●●	1	33%	3	50%	▮▮▮	17%
B Matuidi	2	●●	1	50%	1	20%	▮▮	11%
P Pogba	2	●●	1	50%	2	50%	▮▮	11%
A Lacazette	1	●	1	100%	1	25%	▮	6%
L Remy	1	●	1	100%	1	100%	▮	6%
Y Cabaye	1	●	0	0%	1	16%	▮	6%
A Gignac	1	●	0	0%	1	100%	▮	6%
M Valbuena	1	●	0	50%	1	33%	▮	6%

In France's centralised friendlies played against the teams in Euro 2016 qualifying Group I

BOOKINGS

Matches played	10	▯ 10		▮ 0
Average make-up (▯ 10 ▮ 25)				10

In centralised friendlies against teams in Group I

CORNERS

Avg F	6.7	▮▮▮▮▮▮▮▮▮▮▮	60%
Avg A	4.4	▮▮▮▮▮▮▮	40%

In centralised friendlies. Avg match total 11.1

T hose who fondly remember Romania's run to the 1994 World Cup quarter-finals are likely to be left disappointed by the football this time. While Anghel Iordanescu, the coach from the days of Popescu, Hagi and Dumitrescu, is back in the dugout, the talented players are long gone. However, the expanded format gives them a fair chance of qualification.

How they qualified

It wasn't pretty but it was pretty effective. Romania finished second in a weak section topped by Northern Ireland, with Hungary also qualifying via the playoffs.

They had the best defence in qualifying, conceding just two goals from their ten matches, but the football was dull.

They drew five times, scoring just 11 goals. Nine of their fixtures rewarded punters who backed under 2.5 goals, with the exception a 3-0 win in the Faroe Islands on the final matchday. There were three goalless draws and both teams to score backers collected just twice.

The manager

Iordanescu left football and was involved in politics but he came out of retirement for his third stint as Romania boss after Victor Piturca quit in October 2014 for a more lucrative contract in Saudi Arabia.

A deeply religious man – those who recall USA 94 may remember Iordanescu pacing the touchline clutching a small cross – he had success in club football with Steaua Bucharest, but the manager is best remembered for guiding Romania to the quarter-finals Stateside.

"The greatest day for Romanian people since the revolution," was how Iordanescu described beating Argentina 3-2 in the last 16 before his side suffered penalty heartbreak against Sweden.

Iordanescu was also in charge at France 98, where Romania won their group ahead of England, but he is rumoured to be the lowest-paid coach at Euro 2016, earning a reported £95,000 per year.

FACTFILE

FA founded 1909
www frf.ro
Head coach Anghel Iordanescu
National league Liga I
Date qualified October 11, 2015

Typical starting XI (4-2-3-1) Tatarusanu; Papp, Grigore, Chiriches, Rat; Pintilii, Hoban; Torje, Chipciu, Maxim; Kesuru

Strengths
☑ Strong defence makes Romania difficult to beat
☑ Maxim's set-piece delivery can be their avenue to goal

Weaknesses
☒ Few players ply their trade in major European leagues
☒ There is no obvious threat from the strikers

Star rating ★☆☆☆☆

Fixtures
1 France, 8pm June 10, Saint-Denis
2 Switzerland, 5pm June 15, Paris
3 Albania, 8pm June 19, Lyon
Base Orry-la-ville

Veteran Lucian Sanmartean provides quality

Match winners

Few of Romania's players are based at major European clubs and their approach will be to nullify the opposition.

To that end, the key men will be involved in Romania's defensive organisation, and goalkeeper Ciprian Tatarusanu is the number one for strong Serie A side Fiorentina.

Cultured centre-back Vlad Chiriches had a difficult time at Tottenham and is only a substitute for Napoli but remains pivotal.

Alexandru Maxim is a set-piece specialist, while young attacking midfielder, Nicolae Stanciu, scored on his international debut against Lithuania and is having a storming season for Steaua Bucharest as a number ten.

Veteran playmaker Lucian Sanmartean's incursions off the bench will offer moments of joy in a side otherwise devoid of elegance.

Question marks

There is not a striker worthy of the name in Iordanescu's squad and at one stage during qualifying Romania went more than seven hours of play without scoring.

Romania are not helped by a limited central midfield that usually contains two destroyers in Mihai Pintilii and Ovidiu Hoban, and captain and left-back Razvan Rat will be 35 when the tournament begins.

How to back them

Opening the Euros against France will put Romania firmly in the spotlight but their fate is likely to be decided in the final contest against Albania, where a win could be enough to see them make the knockout phase.

With that in mind, taking Romania, who are unbeaten since June 2014, to be eliminated in the last 16 is one option as they could grind their way out of the group.

However, there is little attacking threat in the squad and under 2.5 goals is a solid bet in all of Romania's games, while France to win to nil at the Stade de France on June 10 is fair enough at evens.

ROMANIA

EUROPEAN CHAMPIONSHIP RECORD

1960	P	W	D	L	GF	GA
Did not qualify	-	-	-	-	-	-
Qualifying	4	1	0	3	3	7

1964	P	W	D	L	GF	GA
Did not qualify	-	-	-	-	-	-
Qualifying	2	1	0	1	3	7

1968	P	W	D	L	GF	GA
Did not qualify	-	-	-	-	-	-
Qualifying	6	3	0	3	18	14

1972	P	W	D	L	GF	GA
Did not qualify	-	-	-	-	-	-
Qualifying	9	4	3	2	15	7

1976	P	W	D	L	GF	GA
Did not qualify	-	-	-	-	-	-
Qualifying	6	1	5	0	11	6

1980	P	W	D	L	GF	GA
Did not qualify	-	-	-	-	-	-
Qualifying	6	2	2	2	9	8

1984	P	W	D	L	GF	GA
Group stage	3	0	1	2	2	4
Qualifying	8	5	2	1	9	3

1988	P	W	D	L	GF	GA
Did not qualify	-	-	-	-	-	-
Qualifying	6	4	1	1	13	3

1992	P	W	D	L	GF	GA
Did not qualify	-	-	-	-	-	-
Qualifying	8	4	2	2	13	7

1996	P	W	D	L	GF	GA
Group stage	3	0	0	3	1	4
Qualifying	10	6	3	1	18	9

2000	P	W	D	L	GF	GA
Quarter-finals	4	1	1	2	4	6
Qualifying	10	7	3	0	25	3

2004	P	W	D	L	GF	GA
Did not qualify	-	-	-	-	-	-
Qualifying	8	4	2	2	21	9

2008	P	W	D	L	GF	GA
Group stage	3	0	2	1	1	3
Qualifying	12	9	2	1	26	7

2012	P	W	D	L	GF	GA
Did not qualify	-	-	-	-	-	-
Qualifying	10	3	5	2	13	9

Totals	P	W	D	L	GF	GA
Finals	13	1	4	8	8	17
Qualifying	105	54	30	21	197	99

Results & goals include extra time

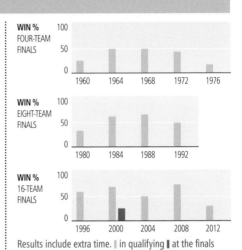

WIN % FOUR-TEAM FINALS				
1960	1964	1968	1972	1976

WIN % EIGHT-TEAM FINALS			
1980	1984	1988	1992

WIN % 16-TEAM FINALS				
1996	2000	2004	2008	2012

Results include extra time. ▌ in qualifying ▌ at the finals

LEGENDARY PLAYER

Gheorghe Hagi had everything – pace, power, touch and vision. He was one of the stars of USA 94, his three goals including an outrageous chip against Colombia during Romania's run to the quarter-finals, their best World Cup performance.

GHEORGHE HAGI   LEGEND

WORLD CUP RECORD

Year	Point of exit		Year	Point of exit
1930	Group stage		1978	Did not qualify
1934	First round		1982	Did not qualify
1938	First round		1986	Did not qualify
1950	Did not enter		1990	Round of 16
1954	Did not qualify		1994	Quarter-finals
1958	Did not qualify		1998	Round of 16
1962	Did not qualify		2002	Did not qualify
1966	Did not qualify		2006	Did not qualify
1970	Group stage		2010	Did not qualify
1974	Did not qualify		2014	Did not qualify

DID YOU KNOW?

Romania have gone 16 European qualifying matches unbeaten – only England, Austria and Italy also made it through Euro 2016 qualifying without defeat

HOW THEY QUALIFIED

Group F	P	W	D	L	F	A	GD	Pts
N Ireland	10	6	3	1	16	8	+8	21
Romania	10	5	5	0	11	2	+9	20
Hungary	10	4	4	2	11	9	+2	16
Finland	10	3	3	4	9	10	-1	12
Faroe Islands	10	2	0	8	6	17	-11	6
Greece	10	1	3	6	7	14	-7	6

Match stats in qualifying

Possession	▮▮▮▮▮▮▮▮▮▮▮	54%
Shots on target	▮▮▮▮▮▮▮▮▮▮▮▮▮	63%
Shots off target	▮▮▮▮▮▮▮▮▮▮▮▮	62%
Corners	▮▮▮▮▮▮▮▮▮▮▮▮	61%

Averages of match totals in qualifying. See pages 228-254 for full qualifying results

Results & prices

		W	D	L
Greece ...... (0) 0-1 (1) .... Romania		10-3	23-10	11-10
Romania ... (1) 1-1 (0) .... Hungary		4-5	13-5	19-4
Finland ..... (0) 0-2 (0) .... Romania		7-4	9-4	19-10
Romania ... (0) 2-0 (0) ... N Ireland		6-10	3-1	13-2
Romania ... (1) 1-0 (0) .... Faroes		2-13	8-1	25-1
N Ireland .. (0) 0-0 (0) .... Romania		7-5	11-5	12-5
Hungary.... (0) 0-0 (0) .... Romania		9-5	21-10	2-1
Romania ... (0) 0-0 (0) .... Greece		3-4	3-1	5-1
Romania ... (0) 1-1 (0) ...... Finland		8-11	13-5	5-1
Faroes .... (0) 0-3 (2) .... Romania		3-10	9-2	14-1

Profit & loss in qualifying 1.13 7.50 -10

Figures based on a £1 level stake using best odds in the Racing Post on day of match. W shows win price, whether home or away, L the price of the opposition

PLAYERS USED IN QUALIFYING

Pos		Club	Age	CAREER P	G	QUALIFYING P	G	🟨	🟥
GK	Costel Pantilimon	Watford	29	21	-	1	-	-	-
GK	Ciprian Tatarusanu	Fiorentina	30	35	-	9	-	1	-
DEF	Laszlo Sepsi	Nuremberg	29	4	-	1	-	1	-
DEF	Paul Papp	Steaua	26	18	3	6	2	1	-
DEF	Florin Gardos	Southampton	27	14	-	1	-	1	-
DEF	Dragos Grigore	Al-Sailiya	29	18	-	10	-	1	-
DEF	Vlad Chiriches	Napoli	26	39	-	10	-	1	-
DEF	Srdjan Luchin	Levski Sofia	30	11	1	1	-	-	-
DEF	Gabriel Tamas	Steaua	32	65	3	2	-	1	-
DEF	Razvan Rat	R. Vallecano	35	108	2	9	-	1	-
DEF	Dorin Goian	Asteras T.	35	60	5	1	-	-	-
DEF	Alexandru Matel	Din Zagreb	26	15	-	1	-	-	-
MID	Christian Tanase	Sivasspor	29	41	6	4	-	1	-
MID	Alexandru Maxim	Stuttgart	25	27	3	9	1	1	-
MID	Andrei Prepelita	Ludogorets	30	6	-	5	-	-	-
MID	Ovidiu Hoban	H. Beer Sheva	33	18	1	8	1	2	-
MID	Mihai Pintilii	Steaua	31	29	1	8	-	4	-
MID	Lucian Sanmartean	Al-Ittihad	36	18	-	7	-	-	-
MID	Gabriel Enache	Steaua	25	3	-	2	-	-	-
MID	Gabriel Torje	Osmanlispor	26	48	10	9	-	3	-
MID	Alexandru Chipciu	Steaua	27	20	3	7	-	3	-
MID	Adrian Popa	Steaua	27	11	-	5	-	1	-
MID	Constantin Budescu	Dalian Yifang	27	4	2	3	2	-	-
ATT	Denis Alibec	Astra Giurgiu	25	1	-	1	-	-	-
ATT	Florin Andone	Cordoba	23	5	1	3	-	-	-
ATT	Ciprian Marica	Steaua	30	70	25	1	1	1	1
ATT	Raul Rusescu	Osmanlispor	27	10	1	3	1	-	-
ATT	Bogdan Stancu	Genclerbirligi	28	39	9	7	2	1	-
ATT	Claudiu Keseru	Ludogorets	29	10	4	6	1	2	-

ROMANIA

CORRECT SCORES

	Competitive	Friendly
1-0	3	2
2-0	4	1
2-1	-	2
3-0	2	-
3-1	-	-
3-2	-	1
4-0	2	1
4-1	-	-
4-2	-	-
4-3	-	-
0-0	3	3
1-1	3	1
2-2	1	1
3-3	-	-
4-4	-	-
0-1	-	-
0-2	1	-
1-2	-	1
0-3	-	-
1-3	1	-
2-3	-	-
0-4	1	-
1-4	1	-
2-4	-	-
3-4	-	1
Other	-	-

Since Euro 2012

HALF-TIME/FULL-TIME DOUBLE RESULTS

Win/Win	8	36%
Draw/Win	3	14%
Lose/Win	0	0%
Win/Draw	1	5%
Draw/Draw	4	18%
Lose/Draw	2	9%
Win/Lose	0	0%
Draw/Lose	0	0%
Lose/Lose	4	18%

Win 1st half	9	41%
Win 2nd half	10	45%
Win both halves	5	23%
Goal both halves	12	55%

Overall
- Win 50%
- Draw 32%
- Lose 18%

WIN 50%

Overall: W11, D7, L4 in 22 competitive games since Euro 2002

CLEAN SHEETS

14 (64%)	Clean sheets	8 (36%)
✓		✗

5 (23%)	Fail to score	17 (77%)
✓		✗

11 (50%)	Win to nil	11 (50%)
✓		✗

2 (9%)	Lose to nil	20 (91%)
✓		✗

UNDER & OVER GOALS

16 (73%)	Over 1.5	6 (27%)
✓		✗

8 (36%)	Over 2.5	14 (64%)
✓		✗

6 (27%)	Over 3.5	16 (73%)
✓		✗

2 (9%)	Over 4.5	20 (91%)
✓		✗

BOTH TEAMS TO SCORE

6 (27%)	Both score	16 (73%)
✓		✗

0 (0%)	& win	22 (100%)
✓		✗

2 (9%)	& lose	20 (91%)
✓		✗

In 22 competitive games since Euro 2012

GOAL TIMES

● GOALS FOR ● GOALS AGAINST

Total match goals by half

14 (61%)	1st half	9 (39%)
F		A

18 (67%)	2nd half	9 (33%)
F		A

Goals for & against by half

14 (44%)	For	18 (56%)
1st		2nd

9 (50%)	Against	9 (50%)
1st		2nd

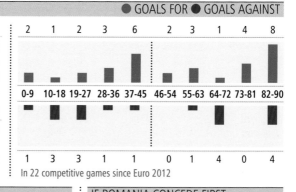

	0-9	10-18	19-27	28-36	37-45	46-54	55-63	64-72	73-81	82-90
For	2	1	2	3	6	2	3	1	4	8
Against	1	3	3	1	1	0	1	4	0	4

In 22 competitive games since Euro 2012

IF ROMANIA SCORE FIRST

They win	11		92%
Draw	1		8%
They lose	0		0%

In 22 competitive games since Euro 2012

IF ROMANIA CONCEDE FIRST

They win	0		0%
Draw	3		43%
They lose	4		57%

Bogdan Stancu (19) celebrates a friendly goal against Italy

GOALSCORERS IN QUALIFYING ● FIRST GOALS

	Goals		1st		Anytime		Percentage of team goals	
B Stancu	2	●●	1	50%	1	14%	▮▮▮▮	18%
P Papp	2	●●	1	50%	1	16%	▮▮▮▮	18%
C Budescu	2	●●	1	50%	1	33%	▮▮▮▮	18%
C Marica	1	●	1	100%	1	100%	▮▮	9%
C Keseru	1	●	1	100%	1	16%	▮▮	9%
R Rusescu	1	●	1	100%	1	33%	▮▮	9%
A Maxim	1	●	0	0%	1	11%	▮▮	9%
O Hoban	1	●	0	0%	1	12%	▮▮	9%

In Euro 2016 qualifying

BOOKINGS

Matches played	10	▢26	▮ 1
Average make-up (	▢10 ▮25)		28.5

In Euro 2016 qualifying

CORNERS

Avg F	5.2	▮▮▮▮▮▮▮▮▮▮▮▮	61%
Avg A	3.3	▮▮▮▮▮▮▮	39%

In Euro 2016 qualifying. Avg match total 8.5

SWIS v ALB 1-0R

The expanded format was always likely to let tournament debutants in and so it has proven for Albania, who were ranked 40th of 54 nations in the February 2014 draw. Just reaching France is a dream come true, particularly after qualifying ahead of arch-rivals Serbia. Tearful skipper Lorik Cana declared: "Serbia will now watch us drinking beer in front of the TV."

How they qualified

Albania made it to France in controversial circumstances and luck played its part from the opening match when they won 1-0 in Portugal against a home side missing their talisman, Cristiano Ronaldo.

However, qualifying was turned on its head in Belgrade after a drone flying a flag depicting 'Greater Albania' was flown over the pitch, sparking a brawl between Serbian and Albanian players and trouble in the stands.

The match was abandoned before the break with the score at 0-0 and Albania were eventually awarded a 3-0 victory by the Court of Arbitration for Sport – Uefa's initial decision was to award Serbia a 3-0 win and then deduct the three points.

Albania finally qualified with a 3-0 win in Armenia. Some Serbs claimed the match was fixed and the head of Armenia's football federation Ruben Hayrapetian said "there was a betrayal".

Albania managed a shot ratio (share of total shots in a game) figure of just 26 per cent in fixtures against teams who finished in the top three of their group after being dominated on the statistics against Portugal and Denmark.

It is easily the lowest shot ratio of the teams heading for France – Ireland are next on 32 per cent. No team qualified with a lower goal average than Albania's 0.88 and none of their players notched twice.

The manager

Much-travelled Italian Gianni De Biasi found his calling when he became Albanian coach

FACTFILE

FA founded 1930
www fshf.org
Head coach Gianni De Biasi
National league Superliga
Date qualified October 11, 2015

Typical starting XI (4-5-1) Berisha; Hysaj, Cana, Mavraj, Agolli; Gashi, Xhaka, Kukeli, Abrashi, Lenjani; Balaj

Strengths

☑ Team unity is everything to Albania
☑ Hysaj has been fantastic for Napoli in Serie A

Weaknesses

☒ Few members of the squad have big-game experience
☒ A lack of goals – none of Albania's players scored twice in qualifying – is a major issue

Star rating ★☆☆☆☆

Fixtures

1 Switzerland, 2pm June 11, Lens

2 France, 8pm June 15, Marseille

3 Romania, 8pm June 19, Lyon

Base Perros-Guirec

Etrit Berisha is likely to have a short but busy tournament

in 2011 and he was granted citizenship last year after marrying a local woman.

De Biasi, along with his assistant, former Tottenham left-back Paolo Tramezzani, has put Albania's success down to a great team ethic and to being given the finances to fly around the world to scout players as far afield as China and Australia.

Match winners

Napoli's Elseid Hysaj is their most valuable player but how much damage can he do from the right-back position? Fellow Serie A-based player, Lazio goalkeeper Etrit Berisha, is also decent, which is just as well as he is set to be busy this summer.

Shkelzen Gashi and Taulant Xhaka are two to keep an eye on, particularly in the Switzerland match when Xhaka will come up against his brother Granit. Teenage winger Milot Rashica has been performing well for Vitesse and is destined for bigger things.

Question marks

There is the obvious problem of the sheer size of the occasion getting to the wide-eyed players and none of Albania's striking options inspire confidence. No player had scored more than three goals from those selected for the friendly matches over Easter.

Gashi, top scorer in Switzerland in 2014 and 2015, had not been as influential for Basel since Urs Fischer replaced Paulo Sousa as manager and De Biasi has made it clear all national team players must be playing at club level so he has moved to the MLS.

Weirdly, Gashi has scored only once for Albania which is totally at odds with his 19-goal league tally for Grasshoppers in 2013-14 and 22 for Basel the season after.

How to back them

Albania beat France at home in a friendly and drew the return but things should be different at Euro 2016, with the Eagles odds-on to finish bottom of Group A.

That is a fair assessment and backing them to be the tournament's lowest scorers at around 6-1 is another wager to consider. Their most likely points will come in the final match against a Scrooge-like Romanian defence and no tournament goals is a runner.

ALBANIA

EUROPEAN CHAMPIONSHIP RECORD

1960	P	W	D	L	GF	GA
Did not enter	-	-	-	-	-	-
Qualifying	-	-	-	-	-	-

1964	P	W	D	L	GF	GA
Did not qualify	-	-	-	-	-	-
Qualifying	2	1	0	1	1	4

1968	P	W	D	L	GF	GA
Did not qualify	-	-	-	-	-	-
Qualifying	4	0	1	3	0	12

1972	P	W	D	L	GF	GA
Did not qualify	-	-	-	-	-	-
Qualifying	6	1	1	4	5	9

1976	P	W	D	L	GF	GA
Did not enter	-	-	-	-	-	-
Qualifying	-	-	-	-	-	-

1980	P	W	D	L	GF	GA
Did not enter	-	-	-	-	-	-
Qualifying	-	-	-	-	-	-

1984	P	W	D	L	GF	GA
Did not qualify	-	-	-	-	-	-
Qualifying	8	0	2	6	4	14

1988	P	W	D	L	GF	GA
Did not qualify	-	-	-	-	-	-
Qualifying	6	0	0	6	2	17

1992	P	W	D	L	GF	GA
Did not qualify	-	-	-	-	-	-
Qualifying	7	1	0	6	2	21

1996	P	W	D	L	GF	GA
Did not qualify	-	-	-	-	-	-
Qualifying	10	2	2	6	10	16

2000	P	W	D	L	GF	GA
Did not qualify	-	-	-	-	-	-
Qualifying	10	1	4	5	8	14

2004	P	W	D	L	GF	GA
Did not qualify	-	-	-	-	-	-
Qualifying	8	2	2	4	11	15

2008	P	W	D	L	GF	GA
Did not qualify	-	-	-	-	-	-
Qualifying	12	2	5	5	12	18

2012	P	W	D	L	GF	GA
Did not qualify	-	-	-	-	-	-
Qualifying	10	2	3	5	7	14

Totals	P	W	D	L	GF	GA
Finals	-	-	-	-	-	-
Qualifying	83	12	20	51	62	154

Results & goals include extra time

WIN % FOUR-TEAM FINALS — 100 / 50 / 0 — 1960, 1964, 1968, 1972, 1976

WIN % EIGHT-TEAM FINALS — 100 / 50 / 0 — 1980, 1984, 1988, 1992

WIN % 16-TEAM FINALS — 100 / 50 / 0 — 1996, 2000, 2004, 2008, 2012

Results include extra time. ▌ in qualifying ▌ at the finals

LEGENDARY PLAYER

LORIK CANA — LEGEND

Panajot Pano was selected by the Albanian FA as their Golden Player to celebrate Uefa's 50th anniversary, but **Lorik Cana**, the first Albanian to play in the Premier League, has captained them to a historic first tournament finals.

WORLD CUP RECORD

Year	Point of exit	Year	Point of exit
1930	Did not enter	1978	Did not enter
1934	Did not enter	1982	Did not qualify
1938	Did not enter	1986	Did not qualify
1950	Did not enter	1990	Did not qualify
1954	Did not enter	1994	Did not qualify
1958	Did not enter	1998	Did not qualify
1962	Did not enter	2002	Did not qualify
1966	Did not qualify	2006	Did not qualify
1970	Did not enter*	2010	Did not qualify
1974	Did not qualify	2014	Did not qualify

*Albania's entry in 1970 was not accepted by Fifa

DID YOU KNOW?

Albania's average of 1.57 points in their completed games was the worst of any side to finish in the top three

HOW THEY QUALIFIED

Group I	P	W	D	L	F	A	GD	Pts
Portugal	8	7	0	1	11	5	+6	21
Albania	8	4	2	2	10	5	+5	14
Denmark	8	3	3	2	8	5	+3	12
Serbia	8	2	1	5	8	13	-5	4
Armenia	8	0	2	6	5	14	-9	2

Serbia deducted 3pts

Match stats in qualifying

Possession	▌▌▌▌▌▌▌▌	44%
Shots on target	▌▌▌▌▌▌▌▌▌	50%
Shots off target	▌▌▌▌▌	33%
Corners	▌▌▌▌▌▌▌	40%

Averages of match totals in qualifying. See pages 228-254 for full qualifying results

Results & prices

	W	D	L
Portugal ... (0) 0-1 (0) ......Albania	12-1	5-1	2-7
Albania ..... (1) 1-1 (0) ....Denmark	13-5	23-10	5-4
Serbia .... (0) 0-3 (0) ......Albania	7-1	3-1	8-15
Albania ..... (0) 2-1 (1) .... Armenia	20-21	12-5	15-4
Denmark... (0) 0-0 (0) ......Albania	11-2	11-4	7-10
Albania ..... (0) 0-1 (0) .... Portugal	5-1	13-5	8-11
Albania ..... (0) 0-2 (0) ....Serbia	15-8	2-1	19-10
Armenia.... (0) 0-3 (2) ......Albania	11-8	23-10	5-2

Profit & loss in qualifying   10.33 3.05 -3.37

Figures based on a £1 level stake using best odds in the Racing Post on day of match. W shows win price, whether home or away, L the price of the opposition. Serbia forfeited their match against Albania and the result is not counted in Albania's P&L figure

PLAYERS USED IN QUALIFYING

				CAREER		QUALIFYING			
Pos		**Club**	**Age**	**P**	**G**	**P**	**G**	▌	▌
GK	Etrit Berisha	Lazio	27	33	-	8	-	1	-
DEF	Berat Djimsiti	Atalanta	23	7	1	4	1	2	-
DEF	Naser Aliji	Basel	22	4	-	1	-	1	-
DEF	Arlind Ajeti	Frosinone	22	8	-	2	-	1	-
DEF	Mergim Mavraj	Cologne	30	24	3	4	1	1	-
DEF	Elseid Hysaj	Napoli	22	18	-	6	-	-	-
DEF	Ansi Agolli	FK Qarabag	33	59	2	7	-	3	-
DEF	Debatik Curri	Flamurtari Vlore	32	44	1	1	-	-	-
DEF	Andi Lila	PAS Giannina	30	57	-	4	-	-	-
DEF	Lorik Cana	Nantes	32	90	1	8	-	2	-
MID	Burim Kukeli	FC Zurich	32	15	-	7	-	2	-
MID	Amir Abrashi	Freiburg	26	17	-	7	-	2	-
MID	Odhise Roshi	Rijeka	25	30	1	5	-	1	-
MID	Ermir Lenjani	Nantes	26	17	2	7	1	-	-
MID	Ergys Kace	PAOK Salonika	22	15	2	2	-	1	-
MID	Taulant Xhaka	Basel	25	11	-	8	-	2	-
MID	Migjen Basha	Lucerne	29	17	3	4	-	1	-
MID	Ledian Memushaj	Pescara	29	13	-	3	-	-	-
MID	Alban Meha	Konyaspor	30	7	2	1	-	-	-
MID	Valdet Rama	1860 Munich	28	15	3	1	-	-	-
MID	Shkelzen Gashi	Colorado Rapids	27	12	1	4	1	-	-
ATT	Armando Sadiku	Vaduz	25	18	3	2	1	-	-
ATT	Bekim Balaj	Rijeka	25	13	1	5	1	-	-
ATT	Hamdi Salihi	Skenderbeu	32	50	11	1	-	-	-
ATT	Sokol Cikalleshi	Istanbul Buyuk.	25	17	2	7	-	1	-

ALBANIA

GROUP A

CORRECT SCORES

	Competitive	Friendly
1-0	3	1
2-0	-	3
2-1	1	-
3-0	1	1
3-1	1	-
3-2	-	-
4-0	-	-
4-1	-	-
4-2	-	-
4-3	-	-
0-0	2	3
1-1	2	1
2-2	-	1
3-3	-	-
4-4	-	-
0-1	2	3
0-2	2	-
1-2	3	1
0-3	-	-
1-3	-	-
2-3	-	-
0-4	-	-
1-4	-	-
2-4	-	-
3-4	-	-
Other	-	-

Since Euro 2012. Abandoned match vs Serbia is not included

HALF-TIME/FULL-TIME DOUBLE RESULTS

Win/Win	2	12%
Draw/Win	3	18%
Lose/Win	1	6%
Win/Draw	2	12%
Draw/Draw	2	12%
Lose/Draw	0	0%
Win/Lose	0	0%
Draw/Lose	5	29%
Lose/Lose	2	12%

Win 1st half	4	24%
Win 2nd half	5	29%
Win both halves	1	6%
Goal both halves	8	47%

Overall
- ● Win 35%
- ● Draw 24%
- ● Lose 41%

WIN 35%

Overall: W6, D4, L7 in 17 competitive games since Euro 2012

CLEAN SHEETS

6 (35%) **Clean sheets** 11 (65%) ✓ ✗

4 (24%) **Win to nil** 13 (76%) ✓ ✗

6 (35%) **Fail to score** 11 (65%) ✓ ✗

4 (24%) **Lose to nil** 13 (76%) ✓ ✗

UNDER & OVER GOALS

10 (59%) **Over 1.5** 7 (41%) ✓ ✗

6 (35%) **Over 2.5** 11 (65%) ✓ ✗

1 (6%) **Over 3.5** 16 (94%) ✓ ✗

0 (0%) **Over 4.5** 17 (100%) ✓ ✗

BOTH TEAMS TO SCORE

7 (41%) **Both score** 10 (59%) ✓ ✗

2 (12%) **& win** 15 (88%) ✓ ✗

3 (18%) **& lose** 14 (82%) ✓ ✗

In 17 competitive games since Euro 2012

GOAL TIMES

Total match goals by half

8 (57%) **1st half** 6 (43%)
F A

8 (44%) **2nd half** 10 (56%)
F A

Goals for & against by half

8 (50%) **For** 8 (50%)
1st 2nd

6 (38%) **Against** 10 (63%)
1st 2nd

● GOALS FOR ● GOALS AGAINST

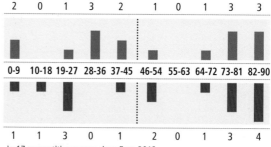

	0-9	10-18	19-27	28-36	37-45	46-54	55-63	64-72	73-81	82-90
For	2	0	1	3	2	1	0	1	3	3
Against	1	1	3	0	1	2	0	1	3	4

In 17 competitive games since Euro 2012

IF ALBANIA SCORE FIRST

They win	5	63%
Draw	2	25%
They lose	1	13%

In 17 competitive games since Euro 2012

IF ALBANIA CONCEDE FIRST

They win	1	14%
Draw	0	0%
They lose	6	86%

Sokol Cikalleshi is one of the few Albanian forward options

GOALSCORERS IN QUALIFYING   ● FIRST GOALS

	Goals		1st		Anytime		Percentage of team goals	
M Mavraj	1 ●		0	0%	1	25%	▮▮▮	14%
B Djimsiti	1 ●		0	0%	1	25%	▮▮▮	14%
S Gashi	1 ●		0	0%	1	25%	▮▮▮	14%
B Balaj	1 ●		1	100%	1	20%	▮▮▮	14%
A Sadiku	1 ●		0	0%	1	50%	▮▮▮	14%
E Lenjani	1 ●		1	100%	1	14%	▮▮▮	14%

In Euro 2016 qualifying. Total team goals does not include goals awarded in abandoned game vs Serbia

BOOKINGS					CORNERS			
Matches played	8	▢ 21	▮ 0		**Avg F**	3	▮▮▮▮▮▮▮	40%
Average make-up (▢ 10 ▮ 25)			26.3		**Avg A**	4.6	▮▮▮▮▮▮▮▮▮▮	60%
In Euro 2016 qualifying					In Euro 2016 qualifying. Avg match total 7.6			

Swis v ALB Swis 1-0
w

Switzerland are becoming tournament regulars having qualified for eight major finals in their last 12 attempts. Now their target is to reach the knockout phase of the European Championship for the first time. The Swiss have a lamentable record of just one victory in nine finals matches and they have scored only five goals, suffering six defeats.

How they qualified

They made a slow start with successive defeats to England and Slovenia but that could have been due to a change of manager after the last World Cup, when the more attack-minded coach Vladimir Petkovic came in for wily fox Ottmar Hitzfeld.

Switzerland rallied to claim second spot and their only other defeat in the group came in a 2-0 loss at Wembley. They finished nine points behind England and the comfortable nature of their qualification possibly had something to do with the soft opponents, an opinion firmed up by third-placed Slovenia's defeat in the playoffs by Ukraine.

The manager

Petkovic, who worked for a homeless charity for many years, won the Coppa Italia with Lazio in 2013, beating local rivals Roma in the final, but he upset his club employers by reportedly negotiating to replace Hitzfeld without their consent.

The manager has come under fire after March friendly losses to Ireland and Bosnia without scoring and said afterwards: "We can and must do better."

Match winners

There are good players throughout the squad. The Swiss are spoilt for choice in the goalkeeping department, with Yann Sommer expected to edge out Borussia Dortmund's Roman Burki for the number one jersey.

Attacking full-backs Stephan Lichtsteiner and Ricardo Rodriguez made the Champions League knockout rounds with Juventus and Wolfsburg respectively and Granit Xhaka is

FACTFILE

FA founded 1895
www football.ch
Head coach Vladimir Petkovic
National league Super League
Date qualified October 9, 2015

....

Typical starting XI (4-3-3) Sommer; Lichtsteiner, Djourou, Schar, Rodriguez; Behrami, Inler, Xhaka; Shaqiri, Seferovic, Mehmedi

....

Strengths
☑ Excellent in the full-back positions
☑ A mainly young side with the potential to improve

Weaknesses
☒ There is no natural leader at centre-back
☒ They lack a goal threat in the striking position

Star rating ★★☆☆☆

....

Fixtures
1 Albania, 2pm June 11, Lens

2 Romania, 5pm June 15, Paris

3 France, 8pm June 19, Lille

Base Montpellier/ Juvignac

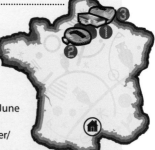

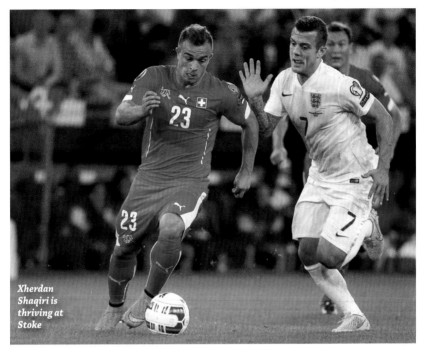

Xherdan Shaqiri is thriving at Stoke

a lovely playmaker, who is entrusted with setting the tempo for his club side, Borussia Monchengladbach.

Teenager Breel Embolo has the scouts flocking to Basel on a regular basis, while the star of the side is Xherdan Shaqiri. Although he struggled for minutes at Bayern Munich and Inter, he was still reluctant to join Stoke. However, it is looking like a good place for him to rebuild his career.

Question marks

Centre-backs Johan Djourou and Fabian Schar rarely convince but the replacements are even worse and until Embolo develops into the real deal there is a lack of genuine class in the striking department.

Eren Derdiyok, Haris Seferovic and Josip Drmic, who is ruled out because of injury, have failed to live up to their early promise.

Home and away defeats to England do not bode well for when the quality of opposition steps up and they may lack a winning mentality. The Swiss had chances against Argentina in the last 16 of the last World Cup but froze on the big occasion.

How to back them

Switzerland should be up to at least matching their exploits at Brazil 2014 in this expanded European Championship, but that is reflected in the prices. The betting is predicting a clash with Poland in the first knockout round.

That would not be too far off a 50-50 tie for a spot in the quarter-finals so the last eight is not beyond the Swiss but their potential on paper is rarely realised on the pitch.

The best bet is for Shaqiri to top-score for his nation once again. Shaqiri did the business at odds of 10-1 at the World Cup and he scored the most goals for Switzerland (four) in qualifying.

The Stoke star also bagged the most Swiss goals in Euro 2012 qualifying (four) and he was only one behind Schar in qualifying for Brazil.

SWITZERLAND

EUROPEAN CHAMPIONSHIP RECORD

1960	P	W	D	L	GF	GA
Did not enter	-	-	-	-	-	-
Qualifying	-	-	-	-	-	-

1964	P	W	D	L	GF	GA
Did not qualify	-	-	-	-	-	-
Qualifying	2	0	1	1	2	4

1968	P	W	D	L	GF	GA
Did not qualify	-	-	-	-	-	-
Qualifying	6	2	1	3	17	13

1972	P	W	D	L	GF	GA
Did not qualify	-	-	-	-	-	-
Qualifying	6	4	1	1	12	5

1976	P	W	D	L	GF	GA
Did not qualify	-	-	-	-	-	-
Qualifying	6	1	1	4	5	10

1980	P	W	D	L	GF	GA
Did not qualify	-	-	-	-	-	-
Qualifying	8	2	0	6	7	18

1984	P	W	D	L	GF	GA
Did not qualify	-	-	-	-	-	-
Qualifying	6	2	2	2	7	9

1988	P	W	D	L	GF	GA
Did not qualify	-	-	-	-	-	-
Qualifying	8	1	5	2	9	9

1992	P	W	D	L	GF	GA
Did not qualify	-	-	-	-	-	-
Qualifying	8	4	2	2	19	7

1996	P	W	D	L	GF	GA
Group stage	3	0	1	2	1	4
Qualifying	8	5	2	1	15	7

2000	P	W	D	L	GF	GA
Did not qualify	-	-	-	-	-	-
Qualifying	8	4	2	2	9	5

2004	P	W	D	L	GF	GA
Group stage	3	0	1	2	1	6
Qualifying	8	4	3	1	15	11

2008	P	W	D	L	GF	GA
Group stage	3	1	0	2	3	3
Qualifying	-	-	-	-	-	-

2012	P	W	D	L	GF	GA
Did not qualify	-	-	-	-	-	-
Qualifying	8	3	2	3	12	10

Totals	P	W	D	L	GF	GA
Finals	9	1	2	6	5	13
Qualifying	82	32	22	28	129	108

Results & goals include extra time

WIN % FOUR-TEAM FINALS — 1960, 1964, 1968, 1972, 1976

WIN % EIGHT-TEAM FINALS — 1980, 1984, 1988, 1992

WIN % 16-TEAM FINALS — 1996, 2000, 2004, 2008, 2012

Results include extra time. █ in qualifying █ at the finals

LEGENDARY PLAYER

His international career ended with him being booed by the Swiss fans, but **Alexander Frei** played at two European Championships and one World Cup, and with 42 goals he is Switzerland's record international goal scorer.

ALEXANDER FREI — LEGEND

WORLD CUP RECORD

Year	Point of exit	Year	Point of exit
1930	Did not enter	1978	Did not qualify
1934	Quarter-finals	1982	Did not qualify
1938	Quarter-finals	1986	Did not qualify
1950	Group stage	1990	Did not qualify
1954	Quarter-finals	1994	Round of 16
1958	Did not qualify	1998	Did not qualify
1962	Group stage	2002	Did not qualify
1966	Group stage	2006	Round of 16
1970	Did not qualify	2010	Group stage
1974	Did not qualify	2014	Round of 16

DID YOU KNOW?

Haris Seferovic was flagged for offside more often than any other player in qualifying – 13 times in eight appearances

HOW THEY QUALIFIED

Group E	P	W	D	L	F	A	GD	Pts
England	10	10	0	0	31	3	+28	30
Switzerland	10	7	0	3	24	8	+16	21
Slovenia	10	5	1	4	18	11	+7	16
Estonia	10	3	1	6	4	9	-5	10
Lithuania	10	3	1	6	7	18	-11	10
San Marino	10	0	1	9	1	36	-35	1

Match stats in qualifying

Possession	▓▓▓▓▓▓▓▓▓▓▓▓▓▓	68%
Shots on target	▓▓▓▓▓▓▓▓▓▓▓▓▓▓▓	74%
Shots off target	▓▓▓▓▓▓▓▓▓▓▓▓▓▓	68%
Corners	▓▓▓▓▓▓▓▓▓▓▓▓▓▓▓	77%

Averages of match totals in qualifying. See pages 228-254 for full qualifying results

Results & prices	W	D	L
Switzerland(0) 0-2 (0) ..... England	13-8	9-4	2-1
Slovenia.... (0) 1-0 (0)Switzerland	7-5	9-4	23-10
San Marino(0) 0-4 (3)Switzerland	1-66	33-1	100-1
Switzerland(0) 4-0 (0) ... Lithuania	1-4	11-2	18-1
Switzerland(2) 3-0 (0) ...... Estonia	2-9	6-1	20-1
Lithuania .. (0) 1-2 (0)Switzerland	2-5	15-4	10-1
Switzerland(0) 3-2 (1) .....Slovenia	8-15	16-5	7-1
England .... (0) 2-0 (0)Switzerland	9-2	11-4	4-5
Switzerland(1) 7-0 (0) San Marino	1-100	66-1	100-1
Estonia ..... (0) 0-1 (0)Switzerland	11-20	16-5	13-2

Profit & loss in qualifying   -1.02 -10 -1.90

Figures based on a £1 level stake using best odds in the Racing Post on day of match. W shows win price, whether home or away, L the price of the opposition

PLAYERS USED IN QUALIFYING

Pos		Club	Age	CAREER P	CAREER G	QUALIFYING P	QUALIFYING G	▢	▧
GK	Yann Sommer	Mgladbach	27	17	-	8	-	-	-
GK	Marwin Hitz	Augsburg	28	2	-	1	-	-	-
GK	Roman Burki	B Dortmund	25	4	-	1	-	-	-
DEF	Timm Klose	Norwich	28	14	-	2	-	-	-
DEF	Johan Djourou	Hamburg	29	59	2	8	1	1	-
DEF	Michael Lang	Basel	25	15	2	2	1	-	-
DEF	Francois Moubandje	Toulouse	25	10	-	3	-	1	-
DEF	Fabian Schar	Hoffenheim	24	19	5	6	2	1	-
DEF	Ricardo Rodriguez	Wolfsburg	23	35	-	8	-	-	-
DEF	Fabian Lustenberger	Hertha Berlin	28	3	-	1	-	-	-
DEF	Philippe Senderos	Grasshoppers	31	56	5	1	-	-	-
DEF	Steve von Bergen	Young Boys	33	49	-	3	-	-	-
DEF	Stefan Lichtsteiner	Juventus	32	80	5	8	-	1	-
MID	Silvan Widmer	Udinese	23	6	-	2	-	-	-
MID	Valentin Stocker	Hertha Berlin	27	33	5	3	1	-	-
MID	Granit Xhaka	Mgladbach	23	41	6	8	1	2	-
MID	Pajtim Kasami	Olympiakos	24	12	2	4	1	-	-
MID	Fabian Frei	Mainz	27	7	1	1	-	-	-
MID	Gelson Fernandes	Rennes	29	55	2	1	-	-	-
MID	Blerim Dzemaili	Genoa	30	46	5	7	1	2	-
MID	Tranquillo Barnetta	Philadelphia U	31	75	10	1	-	-	-
MID	Valon Behrami	Watford	31	64	2	7	-	1	-
MID	Goekhan Inler	Leicester	31	89	7	8	1	-	-
MID	Luca Zuffi	Basel	26	4	-	1	-	-	-
MID	Renato Steffen	Basel	24	4	-	2	-	-	-
MID	Marco Schonbacher	FC Zurich	26	2	-	1	-	-	-
MID	Xherdan Shaqiri	Stoke	24	51	17	9	4	1	-
ATT	Eren Derdiyok	Kasimpasa	27	50	10	2	1	-	-
ATT	Breel Embolo	Basel	19	9	1	5	1	-	-
ATT	Josip Drmic	Mgladbach	23	25	8	9	3	1	-
ATT	Admir Mehmedi	B Leverkusen	25	40	3	8	1	-	-
ATT	Haris Seferovic	E Frankfurt	24	29	7	8	3	-	-

SWITZERLAND

GROUP A

CORRECT SCORES

	Competitive	Friendly
1-0	3	2
2-0	4	1
2-1	3	2
3-0	2	1
3-1	-	-
3-2	1	-
4-0	2	-
4-1	-	-
4-2	-	1
4-3	-	-
0-0	2	1
1-1	1	1
2-2	-	2
3-3	-	-
4-4	1	-
0-1	1	1
0-2	2	1
1-2	-	1
0-3	-	-
1-3	-	-
2-3	-	2
0-4	-	-
1-4	-	-
2-4	-	-
3-4	-	-
Other	2	-

Since Euro 2012

HALF-TIME/FULL-TIME DOUBLE RESULTS

Win/Win	7	28%	Win 1st half	8	33%
Draw/Win	7	28%	Win 2nd half	16	67%
Lose/Win	2	8%	Win both halves	7	29%
Win/Draw	1	4%	Goal both halves	11	46%
Draw/Draw	3	13%			
Lose/Draw	0	0%	**Overall**		
Win/Lose	0	0%	● **Win**	67%	
Draw/Lose	3	13%	○ **Draw**	17%	
Lose/Lose	1	4%	● **Lose**	17%	

Overall: W16, D4, L4 in 24 competitive games since Euro 2012

CLEAN SHEETS

14 (58%) **Clean sheets** 10 (42%) ✓ ✗

12 (50%) **Win to nil** 12 (50%) ✓ ✗

5 (21%) **Fail to score** 19 (79%) ✓ ✗

3 (13%) **Lose to nil** 21 (88%) ✓ ✗

UNDER & OVER GOALS

18 (75%) **Over 1.5** 6 (25%) ✓ ✗

11 (46%) **Over 2.5** 13 (54%) ✓ ✗

6 (25%) **Over 3.5** 18 (75%) ✓ ✗

4 (17%) **Over 4.5** 20 (83%) ✓ ✗

BOTH TEAMS TO SCORE

7 (29%) **Both score** 17 (71%) ✓ ✗

4 (17%) **& win** 20 (83%) ✓ ✗

1 (4%) **& lose** 23 (96%) ✓ ✗

In 24 competitive games since Euro 2012

GOAL TIMES

Total match goals by half

14 (70%) **1st half** 6 (30%)
F A

34 (69%) **2nd half** 15 (31%)
F A

Goals for & against by half

14 (29%) **For** 34 (71%)
1st 2nd

6 (29%) **Against** 15 (71%)
1st 2nd

● GOALS FOR ● GOALS AGAINST

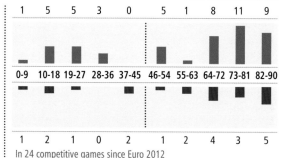

	1	5	5	3	0	5	1	8	11	9
	0-9	10-18	19-27	28-36	37-45	46-54	55-63	64-72	73-81	82-90
	1	2	1	0	2	1	2	4	3	5

In 24 competitive games since Euro 2012

IF SWITZERLAND SCORE FIRST

They win	13		93%
They draw	1		7%
They lose	0		0%

In 24 competitive games since 2012 World Cup

IF SWITZERLAND CONCEDE FIRST

They win	3		38%
They draw	1		13%
They lose	4		50%

Granit Xhaka is a classy playmaker

GOALSCORERS IN QUALIFYING ● FIRST GOALS

	Goals		1st		Anytime		Percentage of team goals	
X Shaqiri	4	●●●●	0	0%	3	33%	▮▮▮	17%
H Seferovic	3	●●●	1	33%	2	25%	▮▮▮	13%
J Drmic	3	●●●	0	0%	2	22%	▮▮▮	13%
F Schar	2	●●	1	50%	2	33%	▮▮	8%
J Djourou	1	●	0	0%	1	12%	▮	4%
B Dzemaili	1	●	0	0%	1	14%	▮	4%
G Inler	1	●	0	0%	1	12%	▮	4%
E Derdiyok	1	●	0	0%	1	50%	▮	4%
V Stocker	1	●	0	0%	1	33%	▮	4%
A Mehmedi	1	●	0	0%	1	12%	▮	4%
P Kasami	1	●	0	0%	1	25%	▮	4%
M Lang	1	●	1	100%	1	50%	▮	4%
G Xhaka	1	●	0	0%	1	12%	▮	4%
B Embolo	1	●	0	0%	1	20%	▮	4%

In Euro 2016 qualifying

BOOKINGS

Matches played	10	☐11	▮ 0
Average make-up (☐10 ▮25)			11

In Euro 2016 qualifying

CORNERS

Avg F	8.3	▮▮▮▮▮▮▮▮▮▮▮▮▮	77%
Avg A	2.5	▮▮▮▮	23%

In Euro 2016 qualifying. Avg match total 10.8

A decent draw makes England value to put Brazil behind them

England always used to be overbacked and underpriced for major tournaments.

However, the globalisation of betting combined with the frustrations of Three Lions supporters means they can now be considered a value bet in certain circumstances, and this appears to be one of those occasions as Roy Hodgson's side look to build on Euro 2016's only perfect qualification campaign.

There remain lingering annoyance from a woeful World Cup campaign which saw England return home from Brazil before the postcards, although only France (69 per cent) and Belgium (64) finished with a better shot ratio than England's 62 per cent of those sides who competed two years ago and will be in action this summer.

It has been widely accepted that England were dreadful at the World Cup but the group, which contained Italy, Uruguay and quarter-finalists Costa Rica, was much tougher than it appeared on paper.

The influential (and often) shrewd Asian syndicates were all over England for their opening game defeat by Italy in Manaus and it could just be that everyone who headed to the Amazon rainforest ending up catching a footballing version of jungle fever.

Matches in Manaus took plenty out of the legs and teams who went north and played further matches (Croatia, Cameroon, Italy, England, Switzerland, Portugal and USA) had a record of P10, W1, D1, L8, F6, A16.

Hodgson has a core of young players who should go well in this tournament and the draw could have been a lot worse than matches against Russia, Wales and Slovakia.

The derby with Wales will dominate the back pages but, as Dragons boss Chris Coleman has continually tried to point out, the Welsh campaign could be much more about the results in their two other fixtures.

Wales defended superbly in the qualifiers and pose a threat on the counter through Gareth Bale but it is a fairly balanced section behind England and the other three nations could take points off each other to help the favourites justify their market status.

Recommended bet

€€€€€ England to win Group B

TO WIN THE GROUP

	bet365	BetBright	Betfair	Betfred	Betway	Boyles	Coral	Hills	Lads	Power	Sky Bet
England	5-6	8-11	3-4	8-11	5-6	4-5	5-6	5-6	5-6	**10-11**	4-5
Russia	10-3	33-10	**10-3**	11-4	3	16-5	11-4	9-4	11-4	13-5	11-4
Wales	7-2	9-2	**11-2**	9-2	9-2	4	**11-2**	5	5	4	5
Slovakia	9	9	6	**10**	8	17-2	7	9	15-2	8	8

Win only. Prices correct March 31

| WAL v SLO 5PM JUNE 11 | ENG v RUS 8PM JUNE 11 | ▶▶▶ | RUS v SLO 2PM JUNE 15 | ENG v WAL 2PM JUNE 16 | ▶▶▶ | RUS v WAL 8PM JUNE 20 | SLO v ENG 8PM JUNE 20 |

England disappointed in Brazil but Roy Hodgson's young side can do far better in France

TO QUALIFY

	bet365	BetBright	Betfair	Betfred	Betway	Boyles	Coral	Hills	Lads	Power	Sky Bet
England	1-10	1-12	1-12	1-10	1-10	1-11	1-14	1-12	**1-8**	1-18	1-12
Russia	**4-11**	7-20	**4-11**	1-3	1-3	**4-11**	3-10	1-4	1-3	3-10	1-3
Wales	2-5	1-2	**4-6**	8-13	8-13	1-2	**4-6**	8-13	**4-6**	4-7	**4-6**
Slovakia	**6-4**	13-10	5-6	6-5	5-6	Evs	Evs	11-10	8-11	Evs	Evs

Win only. Prices correct March 31

5PM JUNE 11 – WALES V SLOVAKIA

	bet365	Betfair	Betfred	Betway	Boyles	Coral	Hills	Lads	Power	Sky Bet
Wales	6-4	5-4	6-4	**8-5**	**8-5**	29-20	29-20	6-4	7-5	11-8
Slovakia	2	**21-10**	2	2	19-10	15-8	2	19-10	15-8	**21-10**
Draw	2	21-10	21-10	2	2	2	15-8	2	**11-5**	21-10

Best prices as decimal odds: Wales 2.6, draw 3.1, Draw 3.2. 102%. Prices correct March 31

8PM JUNE 11 – ENGLAND V RUSSIA

	bet365	Betfair	Betfred	Betway	Boyles	Coral	Hills	Lads	Power	Sky Bet
England	11-10	**6-5**	11-10	21-20	21-20	21-20	23-20	21-20	**6-5**	11-10
Draw	11-5	21-10	11-5	11-5	11-5	21-10	21-10	21-10	11-5	**9-4**
Russia	13-5	9-4	11-4	**3**	14-5	13-5	23-10	14-5	12-5	13-5

England 2.2, draw 3.25, Russia 4. 101%

2PM JUNE 15 – RUSSIA V SLOVAKIA

Slovakia

	Betfair	Betfred	Power
Russia	3-4	**4-5**	**4-5**
Draw	12-5	**5-2**	**5-2**
Slovakia	**19-5**	**19-5**	16-5

Russia 1.8, draw 3.5, Slovakia 4.8. 105%

2PM JUNE 16 – ENGLAND V WALES

	bet365	Betfair	Betfred	Betway	Coral	Power	Sky Bet
England	**5-6**	3-4	4-5	**5-6**	4-5	**5-6**	4-5
Draw	**5-2**	23-10	**5-2**	**5-2**	23-10	23-10	12-5
Wales	10-3	17-5	**18-5**	7-2	10-3	10-3	10-3

England 1.83, draw 3.5, Wales 4.6. 105%

8PM JUNE 20 – SLOVAKIA V ENGLAND

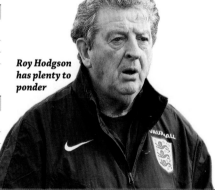

	Betfair	Betfred	Power	Sky Bet
England	**4-6**	4-7	**4-6**	8-15
Draw	13-5	**3**	13-5	11-4
Slovakia	7-2	**5**	7-2	**5**

England 1.67, draw 4, Slovakia 6. 102%

Roy Hodgson has plenty to ponder

8PM JUNE 20 – RUSSIA V WALES

	Betfair	Betfred	Power
Russia	**6-5**	**6-5**	**6-5**
Draw	**11-5**	**11-5**	**11-5**
Wales	23-10	**12-5**	23-10

Russia 2.2, draw 3.2, Wales 3.4. 106%

HOW THEY PERFORMED IN QUALIFYING

			Home			Away							Home	Shots	
	Group/Pos	P	W	D	L	W	D	L	F	A	GD	Pts	Pos%	On	Off
England	Group E	1st	10	5	0	0	5	0	0	31	3	+28	**30**	63.6	47	33
Slovakia	Group C	2nd	10	3	1	1	4	0	1	17	8	+9	**22**	48.2	23	20
Wales	Group B	2nd	10	3	2	0	3	1	1	11	4	+7	**21**	51.4	30	38
Russia	Group G	2nd	9	3	1	1	2	1	1	18	5	+13	**17**	62.8	33	44

Pos% percentage of total possession, **Shots on/off** shots on and off target, **Shots On%** percentage of shots on target (accuracy), **Shots%** percentage of total match shots

If you backed them P/L figures based on a £1 level stake using best odds in the Racing Post on day of match. Percentages represent probablility of victory implied by the win odds. **75%+** matches where the best price

Read → then →	England					Russia					Wales					Slovakia				
	W	D	L	F	A	W	D	L	F	A	W	D	L	F	A	W	D	L	F	A
England						1	0	1	4	2	4	0	0	6	0	2	0	0	4	2
																1	0	0	4	0
Russia	1	0	1	2	4						3	1	0	6	2	1	2	1	2	2
																1	0	0	1	0
Wales	0	0	4	0	6	0	1	3	2	6						1	0	1	6	7
Slovakia	0	0	2	2	4	1	2	1	2	2	1	0	1	7	6					
	0	0	1	0	4	0	0	1	0	1										

Includes all European Championship and World Cup matches since the 2002 World Cup. 90-minute results only. Competitive results above friendly results (in grey)

Euro 2004 qualifying
October 12, 2002
Slovakia .... (1) 1-2 (0) .... England

June 11, 2003
England.......... (0) 2-1 (1)..........Slovakia

Euro 2004 qualifying playoffs
November 15, 2003
Russia .... (0) 0-0 (0) .... Wales

November 19, 2003
Wales............. (0) 0-1 (1)............. Russia

World Cup 2006 qualifying
September 4, 2004
Russia .... (1) 1-1 (0) ....Slovakia

October 9, 2004
England.......... (1) 2-0 (0) .... Wales

September 3, 2005
Wales............. (0) 0-1 (0) .... England

October 12, 2005
Slovakia .... (0) 0-0 (0) .... Russia

Euro 2008 qualifying
October 7, 2006
Wales............. (1) 1-5 (3) ....Slovakia

12 September, 2007
England.......... (2) 3-0 (0) .... Russia
Slovakia .... (1) 2-5 (3) .... Wales

Ashley Young got the only goal when England and Wales last met

October 17, 2007
Russia .... (0) 2-1 (1).......... England

World Cup 2010 qualifying
September 10, 2008
Russia .... (1) 2-1 (0) .... Wales

Friendly
March 28, 2009
England.......... (1) 4-0 (0) ....Slovakia

World Cup 2010 qualifying
September 9, 2009
Wales............. (0) 1-3 (1)............. Russia

Euro 2012 qualifying
September 7, 2010
Russia .... (0) 0-1 (1)..........Slovakia

March 26, 2011
Wales............. (0) 0-2 (2) .... England

September 6, 2011
England.......... (1) 1-0 (0) .... Wales

October 7, 2011
Slovakia .... (0) 0-1 (0) .... Russia

Friendly
May 26, 2014
Russia .... (0) 1-0 (0) ....Slovakia

Away	Shots		Shots overall		If you backed them								
Pos%	On	Off	On%	Shots%	P	75%+	P	50-75%	P	25-50%	P	<25%
62.8	38	35	55.6	77.7	5	+0.60	4	+2.47	1	+2.00	0	0.00
41.0	20	25	48.9	47.8	3	+0.76	2	0.00	2	+0.30	3	+13.00
51.8	21	21	46.4	63.6	2	+0.22	3	+0.27	2	+1.80	3	+2.25
49.8	23	25	44.8	71.8	5	-0.18	1	-1.00	3	-0.85	0	0.00

was 1-3 or shorter **50-75%** matches where the best price was longer than 1-3 and no bigger than Evens **75-25%** matches where the best price was longer than Evens and no bigger than 3-1 **<25%** matches where the best price was longer than 3-1

Only completed matches are included. See pages 228-254 for full qualifying results

ENG V RUSSIA 1-1 ✓

No matter what happens this summer England's campaign surely can't be worse than Brazil 2014, when they were eliminated inside six days. At 28-1, England were their biggest ever price for a World Cup but they still managed to underachieve, with Fleet Street's finest describing their efforts as "traumatic" and "embarrassing".

How they qualified

England bounced back quickly from their South American surrender and qualified as the only team with a 100 per cent record.

Top spot was never in doubt from the moment they triumphed in Switzerland on matchday one and England finished with the best goal difference too: +28 from their ten matches.

The opposition was clearly not up to much but Roy Hodgson's men could only beat what was in front of them and the ease with which they qualified enabled the boss to heavily rotate his team.

Five different right-backs and four left-backs started at least one match and the face of the side has changed plenty since the start of the qualification process.

For instance, it is remarkable to think that Rickie Lambert was involved against the Swiss, squaring the ball to Danny Welbeck for his second goal after joining the fray as a late substitute – at the time of writing he was out to 100-1 to make the Euro 2016 squad.

However, some things never change and Wayne Rooney was England's go-to man in qualifying. He broke Sir Bobby Charlton's scoring record with his seventh and final goal of the qualifying campaign, although four of those strikes were penalties.

The manager

Hodgson was odds-on with bookmakers in January not to see out 2016 in charge of England but everything will depend on the performances in France.

A conservative manager by nature, Hodgson has removed the shackles in recent

Dele Alli and Harry Kane represent England's emerging talents

matches and seems determined to give youth its head. Dele Alli is among those set to take advantage, but will Hodgson stay brave?

Match winners

Historically, Rooney would be the obvious place to start but some are questioning his place in the starting XI after so many of the young guns impressed without the skipper in the 3-2 win over Germany in Berlin in March.

Joe Hart is a solid goalkeeper who rarely lets down the Three Lions but this could be the tournament that launches the talents of an exciting crop of youngsters. John Stones (21 years old), Alli (20), Eric Dier (22), Ross Barkley (22), Harry Kane (22) and Raheem Sterling (21) are all available if Hodgson is prepared to take a chance.

Question marks

The defence is a concern and there is little protection from midfield aside of Dier.

He is yet to appear in a competitive match for the senior team but has been superb for Tottenham and performed with great credit in Berlin. What happens, however, if Dier gets injured or is suspended at any stage?

Rooney could still be considered influential by Hodgson but he has mainly been woeful in major finals, scoring only six goals in five tournaments, four of which came at Euro 2004. The calls are getting louder for the Manchester United man to be axed in favour of Kane and Jamie Vardy.

Kane and Vardy both scored superb goals against the Germans but that result has rapidly raised expectations among the fans.

How to back them

England have never been to the semi-finals of a European Championship on foreign soil but they won't get a better chance than this.

A cracking draw means the Three Lions should be bankers to at least make the quarter-finals – there will be a third-placed side waiting in the last 16 should England top Group B. If they finish second it will be the runners-up in Group F, the weakest section of the lot, so the 4-5 that England manage at least a last-eight spot is a maximum bet.

EUROPEAN CHAMPIONSHIP RECORD

1960	P	W	D	L	GF	GA
Did not enter	-	-	-	-	-	-
Qualifying	-	-	-	-	-	-

1964	P	W	D	L	GF	GA
Did not qualify	-	-	-	-	-	-
Qualifying	2	0	1	1	3	6

1968	P	W	D	L	GF	GA
● Third	2	1	0	1	2	1
Qualifying	8	6	1	1	18	6

1972	P	W	D	L	GF	GA
Did not qualify	-	-	-	-	-	-
Qualifying	8	5	2	1	16	6

1976	P	W	D	L	GF	GA
Did not qualify	-	-	-	-	-	-
Qualifying	6	3	2	1	11	3

1980	P	W	D	L	GF	GA
Group stage	3	1	1	1	3	3
Qualifying	8	7	1	0	22	5

1984	P	W	D	L	GF	GA
Did not qualify	-	-	-	-	-	-
Qualifying	8	5	2	1	23	3

1988	P	W	D	L	GF	GA
Group stage	3	0	0	3	2	7
Qualifying	6	5	1	0	19	1

1992	P	W	D	L	GF	GA
Group stage	3	0	2	1	1	2
Qualifying	6	3	3	0	7	3

1996	P	W	D	L	GF	GA
● Semi-finals	5	2	3	0	8	3
Qualifying	-	-	-	-	-	-

2000	P	W	D	L	GF	GA
Group stage	3	1	0	2	5	6
Qualifying	10	4	4	2	16	5

2004	P	W	D	L	GF	GA
Quarter-finals	4	2	1	1	10	6
Qualifying	8	6	2	0	14	5

2008	P	W	D	L	GF	GA
Did not qualify	-	-	-	-	-	-
Qualifying	12	7	2	3	24	7

2012	P	W	D	L	GF	GA
Quarter-finals	4	2	2	0	5	3
Qualifying	8	5	3	0	17	5

Totals	P	W	D	L	GF	GA
Finals	27	9	9	9	36	31
Qualifying	90	56	24	10	190	55

Results & goals include extra time

WIN % FOUR-TEAM FINALS — bar chart: 1960, 1964, 1968, 1972, 1976

WIN % EIGHT-TEAM FINALS — bar chart: 1980, 1984, 1988, 1992

WIN % 16-TEAM FINALS — bar chart: 1996, 2000, 2004, 2008, 2012

Results include extra time. ▌ in qualifying ▌ at the finals

LEGENDARY PLAYER

Paul Gascoigne's tears at Italia 90 made him a household name and his goal against Scotland in 1996 was the highlight of England's best ever performance at the Euros – he dinked it over Colin Hendry, blasted it in and celebrated in style.

PAUL GASCOIGNE — LEGEND

WORLD CUP RECORD

Year	Point of exit	Year	Point of exit
1930	Did not enter	1978	Did not qualify
1934	Did not enter	1982	Second round
1938	Did not enter	1986	Quarter-finals
1950	Group stage	1990	● Fourth
1954	Quarter-finals	1994	Did not qualify
1958	Group stage	1998	Round of 16
1962	Quarter-finals	2002	Quarter-finals
1966	● Winners	2006	Quarter-finals
1970	Quarter-finals	2010	Round of 16
1974	Did not qualify	2014	Group stage

DID YOU KNOW?

Wayne Rooney put together the longest scoring streak of any player during qualifying, finding the net in seven appearances in succession

GROUP B

HOW THEY QUALIFIED

Group E	P	W	D	L	F	A	GD	Pts
England	10	10	0	0	31	3	+28	30
Switzerland	10	7	0	3	24	8	+16	21
Slovenia	10	5	1	4	18	11	+7	16
Estonia	10	3	1	6	4	9	-5	10
Lithuania	10	3	1	6	7	18	-11	10
San Marino	10	0	1	9	1	36	-35	1

Match stats in qualifying

Possession	▮▮▮▮▮▮▮▮▮▮▮▮	63%
Shots on target	▮▮▮▮▮▮▮▮▮▮▮▮▮▮▮▮▮	88%
Shots off target	▮▮▮▮▮▮▮▮▮▮▮▮▮	68%
Corners	▮▮▮▮▮▮▮▮▮▮▮▮▮▮	76%

Averages of match totals in qualifying. See pages 228-254 for full qualifying results

Results & prices		W	D	L
Switzerland(0) 0-2 (0) .....England	2-1	9-4	13-8
England ....(0) 5-0 (0) San Marino	1-100	40-1	100-1
Estonia .....(0) 0-1 (0) .....England	2-7	5-1	12-1
England ....(0) 3-1 (0) .....Slovenia	4-11	17-4	11-1
England ....(2) 4-0 (0) ...Lithuania	1-7	9-1	28-1
Slovenia....(1) 2-3 (0) .....England	10-11	13-5	19-5
San Marino(0) 0-6 (2) .....England	1-80	40-1	100-1
England ....(0) 2-0 (0)Switzerland	4-5	11-4	9-2
England ....(1) 2-0 (0) .....Estonia	3-20	8-1	25-1
Lithuania ..(0) 0-3 (2) .....England	2-5	4-1	10-1

Profit & loss in qualifying	5.07	-10	-10

Figures based on a £1 level stake using best odds in the Racing Post on day of match. W shows win price, whether home or away, L the price of the opposition

PLAYERS USED IN QUALIFYING

				CAREER		QUALIFYING			
Pos		Club	Age	P	G	P	G		
GK	Jack Butland	Stoke	23	4	-	1	-	-	-
GK	Joe Hart	Man City	29	57	-	9	-	-	-
DEF	Calum Chambers	Arsenal	21	3	-	2	-	-	-
DEF	Chris Smalling	Man Utd	26	23	-	4	-	1	-
DEF	Gary Cahill	Chelsea	30	41	3	8	-	-	-
DEF	John Stones	Everton	22	8	-	3	-	-	-
DEF	Kieran Gibbs	Arsenal	26	10	-	4	-	1	-
DEF	Kyle Walker	Tottenham	26	14	-	1	-	-	-
DEF	Leighton Baines	Everton	31	30	1	3	-	1	-
DEF	Luke Shaw	Man Utd	20	6	-	2	-	-	-
DEF	Nathaniel Clyne	Liverpool	25	11	-	6	-	1	-
DEF	Phil Jagielka	Everton	33	39	3	6	1	1	-
DEF	Phil Jones	Man Utd	24	20	-	4	-	-	-
DEF	Ryan Bertrand	Southampton	26	7	-	1	-	-	-
MID	Adam Lallana	Liverpool	28	21	-	6	-	-	-
MID	Alex O-Chamberlain	Arsenal	22	24	5	7	1	-	-
MID	Andros Townsend	Newcastle	24	10	3	3	1	-	-
MID	Dele Alli	Tottenham	20	6	1	2	-	-	-
MID	Fabian Delph	Man City	26	9	-	6	-	1	-
MID	Jack Wilshere	Arsenal	24	28	2	5	2	1	-
MID	James Milner	Liverpool	30	58	1	6	-	2	-
MID	Jonjo Shelvey	Newcastle	24	6	-	3	-	1	-
MID	Jordan Henderson	Liverpool	25	23	-	6	-	1	-
MID	Michael Carrick	Man Utd	34	34	-	1	-	-	-
MID	Raheem Sterling	Man City	21	20	2	8	2	2	-
MID	Ross Barkley	Everton	22	21	2	5	2	-	-
ATT	Danny Ings	Liverpool	23	1	-	1	-	-	-
ATT	Danny Welbeck	Arsenal	25	34	14	5	6	-	-
ATT	Harry Kane	Tottenham	22	10	4	5	3	-	-
ATT	Jamie Vardy	Leicester	29	6	2	3	-	1	-
ATT	Rickie Lambert	West Brom	34	11	3	2	-	1	-
ATT	Theo Walcott	Arsenal	27	43	8	4	3	-	-
ATT	Wayne Rooney	Man Utd	30	109	51	8	7	-	-

ENGLAND

ENGLAND

CORRECT SCORES

	Competitive	Friendly
1-0	1	2
2-0	4	1
2-1	-	2
3-0	1	1
3-1	1	1
3-2	1	2
4-0	2	-
4-1	1	-
4-2	-	-
4-3	-	-
0-0	2	2
1-1	3	2
2-2	-	2
3-3	-	-
4-4	-	-
0-1	-	1
0-2	-	2
1-2	2	1
0-3	-	-
1-3	-	-
2-3	-	-
0-4	-	-
1-4	-	-
2-4	-	1
3-4	-	-
Other	5	-

Since Euro 2012

HALF-TIME/FULL-TIME DOUBLE RESULTS

Win/Win	10	43%
Draw/Win	5	22%
Lose/Win	1	4%
Win/Draw	2	9%
Draw/Draw	2	9%
Lose/Draw	1	4%
Win/Lose	0	0%
Draw/Lose	1	4%
Lose/Lose	1	4%

Overall: W16, D5, L2 in 23 games since Euro 2012

Win 1st half	12	52%
Win 2nd half	17	74%
Win both halves	10	43%
Goal both halves	16	70%

Overall
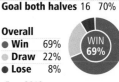
- Win 69%
- Draw 22%
- Lose 8%

CLEAN SHEETS

15 (65%)	**Clean sheets**	8 (35%)
✓		✗
13 (57%)	**Win to nil**	10 (43%)
✓		✗

2 (9%)	**Fail to score**	21 (91%)
✓		✗
0 (0%)	**Lose to nil**	23 (100%)
✓		✗

UNDER & OVER GOALS

20 (87%)	**Over 1.5**	3 (13%)
✓		✗
13 (57%)	**Over 2.5**	10 (43%)
✓		✗
10 (43%)	**Over 3.5**	13 (57%)
✓		✗
7 (30%)	**Over 4.5**	16 (70%)
✓		✗

BOTH TEAMS TO SCORE

8 (35%)	**Both score**	15 (65%)
✓		✗
3 (13%)	**& win**	20 (87%)
✓		✗
2 (9%)	**& lose**	21 (91%)
✓		✗

In 23 competitive games since Euro 2012

GOAL TIMES

● GOALS FOR ● GOALS AGAINST

Total match goals by half

26 (87%)	**1st half**	4 (13%)
F		A
38 (84%)	**2nd half**	7 (16%)
F		A

Goals for & against by half

26 (41%)	**For**	38 (59%)
1st		2nd
4 (36%)	**Against**	7 (64%)
1st		2nd

	0-9	10-18	19-27	28-36	37-45	46-54	55-63	64-72	73-81	82-90
For	3	3	2	9	9	5	6	8	11	8
Against	0	0	0	1	3	1	1	2	1	2

In 23 competitive games since Euro 2012

IF ENGLAND SCORE FIRST

They win	14	87%
Draw	2	13%
They lose	0	0%

In 23 games since Euro 2012

IF ENGLAND CONCEDE FIRST

They win	2	40%
Draw	1	20%
They lose	2	40%

He top-scored in qualifying but Wayne Rooney's record in major tournaments is poor

GOALSCORERS IN QUALIFYING ● FIRST GOALS

	Goals		1st		Anytime		Percentage of team goals	
W Rooney	7	●●●●●●●	3	42%	7	87%		23%
D Welbeck	6	●●●●●●	1	16%	4	80%		19%
T Walcott	3	●●●	1	33%	2	50%		10%
H Kane	3	●●●	1	33%	3	60%		10%
J Wilshere	2	●●	0	0%	1	20%		6%
R Barkley	2	●●	1	50%	2	40%		6%
R Sterling	2	●●	0	0%	2	25%		6%
P Jagielka	1	●	1	100%	1	16%		3%
A Townsend	1	●	0	0%	1	33%		3%
A Oxlade-Chamberlain	1	●	0	0%	1	14%		3%

In Euro 2016 qualifying

BOOKINGS

Matches played	10	☐ 15	▉ 0
Average make-up (☐ 10 ▉ 25)			15

In Euro 2016 qualifying

CORNERS

Avg F	7.3		76%
Avg A	2.3		24%

In Euro 2016 qualifying. Avg match total 9.6

RUSSIA

Eng V Russi 1-1r

They host the World Cup in two years so it would make sense for Russia to use Euro 2016 to build for the future, but if short-termism was a sport Russia would be nailed on to win gold. Manager Leonid Slutsky is only in the job until the end of the European Championships and he is set to rely on one of the oldest teams appearing in France.

How they qualified

The campaign needs to be broken down in two parts, the first under Fabio Capello before his reported £15m payoff, and the final four matches with Slutsky at the helm, when Russia secured automatic qualification behind runaway group winners Austria.

Capello failed to win four of his six matches (admittedly two were against group winners Austria) while Slutsky's side were rampant with four straight successes by an aggregate score of 12-1.

There was more freedom in Russia's play with Slutsky calling the shots, and his decision to use Artem Dzyuba as his main striker paid handsome dividends. The Zenit hitman finished with eight goals, six of which came under the new boss.

The manager

Slutsky is combining national team duties with his main job as CSKA Moscow manager but has said it is impossible to do both roles beyond the Euros.

There is more attacking zest to the side than in the stodgy performances under Capello during their group-stage exit at the World Cup and Slutsky is controversially happy to select nationalised players.

Brazilian-born keeper Guilherme made his debut in March and Roman Neustadter, a former German Under-21 international, is trying to get a Russian passport.

Match winners

What the 6ft 4in Dzyuba lacks in pace he makes up for with the knack of being in the right place at the right time and 2015

FACTFILE

FA founded 1912
www rfs.ru
Head coach Leonid Slutsky
National league Premier League
Date qualified October 12, 2015

Typical starting XI (4-1-4-1) Akinfeev; Smolnikov, Ignashevich, V Berezutski, Kombarov; Denisov; Kokorin, Dzagoev, Shirokov, Shatov; Dzyuba

Strengths
- ☑ Morale is improving under a more popular coach
- ☑ Dzyuba has scored goals at the highest level this season

Weaknesses
- ☒ There is a chronic lack of dynamism throughout the side
- ☒ The centre-backs were past their best some time ago

Star rating ★★☆☆☆

Fixtures

1 England, 8pm June 11, Marseille

2 Slovakia, 2pm June 15, Lille

3 Wales, 8pm June 20, Toulouse

Base Croissy-sur-Seine

Leonid Slutsky revitalised Russia's qualifying campaign

finished gloriously for Russia's lone striker. Not only did he excel with the national team but Dzyuba's tally of six goals in the Champions League group stage – he scored in each of Zenit's last five games in Group H – was bettered only by Robert Lewandowski and Cristiano Ronaldo.

Alan Dzagoev, joint-top goalscorer at Euro 2012, stalled under Capello but is now back in favour and it will be interesting to see whether Aleksandr Kokorin can finally live up to the hype that has surrounded him since a £16m move to Anzhi in 2013.

Question marks

The problem for Russia is their age. Seven of the players who started November's friendly win over Portugal were at least 30, while the qualification-sealing victory over Montenegro featured a defence of right-back Oleg Kuzmin (who was 34 at the time) and long-standing centre-backs Sergei Ignashevich (36) and Alexei Berezutski (33).

To highlight the issue, Kuzmin only made his debut in 2015 and one of the great hopes,

Real Madrid's Denis Cheryshev, went on loan to Valencia to get playing time.

And it doesn't stop there. Igor Denisov will be 32 by the time the action starts in France and his midfield partner Roman Shirokov is set to turn 35 during the tournament.

Ordinarily, keeper Igor Akinfeev would not be considered a weakness but he suffered from the jitters at the last World Cup and despite keeping more clean sheets in the Russian Premier League than any other custodian, he has gone 37 matches without a Champions League shutout.

How to back them

Dzyuba is most likely to notch for the Russians so back him to be their top goalscorer.

He was dumped on loan by former club Spartak to Russian Premier League side Rostov for the second half of the 2014-15 season once it became clear he was controversially signing for rivals Zenit, but Dzyuba has responded excellently since moving to St Petersburg and comes alive in the penalty box.

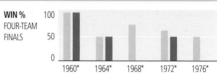

RUSSIA

GROUP B

EUROPEAN CHAMPIONSHIP RECORD

1960*	P	W	D	L	GF	GA
● **Winners**	2	2	0	0	5	1
Qualifying	2	2	0	0	4	1

1964*	P	W	D	L	GF	GA
● Runners-up	2	1	0	1	4	2
Qualifying	4	2	2	0	7	3

1968*	P	W	D	L	GF	GA
● Fourth	2	0	1	1	0	2
Qualifying	8	6	0	2	19	8

1972*	P	W	D	L	GF	GA
● Runners-up	2	1	0	1	1	3
Qualifying	8	5	3	0	16	4

1976*	P	W	D	L	GF	GA
Did not qualify	-	-	-	-	-	-
Qualifying	8	4	1	3	12	10

1980*	P	W	D	L	GF	GA
Did not qualify	-	-	-	-	-	-
Qualifying	6	1	3	2	7	8

1984*	P	W	D	L	GF	GA
Did not qualify	-	-	-	-	-	-
Qualifying	6	4	1	1	11	2

1988*	P	W	D	L	GF	GA
● Runners-up	5	3	1	1	7	4
Qualifying	8	5	3	0	14	3

1992*	P	W	D	L	GF	GA
Group stage	3	0	2	1	1	4
Qualifying	8	5	3	0	13	2

1996	P	W	D	L	GF	GA
Group stage	3	0	1	2	4	8
Qualifying	10	8	2	0	34	5

2000	P	W	D	L	GF	GA
Did not qualify	-	-	-	-	-	-
Qualifying	10	6	1	3	22	12

2004	P	W	D	L	GF	GA
Group stage	3	1	0	2	2	4
Qualifying	10	5	3	2	20	12

2008	P	W	D	L	GF	GA
● Semi-final	5	3	0	2	7	8
Qualifying	12	7	3	2	18	7

2012	P	W	D	L	GF	GA
Group stage	3	1	1	1	5	3
Qualifying	10	7	2	1	17	4

Totals	P	W	D	L	GF	GA
Finals	30	12	6	12	36	39
Qualifying	110	67	27	16	214	81

* Results & goals include extra time. Competed as USSR between 1960-1988 and CIS in 1992

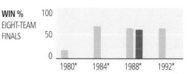

WIN % FOUR-TEAM FINALS — 1960* 1964* 1968* 1972* 1976*

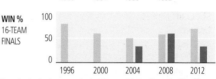

WIN % EIGHT-TEAM FINALS — 1980* 1984* 1988* 1992*

WIN % 16-TEAM FINALS — 1996 2000 2004 2008 2012

Results include extra time. ▌ in qualifying ▌ at the finals.
* Competed as USSR between 1960-1988 and CIS in 1992

LEGENDARY PLAYER

LEV YASHIN — LEGEND

Russia have had some great players – Valentin Ivanov for example – but goalkeeping innovator Lev Yashin stands head and shoulders above the rest. He is still the only keeper to have won the Ballon d'Or (in 1963) and played 78 times for USSR.

WORLD CUP RECORD

Year	Point of exit		Year	Point of exit
1930*	Did not enter		**1978***	Did not qualify
1934*	Did not enter		**1982***	Second round
1938*	Did not enter		**1986***	Round of 16
1950*	Did not enter		**1990***	Group stage
1954*	Did not enter		**1994**	Group stage
1958*	Quarter-finals		**1998**	Did not qualify
1962*	Quarter-finals		**2002**	Group stage
1966*	● Fourth		**2006**	Did not qualify
1970*	Quarter-finals		**2010**	Did not qualify
1974*	Did not qualify		**2014**	Group stage

* Competed as USSR between 1930-1990

DID YOU KNOW?

Seven of Artem Dzyuba's eight goals in qualifying came against the bottom two teams in the group

HOW THEY QUALIFIED

Group G	P	W	D	L	F	A	GD	Pts
Austria	10	9	1	0	22	5	+17	28
Russia	10	6	2	2	21	5	+16	20
Sweden	10	5	3	2	15	9	+6	18
Montenegro	10	3	2	5	10	13	-3	11
Liechtenstein	10	1	2	7	2	26	-24	5
Moldova	10	0	2	8	4	16	-12	2

Match stats in qualifying

Possession	▮▮▮▮▮▮▮▮▮▮▮▮	63%
Shots on target	▮▮▮▮▮▮▮▮▮▮▮▮▮	72%
Shots off target	▮▮▮▮▮▮▮▮▮▮▮▮▮	72%
Corners	▮▮▮▮▮▮▮▮▮▮▮▮	65%

Averages of match totals in qualifying. See pages 228-254 for full qualifying results

Results & prices	W	D	L
Russia.......(1) 4-0 (0)Liechtenstein	1-20	14-1	40-1
Sweden.....(0) 1-1 (1) ....Russia	2-1	9-4	33-20
Russia......(0) 1-1 (0)....Moldova	1-12	12-1	40-1
Austria......(0) 1-0 (0).......Russia	9-5	11-5	19-10
Montenegro(0)0-3 (0).......Russia	11-10	23-10	16-5
Russia......(0) 0-1 (1)......Austria	20-21	12-5	15-4
Russia......(1) 1-0 (0).... Sweden	23-20	9-4	3-1
Liechtenstein(0) 0-7 (3).......Russia	1-7	9-1	33-1
Moldova ...(0) 1-2 (0).......Russia	3-10	5-1	12-1
Russia......(2) 2-0 (0)Montenegro	1-3	9-2	12-1

Profit & loss in qualifying   -2.02 7.25 -1.35

Figures based on a £1 level stake using best odds in the Racing Post on day of match. W shows win price, whether home or away, L the price of the opposition. Montenegro forfeited their match against Russia and the result is not counted in Russia's P&L figure

PLAYERS USED IN QUALIFYING

Pos		Club	Age	CAREER P	G	QUALIFYING P	G	▯	▮
GK	Juri Lodygin	Zenit	26	10	-	2	-	-	-
GK	Igor Akinfeev	CSKA Moscow	30	86	-	10	-	-	-
DEF	Ivan Novoseltsev	Rostov	24	3	-	1	-	-	-
DEF	Georgy Schennikov	CSKA Moscow	25	7	-	1	-	-	-
DEF	Igor Smolnikov	Zenit	27	12	-	7	-	1	-
DEF	Sergey Parshivlyuk	Spartak Moscow	27	3	-	2	-	1	-
DEF	Vladimir Granat	Spartak Moscow	29	9	1	2	-	-	-
DEF	Sergei Ignashevich	CSKA Moscow	36	115	8	9	1	-	-
DEF	Vasili Berezutsky	CSKA Moscow	33	93	4	8	-	-	-
DEF	Oleg Kuzmin	Rubin	35	5	1	3	1	1	-
DEF	Alexei Berezutsky	CSKA Moscow	33	57	-	3	-	-	-
DEF	Nikita Chernov	CSKA Moscow	20	2	-	1	-	-	-
DEF	Yuri Zhirkov	Zenit	32	68	2	3	-	-	-
MID	Dmitri Kombarov	Spartak Moscow	29	38	2	8	1	1	-
MID	Pavel Mamaev	FK Krasnodar	27	10	-	3	-	1	-
MID	Aleksandr Samedov	Lokomotiv Moscow	31	28	3	2	-	-	-
MID	Denis Cheryshev	Valencia	25	9	-	4	-	-	-
MID	Alexei Ionov	Dinamo Moscow	27	11	-	3	-	-	-
MID	Alan Dzagoev	CSKA Moscow	25	49	9	8	1	1	-
MID	Magomed Ozdoev	Rubin	23	6	-	2	-	-	-
MID	Oleg Shatov	Zenit	25	21	2	8	-	1	-
MID	Denis Glushakov	Spartak Moscow	29	42	4	7	-	2	-
MID	Viktor Fayzulin	Zenit	30	20	4	2	-	-	-
MID	Roman Shirokov	CSKA Moscow	34	53	13	7	-	-	-
MID	Igor Denisov	Dinamo Moscow	32	52	-	5	-	1	-
MID	Oleg Ivanov	Terek Grozny	29	3	-	1	-	-	-
MID	Aleksey Miranchuk	Lokomotiv Moscow	20	2	1	1	-	-	-
MID	Dmitri Torbinski	FK Krasnodar	32	28	2	1	-	-	-
mid	Maksim Grigoryev	Lokomotiv Moscow	25	4	-	1	-	-	-
ATT	Artem Dzyuba	Zenit	27	16	8	8	8	-	-
ATT	Fedor Smolov	FK Krasnodar	26	12	5	3	1	-	-
ATT	Aleksandr Kokorin	Zenit	25	37	11	9	3	1	-
ATT	Alexander Kerzhakov	FC Zurich	33	91	30	3	-	-	-
ATT	Dmitriy Poloz	Rostov	24	2	-	1	-	-	-

RUSSIA

CORRECT SCORES

	Competitive	Friendly
1-0	3	2
2-0	2	3
2-1	1	2
3-0	-	1
3-1	1	-
3-2	-	-
4-0	3	1
4-1	1	-
4-2	-	1
4-3	-	-
0-0	-	1
1-1	5	4
2-2	-	1
3-3	-	-
4-4	-	-
0-1	5	-
0-2	-	-
1-2	-	-
0-3	-	-
1-3	-	1
2-3	-	-
0-4	-	-
1-4	-	-
2-4	-	1
3-4	-	-
Other	1	-

Since Euro 2012. Abandoned match vs Montenegro is not included

HALF-TIME/FULL-TIME DOUBLE RESULTS

Win/Win	9	41%
Draw/Win	3	14%
Lose/Win	0	0%
Win/Draw	3	14%
Draw/Draw	2	9%
Lose/Draw	0	9%
Win/Lose	0	0%
Draw/Lose	2	9%
Lose/Lose	3	14%

Win 1st half	12	55%
Win 2nd half	9	41%
Win both halves	6	27%
Goal both halves	9	41%

Overall
- Win 50%
- Draw 32%
- Lose 18%

WIN 50%

Overall: W12, D5, L5 in 22 competitive games since Euro 2012

CLEAN SHEETS

9 (41%)	Clean sheets	13 (59%)
✓		✗

9 (41%)	Win to nil	13 (59%)
✓		✗

5 (23%)	Fail to score	17 (77%)
✓		✗

5 (23%)	Lose to nil	17 (77%)
✓		✗

UNDER & OVER GOALS

14 (64%)	Over 1.5	8 (36%)
✓		✗

7 (32%)	Over 2.5	15 (68%)
✓		✗

6 (27%)	Over 3.5	16 (73%)
✓		✗

2 (9%)	Over 4.5	20 (91%)
✓		✗

BOTH TEAMS TO SCORE

8 (36%)	Both score	14 (64%)
✓		✗

3 (14%)	& win	19 (86%)
✓		✗

0 (0%)	& lose	22 (100%)
✓		✗

In 22 competitive games since 2012 World Cup

GOAL TIMES

● GOALS FOR ● GOALS AGAINST

Total match goals by half

19 (86%)	1st half	3 (14%)
F		A

21 (68%)	2nd half	10 (32%)
F		A

Goals for & against by half

19 (48%)	For	21 (53%)
1st		2nd

3 (23%)	Against	10 (77%)
1st		2nd

6	3	1	3	6	4	2	2	9	4
0-9	10-18	19-27	28-36	37-45	46-54	55-63	64-72	73-81	82-90
1	0	0	1	1	1	1	1	2	5

In 22 competitive games since Euro 2012

IF RUSSIA SCORE FIRST

They win	12		75%
Draw	4		25%
They lose	0		0%

In 22 competitive games since Euro 2012

IF RUSSIA CONCEDE FIRST

They win	0		0%
Draw	1		17%
They lose	5		83%

Artem Dzyuba's winner against Sweden was a key goal in their qualifying group

GOALSCORERS IN QUALIFYING

● FIRST GOALS

	Goals		1st		Anytime		Percentage of team goals	
A Dzyuba	8	●●●●●●●●	3	37%	5	62%		44%
A Kokorin	3	●●●	1	33%	3	33%		17%
O Kuzmin	1	●	1	100%	1	33%		6%
S Ignashevich	1	●	1	100%	1	11%		6%
A Dzagoev	1	●	0	0%	1	12%		6%
D Kombarov	1	●	0	0%	1	12%		6%
F Smolov	1	●	0	0%	1	33%		6%

In Euro 2016 qualifying. Total team goals does not include goals awarded in abandoned game vs Montenegro

BOOKINGS

Matches played	10	☐11	▮ 0
Average make-up (☐10 ▮25)			11

In Euro 2016 qualifying

CORNERS

Avg F	6.2		65%
Avg A	3.3		35%

In Euro 2016 qualifying. Avg match total 9.6

WALES

N ot since 1958 have the Welsh been able to celebrate reaching a major tournament. There was a big party once qualification was secured after several heartbreaking near misses and the excitement reached fever pitch when they were drawn with England. 'Together stronger' is their motto and Wales are determined to make their mark.

How they qualified

Wales eventually finished second to Belgium but they had the better of the head-to-heads against the Red Devils with a goalless draw in Brussels followed by a 1-0 home win as Gareth Bale inevitably turned out to be the match winner in Cardiff.

Chris Coleman's side scored only 11 goals in qualifying – no team in a six-nation section scored fewer and made it to France – but a strong defence laid the foundations for success. They conceded just four goals in their ten fixtures.

The plan was fairly simple: keep it tight and give the ball to Bale, who scored seven of their 11 goals and came up trumps at every opportunity, including in the first game when Wales trailed 1-0 in Andorra before a double from the Real Madrid superstar spared their blushes.

That was one of six Welsh victories, four of which were by one-goal margins.

The manager

Coleman's club managerial career, which took him to Real Sociedad and Larissa in Greece as well as Fulham and Coventry, was fairly unremarkable, but he has rebuilt his reputation since replacing the late Gary Speed in extremely difficult circumstances in 2012.

At the moment Coleman can do no wrong but it was not always so, and after a miserable World Cup qualifying effort there were many calls for Cookie to be handed his P45.

Match winners

You cannot look past Bale, who has revelled

FACTFILE

FA founded 1876
www faw.org.uk
Head coach Chris Coleman
National league Welsh Premier League
Date qualified October 10, 2015

Typical starting XI (5-3-2) Hennessey; Gunter, Chester, Williams, Davies, Taylor; Ramsey, Ledley, Allen; Bale, Robson-Kanu

Strengths

☑ Bale is one of the best players in the world

☑ The Welsh defence was strong in qualifying

Weaknesses

☒ The team could be too reliant on Bale to damage their opponents

☒ There's little depth in the squad to cover injury and suspension

Star rating ★★☆☆☆

Fixtures

1 Slovakia, 5pm June 11, Bordeaux

2 England, 2pm June 16, Lens

3 Russia, 8pm June 20, Toulouse

Base Dinard

in the role of being the most influential player in a team – just as he did in the Premier League – to show the form which earned him his move to the Bernabeu.

From his dribbling ability to his aerial threat, Bale possesses many qualities and Wales will need the Real Madrid man to be at his best to do any significant damage in France.

Centre-back Ashley Williams excelled during the qualifying campaign and Arsenal's Aaron Ramsey is another class act who could become even more important if opponents solely attempt to nullify Bale.

Question marks

A goal each for David Cotterill and Hal Robson-Kanu made them the only players apart from Bale and two-goal Ramsey to score in qualifying and there is a concern that the second match against England will be a distraction when, arguably, the more important fixtures in terms of qualification will be against Slovakia and Russia.

Those who follow the market will have noticed that Wales were friendless in the betting for a number of their qualification matches and their shot ratio against teams who finished in the top three of their group (Belgium and Bosnia) was only 19th best of the 24 qualifiers at 44 per cent.

After the March friendlies, Coleman was bemoaning his side's defending at set-pieces.

How to back them

Greece won Euro 2004 armed with a well-organised defence and a committed midfield and they didn't have anybody close to the level of Bale, but playing that way requires a certain amount of luck and the Dragons are a difficult team to weigh up.

Bookmakers understandably make their qualification prospects a close thing, although betting on the top scorer market is a lot more decisive with Bale a warm order. Bale obviously deserves favouritism but he is likely to be a marked man in France and that could be right up Ramsey's street.

WALES

EUROPEAN CHAMPIONSHIP RECORD

1960	P	W	D	L	GF	GA
Did not enter	-	-	-	-	-	-
Qualifying	-	-	-	-	-	-

1964	P	W	D	L	GF	GA
Did not qualify	-	-	-	-	-	-
Qualifying	2	0	1	1	2	4

1968	P	W	D	L	GF	GA
Did not qualify	-	-	-	-	-	-
Qualifying	6	1	2	3	6	12

1972	P	W	D	L	GF	GA
Did not qualify	-	-	-	-	-	-
Qualifying	6	2	1	3	5	6

1976	P	W	D	L	GF	GA
Did not qualify	-	-	-	-	-	-
Qualifying	8	5	1	2	15	7

1980	P	W	D	L	GF	GA
Did not qualify	-	-	-	-	-	-
Qualifying	6	3	0	3	11	8

1984	P	W	D	L	GF	GA
Did not qualify	-	-	-	-	-	-
Qualifying	6	2	3	1	7	6

1988	P	W	D	L	GF	GA
Did not qualify	-	-	-	-	-	-
Qualifying	6	2	2	2	7	5

1992	P	W	D	L	GF	GA
Did not qualify	-	-	-	-	-	-
Qualifying	6	4	1	1	8	6

1996	P	W	D	L	GF	GA
Did not qualify	-	-	-	-	-	-
Qualifying	10	2	2	6	9	19

2000	P	W	D	L	GF	GA
Did not qualify	-	-	-	-	-	-
Qualifying	8	3	0	5	7	16

2004	P	W	D	L	GF	GA
Did not qualify	-	-	-	-	-	-
Qualifying	10	4	2	4	13	11

2008	P	W	D	L	GF	GA
Did not qualify	-	-	-	-	-	-
Qualifying	12	4	3	5	18	19

2012	P	W	D	L	GF	GA
Did not qualify	-	-	-	-	-	-
Qualifying	8	3	0	5	6	10

Totals	P	W	D	L	GF	GA
Finals	-	-	-	-	-	-
Qualifying	94	35	18	41	114	129

Results & goals include extra time

WIN % FOUR-TEAM FINALS

(bar chart: 1960, 1964, 1968, 1972, 1976; scale 0–100)

WIN % EIGHT-TEAM FINALS

(bar chart: 1980, 1984, 1988, 1992; scale 0–100)

WIN % 16-TEAM FINALS

(bar chart: 1996, 2000, 2004, 2008, 2012; scale 0–100)

Results include extra time. ▮ in qualifying ▮ at the finals

LEGENDARY PLAYER

JOHN CHARLES   LEGEND

John Charles was a key member of the team that reached the quarter-finals of the 1958 World Cup, the only other time Wales have qualified for a major tournament, and he made his mark in Europe with Juventus, winning the Scudetto three times.

WORLD CUP RECORD

Year	Point of exit	Year	Point of exit
1930	Did not enter	1978	Did not qualify
1934	Did not enter	1982	Did not qualify
1938	Did not enter	1986	Did not qualify
1950	Did not qualify	1990	Did not qualify
1954	Did not qualify	1994	Did not qualify
1958	Quarter-finals	1998	Did not qualify
1962	Did not qualify	2002	Did not qualify
1966	Did not qualify	2006	Did not qualify
1970	Did not qualify	2010	Did not qualify
1974	Did not qualify	2014	Did not qualify

DID YOU KNOW?

Real Madrid star Gareth Bale scored seven of Wales's 11 goals in qualifying and was credited for the assist in two more

HOW THEY QUALIFIED

Group B	P	W	D	L	F	A	GD	Pts
Belgium	10	7	2	1	24	5	+19	23
Wales	10	6	3	1	11	4	+7	21
Bosnia-Hz.	10	5	2	3	17	12	+5	17
Israel	10	4	1	5	16	14	+2	13
Cyprus	10	4	0	6	16	17	-1	12
Andorra	10	0	0	10	4	36	-32	0

Match stats in qualifying

Possession	▮▮▮▮▮▮▮▮▮	52%
Shots on target	▮▮▮▮▮▮▮▮▮▮▮▮	68%
Shots off target	▮▮▮▮▮▮▮▮▮▮▮	60%
Corners	▮▮▮▮▮▮▮▮▮▮▮▮	64%

Averages of match totals in qualifying. See pages 228-254 for full qualifying results

Results & prices		W	D	L
Andorra .... (1) 1-2 (1) .... Wales		1-6	10-1	25-1
Wales .... (0) 0-0 (0) . Bosnia-Hz.		13-5	12-5	5-4
Wales .... (2) 2-1 (1) .... Cyprus		4-9	7-2	8-1
Belgium .... (0) 0-0 (0) .... Wales		12-1	5-1	3-10
Israel .... (0) 0-3 (1) .... Wales		14-5	23-10	13-10
Wales .... (1) 1-0 (0) ..... Belgium		17-4	11-4	4-5
Cyprus ...... (0) 0-1 (0) .... Wales		5-6	13-5	9-2
Wales .... (0) 0-0 (0) .... Israel		10-11	13-5	4-1
Bosnia-Hz. (0) 2-0 (0) .... Wales		7-2	13-5	19-20
Wales .... (0) 2-0 (0) .....Andorra		1-20	20-1	80-1

Profit & loss in qualifying 4.54 3 -8.05

Figures based on a £1 level stake using best odds in the Racing Post on day of match. W shows win price, whether home or away, L the price of the opposition

PLAYERS USED IN QUALIFYING

Pos		Club	Age	CAREER		QUALIFYING			
				P	G	P	G	▯	▮
GK	Wayne Hennessey	Crystal Palace	29	56	-	10	-	1	-
DEF	James Collins	West Ham	32	46	3	1	-	-	-
DEF	Jazz Richards	Fulham	25	9	-	4	-	1	-
DEF	Ben Davies	Tottenham	23	19	-	7	-	-	-
DEF	Chris Gunter	Reading	26	66	-	10	-	1	-
DEF	James Chester	West Brom	27	10	-	6	-	1	-
DEF	Ashley Williams	Swansea	31	58	1	10	-	2	-
DEF	Neil Taylor	Swansea	27	27	-	9	-	2	-
MID	Jonathan Williams	MK Dons	22	11	-	2	-	-	-
MID	Aaron Ramsey	Arsenal	25	38	10	8	2	1	-
MID	David Vaughan	Nottm Forest	33	41	1	2	-	1	-
MID	Andy King	Leicester	27	32	2	6	-	-	1
MID	Joe Ledley	Crystal Palace	29	61	4	7	-	2	-
MID	Emyr Huws	Huddersfield	22	6	1	2	-	1	-
MID	Joe Allen	Liverpool	26	25	-	5	-	3	-
MID	Shaun MacDonald	Bournemouth	27	4	-	2	-	-	-
MID	David Edwards	Wolves	30	31	3	5	-	1	-
MID	David Cotterill	Birmingham	28	23	2	2	1	1	-
MID	George Williams	Gillingham	20	7	-	4	-	1	-
MID	Jake Taylor	Exeter	24	1	-	1	-	-	-
ATT	Gareth Bale	Real Madrid	26	54	19	10	7	1	-
ATT	Tom Lawrence	Cardiff	22	4	-	1	-	-	-
ATT	Hal Robson-Kanu	Reading	27	30	2	9	1	1	-
ATT	Sam Vokes	Burnley	26	39	6	6	-	-	-
ATT	Simon Church	MK Dons	27	35	3	7	-	1	-

WALES

CORRECT SCORES

	Competitive	Friendly
1-0	3	-
2-0	1	-
2-1	4	1
3-0	1	-
3-1	-	1
3-2	-	-
4-0	-	-
4-1	-	-
4-2	-	-
4-3	-	-
0-0	3	1
1-1	1	2
2-2	-	-
3-3	-	-
4-4	-	-
0-1	-	1
0-2	3	2
1-2	2	-
0-3	1	-
1-3	-	-
2-3	-	1
0-4	-	-
1-4	-	-
2-4	-	-
3-4	-	-
Other	1	-

Since Euro 2012

HALF-TIME/FULL-TIME DOUBLE RESULTS

Win/Win	3	15%	Win 1st half	4	20%
Draw/Win	4	20%	Win 2nd half	7	35%
Lose/Win	2	10%	Win both halves	1	5%
Win/Draw	0	0%	Goal both halves	10	50%
Draw/Draw	4	20%			
Lose/Draw	0	0%	**Overall**		
Win/Lose	1	5%	● Win	45%	
Draw/Lose	2	10%	● Draw	20%	
Lose/Lose	4	20%	● Lose	35%	

Overall: W9, D4, L7 in 20 competitive games since Euro 2012

CLEAN SHEETS

8 (40%)	Clean sheets	12 (60%)	7 (35%)	Fail to score	13 (65%)
✓		✗	✓		✗
5 (25%)	Win to nil	15 (75%)	4 (20%)	Lose to nil	16 (80%)
✓		✗	✓		✗

UNDER & OVER GOALS

14 (70%)	Over 1.5	6 (30%)
✓		✗
9 (45%)	Over 2.5	11 (55%)
✓		✗
1 (5%)	Over 3.5	19 (95%)
✓		✗
1 (5%)	Over 4.5	19 (95%)
✓		✗

BOTH TEAMS TO SCORE

8 (40%)	Both score	12 (60%)
✓		✗
4 (20%)	& win	16 (80%)
✓		✗
3 (15%)	& lose	17 (85%)
✓		✗

In 20 competitive games since Euro 2012

GOAL TIMES

Total match goals by half

8 (40%)	1st half	12 (60%)
F		A
12 (50%)	2nd half	12 (50%)
F		A

Goals for & against by half

8 (40%)	For	12 (60%)
1st		2nd
12 (50%)	Against	12 (50%)
1st		2nd

● GOALS FOR ● GOALS AGAINST

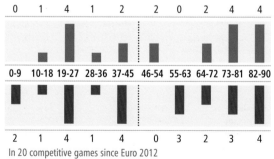

	0-9	10-18	19-27	28-36	37-45	46-54	55-63	64-72	73-81	82-90
For	0	1	4	1	2	2	0	2	4	4
Against	2	1	4	1	4	0	3	2	3	4

In 20 competitive games since Euro 2012

IF WALES SCORE FIRST

They win	6		86%
Draw	0		0%
They lose	1		14%

In 20 competitive games since Euro 2012

IF WALES CONCEDE FIRST

They win	3		30%
Draw	1		10%
They lose	6		60%

Welsh wonder Gareth Bale was quality in qualifying

GOALSCORERS IN QUALIFYING ● FIRST GOALS

	Goals		1st		Anytime		Percentage of team goals	
G Bale	7 ●●●●●●●		2	28%	5	50%	▌▌▌▌▌▌▌▌▌▌▌▌▌	64%
A Ramsey	2 ●●		2	100%	2	25%	▌▌▌	18%
D Cotterill	1 ●		1	100%	1	50%	▌	9%
H Robson-Kanu	1 ●		0	0%	1	11%	▌	9%

In Euro 2016 qualifying

BOOKINGS

Matches played	10	☐21	▌ 1
Average make-up (☐10 ▌25)			23.5

In Euro 2016 qualifying

CORNERS

Avg F	5.8	▌▌▌▌▌▌▌▌▌▌▌	64%
Avg A	3.3	▌▌▌▌▌▌	36%

In Euro 2016 qualifying. Avg match total 9.1

SLOVAKIA

I f you're looking for some Euro 2016 trivia to test your mates, this will almost certainly leave them stumped – which European country went on the longest winning run after the World Cup? Well done to anyone who correctly nailed Slovakia, who made a storming start to the new international cycle with nine straight wins, a run which suggests bookmakers are wrong to mark them down as whipping boys.

GROUP B

How they qualified

Slovakia, as their national-best winning run suggests, started the campaign on fire, with six consecutive qualifying victories as well as three friendly wins, a streak which included a 1-0 triumph in Ukraine and a stunning 2-1 success at home to reigning champions Spain.

Jan Kozak's team got nervous with a first European Championship spot in sight and failed to score in three matches, even losing 1-0 at home to ten-man Belarus, but qualification was secured with a 4-2 win against Luxembourg.

The manager

Kozak, a former Czechoslovakia international who helped the country reach the European Championship semi-finals in 1980, issued a warning to Slovakia's Group B rivals when he said: "It is important that the team has not reached its best. There's still room for improvement."

There is unlikely to be a surprise in the tactics – Kozak will build the team from the back and will rely on counter-attacking.

Match winners

There is a strong spine to the side with goalkeeper Matus Kozacik described as "extraordinary" by his manager after the win over Spain, while Liverpool's Martin Skrtel leads the defence.

The energetic Juraj Kucka is not afraid to get stuck in to opponents, while their standout player is Marek Hamsik, who top-scored in qualifying with five goals.

A gifted if slightly inconsistent playmaker,

FACTFILE

FA founded 1938
www futbalsfz.sk
Head coach Jan Kozak
National league Super Liga
Date qualified October 12, 2015

Typical starting XI (4-2-3-1) Kozacik; Pekarik, Skrtel, Durica, Hubocan; Kucka, Pecovsky; Mak, Hamsik, Weiss; Nemec

Strengths
☑ Hamsik is a classy playmaker
☑ Strong defence stood firm during qualification

Weaknesses
☒ Slovakia lack a renowned striker with Willem II's Nemec leading the line
☒ Counter-attacking team lacks tactical flexibility

Star rating ★★☆☆☆

Fixtures
1 Wales, 5pm June 11, Bordeaux
2 Russia, 2pm June 15, Lille
3 England, 8pm June 20, Saint-Etienne
Base Vichy

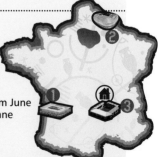

Jan Kozak will set his team up to hit on the break

Hamsik has thrived at Napoli this season and is the man who usually makes Slovakia tick.

Also watch out for Vladimir Weiss – the one-time Manchester City winger was credited by Uefa with six assists in qualifying and should be playing his club football at a higher level but he decided to take the big money on offer in the Qatari championship.

Question marks

Playing on the break is all well and good when you score first and opponents have to come on to you, but what happens if you need to chase the game? Slovakia scored first seven times in qualifying and won the lot, but failed to score in the three other matches.

Kozak would love a high-quality striker – journeyman Adam Nemec often leads the line – and Sydney's Filip Holosko turned down the chance to play in the March friendlies to concentrate on club football.

Robert Vittek, who turned 34 on April 1, may yet get his fair share of minutes given the lack of options elsewhere but he is not the same player who scored four times as Slovakia made the knockout phase of the 2010 World Cup.

How to back them

Bookmakers may be wrong to be so dismissive of Slovakia. The Group B outsiders have the potential to make life tricky for at least Russia and Wales so a lay of them to finish bottom of the section looks a strong play – there is not much between Slovakia and the other two.

They are bigger than 21-10 to win their opening match against Wales in Bordeaux on June 11 which looks on the large side, although a safer wager is to take Slovakia on the draw no bet as the outsiders in a clash of counter-attacking sides that looks destined to be tight.

SLOVAKIA

EUROPEAN CHAMPIONSHIP RECORD

1960*	P	W	D	L	GF	GA
● Third	2	1	0	1	2	3
Qualifying	6	4	1	1	16	5

1964*	P	W	D	L	GF	GA
Did not qualify	-	-	-	-	-	-
Qualifying	2	0	1	1	2	3

1968*	P	W	D	L	GF	GA
Did not qualify	-	-	-	-	-	-
Qualifying	6	3	1	2	8	4

1972*	P	W	D	L	GF	GA
Did not qualify	-	-	-	-	-	-
Qualifying	6	4	1	1	11	4

1976*	P	W	D	L	GF	GA
● Winners	2	1	1	0	5	3
Qualifying	8	5	2	1	19	7

1980*	P	W	D	L	GF	GA
● Third	4	1	2	1	5	4
Qualifying	6	5	0	1	17	4

1984*	P	W	D	L	GF	GA
Did not qualify	-	-	-	-	-	-
Qualifying	8	3	4	1	15	7

1988*	P	W	D	L	GF	GA
Did not qualify	-	-	-	-	-	-
Qualifying	6	2	3	1	7	5

1992*	P	W	D	L	GF	GA
Did not qualify	-	-	-	-	-	-
Qualifying	8	5	0	3	12	9

1996	P	W	D	L	GF	GA
Did not qualify	-	-	-	-	-	-
Qualifying	10	4	2	4	14	18

2000	P	W	D	L	GF	GA
Did not qualify	-	-	-	-	-	-
Qualifying	10	5	2	3	12	9

2004	P	W	D	L	GF	GA
Did not qualify	-	-	-	-	-	-
Qualifying	8	3	1	4	11	9

2008	P	W	D	L	GF	GA
Did not qualify	-	-	-	-	-	-
Qualifying	12	5	1	6	33	23

2012	P	W	D	L	GF	GA
Did not qualify	-	-	-	-	-	-
Qualifying	10	4	3	3	7	10

Totals	P	W	D	L	GF	GA
Finals	8	3	3	2	12	10
Qualifying	106	52	22	32	184	117

* Results & goals include extra time. Competed as part of Czechoslovakia 1960-1992

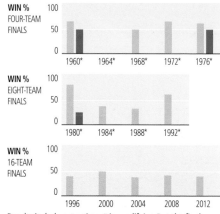

WIN % FOUR-TEAM FINALS	1960* 1964* 1968* 1972* 1976*
WIN % EIGHT-TEAM FINALS	1980* 1984* 1988* 1992*
WIN % 16-TEAM FINALS	1996 2000 2004 2008 2012

Results include extra time. ▮ in qualifying ▮ at the finals.
* Competed as part of Czechoslovakia 1960-1992

LEGENDARY PLAYER

Robert Vittek is a bit-part player these days but he was Slovakia's star man at the 2010 World Cup. His four goals included one in each half as they knocked out defending champions Italy to reach the last 16 in their only previous tournament finals.

ROBERT VITTEK — LEGEND

WORLD CUP RECORD

Year	Point of exit	Year	Point of exit
1930*	Did not enter	1978*	Did not qualify
1934*	● Runners-up	1982*	First round
1938*	Quarter-finals	1986*	Did not qualify
1950*	Did not enter	1990*	Quarter-finals
1954*	First round	1994*	Did not qualify
1958*	First round	1998	Did not qualify
1962*	● Runners-up	2002	Did not qualify
1966*	Did not qualify	2006	Did not qualify
1970*	Group stage	2010	Round of 16
1974*	Did not qualify	2014	Did not qualify

* Competed as part of Czechoslovakia between 1930-1994

DID YOU KNOW?

Only Hallur Hansson of the Faroe Islands saw more yellow cards than Martin Skrtel's five in qualifying

HOW THEY QUALIFIED

Group C	P	W	D	L	F	A	GD	Pts
Spain	10	9	0	1	23	3	+20	27
Slovakia	10	7	1	2	17	8	+9	22
Ukraine	10	6	1	3	14	4	+10	19
Belarus	10	3	2	5	8	14	-6	11
Luxembourg	10	1	1	8	6	27	-21	4
Macedonia	10	1	1	8	6	18	-12	4

Match stats in qualifying

Possession	▌▌▌▌▌▌▌▌	45%
Shots on target	▌▌▌▌▌▌▌▌▌▌▌	61%
Shots off target	▌▌▌▌▌▌▌	40%
Corners	▌▌▌▌▌▌	37%

Averages of match totals in qualifying. See pages 228-254 for full qualifying results

Results & prices

	W	D	L
Ukraine.....(0) 0-1 (1) .....Slovakia	5-1	29-10	7-10
Slovakia....(1) 2-1 (0) ....Spain	9-1	15-4	2-5
Belarus .....(0) 1-3 (0).....Slovakia	13-10	12-5	5-2
Macedonia(0) 0-2 (2) .....Slovakia	Evs	12-5	18-5
Slovakia....(3) 3-0 (0)Luxembourg	1-7	9-1	25-1
Slovakia....(2) 2-1 (0) Macedonia	2-7	5-1	15-1
Spain ....(2) 2-0 (0) .....Slovakia	14-1	11-2	1-3
Slovakia....(0) 0-0 (0) ......Ukraine	13-8	11-5	21-10
Slovakia....(0) 0-1 (1) ...... Belarus	3-5	16-5	6-1
Luxembourg(0)2-4 (3) .....Slovakia	1-3	9-2	11-1

Profit & loss in qualifying 14.06 -6.80 -1.67

Figures based on a £1 level stake using best odds in the Racing Post on day of match. W shows win price, whether home or away, L the price of the opposition

PLAYERS USED IN QUALIFYING

Pos		Club	Age	CAREER P	G	QUALIFYING P	G	 ▯	◼
GK	Matus Kozacik	Viktoria Plzen	32	15	-	10	-	1	-
DEF	Martin Skrtel	Liverpool	31	79	5	8	-	5	-
DEF	Kornel Salata	S. Bratislava	31	36	2	4	1	-	-
DEF	Lukas Tesak	Kairat	31	3	-	1	-	1	-
DEF	Tomas Hubocan	Din. Moscow	30	44	-	9	-	1	-
DEF	Jan Durica	Loko Moscow	34	77	4	5	-	1	-
DEF	Norbert Gyomber	Roma	23	12	-	6	-	3	-
DEF	Peter Pekarik	Hertha Berlin	29	65	2	8	1	1	-
MID	Miroslav Stoch	Bursaspor	26	52	6	7	1	1	-
MID	Robert Mak	PAOK Salonika	25	26	7	9	2	-	-
MID	Vladimir Weiss	Al-Gharafa	26	50	4	8	1	2	-
MID	Marek Hamsik	Napoli	28	85	17	10	5	1	-
MID	Filip Kiss	Haugesund	25	8	-	4	-	1	-
MID	Juraj Kucka	Milan	29	45	4	9	2	4	-
MID	Viktor Pecovsky	Zilina	33	30	1	9	-	-	-
MID	Jan Gregus	Jablonec	25	5	-	1	-	-	-
MID	Ondrej Duda	Legia Warsaw	21	9	1	3	-	-	-
MID	Patrik Hrosovsky	Viktoria Plzen	24	9	-	3	-	-	-
MID	Dusan Svento	Cologne	30	36	1	4	-	-	-
MID	Erik Sabo	PAOK Salonika	24	8	-	2	-	-	-
MID	Filip Holosko	Sydney FC	32	65	8	1	-	-	-
MID	Stanislav Sestak	Ferencvaros	33	63	13	3	1	1	-
ATT	Martin Jakubko	Ruzomberok	36	41	9	2	-	-	-
ATT	Robert Vittek	S. Bratislava	34	82	23	1	-	-	-
ATT	Adam Nemec	Willem II	30	20	4	7	3	1	-
ATT	Michal Duris	Mlada Boleslav	28	23	3	6	-	-	-

SOCCERBASE.COM

SLOVAKIA

CORRECT SCORES

	Competitive	Friendly
1-0	2	2
2-0	2	2
2-1	3	1
3-0	1	-
3-1	1	3
3-2	-	1
4-0	-	-
4-1	-	-
4-2	1	-
4-3	-	-
0-0	1	2
1-1	3	1
2-2	1	1
3-3	-	-
4-4	-	-
0-1	3	1
0-2	1	-
1-2	1	1
0-3	-	1
1-3	-	-
2-3	-	-
0-4	-	-
1-4	-	-
2-4	-	-
3-4	-	-
Other	-	-

Since Euro 2012

HALF-TIME/FULL-TIME DOUBLE RESULTS

Win/Win	8	40%
Draw/Win	2	10%
Lose/Win	0	0%
Win/Draw	1	5%
Draw/Draw	3	15%
Lose/Draw	1	5%
Win/Lose	1	5%
Draw/Lose	1	5%
Lose/Lose	3	15%

Win 1st half	10	50%
Win 2nd half	4	20%
Win both halves	1	5%
Goal both halves	8	40%

Overall
- ● **Win** 50%
- ● **Draw** 25%
- ● **Lose** 25%

WIN 50%

Overall: W10, D5, L5 in 20 competitive games since Euro 2012

CLEAN SHEETS

7 (35%)	**Clean sheets**	13 (65%)
✓		✗
6 (30%)	**Win to nil**	14 (70%)
✓		✗

5 (25%)	**Fail to score**	15 (75%)
✓		✗
4 (20%)	**Lose to nil**	16 (80%)
✓		✗

UNDER & OVER GOALS

14 (70%)	**Over 1.5**	6 (30%)
✓		✗
8 (40%)	**Over 2.5**	12 (60%)
✓		✗
3 (15%)	**Over 3.5**	17 (85%)
✓		✗
1 (5%)	**Over 4.5**	19 (95%)
✓		✗

BOTH TEAMS TO SCORE

10 (50%)	**Both score**	10 (50%)
✓		✗
5 (25%)	**& win**	15 (75%)
✓		✗
1 (5%)	**& lose**	19 (95%)
✓		✗

In 20 competitive games since Euro 2012

GOAL TIMES

● GOALS FOR ● GOALS AGAINST

Total match goals by half

20 (74%)	**1st half**	7 (26%)
F		A
8 (42%)	**2nd half**	11 (58%)
F		A

4	4	3	3	6	0	0	1	3	4
0-9	10-18	19-27	28-36	37-45	46-54	55-63	64-72	73-81	82-90
1	2	1	2	1	1	2	3	2	3

Goals for & against by half

20 (71%)	**For**	8 (29%)
1st		2nd
7 (39%)	**Against**	11 (61%)
1st		2nd

In 20 competitive games since Euro 2012

IF SLOVAKIA SCORE FIRST

They win	10		83%
Draw	1		8%
They lose	1		8%

In 20 competitive games since Euro 2012

IF SLOVAKIA CONCEDE FIRST

They win	0		0%
Draw	3		43%
They lose	4		57%

*Marek Hamsik is
Slovakia's class act*

GOALSCORERS IN QUALIFYING ● FIRST GOALS

	Goals		1st		Anytime		Percentage of team goals	
M Hamsik	5	●●●●●	2	40%	3	30%		29%
A Nemec	3	●●●	1	33%	3	42%		18%
J Kucka	2	●●	2	100%	2	22%		12%
R Mak	2	●●	1	50%	2	22%		12%
S Sestak	1	●	0	0%	1	33%		6%
P Pekarik	1	●	0	0%	1	12%		6%
M Stoch	1	●	0	0%	1	14%		6%
V Weiss	1	●	0	0%	1	12%		6%
K Salata	1	●	1	100%	1	25%		6%

In Euro 2016 qualifying

BOOKINGS

Matches played   10   ☐24   ■ 0
Average make-up (☐10 ■25)   24

In Euro 2016 qualifying

CORNERS

Avg F   3.7   37%
Avg A   6.2   63%

In Euro 2016 qualifying. Avg match total 9.9

North's party to finish early despite brilliant qualifying campaign

A bet on **Northern Ireland** to finish bottom of Group C won't win many points for originality, but it should at least win.

Northern Ireland have done wonderfully well to reach the finals and there is no question that coach Michael O'Neill, who guided them to France as group winners, is a shrewd operator.

However, it could be argued the rest of the group imploded. Favourites Greece finished bottom, Hungary used three different managers and Romania also went through a coaching change, while Northern Ireland's continuity helped them come out on top.

The really hard work begins now and O'Neill's men could barely have received a tougher draw than world champions Germany, Poland, who were possibly the best side in pot three of the seeding system, and a Ukraine outfit who are probably the strongest of the playoff winners.

Facing Germany last is a bonus as they could rest key men if qualification is in the bag, but it does mean that Ukraine meet Poland in the final round of fixtures and it is easy to imagine a scenario where a draw is mutually beneficial for both sides to qualify.

Germany should top the group. They took their eye off the ball in qualifying but possess world-class quality all over the pitch and although they are unlikely to start with a natural number nine, the likes of Thomas Muller, Mario Gotze and Marco Reus should be able to finish off the excellent approach play of Toni Kroos and Mesut Ozil.

Poland, who beat the Germans at home in qualifying, have no such concerns in the striking position and possess perhaps the best all-round centre forward in Europe in the shape of Bayern Munich hotshot Robert Lewandowski.

Ukraine have a twin threat from wide in Andrei Yarmolenko and Yevhen Konoplyanka and were also strong defensively in qualifying, conceding only four goals despite facing two matches against reigning champions Spain.

On paper this group deserves three qualifiers for the last 16 but that trio is unlikely to include Northern Ireland.

Recommended bet

€€€€€ Northern Ireland to finish bottom

TO WIN THE GROUP

	bet365	BetBright	Betfair	Betfred	Betway	Boyles	Coral	Hills	Lads	Power	Sky Bet
Germany	2-5	1-3	4-11	4-11	4-11	3-10	3-10	1-3	4-11	4-11	1-3
Poland	10-3	9-2	9-2	7-2	9-2	9-2	5	9-2	9-2	9-2	6
Ukraine	9	7	6	7	6	15-2	13-2	6	6	11-2	5
N Ireland	20	25	25	28	25	28	33	25	22	25	16

Win only. Prices correct March 31

Qualification was a historic achievement but Northern Ireland may struggle in a tough group

TO QUALIFY

	bet365	BetBright	Betfair	Betfred	Betway	Boyles	Coral	Hills	Lads	Power	Sky Bet
Germany	1-50	1-100	**1-33**	1-50	1-50	1-66	1-50	1-50	1-50	1-80	1-50
Poland	2-9	2-9	1-3	3-10	1-5	2-7	1-3	2-7	4-11	3-10	**1-2**
Ukraine	**8-13**	8-15	2-5	4-9	**8-13**	1-2	2-5	4-11	1-2	4-11	2-5
N Ireland	2	23-10	9-4	9-4	2	11-5	11-5	**11-4**	2	2	2

Win only. Prices correct March 31

5PM JUNE 12 – POLAND V N IRELAND

	bet365	Betfair	Betfred	Betway	Boyles	Coral	Hills	Lads	Power	Sky Bet
Poland	4-5	17-20	5-6	4-5	5-6	**10-11**	4-5	4-5	4-5	5-6
Draw	**5-2**	9-4	12-5	12-5	23-10	12-5	11-5	23-10	23-10	12-5
N Ireland	7-2	3	18-5	**4**	18-5	14-5	7-2	**4**	7-2	7-2

Best prices as decimal odds: Poland 1.91, draw 3.5, N Ireland 5. 101%. Prices correct March 31

8PM JUNE 12 – GERMANY V UKRAINE

	bet365	Betfair	Betfred	Betway	Boyles	Coral	Hills	Lads	Power	Sky Bet
Germany	1-2	8-15	1-2	8-15	1-2	4-9	**11-20**	8-15	1-2	8-15
Draw	14-5	27-10	3	3	**31-10**	3	13-5	3	3	3
Ukraine	**13-2**	5	6	23-4	11-2	6	5	11-2	11-2	5

Germany 1.55, draw 4.1, Ukraine 7.5. 102%

Andriy Yarmolenko is Ukraine's main man

5PM JUNE 16 – UKRAINE V N IRELAND

	Betfair	Betfred	Power
Ukraine	**19-20**	**19-20**	**19-20**
Draw	12-5	12-5	23-10
N Ireland	14-5	3	14-5

Ukraine 1.95, draw 3.4, N Ireland 4. 106%

8PM JUNE 16 – GERMANY V POLAND

	Betfair	Betfred	Power
Germany	8-15	**4-7**	8-15
Draw	14-5	3	14-5
Poland	5	5	**5**

Germany 1.57, draw 4, Poland 6. 105%

5PM JUNE 21 – UKRAINE V POLAND

	Betfair	Betfred	Power
Poland	6-4	6-4	6-4
Ukraine	7-4	15-8	7-4
Draw	11-5	9-4	11-5

Poland 2.5, draw 2.88, Draw 3.25. 106%

5PM JUNE 21 – N IRELAND V GERMANY

	Betfair	Betfred	Power
Germany	2-9	2-9	2-9
Draw	5	11-2	5
N Ireland	10	11	10

Germany 1.22, draw 6.5, N Ireland 12. 106%

HOW THEY PERFORMED IN QUALIFYING

	Group/Pos		P	Home			Away			F	A	GD	Pts	Home Pos%	Shots On	Off
				W	D	L	W	D	L							
Germany	Group D	1st	10	4	1	0	3	0	2	24	9	+15	22	72.0	47	56
Poland	Group D	2nd	10	4	1	0	2	2	1	33	10	+23	21	49.0	39	28
N Ireland	Group F	1st	10	3	2	0	3	1	1	16	8	+8	21	46.0	23	38
Ukraine	Group C	3rd	10	3	0	2	3	1	1	14	4	+10	19	57.4	31	51

Pos% percentage of total possession, **Shots on/off** shots on and off target, **Shots On%** percentage of shots on target (accuracy), **Shots%** percentage of total match shots

If you backed them P/L figures based on a £1 level stake using best odds in the Racing Post on day of match. Percentages represent probablility of victory implied by the win odds. **75%+** matches where the best price

	Germany					Ukraine					Poland					N Ireland				
	W	D	L	F	A	W	D	L	F	A	W	D	L	F	A	W	D	L	F	A
Germany						-	-	-	-	-	3	0	1	6	3	-	-	-	-	-
						0	1	0	3	3	0	2	0	2	2	1	0	0	4	1
Ukraine	-	-	-	-	-						2	0	0	4	1	0	2	0	0	0
	0	1	0	3	3						1	1	0	2	1	-	-	-	-	-
Poland	1	0	3	3	6	0	0	2	1	4						2	1	1	7	4
	0	2	0	2	2	0	1	1	1	2						-	-	-	-	-
N Ireland	-	-	-	-	-	0	2	0	0	0	1	1	2	4	7					
	0	0	1	1	4	-	-	-	-	-	-	-	-	-	-					

Includes all European Championship and World Cup matches since the 2002 World Cup. 90-minute results only. Competitive results above friendly results (in grey)

Euro 2004 qualifying
October 16, 2002
N Ireland........ (0) 0-0 (0) ....Ukraine

September 6, 2003
Ukraine .... (0) 0-0 (0) .... N Ireland

World Cup 2006 qualifying
September 4, 2004
N Ireland........ (0) 0-3 (2) .... Poland

March 30, 2005
Poland............ (0) 1-0 (0) .... N Ireland

Friendly
June 4, 2005
N Ireland........ (1) 1-4 (1)..........Germany

World Cup 2006 group stage
June 14, 2006
Germany .... (0) 1-0 (0) .... Poland

Euro 2008 group stage
June 8, 2008
Germany .... (1) 2-0 (0) .... Poland

Friendly
August 20, 2008
Ukraine .... (1) 1-0 (0) .... Poland

World Cup 2010 qualifying
March 28, 2009
N Ireland........ (1) 3-2 (1)............ Poland

September 5, 2009
Poland............ (0) 1-1 (1)........ N Ireland

Friendly
September 4, 2010
Poland............ (1) 1-1 (0) ....Ukraine

September 6, 2011
Poland............ (0) 2-2 (0) ....Germany

November 11, 2011
Ukraine .... (3) 3-3 (1)........Germany

World Cup 2014 qualifying
March 22, 2013
Poland............ (1) 1-3 (3) ....Ukraine

Mario Gotze makes it three for Germany against Poland

October 11, 2013
Ukraine .... (0) 1-0 (0) .... Poland

Friendly
May 13, 2014
Germany .... (0) 0-0 (0) .... Poland

Euro 2016 qualifying
October 11, 2014
Poland............ (0) 2-0 (0) ....Germany

September 4, 2015
Germany .... (2) 3-1 (1)............ Poland

Away	Shots		Shots overall		If you backed them							
Pos%	On	Off	On%	Shots%	P	75%+	P	50-75%	P	25-50%	P	<25%
72.0	42	36	49.2	77.0	7	-0.30	3	-1.56	0	0.00	0	0.00
51.0	36	30	56.4	58.8	3	+0.39	3	+0.86	2	-2.00	2	+5.00
41.6	18	22	40.6	56.7	1	+0.29	1	+0.70	5	+0.43	3	+13.00
58.2	17	33	36.4	67.0	2	+0.38	4	+0.40	3	-0.62	1	-1.00

was 1-3 or shorter **50-75%** matches where the best price was longer than 1-3 and no bigger than Evens **75-25%** matches where the best price was longer than Evens and no bigger than 3-1 **<25%** matches where the best price was longer than 3-1

Only completed matches are included. See pages 228-254 for full qualifying results

GERMANY

GER v UKR 2-0 R

It seemed impossible to claim the World Cup-European Championship double until France did it in 1998 and 2000. Spain bettered that with a hat-trick of titles in 2008, 2010 and 2012, and now Germany are out to prove that winning is a habit after Joachim Low's side became Europe's first ever World Cup winners on South American soil two years ago.

How they qualified

Germany took a while to come down from the euphoria of their World Cup-winning success against Argentina at the Maracana but they finished top of Group D by one point.

Qualification was not without its blips, however. Germany suffered defeats in Poland and Ireland and appeared to be playing in second gear for most of their matches, although the attacking performance in the 3-2 victory in Scotland was scintillating at times.

Germany also finished with the best shot ratio of any qualifier in matches against top-three sides. Their figure of 77 per cent was four percentage points higher than next-best Portugal and nobody else managed more than 69.

The manager

Before Brazil, Low looked destined to be a nearly man after leading Germany to the final of Euro 2008 and the semi-finals of the 2010 World Cup and Euro 2012. But the 7-1 demolition of hosts Brazil in the semi-finals of the last World Cup was one of the most astonishing results in football history.

Tactically, Low has moved Germany away from their traditional power game to a more possession-based plan modelled on Pep Guardiola's approach, and the Germany boss openly admits to referring to Spain as the role models for his side.

"It's not necessary to have the big, bulky striker up front anymore," said Low in reference to his preferred false nine system, which relies on a more mobile player like Mario Gotze to seek out space against opponents defending deep.

FACTFILE

FA founded 1900
www dfb.de
Head coach Joachim Low
National league Bundesliga
Date qualified October 11, 2015

Typical starting XI (4-2-3-1) Neuer; Rudy, Boateng, Hummels, Hector; Kroos, Schweinsteiger; Muller, Ozil, Reus; Gotze

Strengths
☑ The depth and quality of their midfield is magnificent
☑ Nobody is better between the sticks than Neuer

Weaknesses
☒ The full-backs can be exposed defensively
☒ They may not possess the hunger that we saw in Brazil

Star rating ★★★★★

Fixtures

1 Ukraine, 8pm June 12, Lille

2 Poland, 8pm June 16, Saint-Denis

3 N Ireland, 5pm June 21, Paris

Base Evian-les-Bains

Mario Gotze's World Cup-winning goal

This was explained by Urs Siegenthaler, the German FA's chief scout, to journalist Raphael Honigstein in a blog for ESPN when he said: "Would you rather take a Smart car or a van to look for a parking space in town?"

And it was substitute Gotze's extra-time goal in the final that won the World Cup.

Match winners

The midfield is outrageously gifted and could be considered Germany's best ever.

Toni Kroos and Sami Khedira or Bastian Schweinsteiger sit deep, allowing Mesut Ozil, Thomas Muller and Marco Reus to join in support of Gotze. Ilkay Gundogan Gundogan and Reus missed the World Cup because of injury so Germany are arguably even stronger than two years ago.

With poacher Miroslav Klose retired from international football, Plan B in attack is now burly Besiktas bruiser Mario Gomez.

They also have the planet's best goalkeeper in Manuel Neuer and a World Cup-winning centre-back pairing of Mats Hummels and Jerome Boateng.

Question marks

Low has struggled to find an adequate right-back to fill the void left by Philipp Lahm's international retirement and Cologne left-back Jonas Hector is short of experience.

How to back them

Germany must be on every shortlist to win the competition, although the draw could have been kinder.

The market suggests a quarter-final date with Belgium and a semi-final against France so there could be plenty of work to be done if they are to make it to the final in Paris.

Thomas Muller, who scored nine times in qualifying, is the obvious place to look for a leading goalscorer but Marco Reus is one to watch, as Low prefers a shared approach to attacking with all of the forward-thinking players involved.

GERMANY

EUROPEAN CHAMPIONSHIP RECORD

1960*	P	W	D	L	GF	GA
Did not enter	-	-	-	-	-	-
Qualifying	-	-	-	-	-	-

1964*	P	W	D	L	GF	GA
Did not enter	-	-	-	-	-	-
Qualifying	-	-	-	-	-	-

1968*	P	W	D	L	GF	GA
Did not qualify	-	-	-	-	-	-
Qualifying	4	2	1	1	9	2

1972*	P	W	D	L	GF	GA
● Winners	2	2	0	0	5	1
Qualifying	8	5	3	0	13	3

1976*	P	W	D	L	GF	GA
● Runners-up	2	1	1	0	6	4
Qualifying	8	4	4	0	17	5

1980*	P	W	D	L	GF	GA
● Winners	4	3	1	0	6	3
Qualifying	6	4	2	0	17	1

1984*	P	W	D	L	GF	GA
Group stage	3	1	1	1	2	2
Qualifying	8	5	1	2	15	5

1988*	P	W	D	L	GF	GA
● Semi-finals	4	2	1	1	6	3
Qualifying	-	-	-	-	-	-

1992	P	W	D	L	GF	GA
● Runners-up	5	2	1	2	7	8
Qualifying	6	5	0	1	13	4

1996	P	W	D	L	GF	GA
● Winners	6	4	2	0	10	3
Qualifying	10	8	1	1	27	10

2000	P	W	D	L	GF	GA
Group stage	3	0	1	2	1	5
Qualifying	8	6	1	1	20	4

2004	P	W	D	L	GF	GA
Group stage	3	0	2	1	2	3
Qualifying	8	5	3	0	13	4

2008	P	W	D	L	GF	GA
● Runners-up	6	4	0	2	10	7
Qualifying	12	8	3	1	35	7

2012	P	W	D	L	GF	GA
● Semi-finals	5	4	0	1	10	6
Qualifying	10	10	0	0	34	7

Totals	P	W	D	L	GF	GA
Finals	62	34	17	11	111	48
Qualifying	88	62	19	7	213	52

* Results & goals include extra time. Competed as East & West Germany 1960-1990. West Germany's record shown (East Germany never qualified for European Championship finals)

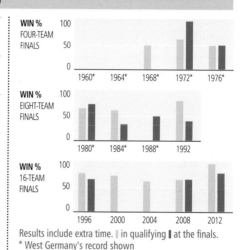

WIN % FOUR-TEAM FINALS				
1960*	1964*	1968*	1972*	1976*

WIN % EIGHT-TEAM FINALS			
1980*	1984*	1988*	1992

WIN % 16-TEAM FINALS				
1996	2000	2004	2008	2012

Results include extra time. ▌ in qualifying ▌ at the finals.
* West Germany's record shown

LEGENDARY PLAYER

FRANZ BECKENBAUER LEGEND

A true giant of the game, **Franz Beckenbauer** captained the West German side that won the European Championships in 1972 and the 1974 World Cup. Then as coach, Der Kaiser steered West Germany to glory at the 1990 World Cup.

WORLD CUP RECORD

Year	Point of exit		Year	Point of exit
1930*	Did not enter		1978*	Second round
1934*	● Third		1982*	● Runners-up
1938*	First round		1986*	● Runners-up
1950*	Banned		1990*	● **Winners**
1954*	● **Winners**		1994	Quarter-finals
1958*	● Fourth		1998	Quarter-finals
1962*	Quarter-finals		2002	● Runners-up
1966*	● Runners-up		2006	● Third
1970*	● Third		2010	● Third
1974*	● **Winners**		2014	● **Winners**

* West Germany's record shown between 1950-1990

DID YOU KNOW?

Germany's 2.2 points per game in qualifying is their lowest average in the Euros since reunification

HOW THEY QUALIFIED

Group D	P	W	D	L	F	A	GD	Pts
Germany	10	7	1	2	24	9	+15	22
Poland	10	6	3	1	33	10	+23	21
Ireland	10	5	3	2	19	7	+12	18
Scotland	10	4	3	3	22	12	+10	15
Georgia	10	3	0	7	10	16	-6	9
Gibraltar	10	0	0	10	2	56	-54	0

Match stats in qualifying

Possession	▮▮▮▮▮▮▮▮▮▮▮▮	72%
Shots on target	▮▮▮▮▮▮▮▮▮▮▮▮	73%
Shots off target	▮▮▮▮▮▮▮▮▮▮▮▮	81%
Corners	▮▮▮▮▮▮▮▮▮▮▮▮	79%

Averages of match totals in qualifying. See pages 228-254 for full qualifying results

Results & prices	W	D	L
Germany...(1) 2-1 (0)....Scotland	1-6	15-2	18-1
Poland......(0) 2-0 (0)....Germany	8-15	10-3	6-1
Germany...(0) 1-1 (0).......Ireland	2-7	21-4	14-1
Germany...(3) 4-0 (0)....Gibraltar	1-100	50-1	200-1
Georgia....(0) 0-2 (2)....Germany	2-13	9-1	25-1
Gibraltar..(0) 0-7 (1)....Germany	1-100	80-1	150-1
Germany...(2) 3-1 (1).......Poland	3-10	5-1	10-1
Scotland ...(2) 2-3 (2)....Germany	4-9	15-4	15-2
Ireland......(0) 1-0 (0)....Germany	8-15	7-2	13-2
Germany...(0) 2-1 (0).....Georgia	1-16	18-1	66-1

Profit & loss in qualifying -1.86 -3.75 4.50

Figures based on a £1 level stake using best odds in the Racing Post on day of match. W shows win price, whether home or away, L the price of the opposition

PLAYERS USED IN QUALIFYING — CAREER — QUALIFYING

Pos		Club	Age	P	G	P	G	☐	■
GK	Roman Weidenfeller	B Dortmund	35	5	-	1	-	-	-
GK	Manuel Neuer	Bayern Munich	30	64	-	9	-	-	-
DEF	Shkodran Mustafi	Valencia	24	10	-	1	-	-	-
DEF	Jonas Hector	Cologne	26	12	1	7	-	-	-
DEF	Antonio Rudiger	Roma	23	9	-	2	-	-	-
DEF	Mats Hummels	B Dortmund	27	46	4	7	-	3	-
DEF	Benedikt Howedes	Schalke	28	32	2	1	-	-	-
DEF	Matthias Ginter	B Dortmund	22	9	-	4	-	-	-
DEF	Erik Durm	B Dortmund	24	7	-	4	-	1	-
DEF	Jerome Boateng	Bayern Munich	27	57	-	10	-	1	-
DEF	Sebastian Rudy	Hoffenheim	26	10	-	4	-	-	-
MID	Andre Schurrle	Wolfsburg	25	50	20	7	3	-	-
MID	Marco Reus	B Dortmund	27	29	9	4	1	-	-
MID	Mesut Ozil	Arsenal	27	72	19	6	-	-	-
MID	Sami Khedira	Juventus	29	58	5	2	-	-	-
MID	Toni Kroos	Real Madrid	26	64	11	9	1	1	-
MID	Emre Can	Liverpool	22	5	-	2	-	-	-
MID	Christoph Kramer	Bayer Leverkusen	25	12	-	3	-	-	-
MID	Mario Gotze	Bayern Munich	24	50	17	9	3	-	-
MID	Lars Bender	Bayer Leverkusen	27	19	4	1	-	-	-
MID	Bastian Schweinsteiger	Man Utd	31	114	23	4	-	2	-
MID	Ilkay Gundogan	B Dortmund	25	16	4	5	2	-	-
MID	Julian Draxler	Wolfsburg	22	17	1	2	-	-	-
MID	Karim Bellarabi	Bayer Leverkusen	26	10	1	7	1	1	-
MID	Patrick Herrmann	Mgladbach	25	2	-	1	-	-	-
MID	Thomas Muller	Bayern Munich	26	70	31	9	9	1	-
ATT	Max Kruse	Wolfsburg	28	14	4	5	3	-	-
ATT	Lukas Podolski	Galatasaray	31	127	48	7	-	-	-
ATT	Kevin Volland	Hoffenheim	23	6	-	2	-	-	-

GERMANY

CORRECT SCORES

	Competitive	Friendly
1-0	2	3
2-0	1	-
2-1	3	1
3-0	5	-
3-1	1	-
3-2	1	-
4-0	2	-
4-1	1	1
4-2	-	1
4-3	-	-
0-0	2	2
1-1	1	1
2-2	1	2
3-3	-	1
4-4	1	-
0-1	1	-
0-2	1	1
1-2	-	1
0-3	-	-
1-3	-	1
2-3	-	1
0-4	-	-
1-4	-	-
2-4	-	1
3-4	-	1
Other	4	1

Since Euro 2012

HALF-TIME/FULL-TIME DOUBLE RESULTS

Win/Win	16	59%
Draw/Win	3	11%
Lose/Win	1	4%
Win/Draw	1	4%
Draw/Draw	4	15%
Lose/Draw	0	0%
Win/Lose	0	0%
Draw/Lose	2	7%
Lose/Lose	0	0%

Win 1st half	17	63%
Win 2nd half	15	56%
Win both halves	11	41%
Goal both halves	17	63%

Overall
- Win 74%
- Draw 19%
- Lose 7%

WIN 74%

Overall: W20, D5, L2 in 27 competitive games since Euro 2012

CLEAN SHEETS

13 (48%) **Clean sheets** 14 (52%)
11 (41%) **Win to nil** 16 (59%)

4 (15%) **Fail to score** 23 (85%)
2 (7%) **Lose to nil** 25 (93%)

UNDER & OVER GOALS

22 (81%) **Over 1.5** 5 (19%)
19 (70%) **Over 2.5** 8 (30%)
11 (41%) **Over 3.5** 16 (59%)
7 (26%) **Over 4.5** 20 (74%)

BOTH TEAMS TO SCORE

12 (44%) **Both score** 15 (56%)
9 (33%) **& win** 18 (67%)
0 (0%) **& lose** 27 (100%)

In 27 competitive games since Euro 2012

GOAL TIMES

Total match goals by half

36 (88%) **1st half** 5 (12%)
42 (70%) **2nd half** 18 (30%)

Goals for & against by half

36 (46%) **For** 42 (54%)
1st / 2nd
5 (22%) **Against** 18 (78%)
1st / 2nd

● GOALS FOR ● GOALS AGAINST

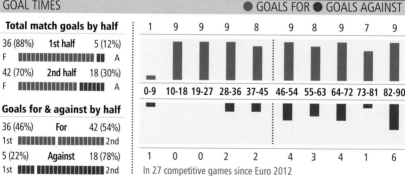

	0-9	10-18	19-27	28-36	37-45	46-54	55-63	64-72	73-81	82-90
For	1	9	9	9	8	9	8	9	7	9
Against	1	0	0	2	2	4	3	4	1	6

In 27 competitive games since Euro 2012

IF GERMANY SCORE FIRST

They win	19	86%
They draw	3	14%
They lose	0	0%

In 27 competitive games since 2012 World Cup

IF GERMANY CONCEDE FIRST

They win	1	33%
They draw	0	0%
They lose	2	67%

Thomas Muller sends Georgia's keeper the wrong way to score from the spot

GOALSCORERS IN QUALIFYING ● FIRST GOALS

	Goals		1st		Anytime	Percentage of team goals	
T Muller	9	●●●●●●○○○	5	55%	6	66%	38%
M Kruse	3	●●●	0	0%	2	40%	13%
A Schurrle	3	●●●	1	33%	1	14%	13%
M Gotze	3	●●●	0	0%	2	22%	13%
I Gundogan	2	●●	0	0%	2	40%	8%
T Kroos	1	●	1	100%	1	11%	4%
M Reus	1	●	1	100%	1	25%	4%
K Bellarabi	1	●	0	0%	1	14%	4%

In Euro 2016 qualifying

BOOKINGS

Matches played	10	☐ 10	▮ 0
Average make-up	(☐ 10	▮ 25)	10

In Euro 2016 qualifying

CORNERS

Avg F	9.2		79%
Avg A	2.4		21%

In Euro 2016 qualifying. Avg match total 11.6

UKRAINE

GER v ukr 2-0 ᴿ

I f at first you don't succeed, try, try again. Or in Ukraine's case try again, and again, and again – the Zbirna finally made it through a playoff after losing all five of their two-legged ties since their attempt to reach the 1998 World Cup. After breaking their playoff hoodoo, the knockout phase is the aim for Ukraine, who disappointed as co-hosts of the Euros on their debut in 2012.

How they qualified

There were wild scenes after Ukraine's 3-1 aggregate success in the playoffs against Slovenia, which came after they only narrowly missed out on automatic qualification as the best third-placed side.

Ukraine failed to score in their four matches against the top two – Spain and Slovakia – but they played well against the reigning champions and were unfortunate to collect just one point from that quartet of fixtures.

They won the rest of their group games but their 12 matches produced just 22 goals, and six of those came against Luxembourg.

The manager

Christmas came late for Mikhail Fomenko when he was appointed as manager on Boxing Day 2012. He got the job almost by default – he was put in charge of finding a new boss but nobody was deemed suitable after Andriy Shevchenko and Harry Redknapp reportedly turned it down.

Fomenko has had a varied career which includes a spell as Iraq manager in the early nineties but, despite good results with the national team, he is not loved by the public.

Like so many previous Ukraine coaches he is a disciple of Valeriy Lobanovskyi and there had been rumours he could be replaced by his assistant Shevchenko after failing to show at the Euro 2016 draw. However, the 67-year-old remains in situ.

Match winners

Wing wizards Andriy Yarmolenko and Yevhen Konoplyanka are incredibly

FACTFILE

FA founded 1991
www ffu.org.ua
Head coach Mikhail Fomenko
National league Premier League
Date qualified November 17, 2015

Typical starting XI (4-1-2-3) Pyatov; Fedetskiy, Khacheridi, Rakitskiy, Shevchuk; Stepanenko; Rotan, Sydorchuk; Yarmolenko, Zozulya, Konoplyanka

Strengths
☑ The two wingers are wonderful
☑ Ukraine will be well organised defensively

Weaknesses
☒ They lack a true international-class striker
☒ Ukraine may not possess the self-belief to compete at this level

Star rating

Fixtures
1 Germany, 8pm June 12, Lille
2 N Ireland, 5pm June 16, Lyon
3 Poland, 5pm June 21, Marseille
Base Aix-en-Provence

Ukraine celebrate reaching the finals

influential and virtually everything goes through the pair, who play for Dynamo Kiev and Seville respectively.

Both are deployed as inverted wingers so cut in from wide positions on to their favoured feet and respected website transfermarkt.com rates each player at £19m. The next best is centre-back Yaroslav Rakitsky at just £7m.

The side is built around the dynamic duo and the eight other outfield players sacrifice themselves to give Yarmolenko and Konoplyanka the freedom to wreak maximum damage.

Question marks

There is a general lack of depth for the main starters and Fomenko is struggling for a first-choice forward. Roman Zozulya started most frequently in qualifying but has inevitably failed to live up to the early comparisons with Shevchenko, while Artem Kravets moved from Dynamo Kiev's bench to Stuttgart in January in a bid to win a starting berth.

Zozulya, Kravets and beanpole striker Pylyp Budkivskyi were the three forwards chosen for the March friendlies after Yevhen Seleznyov was overlooked following a controversial transfer switch from Dnipro to Russian side Kuban Krasnodar.

How to back them

Yarmolenko notched six times in qualifying compared to Konoplyanka's two so he is sure to be the most popular of the pair to top Ukraine's scoring charts, but bear in mind the Dynamo Kiev man appeared to be jocked off penalty duty after missing from the spot against Macedonia.

Ukraine to score exactly four points and finish third in the group could be the bets.

They have never beaten opening opponents Germany but should have too much class for Northern Ireland in Lyon. That could set up an intriguing final-day clash with Poland where, potentially, a point each will take the old enemies through together. However, the Poles are likely to have the better goal difference by then.

UKRAINE

GROUP C

EUROPEAN CHAMPIONSHIP RECORD

1960*
● **Winners**

	P	W	D	L	GF	GA
Winners	2	2	0	0	5	1
Qualifying	2	2	0	0	4	1

1964*

	P	W	D	L	GF	GA
● Runners-up	2	1	0	1	4	2
Qualifying	4	2	2	0	7	3

1968*

	P	W	D	L	GF	GA
● Fourth	2	0	1	1	0	2
Qualifying	8	6	0	2	19	8

1972*

	P	W	D	L	GF	GA
● Runners-up	2	1	0	1	1	3
Qualifying	8	5	3	0	16	4

1976*

	P	W	D	L	GF	GA
Did not qualify	-	-	-	-	-	-
Qualifying	8	4	1	3	12	10

1980*

	P	W	D	L	GF	GA
Did not qualify	-	-	-	-	-	-
Qualifying	6	1	3	2	7	8

1984*

	P	W	D	L	GF	GA
Did not qualify	-	-	-	-	-	-
Qualifying	6	4	1	1	11	2

1988*

	P	W	D	L	GF	GA
● Runners-up	5	3	1	1	7	4
Qualifying	8	5	3	0	14	3

1992*

	P	W	D	L	GF	GA
Group stage	3	0	2	1	1	4
Qualifying	8	5	3	0	13	2

1996

	P	W	D	L	GF	GA
Did not qualify	-	-	-	-	-	-
Qualifying	10	4	1	5	11	15

2000

	P	W	D	L	GF	GA
Did not qualify	-	-	-	-	-	-
Qualifying	12	5	6	1	16	7

2004

	P	W	D	L	GF	GA
Did not qualify	-	-	-	-	-	-
Qualifying	8	2	4	2	11	10

2008

	P	W	D	L	GF	GA
Did not qualify	-	-	-	-	-	-
Qualifying	12	5	2	5	18	16

2012

	P	W	D	L	GF	GA
Group stage	3	1	0	2	2	4
Qualifying	-	-	-	-	-	-

Totals

	P	W	D	L	GF	GA
Finals	19	8	4	7	20	20
Qualifying	100	50	29	21	159	89

* Results & goals include extra time. Competed as part of USSR between 1960-1988 and CIS in 1992

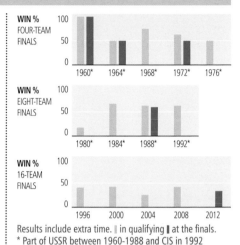

WIN % FOUR-TEAM FINALS — 1960* 1964* 1968* 1972* 1976*

WIN % EIGHT-TEAM FINALS — 1980* 1984* 1988* 1992*

WIN % 16-TEAM FINALS — 1996 2000 2004 2008 2012

Results include extra time. ▌ in qualifying ▌ at the finals.
* Part of USSR between 1960-1988 and CIS in 1992

LEGENDARY PLAYER

ANDRIY SHEVCHENKO LEGEND

Andriy Shevchenko flopped in England but the 2004 Ballon d'Or winner is Ukraine's all-time top scorer and grabbed goals in their first wins at the World Cup, in Germany in 2006, and the European Championships, when they co-hosted in 2012.

WORLD CUP RECORD

Year	Point of exit	Year	Point of exit
1930*	Did not enter	1978*	Did not qualify
1934*	Did not enter	1982*	Second round
1938*	Did not enter	1986*	Round of 16
1950*	Did not enter	1990*	Group stage
1954*	Did not enter	1994	Did not enter
1958*	Quarter-finals	1998	Did not qualify
1962*	Quarter-finals	2002	Did not qualify
1966*	● Fourth	2006	Quarter-finals
1970*	Quarter-finals	2010	Did not qualify
1974*	Did not qualify	2014	Did not qualify

* Competed as part of USSR between 1930-1990

DID YOU KNOW?

Andriy Yarmolenko played all but 25 minutes of Ukraine's qualifying campaign without receiving a single caution

HOW THEY QUALIFIED

Group C	P	W	D	L	F	A	GD	Pts
Spain	10	9	0	1	23	3	+20	27
Slovakia	10	7	1	2	17	8	+9	22
Ukraine	10	6	1	3	14	4	+10	19
Belarus	10	3	2	5	8	14	-6	11
Luxembourg	10	1	1	8	6	27	-21	4
Macedonia	10	1	1	8	6	18	-12	4

Results & prices

	W	D	L
Austria......(1) 1-1 (1) ..... Sweden	11-5	23-10	6-4
Sweden.....(0) 1-1 (1) ....Russia	33-20	9-4	2-1
Sweden.....(1) 2-0 (0) Liechtenstein	1-25	14-1	66-1
Montenegro(0) 1-1 (1) ..... Sweden	7-5	9-4	23-10
Moldova.....(0) 0-2 (0) ..... Sweden	4-9	15-4	9-1
Sweden.....(3) 3-1 (0) Montenegro	1-2	7-2	8-1
Russia.......(1) 1-0 (0) ..... Sweden	3-1	9-4	23-20
Sweden.....(0) 1-4 (2) ......Austria	5-4	5-2	13-5
Liechtenstein(0) 0-2 (1) ..... Sweden	1-8	10-1	33-1
Sweden.....(1) 2-0 (0) ....Moldova	1-5	13-2	20-1
Sweden.....(1) 2-0 (0) ....Denmark	7-5	9-4	5-2

Match stats in qualifying

Possession	▊▊▊▊▊▊▊▊▊░░░░░░	53%
Shots on target	▊▊▊▊▊▊▊▊▊░░░░░░	56%
Shots off target	▊▊▊▊▊▊▊▊▊░░░░░░	55%
Corners	▊▊▊▊▊▊▊▊▊░░░░░░	54%

Averages of match totals in qualifying. See pages 228-254 for full qualifying results

Profit & loss in qualifying   -3.29   1.3   -6.25

Figures based on a £1 level stake using best odds in the Racing Post on day of match. W shows win price, whether home or away, L the price of the opposition

PLAYERS USED IN QUALIFYING

Pos		Club	Age	CAREER P	CAREER G	QUALIFYING P	QUALIFYING G	▯	▮
GK	Andriy Pyatov	Shakhtar	31	62	-	12	-	-	-
DEF	Yevhen Khacheridi	Dynamo Kiev	28	40	3	10	-	4	-
DEF	Viacheslav Shevchuk	Shakhtar	37	52	-	12	-	-	-
DEF	Artem Fedetskyi	Dnipro	31	46	2	11	-	5	-
DEF	Oleksandr Kucher	Shakhtar	33	49	2	6	-	3	-
DEF	Yaroslav Rakitskiy	Shakhtar	26	38	4	9	-	2	-
DEF	Mykola Morozyuk	Dynamo Kiev	28	13	1	2	-	-	-
MID	Oleksandr Karavayev	Shakhtar	24	2	-	2	-	-	-
MID	Alexander Zinchenko	FC Ufa	19	1	-	1	-	-	-
MID	Ruslan Malinovsky	Genk	23	3	-	2	-	-	-
MID	Serhiy Rybalka	Dynamo Kiev	26	8	-	6	-	2	-
MID	Anatolii Tymoschuk	Kairat	37	142	4	5	-	-	-
MID	Roman Bezus	Dnipro	25	19	4	1	-	1	-
MID	Kyrylo Kovalchuk	Karsiyaka	29	4	-	2	-	-	-
MID	Artem Gromov	Poltava	26	2	-	1	-	-	-
MID	Edmar	Dnipro	35	15	1	3	-	1	-
MID	Serhiy Sydorchuk	Dynamo Kiev	25	10	2	7	2	3	-
MID	Oleg Gusev	Dynamo Kiev	33	98	13	2	-	-	-
MID	Taras Stepanenko	Shakhtar	26	27	2	9	-	3	-
MID	Ruslan Rotan	Dnipro	34	86	7	8	-	2	-
MID	Denys Garmash	Dynamo Kiev	26	26	2	6	1	1	1
MID	Denys Oliynyk	Vitesse Arn.	28	12	-	1	-	-	-
MID	Yevhen Konoplyanka	Seville	26	51	11	11	2	2	-
MID	Andriy Yarmolenko	Dynamo Kiev	26	57	23	12	6	-	-
ATT	Artem Kravets	Stuttgart	27	13	4	8	3	1	-
ATT	Yevhen Seleznev	Kuban	30	48	11	5	2	1	-
ATT	Roman Zozulya	Dnipro	26	24	3	5	-	1	-
ATT	Oleksandr Gladkiy	Shakhtar	28	11	1	2	-	-	-
ATT	Pylyp Budkivsky	Zorya Luhansk	24	6	-	4	-	1	-

UKRAINE

CORRECT SCORES

	Competitive	Friendly
1-0	2	4
2-0	4	3
2-1	1	2
3-0	2	-
3-1	2	-
3-2	-	-
4-0	1	-
4-1	-	-
4-2	-	-
4-3	-	-
0-0	3	3
1-1	2	1
2-2	-	-
3-3	-	-
4-4	-	-
0-1	4	-
0-2	-	-
1-2	-	-
0-3	1	-
1-3	-	-
2-3	-	-
0-4	-	-
1-4	-	-
2-4	-	-
3-4	-	-
Other	2	-

Since Euro 2012

HALF-TIME/FULL-TIME DOUBLE RESULTS

Win/Win	7	29%
Draw/Win	7	29%
Lose/Win	0	0%
Win/Draw	1	4%
Draw/Draw	3	13%
Lose/Draw	1	4%
Win/Lose	0	0%
Draw/Lose	0	0%
Lose/Lose	5	21%

Win 1st half	8	33%
Win 2nd half	12	50%
Win both halves	4	17%
Goal both halves	8	33%

Overall
- Win 58%
- Draw 21%
- Lose 21%

WIN 58%

Overall: W14, D5, L5 in 24 competitive games since Euro 2012

CLEAN SHEETS

14 (58%) **Clean sheets** 10 (42%) ✓ ✗

11 (46%) **Win to nil** 13 (54%) ✓ ✗

8 (33%) **Fail to score** 16 (67%) ✓ ✗

5 (21%) **Lose to nil** 19 (79%) ✓ ✗

UNDER & OVER GOALS

15 (63%) **Over 1.5** 9 (38%) ✓ ✗

9 (38%) **Over 2.5** 15 (63%) ✓ ✗

5 (21%) **Over 3.5** 19 (79%) ✓ ✗

2 (8%) **Over 4.5** 22 (92%) ✓ ✗

BOTH TEAMS TO SCORE

5 (21%) **Both score** 19 (79%) ✓ ✗

3 (13%) **& win** 21 (88%) ✓ ✗

0 (0%) **& lose** 24 (100%) ✓ ✗

In 24 competitive games since Euro 2012

GOAL TIMES

Total match goals by half

17 (68%) **1st half** 8 (32%)
F A

30 (88%) **2nd half** 4 (12%)
F A

Goals for & against by half

17 (36%) **For** 30 (64%)
1st 2nd

8 (67%) **Against** 4 (33%)
1st 2nd

● GOALS FOR ● GOALS AGAINST

3	3	3	3	5	8	7	3	2	10
0-9	10-18	19-27	28-36	37-45	46-54	55-63	64-72	73-81	82-90
0	3	2	2	1	0	1	1	1	1

In 24 competitive games since Euro 2012

IF UKRAINE SCORE FIRST

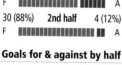

They win	14	93%
Draw	1	7%
They lose	0	0%

In 24 competitive games since Euro 2012

IF UKRAINE CONCEDE FIRST

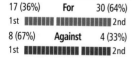

They win	0	0%
Draw	1	17%
They lose	5	83%

УКРАЇНА

Andriy Yarmolenko's late goal put Ukraine's playoff against Slovenia beyond doubt

GOALSCORERS IN QUALIFYING

● FIRST GOALS

	Goals		1st		Anytime		Percentage of team goals	
A Yarmolenko	6	●●●●●●	2	33%	4	33%		35%
A Kravets	3	●●●	2	66%	3	37%		18%
Y Seleznev	2	●●	1	50%	2	40%		12%
Y Konoplyanka	2	●●	0	0%	2	18%		12%
S Sydorchuk	2	●●	1	50%	2	28%		12%
D Harmash	1	●	0	0%	1	16%		6%

In Euro 2016 qualifying

BOOKINGS

Matches played	12	▢33	▮ 1
Average make-up (▢10 ▮25)			29.6

In Euro 2016 qualifying

CORNERS

Avg F	6.6		64%
Avg A	3.7		36%

In Euro 2016 qualifying. Avg match total 10.3

POLAND

POL v N.Ireland ~~[crossed out]~~ 1-0

Poland were the great entertainers in qualifying but they have a lamentable record in the main event, with just two finals appearances and no wins in six matches despite being at home in 2008. However, Poland were third at the 1974 and 1982 World Cups so they do have pedigree. Some rate them dark horses in France – but first they have to win a game...

How they qualified

Poland were fun to watch and finished just a point behind Germany – a 2-0 home success against the world champions was a massive result.

Poland's sole defeat was in the reverse fixture against the Germans but they scored a qualifying-high 33 goals. Their ten matches also produced the most goals of any team to make it to France (43) and Robert Lewandowski topped the continent's charts with a whopping 13 goals.

Lewandowski also produced the most shots on target (25), although it is worth remembering that 7-0 and 8-1 wins over Gibraltar helped boost those figures.

Six of Lewandowski's goals came against the minnows but he also delivered when it mattered, his two goals against Scotland and his strike against Ireland late in qualifying helped seal Poland's place at the finals.

The manager

Adam Nawalka's revival of fallen giants Gornik Zabrze provided him with the platform to take charge of the Polish national side. He has a number of choices of formation in France and 4-4-2 is an option if the team needs to be aggressive.

Much will depend on where Ajax's Arkadiusz Milik plays. He came through at Gornik when Nawalka was in charge and is used on the left in a 4-2-3-1, central in a 4-4-1-1 or alongside skipper Lewandowski in a two-pronged attack.

Giving Lewandowski the captaincy was one of the biggest decisions Nawalka has had to make in his time as Poland manager after

---

FACTFILE

FA founded 1919
www pzpn.pl
Head coach Adam Nawalka
National league Ekstraklasa
Date qualified October 11, 2015

....

Typical starting XI (4-4-1-1) Fabianski; Piszczek, Glik, Szukala, Wawrzyniak; Grosicki, Krychowiak, Maczynski, Rybus; Milik; Lewandowski

....

Strengths
☑ Lewandowski is one of the world's best strikers
☑ The side has a strong spine

Weaknesses
☒ Poland don't keep many clean sheets
☒ Not all of their first-choice XI are regulars for their club sides

Star rating ★★★☆☆

....

Fixtures

1 N Ireland, 5pm June 12, Nice

2 Germany, 8pm June 16, Saint-Denis

3 Ukraine, 5pm June 21, Marseille

Base La Baule

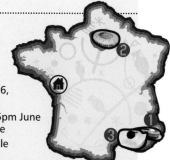

Poland celebrate reaching the finals

Jakub Blaszczykowski was stripped of the role following a long spell on the sidelines with injury.

The former Borussia Dortmund team-mates don't get on at the best of times and things have reportedly got worse between the pair since Lewandowski was handed the armband.

Match winners

It's easy to see why Nawalka wanted to do everything in his power to make Lewandowski feel important, given he is one of the world's most complete strikers.

The Bayern Munich star is a tremendous talent who will always give Poland a chance and those who believed Lewandowski didn't always put in his best efforts for the national team have been silenced in the last couple of years.

Lewandowski leads the line expertly and forms the final element of a strong spine that includes a few different top-level goalkeeping options, Torino's warrior-like centre-back Kamil Glik and Seville's highly rated midfielder Grzegorz Krychowiak.

Question marks

The big question is whether Poland's bit-part players outside of their four or five top men can keep the mistakes to a minimum, particularly at the back where Glik is struggling for a reliable partner.

There have also been question marks surrounding the left-back slot and Blaszczykowski's position within the side.

The Fiorentina loanee is still one of Poland's better players but he was upset at losing the captaincy and has struggled with injuries over a sustained period.

How to back them

Poland have the potential to be quarter-finalists and the draw suggests a last-16 tie with Switzerland should both, as expected, finish second in their sections. However, the best bet is the 10-11 that they beat Northern Ireland in their first match – the brilliance of Lewandowski will be difficult to stop as Ireland and Scotland can testify.

POLAND

EUROPEAN CHAMPIONSHIP RECORD

1960	P	W	D	L	GF	GA
Did not qualify	-	-	-	-	-	-
Qualifying	2	0	0	2	2	7

1964	P	W	D	L	GF	GA
Did not qualify	-	-	-	-	-	-
Qualifying	2	0	0	2	0	4

1968	P	W	D	L	GF	GA
Did not qualify	-	-	-	-	-	-
Qualifying	6	3	1	2	13	9

1972	P	W	D	L	GF	GA
Did not qualify	-	-	-	-	-	-
Qualifying	6	2	2	2	10	6

1976	P	W	D	L	GF	GA
Did not qualify	-	-	-	-	-	-
Qualifying	6	3	2	1	9	5

1980	P	W	D	L	GF	GA
Did not qualify	-	-	-	-	-	-
Qualifying	8	5	2	1	13	4

1984	P	W	D	L	GF	GA
Did not qualify	-	-	-	-	-	-
Qualifying	6	1	2	3	6	9

1988	P	W	D	L	GF	GA
Did not qualify	-	-	-	-	-	-
Qualifying	8	3	2	3	9	11

1992	P	W	D	L	GF	GA
Did not qualify	-	-	-	-	-	-
Qualifying	6	2	3	1	8	6

1996	P	W	D	L	GF	GA
Did not qualify	-	-	-	-	-	-
Qualifying	10	3	4	3	14	12

2000	P	W	D	L	GF	GA
Did not qualify	-	-	-	-	-	-
Qualifying	8	4	1	3	12	8

2004	P	W	D	L	GF	GA
Did not qualify	-	-	-	-	-	-
Qualifying	8	4	1	3	11	7

2008	P	W	D	L	GF	GA
Group stage	3	0	1	2	1	4
Qualifying	14	8	4	2	24	12

2012	P	W	D	L	GF	GA
Group stage	3	0	2	1	2	3
Qualifying	-	-	-	-	-	-

Totals	P	W	D	L	GF	GA
Finals	6	0	3	3	3	7
Qualifying	90	38	24	28	131	100

Results & goals include extra time

WIN % FOUR-TEAM FINALS — 100 / 50 / 0
1960 1964 1968 1972 1976

WIN % EIGHT-TEAM FINALS — 100 / 50 / 0
1980 1984 1988 1992

WIN % 16-TEAM FINALS — 100 / 50 / 0
1996 2000 2004 2008 2012

Results include extra time. ▌in qualifying ▌at the finals

LEGENDARY PLAYER

With seven goals, **Grzegorz Lato** was top scorer at the 1974 World Cup, where Poland finished third, and he was in the team when they repeated the feat in 1982. He ended his career with 45 international goals from 100 appearances.

GRZEGORZ LATO
LEGEND

WORLD CUP RECORD

Year	Point of exit	Year	Point of exit
1930	Did not enter	1978	Second round
1934	Did not enter	1982	● Third
1938	First round	1986	Round of 16
1950	Did not enter	1990	Did not qualify
1954	Did not enter	1994	Did not qualify
1958	Did not qualify	1998	Did not qualify
1962	Did not qualify	2002	Group stage
1966	Did not qualify	2006	Group stage
1970	Did not qualify	2010	Did not qualify
1974	● Third	2014	Did not qualify

DID YOU KNOW?

Nine of Robert Lewandowski's record-equalling haul of 13 goals in the qualifying campaign came against Gibraltar and Georgia, the bottom two in their group

HOW THEY QUALIFIED

Group D	P	W	D	L	F	A	GD	Pts
Germany	10	7	1	2	24	9	+15	22
Poland	10	6	3	1	33	10	+23	21
Ireland	10	5	3	2	19	7	+12	18
Scotland	10	4	3	3	22	12	+10	15
Georgia	10	3	0	7	10	16	-6	9
Gibraltar	10	0	0	10	2	56	-54	0

Match stats in qualifying

Possession	▮▮▮▮▮▮▮▮	50%
Shots on target	▮▮▮▮▮▮▮▮▮▮▮	64%
Shots off target	▮▮▮▮▮▮▮▮▮	53%
Corners	▮▮▮▮▮▮▮▮▮	54%

Averages of match totals in qualifying. See pages 228-254 for full qualifying results

Results & prices		W	D	L
Gibraltar ... (0) 0-7 (1) ...... Poland		1-12	14-1	30-1
Poland ...... (0) 2-0 (0) .... Germany		6-1	10-3	8-15
Poland ...... (1) 2-2 (1) .... Scotland		19-20	5-2	15-4
Georgia .... (0) 0-4 (0) ...... Poland		19-20	12-5	15-4
Ireland ...... (0) 1-1 (1) ...... Poland		21-10	9-4	13-8
Poland ...... (0) 4-0 (0) ..... Georgia		3-10	19-4	12-1
Germany ... (2) 3-1 (1) ...... Poland		10-1	5-1	3-10
Poland ...... (4) 8-1 (0) .... Gibraltar		1-100	50-1	150-1
Scotland ... (1) 2-2 (1) .... Poland		17-10	9-4	19-10
Poland ...... (2) 2-1 (1) ...... Ireland		91-100	5-2	15-4

Profit & loss in qualifying	4.25	0	-8.70

Figures based on a £1 level stake using best odds in the Racing Post on day of match. W shows win price, whether home or away, L the price of the opposition

PLAYERS USED IN QUALIFYING

Pos		Club	Age	CAREER		QUALIFYING			
				P	G	P	G	▯	▮
GK	Lukasz Fabianski	Swansea	31	29	-	6	-	-	-
GK	Wojciech Szczesny	Roma	26	25	-	4	-	-	-
DEF	Marcin Komorowski	Terek Grozny	32	13	1	1	-	-	-
DEF	Michal Pazdan	Legia Warsaw	28	16	-	3	-	-	-
DEF	Lukasz Szukala	Osmanlispor	32	17	1	9	1	2	-
DEF	Jakub Wawrzyniak	Lechia Gdansk	32	48	1	5	-	-	-
DEF	Lucasz Piszczek	B Dortmund	31	45	2	7	-	1	-
DEF	Pawel Olkowski	Cologne	26	13	-	6	-	-	-
DEF	Artur Jedrzejczyk	Legia Warsaw	28	17	2	3	-	-	-
DEF	Kamil Glik	Torino	28	39	3	9	1	4	-
MID	Tomasz Jodlowiec	Legia Warsaw	30	42	1	6	-	1	-
MID	Maciej Rybus	Terek Grozny	26	41	2	8	-	2	-
MID	Grzegorz Krychowiak	Seville	26	33	2	10	2	2	-
MID	Mateusz Klich	Kaiserslautern	25	10	1	1	-	1	-
MID	Kamil Grosicki	Rennes	28	37	8	9	4	1	-
MID	Jakub Blaszczykowski	Fiorentina	30	77	16	5	1	-	-
MID	Slawomir Peszko	Lechia Gdansk	31	35	2	4	1	2	-
MID	Karol Linetty	Lech Poznan	21	9	1	2	-	1	-
MID	Filip Starzynski	Zaglebie Lubin	25	2	1	1	-	-	-
MID	Krzysztof Maczynski	Wisla Krakow	29	14	1	8	1	-	-
MID	Sebastian Mila	Lechia Gdansk	33	38	8	5	2	1	-
MID	Michal Zyro	Wolves	23	4	-	1	-	-	-
MID	Bartosz Kapustka	Cracovia	19	5	2	1	1	-	-
MID	Piotr Zielinski	Empoli	22	13	3	1	-	-	-
MID	Michal Kucharczyk	Legia Warsaw	25	9	1	1	-	-	-
MID	Waldemar Sobota	St Pauli	29	17	4	3	-	-	-
ATT	Arkadiusz Milik	Ajax	22	24	10	9	6	-	-
ATT	Robert Lewandowski	Bayern Munich	27	75	34	10	13	1	-

SOCCERBASE.COM

POLAND

CORRECT SCORES

	Competitive	Friendly
1-0	-	3
2-0	2	1
2-1	1	1
3-0	-	1
3-1	-	1
3-2	-	1
4-0	2	-
4-1	-	1
4-2	-	1
4-3	-	-
0-0	-	3
1-1	4	-
2-2	3	1
3-3	-	-
4-4	-	-
0-1	1	2
0-2	1	2
1-2	-	-
0-3	-	-
1-3	2	1
2-3	-	-
0-4	-	-
1-4	-	-
2-4	-	-
3-4	-	-
Other	4	1

Since Euro 2012

HALF-TIME/FULL-TIME DOUBLE RESULTS

Win/Win	6	30%	Win 1st half	7	35%
Draw/Win	3	15%	Win 2nd half	10	50%
Lose/Win	0	0%	Win both halves	5	25%
Win/Draw	1	5%	Goal both halves	12	60%
Draw/Draw	4	20%			
Lose/Draw	2	10%	**Overall**		
Win/Lose	0	0%	● Win	45%	
Draw/Lose	1	5%	● Draw	35%	
Lose/Lose	3	15%	● Lose	20%	

WIN 45%

Overall: W9, D7, L4 in 20 competitive games since Euro 2012

CLEAN SHEETS

6 (30%)	Clean sheets	14 (70%)
✓ ▮▮▮▮▮▮		✗
6 (30%)	Win to nil	14 (70%)
✓ ▮▮▮▮▮▮		✗

2 (10%)	Fail to score	18 (90%)
✓ ▮▮		✗
2 (10%)	Lose to nil	18 (90%)
✓ ▮▮		✗

UNDER & OVER GOALS

19 (95%)	Over 1.5	1 (5%)
✓ ▮▮▮▮▮▮▮▮▮▮▮▮▮▮▮▮▮▮▮		✗
12 (60%)	Over 2.5	8 (40%)
✓ ▮▮▮▮▮▮▮▮▮▮▮▮		✗
11 (55%)	Over 3.5	9 (45%)
✓ ▮▮▮▮▮▮▮▮▮▮▮		✗
4 (20%)	Over 4.5	16 (80%)
✓ ▮▮▮▮		✗

BOTH TEAMS TO SCORE

12 (60%)	Both score	8 (40%)
✓ ▮▮▮▮▮▮▮▮▮▮▮▮		✗
3 (15%)	& win	17 (85%)
✓ ▮▮▮		✗
2 (10%)	& lose	18 (90%)
✓ ▮▮		✗

In 20 competitive games since Euro 2012

GOAL TIMES

Total match goals by half		
21 (58%)	1st half	15 (42%)
F ▮▮▮▮▮▮▮▮▮▮▮▮ ▮▮▮▮▮▮▮▮ A		
30 (81%)	2nd half	7 (19%)
F ▮▮▮▮▮▮▮▮▮▮▮▮▮▮▮▮ ▮▮▮▮ A		

Goals for & against by half		
21 (41%)	For	30 (59%)
1st ▮▮▮▮▮▮▮▮ ▮▮▮▮▮▮▮▮▮▮▮▮ 2nd		
15 (68%)	Against	7 (32%)
1st ▮▮▮▮▮▮▮▮▮▮▮▮▮▮▮▮ ▮▮▮▮▮ 2nd		

● GOALS FOR ● GOALS AGAINST

4	8	3	5	1	6	6	4	5	9

0-9	10-18	19-27	28-36	37-45	46-54	55-63	64-72	73-81	82-90
2	4	3	1	5	0	2	1	0	4

In 20 competitive games since Euro 2012

IF POLAND SCORE FIRST

They win	9	▮▮▮▮▮▮▮▮▮▮▮▮▮	64%
Draw	5	▮▮▮▮▮▮▮	36%
They lose	0		0%

In 20 competitive games since Euro 2012

IF POLAND CONCEDE FIRST

They win	0		0%
Draw	2	▮▮▮▮▮	33%
They lose	4	▮▮▮▮▮▮▮▮▮▮▮	67%

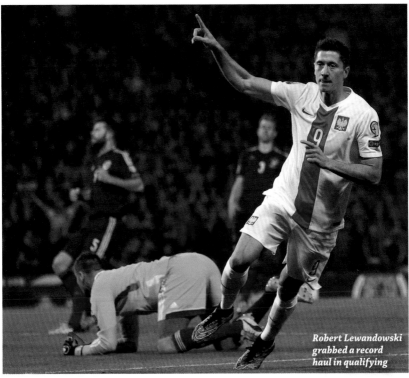

Robert Lewandowski grabbed a record haul in qualifying

GOALSCORERS IN QUALIFYING

● FIRST GOALS

	Goals		1st		Anytime		Percentage of team goals	
R Lewandowski	13	●●●●●●●●●●●●●	1	7%	6	60%		39%
A Milik	6	●●●●●●●	2	33%	5	55%		18%
K Grosicki	4	●●●●	2	50%	2	22%		12%
S Mila	2	●●	0	0%	2	40%		6%
G Krychowiak	2	●●	1	50%	2	20%		6%
J Blaszczykowski	1	●	0	0%	1	20%		3%
S Peszko	1	●	1	100%	1	25%		3%
K Glik	1	●	1	100%	1	11%		3%
K Maczynski	1	●	1	100%	1	12%		3%
L Szukala	1	●	0	0%	1	11%		3%
B Kapustka	1	●	0	0%	1	100%		3%

In Euro 2016 qualifying

BOOKINGS

Matches played	10	☐19	▮ 0
Average make-up (☐10 ▮25)			19

In Euro 2016 qualifying

CORNERS

Avg F	5.2		54%
Avg A	4.4		46%

In Euro 2016 qualifying. Avg match total 9.6

Northern Ireland reached the Euros by upsetting the odds to finish top of qualifying Group F and they will have to upset the odds again, with bookmakers making Michael O'Neill's side rank outsiders. But that won't bother the supporters heading to the party looking for a shock to match the win over hosts Spain at the 1982 World Cup.

How they qualified

It looked likely to be another bleak campaign when Northern Ireland were losing 1-0 to Hungary in their opening qualifier before two late goals turned the match around. O'Neill's side lost just one of their matches, away to Romania, as they defied pre-tournament odds of 33-1 to win their group.

To put their achievement into context, it's worth remembering that Northern Ireland were 6-1 just to qualify for Euro 2016.

The manager

O'Neill enjoyed huge success with Shamrock Rovers in the League of Ireland, where he not only won the title but also guided them to the Europa League group stage. They finished pointless but it was the first time an Irish club had gone so far in the competition.

And O'Neill's reputation has since soared thanks to his work with the Northern Irish national team. Their Football Association will be crossing their fingers that no club side comes in for the gaffer after the tournament.

Steven Davis explained what makes O'Neill so special in a January interview with the Belfast Telegraph: "Michael's influence has been huge. He has put the blocks in place for us to be a success. Everything we have done from the preparation for matches to the atmosphere created in the squad has been down to Michael.

"Tactically his knowledge is excellent and anything that he tells us has a method behind it."

Match winners

Kyle Lafferty excelled in qualifying, scoring

FACTFILE

FA founded 1880
www irishfa.com
Head coach Michael O'Neill
National league NIFL Premiership
Date qualified October 8, 2015

....

Typical starting XI (4-1-4-1) McGovern; McLaughlin, McAuley, Evans, *Brunt; Baird; McGinn, Norwood, Davis, Dallas; Lafferty.
*Brunt is injured – the next most frequent starter at left-back was Shane Ferguson

....

Strengths
- ☑ O'Neill has created a club-like atmosphere in the squad
- ☑ Northern Ireland will pose a threat from set-pieces

Weaknesses
- ☒ A number of the players ply their trade outside the top flight
- ☒ Scoring goals could well be a major problem

Star rating ★☆☆☆☆

....

Fixtures
1 Poland, 5pm June 12, Nice
2 Ukraine, 5pm June 16, Lyon
3 Germany, 5pm June 21, Paris
Base Saint-Georges-de-Reneins

Northern Ireland coach Michael O'Neill has fostered a club-like team spirit

seven of Northern Ireland's 16 goals, and he might be one of those types who does better for his country rather than club.

The two best players are Davis and Jonny Evans. Evans left Manchester United for regular playing time at West Brom and looks a class above the majority of his Albion team-mates, while Davis is a much underrated midfield schemer for Southampton who will be looking to dictate play for O'Neill's side.

Set-pieces will be a huge part of the plan and centre-back Gareth McAuley proved that in qualifying with three goals.

Question marks

Keeper Michael McGovern plays for Hamilton, right-back Conor McLaughlin is at Fleetwood, Chris Baird was barely used by Derby and Lafferty likewise at Norwich so, quite clearly, matches against Germany, Ukraine and Poland will be a massive step up for some of these players and a different level entirely from what was a soft group given

Greece's pathetic performances.

Left-back Chris Brunt, one of seven Premier League players in the regular squad, has been ruled out with a knee injury, news O'Neill called a "devastating blow."

Lafferty aside, it is difficult to see where the goals will come from unless QPR's March debutant Conor Washington comes good and Northern Ireland managed to keep only one clean sheet in their last seven qualifiers.

How to back them

This may be a step too far for Northern Ireland and a pointless campaign is possible even if Germany have top spot wrapped up before the final group game.

Northern Ireland look worth backing to come last in a very difficult section, while Lafferty looks too short to finish as their top scorer despite a solid international record. Maybe split stakes on McAuley and Evans, with one goal potentially enough to land the bet and set-pieces a real strength of the side.

EUROPEAN CHAMPIONSHIP RECORD

1960	P	W	D	L	GF	GA
Did not enter	-	-	-	-	-	-
Qualifying	-	-	-	-	-	-

1964	P	W	D	L	GF	GA
Did not qualify	-	-	-	-	-	-
Qualifying	4	2	1	1	5	2

1968	P	W	D	L	GF	GA
Did not qualify	-	-	-	-	-	-
Qualifying	6	1	1	4	2	8

1972	P	W	D	L	GF	GA
Did not qualify	-	-	-	-	-	-
Qualifying	6	2	2	2	10	6

1976	P	W	D	L	GF	GA
Did not qualify	-	-	-	-	-	-
Qualifying	6	3	0	3	8	5

1980	P	W	D	L	GF	GA
Did not qualify	-	-	-	-	-	-
Qualifying	8	4	1	3	8	14

1984	P	W	D	L	GF	GA
Did not qualify	-	-	-	-	-	-
Qualifying	8	5	1	2	8	5

1988	P	W	D	L	GF	GA
Did not qualify	-	-	-	-	-	-
Qualifying	6	1	1	4	2	10

1992	P	W	D	L	GF	GA
Did not qualify	-	-	-	-	-	-
Qualifying	8	2	3	3	11	11

1996	P	W	D	L	GF	GA
Did not qualify	-	-	-	-	-	-
Qualifying	10	5	2	3	20	15

2000	P	W	D	L	GF	GA
Did not qualify	-	-	-	-	-	-
Qualifying	8	1	2	5	4	19

2004	P	W	D	L	GF	GA
Did not qualify	-	-	-	-	-	-
Qualifying	8	0	3	5	0	8

2008	P	W	D	L	GF	GA
Did not qualify	-	-	-	-	-	-
Qualifying	12	6	2	4	17	14

2012	P	W	D	L	GF	GA
Did not qualify	-	-	-	-	-	-
Qualifying	10	2	3	5	9	13

Totals	P	W	D	L	GF	GA
Finals	-	-	-	-	-	-
Qualifying	100	34	22	44	104	130

Results & goals include extra time

WIN % FOUR-TEAM FINALS — 100 / 50 / 0 — 1960 1964 1968 1972 1976

WIN % EIGHT-TEAM FINALS — 100 / 50 / 0 — 1980 1984 1988 1992

WIN % 16-TEAM FINALS — 100 / 50 / 0 — 1996 2000 2004 2008 2012

Results include extra time. ▌ in qualifying ▌ at the finals

LEGENDARY PLAYER

George Best was a genius, but **Billy Bingham** was there for all of the national team's biggest moments, playing at Sweden 1958 and then, as manager, leading Northern Ireland to two Home Championships and qualification for the 1982 and 1986 World Cups.

BILLY BINGHAM LEGEND

WORLD CUP RECORD

Year	Point of exit	Year	Point of exit
1930*	Did not enter	1978	Did not qualify
1934*	Did not qualify	1982	Second round
1938*	Did not qualify	1986	Group stage
1950*	Did not qualify	1990	Did not qualify
1954	Did not qualify	1994	Did not qualify
1958	Quarter-finals	1998	Did not qualify
1962	Did not qualify	2002	Did not qualify
1966	Did not qualify	2006	Did not qualify
1970	Did not qualify	2010	Did not qualify
1974	Did not qualify	2014	Did not qualify

* Competed as part of Ireland between 1930-1950

DID YOU KNOW?

David Healy's record 13 goals in qualifying for Euro 2008 was over a third of his international career total

GROUP C

HOW THEY QUALIFIED

Group F	P	W	D	L	F	A	GD	Pts
N Ireland	**10**	**6**	**3**	**1**	**16**	**8**	**+8**	**21**
Romania	**10**	**5**	**5**	**0**	**11**	**2**	**+9**	**20**
Hungary	**10**	**4**	**4**	**2**	**11**	**9**	**+2**	**16**
Finland	10	3	3	4	9	10	-1	12
Faroe Islands	10	2	0	8	6	17	-11	6
Greece	10	1	3	6	7	14	-7	6

Match stats in qualifying

Possession	44%
Shots on target	55%
Shots off target	58%
Corners	56%

Averages of match totals in qualifying. See pages 228-254 for full qualifying results

Results & prices	W	D	L
Hungary....(0) 1-2 (0)... N Ireland	7-1	10-3	1-2
N Ireland ..(2) 2-0 (0)....... Faroes	2-7	19-4	14-1
Greece......(0) 0-2 (1)... N Ireland	7-1	10-3	8-15
Romania...(0) 2-0 (0)... N Ireland	13-2	3-1	6-10
N Ireland ..(2) 2-1 (0)...... Finland	9-5	11-5	19-10
N Ireland ..(0) 0-0 (0).... Romania	12-5	11-5	7-5
Faroes.......(1) 1-3 (1)... N Ireland	7-10	3-1	11-2
N Ireland ..(0) 1-1 (0).... Hungary	13-8	23-10	21-10
N Ireland ..(1) 3-1 (0).......Greece	13-8	19-10	12-5
Finland .....(0) 1-1 (1)... N Ireland	27-10	9-4	5-4
Profit & loss in qualifying	**14.42**	**-0.25**	**-8.40**

Figures based on a £1 level stake using best odds in the Racing Post on day of match. W shows win price, whether home or away, L the price of the opposition

PLAYERS USED IN QUALIFYING

			CAREER			QUALIFYING			
Pos		**Club**	**Age**	**P**	**G**	**P**	**G**	▯	▮
GK	Michael McGovern	Hamilton	31	10	-	5	-	-	-
GK	Roy Carroll	Notts County	38	43	-	5	-	-	-
DEF	Aaron Hughes	Melbourne City	36	98	1	4	-	-	-
DEF	Chris Baird	Fulham	34	76	-	9	-	2	1
DEF	Conor McLaughlin	Fleetwood	24	16	-	9	-	3	-
DEF	Craig Cathcart	Watford	27	26	2	4	1	-	-
DEF	Gareth McAuley	West Brom	36	60	7	10	3	-	-
DEF	Jonny Evans	West Brom	28	47	1	4	-	-	-
DEF	Luke McCullough	Doncaster	22	5	-	2	-	-	-
DEF	Patrick McNair	Man Utd	21	7	-	3	-	-	-
DEF	Ryan McGivern	Port Vale	26	23	-	2	-	-	-
MID	Ben Reeves	MK Dons	24	2	-	1	-	-	-
MID	Chris Brunt	West Brom	31	54	1	8	-	2	-
MID	Corry Evans	Blackburn	25	32	1	7	-	-	-
MID	Niall McGinn	Aberdeen	28	41	2	8	1	-	-
MID	Oliver Norwood	Reading	25	32	-	10	-	1	-
MID	Pat McCourt	Luton	32	18	2	1	-	-	-
MID	Sammy Clingan	Unattached	32	39	-	1	-	-	-
MID	Shane Ferguson	Millwall	24	24	1	5	-	1	-
MID	Steve Davis	Southampton	31	81	8	9	2	-	-
MID	Stuart Dallas	Leeds	25	12	1	6	-	-	-
MID	Jamie Ward	Nottm Forest	30	20	2	6	1	-	-
ATT	Josh Magennis	Kilmarnock	25	18	1	7	1	1	-
ATT	Billy McKay	Dundee Utd	27	11	-	2	-	-	-
ATT	Kyle Lafferty	Birmingham	28	49	16	9	7	3	-
ATT	Liam Boyce	Ross County	25	7	-	1	-	-	-

CORRECT SCORES

	Competitive	Friendly
1-0	1	2
2-0	2	-
2-1	2	-
3-0	-	-
3-1	2	-
3-2	-	-
4-0	-	-
4-1	-	-
4-2	-	-
4-3	-	-
0-0	1	2
1-1	6	2
2-2	-	-
3-3	-	1
4-4	-	-
0-1	-	3
0-2	4	1
1-2	-	-
0-3	-	-
1-3	-	-
2-3	1	-
0-4	-	-
1-4	-	-
2-4	1	-
3-4	-	-
Other	-	-

Since Euro 2012

HALF-TIME/FULL-TIME DOUBLE RESULTS

Win/Win	5	25%	Win 1st half	8	40%
Draw/Win	2	10%	Win 2nd half	6	30%
Lose/Win	0	0%	Win both halves	2	10%
Win/Draw	3	15%	Goal both halves	12	60%
Draw/Draw	2	10%			
Lose/Draw	2	10%	**Overall**		
Win/Lose	0	0%	● Win	35%	
Draw/Lose	5	25%	● Draw	35%	
Lose/Lose	1	5%	● Lose	30%	

WIN 35%

Overall: W7, D7, L6 in 20 competitive games since Euro 2012

CLEAN SHEETS

4 (20%) **Clean sheets** 16 (80%) ✓ ✗

5 (25%) **Fail to score** 15 (75%) ✓ ✗

3 (15%) **Win to nil** 17 (85%) ✓ ✗

4 (20%) **Lose to nil** 16 (80%) ✓ ✗

UNDER & OVER GOALS

18 (90%) **Over 1.5** 2 (10%) ✓ ✗

6 (30%) **Over 2.5** 14 (70%) ✓ ✗

4 (20%) **Over 3.5** 16 (80%) ✓ ✗

2 (10%) **Over 4.5** 18 (90%) ✓ ✗

BOTH TEAMS TO SCORE

12 (60%) **Both score** 8 (40%) ✓ ✗

4 (20%) **& win** 16 (80%) ✓ ✗

2 (10%) **& lose** 18 (90%) ✓ ✗

In 20 competitive games since Euro 2012

GOAL TIMES

Total match goals by half

13 (68%) **1st half** 6 (32%)
F ▬▬▬▬▬▬▬ A

12 (39%) **2nd half** 19 (61%)
F ▬▬▬▬▬▬▬ A

Goals for & against by half

13 (52%) **For** 12 (48%)
1st ▬▬▬▬▬▬ 2nd

6 (24%) **Against** 19 (76%)
1st ▬▬▬▬▬▬ 2nd

● GOALS FOR ● GOALS AGAINST

	0-9	10-18	19-27	28-36	37-45	46-54	55-63	64-72	73-81	82-90
For	2	3	1	5	2	3	1	2	2	4
Against	1	0	1	2	2	0	1	1	9	8

In 20 competitive games since Euro 2012

IF NORTHERN IRELAND SCORE FIRST

They win	6	60%
Draw	3	30%
They lose	1	10%

In 20 competitive games since Euro 2012

IF NORTHERN IRELAND CONCEDE FIRST

They win	1	11%
Draw	3	33%
They lose	5	56%

Kyle Lafferty scores against Finland

GOALSCORERS IN QUALIFYING

● **FIRST GOALS**

	Goals		1st		Anytime		Percentage of team goals	
K Lafferty	7	●●●●●●●	1	14%	6	66%		44%
G McAuley	3	●●●	2	66%	2	20%		19%
S Davis	2	●●	1	50%	1	11%		13%
J Ward	1	●	1	100%	1	16%		6%
C Cathcart	1	●	1	100%	1	25%		6%
J Magennis	1	●	0	0%	1	14%		6%
N McGinn	1	●	0	0%	1	12%		6%

In Euro 2016 qualifying

BOOKINGS

Matches played	10	☐ 13	▮ 1
Average make-up (☐ 10 ▮ 25)			15.5

In Euro 2016 qualifying

CORNERS

Avg F	5.4		56%
Avg A	4.2		44%

In Euro 2016 qualifying. Avg match total 9.6

Croatia's classy midfield can cash in against the gung-ho Czechs

This is a fascinating group but, unfortunately, intrigue is not usually a word associated with finding a punting gem.

Spain deserve to be favourites but this section is no gimme for the European champions with tricky matches against Czech Republic, Turkey and **Croatia**.

La Roja have been slow starters in recent tournaments and should that be the case again, Vicente del Bosque will have to work overtime on Spain's confidence after their shambolic defence of the World Cup in Brazil.

On the plus side for Spain, Gerard Pique alongside Sergio Ramos forms the strongest centre-back pairing in international football, while Sergio Busquets and Andres Iniesta are part of Barcelona's brilliant midfield.

If Del Bosque can find the solution to their striking problems, Spain may yet land a hat-trick of European titles but anyone who fancies them to go well would be better off sticking to the outright market rather than backing them in this awkward group.

Croatia have a magnificent midfield themselves with Luka Modric alongside Ivan Rakitic, while they also have a genuine goal threat in Mario Mandzukic.

But there are question marks. Do they have the defence to top the group? Is manager Ante Cacic good enough to win the tactical battles?

The answers are difficult to give at the moment but it may not be an issue in their second match against gung-ho Czech Republic. If, as expected, Croatia dominate the midfield battle, they can control the game and Mandzukic should fill his boots on June 17 in Saint-Etienne.

The Czechs, who meet Spain at what might be the right time – first up – are a dangerous team themselves but a lack of clean sheets must be a concern at this level and Turkey could even reverse the qualification form.

Turkey were all over the place early doors but got their act together and are a different beast now to the team who were turned over 3-0 in Iceland and beaten 2-1 at home by Czech Republic in 2014.

Recommended bet
€€€€ Croatia to beat Czech Rep on June 17

TO WIN THE GROUP

	bet365	BetBright	Betfair	Betfred	Betway	Boyles	Coral	Hills	Lads	Power	Sky Bet
Spain	1-2	4-7	**4-6**	8-15	4-7	8-15	4-7	4-7	4-7	8-15	**4-6**
Croatia	3	33-10	3	**7-2**	10-3	10-3	3	**7-2**	**7-2**	**7-2**	3
Czech Rep	9	15-2	8	8	7	8	8	7	6	15-2	8
Turkey	**10**	8	13-2	13-2	8	17-2	8	7	9	15-2	13-2

Win only. Prices correct March 31

| TUR v CRO | SPA v CZE | ▶▶▶ | CZE v CRO | SPA v TUR | ▶▶▶ | CZE v TUR | CRO v SPA |
| 2PM JUNE 12 | 2PM JUNE 13 | | 5PM JUNE 17 | 8PM JUNE 17 | | 8PM JUNE 21 | 8PM JUNE 21 |

With the likes of Barcelona's Ivan Rakitic in the side, Croatia have a midfield to be feared

TO QUALIFY

	bet365	BetBright	Betfair	Betfred	Betway	Boyles	Coral	Hills	Lads	Power	Sky Bet
Spain	1-33	1-50	3-50	1-20	1-25	1-33	1-25	**1-16**	1-20	1-25	**1-16**
Croatia	4-11	2-5	2-5	4-11	2-5	3-10	1-3	**4-9**	4-11	2-5	2-7
Turkey	**10-11**	5-6	8-11	5-6	5-6	**10-11**	5-6	8-13	9-10	8-11	8-11
Czech Rep	**10-11**	4-5	5-6	**10-11**	4-5	4-5	4-5	8-11	4-6	8-11	**10-11**

Win only. Prices correct March 31

2PM JUNE 12 – TURKEY V CROATIA

	bet365	Betfair	Betfred	Betway	Boyles	Coral	Hills	Lads	Power	Sky Bet
Croatia	6-5	11-10	6-5	6-5	6-5	11-10	23-20	23-20	**5-4**	6-5
Draw	21-10	21-10	11-5	11-5	11-5	**9-4**	21-10	21-10	11-5	11-5
Turkey	**5-2**	12-5	12-5	**5-2**	12-5	9-4	23-10	**5-2**	21-10	12-5

Best prices as decimal odds: Croatia 2.25, draw 3.25, Turkey 3.5. 104%. Prices correct March 31

2PM JUNE 13 – SPAIN V CZECH REP

	bet365	Betfair	Betfred	Betway	Boyles	Coral	Hills	Lads	Power	Sky Bet
Spain	**4-7**	**4-7**	8-15	8-15	8-15	1-2	8-15	8-15	1-2	8-15
Draw	**3**	11-4	**3**	**3**	**3**	14-5	11-4	14-5	**3**	**3**
Czech Rep	9-2	9-2	11-2	**23-4**	5	11-2	5	11-2	11-2	5

Spain 1.57, draw 4, Czech Rep 6.75. 103%

5PM JUNE 17 – CZECH REP V CROATIA

	Betfair	Betfred	Power
Croatia	**13-10**	**13-10**	**13-10**
Draw	21-10	**11-5**	21-10
Czech Rep	21-10	**11-5**	21-10

Croatia 2.3, draw 3.2, Czech Rep 3.2. 106%

8PM JUNE 17 – SPAIN V TURKEY

	Betfair	Betfred	Power
Spain	3-5	**8-13**	3-5
Draw	11-4	**11-4**	27-10
Turkey	9-2	**9-2**	9-2

Spain 1.62, draw 3.75, Turkey 5.5. 107%

8PM JUNE 21 – CROATIA V SPAIN

	Betfair	Betfred	Power
Spain	Evs	**21-20**	Evs
Draw	**9-4**	9-4	**9-4**
Croatia	27-10	**11-4**	27-10

Spain 2.05, draw 3.25, Croatia 3.75. 106%

8PM JUNE 21 – CZECH REP V TURKEY

	Betfair	Betfred	Power
Czech Rep	6-4	**6-4**	**6-4**
Turkey	9-5	**15-8**	9-5
Draw	21-10	**11-5**	21-10

Czech Rep 2.5, draw 2.88, Draw 3.2. 106%

Spain are bidding to win a third successive European Championship

HOW THEY PERFORMED IN QUALIFYING

	Group/Pos	P	Home W	D	L	Away W	D	L	F	A	GD	Pts	Home Pos%	Shots On	Off
Spain	Group C 1st	10	5	0	0	4	0	1	23	3	+20	**27**	72.4	27	39
Czech Rep	Group A 1st	10	3	1	1	4	0	1	19	14	+5	**22**	59.2	18	41
Croatia	Group H 2nd	10	4	1	0	2	2	1	20	5	+15	**21**	59.2	28	40
Turkey	Group A 3rd	10	3	1	1	2	2	1	14	9	+5	**18**	56.6	33	30

Pos% percentage of total possession, **Shots on/off** shots on and off target, **Shots On%** percentage of shots on target (accuracy), **Shots%** percentage of total match shots

If you backed them P/L figures based on a £1 level stake using best odds in the Racing Post on day of match. Percentages represent probablility of victory implied by the win odds. **75%+** matches where the best price

	Spain					Czech Rep					Turkey					Croatia				
	W	D	L	F	A	W	D	L	F	A	W	D	L	F	A	W	D	L	F	A
Spain						2	0	0	4	1	2	0	0	3	1	1	0	0	1	0
						-	-	-	-	-	-	-	-	-	-	1	0	0	2	1
Czech Rep	0	0	2	1	4						1	0	2	4	6	-	-	-	-	-
	-	-	-	-	-						2	1	1	9	4	0	0	1	2	4
Turkey	0	0	2	1	3	2	0	1	6	4						0	2	1	1	4
	-	-	-	-	-	1	1	2	4	9						0	1	0	2	2
Croatia	0	0	1	0	1	-	-	-	-	-	1	2	0	3	0					
	0	0	1	1	2	1	0	0	4	2	0	1	0	2	2					

Includes all European Championship and World Cup matches since the 2002 World Cup. 90-minute results only. Competitive results above friendly results (in grey)

Friendly
April 30, 2003
Czech Rep ...... (4) 4-0 (0) ....Turkey

March 31, 2004
Croatia .... (1) 2-2 (0) ....Turkey

March 1, 2006
Turkey .... (0) 2-2 (1).......Czech Rep

June 7, 2006
Spain.............. (0) 2-1 (1)............Croatia

Euro 2008 group stage
June 15, 2008
Turkey .... (0) 3-2 (1).......Czech Rep

Euro 2008 quarter-finals
June 20, 2008
Croatia .... (0) 1-1 (0) ....Turkey
AET 0-0 90 mins. Turkey won 3-1 on pens

World Cup 2010 qualifying
March 28, 2009
Spain.............. (0) 1-0 (0) ....Turkey

April 1, 2009
Turkey .... (1) 1-2 (0) .... Spain

Friendly
May 22, 2010
Turkey .... (1) 2-1 (0) ......Czech Rep

February 9, 2011
Croatia .... (2) 4-2 (2) ......Czech Rep

Euro 2012 qualifying
March 25, 2011
Spain.............. (0) 2-1 (1).......Czech Rep

October 7, 2011
Czech Rep ...... (0) 0-2 (2) .... Spain

Euro 2012 qualifying playoffs
November 11, 2011
Turkey .... (0) 0-3 (2) ....Croatia

November 15, 2011
Croatia .... (0) 0-0 (0) ....Turkey

Euro 2012 group stage
June 18, 2012
Croatia .... (0) 0-1 (0) .... Spain

Friendly
February 6, 2013
Turkey .... (0) 0-2 (2) ......Czech Rep

Euro 2016 qualifying
October 10, 2014
Turkey .... (1) 1-2 (1).......Czech Rep

October 10, 2015
Czech Rep ...... (0) 0-2 (0) ....Turkey

Turkey's Hakan Calhanoglu tries his luck against the Czechs

Away	Shots		Shots overall		If you backed them							
Pos%	On	Off	On%	Shots%	P	75%+	P	50-75%	P	25-50%	P	<25%
69.2	32	31	45.7	65.2	8	+1.37	1	-1.00	1	+1.63	0	0.00
47.8	22	17	40.8	53.6	2	-0.80	3	+1.85	3	+0.50	2	+11.33
61.4	20	39	37.8	68.6	4	+0.67	2	-0.50	4	-1.70	0	0.00
50.4	21	38	44.3	60.1	2	-0.75	3	+0.07	4	+2.30	1	-1.00

was 1-3 or shorter **50-75%** matches where the best price was longer than 1-3 and no bigger than Evens **75-25%** matches where the best price was longer than Evens and no bigger than 3-1 **<25%** matches where the best price was longer than 3-1

Only completed matches are included. See pages 228-254 for full qualifying results

Spain v Czech 1-0 R

N ick Saban, an NFL boss once described as the most powerful coach in sport, said: "One thing about championship teams is that they're resilient. No matter what is thrown at them, no matter how deep the hole, they find a way to bounce back." Spain are a championship team but what will confirm La Roja as the greatest of all time is if they can bounce back.

How they qualified

Getting knocked out of the World Cup after two matches left its mark on Spain, and the hangover from the humiliation of losing 5-1 to Holland was clearly evident in a 2-1 loss to Slovakia in their second qualifier.

Those were the last competitive goals Spain conceded, though as Vicente del Bosque's side rallied to win eight straight matches to nil and top their group comfortably.

Even so, goals were difficult to come by – Valencia's Paco Alcacer topped the charts with five – and Spain have lost high-profile friendlies against France, Germany and Holland without scoring.

The manager

Del Bosque has won the lot – La Liga and the Champions League with Real Madrid and the European Championship and World Cup with the national team – and the 65-year-old is expected to retire at the end of this tournament.

A fiercely loyal man, it was his misplaced trust in the old guard that ultimately cost Spain in Brazil after he selected 16 players in 2014 who had been crowned champions in South Africa four years earlier.

Match winners

Despite the departures of the likes of Xabi Alonso and Xavi, Spain's midfield remains the heartbeat of the side with Andres Iniesta the inspiration. Koke, Isco and Thiago Alcantara are part of an emerging force that still includes David Silva, Cesc Fabregas and Santi Cazorla.

Sergio Ramos and Gerard Pique are world-

FACTFILE

FA founded 1913
www rfef.es
Head coach Vicente Del Bosque
National league Primera Division
Date qualified October 9, 2015

Typical starting XI (4-1-2-3) Casillas; Juanfran, Ramos, Pique, Alba; Busquets; Fabregas, Iniesta; Silva, Costa, Pedro

Strengths

☑ The midfield is packed with world-class talent and can dominate opponents
☑ There's no better centre-back pairing than Ramos and Pique

Weaknesses

☒ Friction between the Barca-Real Madrid players is not good for morale
☒ Del Bosque needs to sort out the striking position

Star rating ★★★★☆

Fixtures

1 Czech Rep, 2pm June 13, Toulouse

2 Turkey, 8pm June 17, Nice

3 Croatia, 8pm June 21, Bordeaux

Base Saint-Martin-de-Re

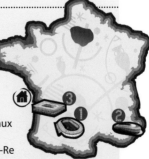

Vicente Del Bosque has won it all but his faith in the old guard cost Spain at the last World Cup

class centre-backs and there is talent in the forward positions even though Alcacer, Alvaro Morata and Diego Costa have failed to nail down the number nine position.

Despite Del Bosque's loyal nature, he could ditch captain Iker Casillas, who has made mistakes for Porto, in favour of the much superior goalkeeper David de Gea.

Question marks

That centre-forward role remains a headache for Del Bosque, who could be tempted to use Fabregas, Pedro or one of his other midfielders as a false nine – Aritz Aduriz, 35, was called up for the March friendlies which serves to highlight the striking concerns.

Pique and Ramos form a partnership at the heart of the defence but they have been involved in a public spat that has turned political, with Pique's pro-Catalan independence stance causing problems for the Barcelona defender at national level.

How to back them

Spain have been slow starters in recent tournaments, with a draw against Italy at Euro 2012 and losses to Switzerland and Holland in the World Cups of 2010 and 2014, so don't lump on them to win in Toulouse against Czech Republic on June 13.

La Roja were 20-23 against Italy, 2-7 against the Swiss and went off 17-20 for the Dutch disaster and don't make much appeal at 4-7 to beat the Czechs.

That said, the group, which also contains Turkey and Croatia, is one that Spain should win and there would then be a third-placed side waiting in the last 16.

The market also predicts a quarter-final with either Poland or Switzerland and it could have been much worse for La Roja.

They look likely to be the strongest side in the top half of the knockout draw which makes them ideal candidates in the 'name the finalists' market.

SPAIN

EUROPEAN CHAMPIONSHIP RECORD

1960	P	W	D	L	GF	GA
Withdrew	-	-	-	-	-	-
Qualifying	2	2	0	0	7	2

1964	P	W	D	L	GF	GA
● Winners	2	2	0	0	4	2
Qualifying	6	4	1	1	16	5

1968	P	W	D	L	GF	GA
Did not qualify	-	-	-	-	-	-
Qualifying	8	3	2	3	7	5

1972	P	W	D	L	GF	GA
Did not qualify	-	-	-	-	-	-
Qualifying	6	3	2	1	14	3

1976	P	W	D	L	GF	GA
Did not qualify	-	-	-	-	-	-
Qualifying	8	3	4	1	11	9

1980	P	W	D	L	GF	GA
Group stage	3	0	1	2	2	4
Qualifying	6	4	1	1	13	5

1984	P	W	D	L	GF	GA
● Runners-up	5	1	3	1	4	5
Qualifying	8	6	1	1	24	8

1988	P	W	D	L	GF	GA
Group stage	3	1	0	2	3	5
Qualifying	6	5	0	1	14	6

1992	P	W	D	L	GF	GA
Did not qualify	-	-	-	-	-	-
Qualifying	7	3	0	4	17	12

1996	P	W	D	L	GF	GA
Quarter-finals	4	1	3	0	4	3
Qualifying	10	8	2	0	25	4

2000	P	W	D	L	GF	GA
Quarter-finals	4	2	0	2	7	7
Qualifying	8	7	0	1	42	5

2004	P	W	D	L	GF	GA
Group stage	3	1	1	1	2	2
Qualifying	10	7	2	1	21	5

2008	P	W	D	L	GF	GA
● Winners	6	5	1	0	12	3
Qualifying	12	9	1	2	23	8

2012	P	W	D	L	GF	GA
● Winners	6	4	2	0	12	1
Qualifying	8	8	0	0	26	6

Totals	P	W	D	L	GF	GA
Finals	36	17	11	8	50	32
Qualifying	105	72	16	17	260	83

Results & goals include extra time

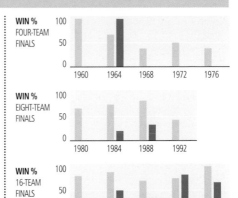

WIN % FOUR-TEAM FINALS — 1960, 1964, 1968, 1972, 1976

WIN % EIGHT-TEAM FINALS — 1980, 1984, 1988, 1992

WIN % 16-TEAM FINALS — 1996, 2000, 2004, 2008, 2012

Results include extra time. ▨ in qualifying ▮ at the finals

LEGENDARY PLAYER

Xavi was at the heart of the Spanish team that won the Euros in 2008 and 2012 either side of the 2010 World Cup. After a stellar career at Barcelona, he is Spain's most decorated footballer and is considered to be one of the best midfielders of all time.

XAVI HERNANDEZ · LEGEND

WORLD CUP RECORD

Year	Point of exit	Year	Point of exit
1930	Did not enter	1978	Group stage
1934	Quarter-finals	1982	Second round
1938	Did not enter	1986	Quarter-finals
1950	● Fourth	1990	Round of 16
1954	Did not qualify	1994	Quarter-finals
1958	Did not qualify	1998	Group stage
1962	Group stage	2002	Quarter-finals
1966	Group stage	2006	Round of 16
1970	Did not qualify	2010	● Winners
1974	Did not qualify	2014	Group stage

DID YOU KNOW?

Jesus Maria Pereda scored for Spain in the sixth minute of the 1964 final – that is still the fastest goal in a European Championship final

HOW THEY QUALIFIED

Group C	P	W	D	L	F	A	GD	Pts
Spain	10	9	0	1	23	3	+20	27
Slovakia	10	7	1	2	17	8	+9	22
Ukraine	10	6	1	3	14	4	+10	19
Belarus	10	3	2	5	8	14	-6	11
Luxembourg	10	1	1	8	6	27	-21	4
Macedonia	10	1	1	8	6	18	-12	4

Match stats in qualifying

Possession	▊▊▊▊▊▊▊▊▊▊▊	71%
Shots on target	▊▊▊▊▊▊▊▊▊▊	66%
Shots off target	▊▊▊▊▊▊▊▊▊	65%
Corners	▊▊▊▊▊▊▊▊▊	67%

Averages of match totals in qualifying. See pages 228-254 for full qualifying results

Results & prices	W	D	L
Spain........(3) 5-1 (1) Macedonia	1-12	12-1	33-1
Slovakia....(1) 2-1 (0).........Spain	2-5	15-4	9-1
Luxembourg(0)0-4(2).........Spain	1-25	20-1	66-1
Spain........(2) 3-0 (0)......Belarus	1-10	12-1	40-1
Spain........(1) 1-0 (0)......Ukraine	3-10	9-2	13-1
Belarus.....(0) 0-1 (1).........Spain	1-3	9-2	11-1
Spain........(2) 2-0 (0).....Slovakia	1-3	11-2	14-1
Macedonia(0) 0-1 (1).........Spain	1-6	7-1	25-1
Spain........(1) 4-0 (0)Luxembourg	1-50	40-1	80-1
Ukraine.....(0) 0-1 (1).........Spain	13-8	23-10	21-10
Profit & loss in qualifying	**2**	**-10**	**0**

Figures based on a £1 level stake using best odds in the Racing Post on day of match. W shows win price, whether home or away, L the price of the opposition

PLAYERS USED IN QUALIFYING

Pos		Club	Age	CAREER P	CAREER G	QUALIFYING P	QUALIFYING G	▯	▮
GK	David de Gea	Man Utd	25	8	-	3	-	1	-
GK	Iker Casillas	Porto	35	166	-	7	-	-	-
DEF	Mario Gaspar	Villarreal	25	3	2	1	1	-	-
DEF	Nacho	Real Madrid	26	4	-	1	-	-	-
DEF	Cesar Azpilicueta	Chelsea	26	14	-	1	-	-	-
DEF	Dani Carvajal	Real Madrid	24	5	-	2	-	-	-
DEF	Gerard Pique	Barcelona	29	76	4	8	-	1	-
DEF	Jordi Alba	Barcelona	27	42	6	9	1	-	-
DEF	Juan Bernat	Bayern Munich	23	7	1	4	1	-	-
DEF	Marc Bartra	Barcelona	25	9	-	3	-	-	-
DEF	Mikel San Jose	Ath Bilbao	27	5	-	1	-	1	-
DEF	Raul Albiol	Napoli	30	51	-	2	-	-	-
DEF	Sergio Ramos	Real Madrid	30	131	10	6	1	1	-
DEF	Juanfran	Atl Madrid	31	17	-	7	-	-	-
DEF	Xabier Etxeita	Ath Bilbao	28	1	-	1	-	-	-
MID	Vitolo	Seville	26	3	-	1	-	-	-
MID	Isco	Real Madrid	24	14	1	6	1	-	-
MID	Koke	Atl Madrid	24	22	-	7	-	1	-
MID	Andres Iniesta	Barcelona	32	107	13	5	1	-	-
MID	Bruno	Villarreal	31	6	-	1	-	-	-
MID	Cesc Fabregas	Chelsea	29	103	14	6	-	1	-
MID	David Silva	Man City	30	96	23	8	3	2	-
MID	Juan Mata	Man Utd	28	41	10	3	-	-	-
MID	Santi Cazorla	Arsenal	31	78	14	7	2	1	-
MID	Sergi Busquets	Barcelona	27	83	2	10	2	-	-
MID	Thiago	B Munich	25	7	-	1	-	1	-
ATT	Pedro	Chelsea	28	56	16	8	2	2	-
ATT	Jose Callejon	Napoli	29	2	-	1	-	-	-
ATT	Nolito	Celta Vigo	29	6	-	2	-	-	-
ATT	Alvaro Morata	Juventus	23	8	1	4	1	1	-
ATT	Diego Costa	Chelsea	27	10	1	4	1	3	-
ATT	Paco Alcacer	Valencia	23	13	6	8	5	-	-
ATT	Munir El Haddadi	Barcelona	20	1	-	1	-	-	-
ATT	Rodrigo	Valencia	25	1	-	1	-	-	-

CORRECT SCORES

	Competitive	Friendly
1-0	6	1
2-0	3	5
2-1	2	4
3-0	3	-
3-1	-	1
3-2	-	-
4-0	3	-
4-1	-	-
4-2	-	-
4-3	-	-
0-0	1	1
1-1	2	1
2-2	-	1
3-3	-	-
4-4	-	-
0-1	-	3
0-2	1	1
1-2	1	-
0-3	1	-
1-3	-	-
2-3	-	-
0-4	-	-
1-4	-	-
2-4	-	-
3-4	-	-
Other	3	2

Since Euro 2012

HALF-TIME/FULL-TIME DOUBLE RESULTS

Win/Win	16	62%	Win 1st half	17	65%
Draw/Win	3	12%	Win 2nd half	13	50%
Lose/Win	0	0%	Win both halves	10	38%
Win/Draw	1	4%	Goal both halves	15	58%
Draw/Draw	2	8%			
Lose/Draw	0	0%	**Overall**		
Win/Lose	0	0%	● Win	73%	
Draw/Lose	1	4%	● Draw	12%	
Lose/Lose	3	12%	● Lose	15%	

WIN 73%

Overall: W19, D3, L4 in 26 games since Euro 2012

CLEAN SHEETS

17 (65%)	**Clean sheets**	9 (35%)	3 (12%)	**Fail to score**	23 (88%)
✓		✗	✓		✗
16 (62%)	**Win to nil**	10 (38%)	2 (8%)	**Lose to nil**	24 (92%)
✓		✗	✓		✗

UNDER & OVER GOALS

19 (73%)	**Over 1.5**	7 (27%)
✓		✗
13 (50%)	**Over 2.5**	13 (50%)
✓		✗
6 (23%)	**Over 3.5**	20 (77%)
✓		✗
3 (12%)	**Over 4.5**	23 (88%)
✓		✗

BOTH TEAMS TO SCORE

7 (27%)	**Both score**	19 (73%)
✓		✗
3 (12%)	**& win**	23 (88%)
✓		✗
2 (8%)	**& lose**	24 (92%)
✓		✗

In 26 competitive games since Euro 2012

GOAL TIMES

Total match goals by half

28 (80%) **1st half** 7 (20%)
F ▮▮▮▮▮▮▮▮▮▮ A

28 (74%) **2nd half** 10 (26%)
F ▮▮▮▮▮▮▮▮▮▮ A

Goals for & against by half

28 (50%) **For** 28 (50%)
1st ▮▮▮▮▮▮▮▮▮▮ 2nd

7 (41%) **Against** 10 (59%)
1st ▮▮▮▮▮▮▮▮▮▮ 2nd

● GOALS FOR ● GOALS AGAINST

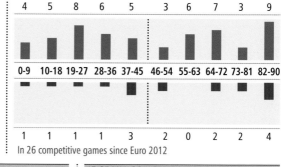

	4	5	8	6	5	3	6	7	3	9
	0-9	10-18	19-27	28-36	37-45	46-54	55-63	64-72	73-81	82-90
	1	1	1	1	3	2	0	2	2	4

In 26 competitive games since Euro 2012

IF SPAIN SCORE FIRST

They win	19		86%
Draw	2		9%
They lose	1		5%

In 26 competitive games since Euro 2012

IF SPAIN CONCEDE FIRST

They win	0		0%
Draw	0		0%
They lose	3		100%

GROUP D

Paco Alcacer in last summer's friendly win over Costa Rica

GOALSCORERS IN QUALIFYING

● FIRST GOALS

	Goals		1st		Anytime		Percentage of team goals	
F Alcacer	5	●●●●●	0	0%	4	50%	▮▮▮▮	22%
D Silva	3	●●●	2	66%	3	37%	▮▮▮	13%
S Cazorla	2	●●	1	50%	1	14%	▮▮	9%
S Busquets	2	●●	0	0%	2	20%	▮▮	9%
Pedro	2	●●	0	0%	2	25%	▮▮	9%
S Ramos	1	●	1	100%	1	16%	▮	4%
A Iniesta	1	●	0	0%	1	20%	▮	4%
D Costa	1	●	0	0%	1	25%	▮	4%
J Alba	1	●	1	100%	1	11%	▮	4%
Mario	1	●	1	100%	1	100%	▮	4%
Isco	1	●	1	100%	1	16%	▮	4%
A Morata	1	●	1	100%	1	25%	▮	4%
J Bernat	1	●	0	0%	1	25%	▮	4%

In Euro 2016 qualifying

BOOKINGS

Matches played	10	▢18		▮ 0
Average make-up (▢ 10 ▮ 25)				18

In Euro 2016 qualifying

CORNERS

Avg F	7.4	▮▮▮▮▮▮▮▮▮▮▮▮	67%
Avg A	3.7	▮▮▮▮▮▮	33%

In Euro 2016 qualifying. Avg match total 11.1

CZECH REPUBLIC

Spain v Czech 1-0 R

The Euros and Czech Republic go together like eggs and bacon. The country has been synonymous with the finals since Antonin Panenka's chipped penalty won the tournament in 1976. Since the dissolution of Czechoslovakia, Czech Republic have qualified for all six tournaments, and goals look guaranteed from the entertainers.

How they qualified

Few countries can be more proud of their qualifying achievements. The Czechs topped a group that contained Holland and Turkey, as well as surprise package Iceland.

Both teams scored in nine of their ten matches – Czech Republic conceded 14 goals in those games, achieving success despite failing to keep a single clean sheet.

It was often great to watch and qualification was secured with two matches to spare, but there was a certain amount of luck required in a number of the triumphs, something that Pavel Vrba unashamedly admitted.

The manager

Vrba deserves his own book, with the 52-year-old earning comparisons with Brian Clough (for his success with small teams), Arsene Wenger (for his belief in the beautiful game) and Sir Alex Ferguson (for his record-breaking reign with Viktoria Plzen).

He won the Slovak league with Zilina in 2007 but it was with Plzen that Vrba made his mark from 2008-2013 as he guided the club to dizzy heights of the Champions League.

Plzen the domestic cup for the first time in their history under Vrba and he then led them to their first title in 2011, before claiming the championship again in 2013.

Match winners

As Vrba acknowledged last year, the Czechs have few world-class talents these days: "Some ten to 15 years ago, we had players at top European clubs. This situation is different."

Arsenal custodian Petr Cech is superb but

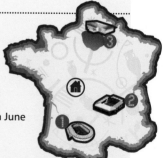

GROUP D

Pavel Kaderabek scores against the Dutch

there are not many members of the group who ply their trade at the highest level.

Fifteen members of the regular squad are based domestically, although Sparta Prague's excellent Europa League run suggests the Czech Liga standard is beginning to rise.

Veteran Tomas Rosicky, if fit, remains influential and Borek Dockal is capable of grabbing important goals from midfield for club and country. It was Dockal who notched the first of three Sparta away goals at Lazio which enabled them to reach the Europa League quarter-finals and he struck against Holland, Iceland and Turkey in qualifying.

Attacking right-back Pavel Kaderabek has struggled for Hoffenheim this term but was impressive during last summer's European Under-21 Championship.

Question marks

Rosicky has been dogged by injury problems so 34-year-old Jaroslav Plasil may have to take over playmaking responsibilities and another golden oldie, David Lafata, is the man most likely to lead the line.

The team is committed to attack and, as we went to press, had never kept a clean sheet under Vrba – the Czechs' last shutout was back in November 2013 against Canada.

Centre-back Marek Suchy is also suspended for the opener against Spain, although it could be argued facing the champions first is a plus, despite his absence.

How to back them

If the Czechs sneak into the knockout rounds they would be fair runners to concede the most goals but they will probably have to edge out Turkey or Croatia to reach the last 16 alongside Spain.

A safer play is to back over 2.5 goals in all of the Czech Republic group matches – Vrba's Plzen side played six Champions League games in 2013 and there were 23 goals.

EUROPEAN CHAMPIONSHIP RECORD

1960*	P	W	D	L	GF	GA
● Third	2	1	0	1	2	3
Qualifying	6	4	1	1	16	5

1964*	P	W	D	L	GF	GA
Did not qualify	-	-	-	-	-	-
Qualifying	2	0	1	1	2	3

1968*	P	W	D	L	GF	GA
Did not qualify	-	-	-	-	-	-
Qualifying	6	3	1	2	8	4

1972*	P	W	D	L	GF	GA
Did not qualify	-	-	-	-	-	-
Qualifying	6	4	1	1	11	4

1976*	P	W	D	L	GF	GA
● Winners	2	1	1	0	5	3
Qualifying	8	5	2	1	19	7

1980*	P	W	D	L	GF	GA
● Third	4	1	2	1	5	4
Qualifying	6	5	0	1	17	4

1984*	P	W	D	L	GF	GA
Did not qualify	-	-	-	-	-	-
Qualifying	8	3	4	1	15	7

1988*	P	W	D	L	GF	GA
Did not qualify	-	-	-	-	-	-
Qualifying	6	2	3	1	7	5

1992*	P	W	D	L	GF	GA
Did not qualify	-	-	-	-	-	-
Qualifying	8	5	0	3	12	9

1996	P	W	D	L	GF	GA
● Runners-up	6	2	2	2	7	8
Qualifying	10	6	3	1	21	6

2000	P	W	D	L	GF	GA
Group stage	3	1	0	2	3	3
Qualifying	10	10	0	0	26	5

2004	P	W	D	L	GF	GA
● Semi-finals	5	4	0	1	10	5
Qualifying	8	7	1	0	23	5

2008	P	W	D	L	GF	GA
Group stage	3	1	0	2	4	6
Qualifying	12	9	2	1	27	5

2012	P	W	D	L	GF	GA
Quarter-finals	4	2	0	2	4	6
Qualifying	10	6	1	3	15	8

Totals	P	W	D	L	GF	GA
Finals	29	13	5	11	40	38
Qualifying	106	69	20	17	219	77

* Results & goals include extra time. Competed as Czechoslovakia between 1960-1992

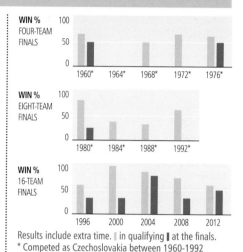

WIN %
FOUR-TEAM FINALS
1960* 1964* 1968* 1972* 1976*

WIN %
EIGHT-TEAM FINALS
1980* 1984* 1988* 1992*

WIN %
16-TEAM FINALS
1996 2000 2004 2008 2012

Results include extra time. ▌ in qualifying ▌ at the finals.
* Competed as Czechoslovakia between 1960-1992

LEGENDARY PLAYER

ANTONIN PANENKA   LEGEND

Pavel Nedved and Josef Masopust played in major finals and won Uefa's Ballon d'Or, but it was **Antonin Panenka** who delivered the Czechs their only tournament victory, with his cheeky penalty in the shootout that settled the Euro 76 final.

WORLD CUP RECORD

Year	Point of exit	Year	Point of exit
1930*	Did not enter	1978*	Did not qualify
1934*	Runners-up	1982*	First round
1938*	Quarter-finals	1986*	Did not qualify
1950*	Did not enter	1990*	Quarter-finals
1954*	First round	1994*	Did not qualify
1958*	First round	1998	Did not qualify
1962*	● Runners-up	2002	Did not qualify
1966*	Did not qualify	2006	Group stage
1970*	Group stage	2010	Did not qualify
1974*	Did not qualify	2014	Did not qualify

* Competed as Czechoslovakia between 1930-1994

DID YOU KNOW?

The Czechs had the worst defensive record in qualifying of any team to reach France

GROUP D

HOW THEY QUALIFIED

Group A	P	W	D	L	F	A	GD	Pts
Czech Rep	10	7	1	2	19	14	+5	22
Iceland	10	6	2	2	17	6	+11	20
Turkey	10	5	3	2	14	9	+5	18
Holland	10	4	1	5	17	14	+3	13
Kazakhstan	10	1	2	7	7	18	-11	5
Latvia	10	0	5	5	6	19	-13	5

Match stats in qualifying

Possession	▮▮▮▮▮▮▮▮▮▮▮	54%
Shots on target	▮▮▮▮▮▮▮▮▮▮	53%
Shots off target	▮▮▮▮▮▮▮▮▮▮	54%
Corners	▮▮▮▮▮▮▮▮▮▮▮▮	63%

Averages of match totals in qualifying. See pages 228-254 for full qualifying results

Results & prices

	W	D	L
Czech Rep. (1) 2-1 (0) ......Holland	10-3	13-5	1-1
Turkey.......(1) 1-2 (1) . Czech Rep	5-2	23-10	13-10
Kazakhstan(0) 2-4 (2) . Czech Rep	9-20	15-4	7-1
Czech Rep. (1) 2-1 (1) ...... Iceland	4-5	11-4	9-2
Czech Rep. (0) 1-1 (1) .... Latvia	1-4	11-2	18-1
Iceland......(0) 2-1 (0). Czech Rep	13-8	11-5	15-8
Czech Rep. (0) 2-1 (1) Kazakhstan	1-5	13-2	18-1
Latvia ....(0) 1-2 (2) . Czech Rep	6-10	16-5	6-1
Czech Rep. (0) 0-2 (0) ....Turkey	7-4	23-10	9-5
Holland.....(0) 2-3 (2) . Czech Rep	8-1	4-1	4-9

Profit & loss in qualifying   12.88 -3.50 -4.32

Figures based on a £1 level stake using best odds in the Racing Post on day of match. W shows win price, whether home or away, L the price of the opposition

PLAYERS USED IN QUALIFYING

Pos		Club	Age	Career P	Career G	Qualifying P	Qualifying G	🟦	■
GK	Petr Cech	Arsenal	34	118	-	9	-	-	-
GK	Tomas Vaclik	Basel	27	6	-	1	-	-	-
DEF	Daniel Pudil	Sheff Wed	30	31	2	1	-	-	-
DEF	David Limbersky	Viktoria Plzen	32	35	1	7	1	2	-
DEF	Marek Suchy	Basel	28	26	-	4	-	-	1
DEF	Michal Kadlec	Fenerbahce	31	63	8	6	-	-	-
DEF	Pavel Kaderabek	Hoffenheim	24	15	2	9	2	-	-
DEF	Theo Gebre Selassie	Werder Bremen	29	33	1	3	-	1	-
DEF	Tomas Kalas	Middlesbrough	23	3	-	1	-	-	-
DEF	Tomas Sivok	Bursaspor	32	52	5	4	1	-	-
DEF	Vaclav Prochazka	Osmanlispor	32	15	-	9	-	1	-
DEF	Filip Novak	Midtjylland	25	2	-	1	-	1	-
MID	Borek Dockal	Sparta Prague	27	23	6	9	4	3	-
MID	Daniel Kolar	Viktoria Plzen	30	26	2	3	-	1	-
MID	David Pavelka	Kasimpasa	25	5	-	4	-	1	-
MID	Jan Kopic	Viktoria Plzen	26	2	-	1	-	-	-
MID	Jaroslav Plasil	Bordeaux	34	97	6	5	-	-	-
MID	Jiri Skalak	Brighton	24	7	-	3	-	1	-
MID	Ladislav Krejci	Sparta Prague	23	20	4	9	1	2	-
MID	Lukas Vacha	Sparta Prague	27	8	-	4	-	-	-
MID	Milan Petrzela	Viktoria Plzen	32	17	-	1	-	-	-
MID	Ondrej Vanek	Viktoria Plzen	25	8	-	1	-	-	-
MID	Tomas Rosicky	Arsenal	35	100	22	5	-	1	-
MID	Vaclav Pilar	Viktoria Plzen	27	22	5	6	2	-	-
MID	Vladimir Darida	Hertha Berlin	25	33	1	10	1	1	-
MID	Josef Sural	Sparta Prague	26	9	1	4	1	-	-
ATT	David Lafata	Sparta Prague	34	37	8	7	1	-	-
ATT	Matej Vydra	Reading	24	17	5	2	-	-	-
ATT	Milan Skoda	Slavia Prague	30	7	2	5	2	-	-
ATT	Tomas Necid	Bursaspor	26	36	9	5	1	-	-
ATT	Vaclav Kadlec	Midtjylland	24	11	2	1	-	-	-

CZECH REPUBLIC

CORRECT SCORES

	Competitive	Friendly
1-0	1	-
2-0	-	2
2-1	5	-
3-0	1	1
3-1	1	-
3-2	1	-
4-0	-	-
4-1	1	1
4-2	1	-
4-3	-	-
0-0	3	1
1-1	1	2
2-2	-	2
3-3	-	-
4-4	-	-
0-1	-	4
0-2	1	-
1-2	3	1
0-3	1	-
1-3	-	1
2-3	-	-
0-4	-	-
1-4	-	-
2-4	-	-
3-4	-	-
Other	-	-

Since Euro 2012

HALF-TIME/FULL-TIME DOUBLE RESULTS

Win/Win	5	25%	**Win 1st half**	6	30%
Draw/Win	5	25%	**Win 2nd half**	8	40%
Lose/Win	1	5%	**Win both halves**	1	5%
Win/Draw	0	0%	**Goal both halves**	12	60%
Draw/Draw	3	15%			
Lose/Draw	1	5%	**Overall**		
Win/Lose	1	5%	● **Win**	55%	
Draw/Lose	3	15%	● **Draw**	20%	
Lose/Lose	1	5%	● **Lose**	25%	

WIN 55%

Overall: W11, D4, L5 in 20 competitive games since Euro 2012

CLEAN SHEETS

5 (25%)	**Clean sheets**	15 (75%)	5 (25%)	**Fail to score**	15 (75%)
✓		✗	✓		✗
2 (10%)	**Win to nil**	18 (90%)	2 (10%)	**Lose to nil**	18 (90%)
✓		✗	✓		✗

UNDER & OVER GOALS

16 (80%)	**Over 1.5**	4 (20%)
✓		✗
14 (70%)	**Over 2.5**	6 (30%)
✓		✗
4 (20%)	**Over 3.5**	16 (80%)
✓		✗
3 (15%)	**Over 4.5**	17 (85%)
✓		✗

BOTH TEAMS TO SCORE

13 (65%)	**Both score**	7 (35%)
✓		✗
9 (45%)	**& win**	11 (55%)
✓		✗
3 (15%)	**& lose**	17 (85%)
✓		✗

In 20 competitive games since Euro 2012

GOAL TIMES

Total match goals by half

13 (68%)	**1st half**	6 (32%)
F		A
19 (53%)	**2nd half**	17 (47%)
F		A

Goals for & against by half

13 (41%)	**For**	19 (59%)
1st		2nd
6 (26%)	**Against**	17 (74%)
1st		2nd

● GOALS FOR ● GOALS AGAINST

1	3	4	3	2	4	4	3	2	6
0-9	10-18	19-27	28-36	37-45	46-54	55-63	64-72	73-81	82-90
2	0	1	2	1	3	4	2	3	5

In 20 competitive games since Euro 2012

IF CZECH REPUBLIC SCORE FIRST

They win	8		80%
Draw	0		0%
They lose	2		20%

In 20 competitive games since Euro 2012

IF CZECH REPUBLIC CONCEDE FIRST

They win	3		43%
Draw	1		14%
They lose	3		43%

Borek Dockal scored against each of the other three sides in the top four of qualifying Group D

GOALSCORERS IN QUALIFYING

● FIRST GOALS

	Goals		1st		Anytime	Percentage of team goals	
B Dockal	4	●●●●	3	75%	4 44%	▊▊▊▊	21%
V Pilar	2	●●	0	0%	2 33%	▊	11%
P Kaderabek	2	●●	1	50%	2 22%	▊	11%
M Skoda	2	●●	0	0%	1 20%	▊	11%
T Sivok	1	●	0	0%	1 25%	▊	5%
D Limbersky	1	●	1	100%	1 14%	▊	5%
D Lafata	1	●	0	0%	1 14%	▊	5%
T Necid	1	●	0	0%	1 20%	▊	5%
L Krejci	1	●	0	0%	1 11%	▊	5%
V Darida	1	●	0	0%	1 10%	▊	5%
J Sural	1	●	0	0%	1 25%	▊	5%

In Euro 2016 qualifying

BOOKINGS

Matches played	10	☐ 15	▊ 1
Average make-up (☐ 10 ▊ 25)			17.5

In Euro 2016 qualifying

CORNERS

Avg F	5.9	▊▊▊▊▊▊▊▊▊▊▊▊	63%
Avg A	3.4	▊▊▊▊▊▊▊	37%

In Euro 2016 qualifying. Avg match total 9.3

DON'T
KNOW YOUR
NEUER
FROM YOUR
NAPOLEON,
YOUR
EVRA
FROM YOUR
ESCARGOT?
DON'T
WORRY.

TURKEY

The Emperor strikes back. Fatih Terim, Turkey's charismatic coach, was in charge the last time they qualified for a major tournament, when they reached the semi-finals of Euro 2008. Positive vibes are oozing out of the camp and Terim insists "we will not fear anyone" despite a tough draw alongside Spain, Croatia and Czech Republic.

How they qualified

Turkey were definitely the team to avoid from the bottom pot of seeds after finishing the qualifying campaign in ruthless fashion. Even so, they reached the finals via the backdoor after using up all their lives.

They qualified as the best third-placed team on a dramatic final matchday, going through thanks to a last-gasp Selcuk Inan free kick in a 1-0 win over Iceland.

France looked as far away as Pluto at one stage as Turkey opened up with one point from a possible nine, but after starting with two consecutive defeats, Terim's team finished unbeaten and they scored in every game bar the 3-0 hammering in Iceland on matchday one.

Good fortune was with Turkey, who saved their campaign with a 3-0 thrashing of Holland before beating Czech Republic and Iceland, who had already qualified.

The manager

Nicknamed the Emperor, Terim is in his third spell in charge of the Turkish team. And he needed all of his experience to calm a feud between Hakan Calhanoglu, Omer Toprak and Gokhan Tore, which surely harmed the early part of qualifying.

Calhanoglu alleges he and Toprak were threatened while on international duty in their hotel room by a gun-wielding friend of Tore who was upset at a new relationship between Toprak and Tore's ex-girlfriend.

Toprak and Calhanoglu refused to play for the national team for a while after Tore was recalled to the squad by Terim, who said: "If we got rid of everyone who made a mistake

FACTFILE

FA founded 1923
www tff.org
Head coach Fatih Terim
National league Super Lig
Date qualified October 13, 2015

Typical starting XI (4-2-3-1) Babacan; Gonul, Aziz, Balta, Erkin; Inan, Tufan; Calhanoglu, Ozyakup, Turan; Yilmaz

Strengths

☑ Inan and Calhanoglu are set-piece specialists
☑ Turan has the ability to turn matches on his own

Weaknesses

☒ Too many players are based in a sub-standard Turkish league
☒ Turkey are capable of some shocking performances

Star rating ★★☆☆☆

Fixtures

1 Croatia, 2pm June 12, Paris

2 Spain, 8pm June 17, Nice

3 Czech Rep, 8pm June 21, Lens

Base Saint-Cyr-sur-Mer

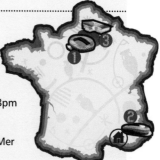

Brilliant:
Arda Turan

we wouldn't be able to pick a team." Terim is not to everyone's taste but Calhanoglu has since been persuaded to return and the boss showed with a semi-final appearance at Euro 2008 that it would be wrong to underestimate him.

Match winners

The majority of the squad are based in Turkey. Galatasaray's Burak Yilmaz is a target-man figure in Terim's 4-2-3-1 formation while Inan has shown his worth from midfield.

However, the best players are housed abroad. The brilliant Arda Turan is now at Barcelona having left Atletico Madrid, and Calhanoglu plays for Bayer Leverkusen, while Yilmaz took the Chinese Yuan and headed to the Far East.

Turan can find spaces in the tiniest of areas, Calhanoglu is raw but classy and Yilmaz guarantees goals.

Question marks

Turkey were wildly inconsistent in qualifying and there is no margin for error in a difficult group. They simply cannot put in the kind of performances that saw them frozen out in Iceland and pick up just two points from six against Latvia.

The defence would be improved by having Toprak in it and there has to be some concern about the team harmony when the squad must stay together for such a long period.

Galatasaray and Fenerbahce, who make up a fair chunk of the squad, were both eliminated earlier than they would have liked in the Champions League.

How to back them

Back Yilmaz to be Turkey's top goalscorer. He has a good record at international level and in his last full five campaigns in Turkey (2010-11 to 2014-15) he notched league tallies of 19, 33, 24, 16 and 16, winning the Super Lig Golden Boot in 2012 and 2013.

Yilmaz was Turkey's top scorer in qualifying with four goals and there are few alternatives to be the main striker this summer.

TURKEY

EUROPEAN CHAMPIONSHIP RECORD

1960	P	W	D	L	GF	GA
Did not qualify	-	-	-	-	-	-
Qualifying	2	1	0	1	2	3

1964	P	W	D	L	GF	GA
Did not qualify	-	-	-	-	-	-
Qualifying	2	0	0	2	0	7

1968	P	W	D	L	GF	GA
Did not qualify	-	-	-	-	-	-
Qualifying	6	1	2	3	3	8

1972	P	W	D	L	GF	GA
Did not qualify	-	-	-	-	-	-
Qualifying	6	2	1	3	5	13

1976	P	W	D	L	GF	GA
Did not qualify	-	-	-	-	-	-
Qualifying	6	2	2	2	5	10

1980	P	W	D	L	GF	GA
Did not qualify	-	-	-	-	-	-
Qualifying	6	3	1	2	5	5

1984	P	W	D	L	GF	GA
Did not qualify	-	-	-	-	-	-
Qualifying	8	3	1	4	8	16

1988	P	W	D	L	GF	GA
Did not qualify	-	-	-	-	-	-
Qualifying	6	0	2	4	2	16

1992	P	W	D	L	GF	GA
Did not qualify	-	-	-	-	-	-
Qualifying	6	0	0	6	1	14

1996	P	W	D	L	GF	GA
Group stage	3	0	0	3	0	5
Qualifying	8	4	3	1	16	8

2000	P	W	D	L	GF	GA
Quarter-finals	4	1	1	2	3	4
Qualifying	10	5	4	1	16	7

2004	P	W	D	L	GF	GA
Did not qualify	-	-	-	-	-	-
Qualifying	10	6	2	2	19	8

2008	P	W	D	L	GF	GA
● Semi-finals	5	2	1	2	8	9
Qualifying	12	7	3	2	25	11

2012	P	W	D	L	GF	GA
Did not qualify	-	-	-	-	-	-
Qualifying	12	5	3	4	13	14

Totals	P	W	D	L	GF	GA
Finals	12	3	2	7	11	18
Qualifying	100	39	24	37	120	140

Results & goals include extra time

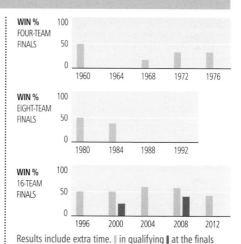

WIN % 100
FOUR-TEAM 50
FINALS 0
1960 1964 1968 1972 1976

WIN % 100
EIGHT-TEAM 50
FINALS 0
1980 1984 1988 1992

WIN % 100
16-TEAM 50
FINALS 0
1996 2000 2004 2008 2012

Results include extra time. ▌in qualifying ▌at the finals

LEGENDARY PLAYER

Turkey's record scorer, **Hakan Sukur** bagged a brace en route to the quarters at Euro 2000 but he is best remembered for scoring the fastest goal in World Cup history, 10.8 seconds into the third-place playoff against South Korea in 2002.

HAKAN SUKUR — LEGEND

WORLD CUP RECORD

Year	Point of exit	Year	Point of exit
1930	Did not enter	1978	Did not qualify
1934	Withdrew	1982	Did not qualify
1938	Did not enter	1986	Did not qualify
1950	Withdrew	1990	Did not qualify
1954	First round	1994	Did not qualify
1958	Withdrew	1998	Did not qualify
1962	Did not qualify	2002	● Third
1966	Did not qualify	2006	Did not qualify
1970	Did not qualify	2010	Did not qualify
1974	Did not qualify	2014	Did not qualify

DID YOU KNOW?

At Euro 2008 Turkey won the only penalty shootout in their history against Croatia, who will be their first opponents in France

GROUP D

HOW THEY QUALIFIED

Group A	P	W	D	L	F	A	GD	Pts
Czech Rep	10	7	1	2	19	14	+5	22
Iceland	10	6	2	2	17	6	+11	20
Turkey	10	5	3	2	14	9	+5	18
Holland	10	4	1	5	17	14	+3	13
Kazakhstan	10	1	2	7	7	18	-11	5
Latvia	10	0	5	5	6	19	-13	5

Match stats in qualifying

Possession	▮▮▮▮▮▮▮▮▮▮▮	54%
Shots on target	▮▮▮▮▮▮▮▮▮▮▮▮	61%
Shots off target	▮▮▮▮▮▮▮▮▮▮▮▮	59%
Corners	▮▮▮▮▮▮▮▮▮	48%

Averages of match totals in qualifying. See pages 228-254 for full qualifying results

Results & prices	W	D	L
Iceland......(1) 3-0 (0) ....Turkey	11-10	12-5	16-5
Turkey.......(1) 1-2 (1) . Czech Rep	13-10	23-10	5-2
Latvia ......(0) 1-1 (0) ....Turkey	4-6	29-10	21-4
Turkey.......(2) 3-1 (0) Kazakhstan	1-4	11-2	18-1
Holland.....(0) 1-1 (1) ....Turkey	6-1	10-3	4-7
Kazakhstan(0) 0-1 (0) ....Turkey	1-2	7-2	15-2
Turkey......(0) 1-1 (0) .... Latvia	1-4	11-2	17-1
Turkey.......(2) 3-0 (0) ....Holland	5-2	5-2	5-4
Czech Rep.(0) 0-2 (0) ....Turkey	9-5	23-10	7-4
Turkey.......(0) 1-0 (0) ..... Iceland	4-7	16-5	7-1

Profit & loss in qualifying 0.62 4.73 -2.30

Figures based on a £1 level stake using best odds in the Racing Post on day of match. W shows win price, whether home or away, L the price of the opposition

PLAYERS USED IN QUALIFYING

				CAREER		QUALIFYING			
Pos		Club	Age	P	G	P	G	▯	▮
GK	Volkan Babacan	Istanbul Buyuk.	27	14	-	8	-	-	-
GK	Onur Kivrak	Trabzonspor	28	12	-	1	-	-	-
GK	Tolga Zengin	Besiktas	32	9	-	1	-	-	-
DEF	Caner Erkin	Fenerbahce	27	44	2	9	-	-	-
DEF	Emre Tasdemir	Bursaspor	20	4	-	1	-	-	-
DEF	Sener Ozbayrakli	Fenerbahce	26	7	-	4	-	2	-
DEF	Semih Kaya	Galatasaray	25	23	-	4	-	-	-
DEF	Serdar Aziz	Bursaspor	25	9	1	7	1	-	-
DEF	Gokhan Gonul	Fenerbahce	31	55	1	5	-	1	-
DEF	Ersan Gulum	Hebei China	29	7	-	2	-	-	-
DEF	Omer Toprak	B Leverkusen	26	23	2	1	-	1	1
DEF	Hakan Balta	Galatasaray	33	44	2	6	-	1	-
MID	Olcan Adin	Galatasaray	30	10	1	2	-	-	-
MID	Hakan Calhanoglu	B Leverkusen	22	16	5	7	1	-	-
MID	Selcuk Inan	Galatasaray	31	50	8	9	3	-	-
MID	Mehmet Topal	Fenerbahce	30	56	-	9	-	1	-
MID	Emre Belozoglu	Istanbul Buyuk.	35	94	9	1	-	-	-
MID	Ozan Tufan	Fenerbahce	21	21	1	10	-	2	-
MID	Volkan Sen	Fenerbahce	28	14	-	7	-	1	-
MID	Gokhan Tore	Besiktas	24	26	-	7	-	2	1
MID	Hamit Altintop	Galatasaray	33	82	7	1	-	1	-
MID	Oguzhan Ozyakup	Besiktas	23	17	1	5	1	2	-
MID	Bilal Kisa	Galatasaray	32	14	1	1	1	1	-
MID	Olcay Sahan	Besiktas	29	22	2	4	-	-	-
MID	Arda Turan	Barcelona	29	89	17	9	2	4	-
MID	Mehmet Ekici	Trabzonspor	26	12	-	1	-	-	-
ATT	Cenk Tosun	Besiktas	25	7	3	2	-	1	-
ATT	Colin Kazim-Richards	Celtic	29	37	2	1	-	-	-
ATT	Mustafa Pektemek	Besiktas	27	12	3	1	-	-	-
ATT	Burak Yilmaz	Beijing Guoan	30	42	19	6	4	-	-
ATT	Muhammet Demir	Trabzonspor	24	2	-	1	-	-	-
ATT	Adem Buyuk	Kasimpasa	28	2	-	1	-	-	-
ATT	Umut Bulut	Galatasaray	33	38	10	6	1	-	-

TURKEY

CORRECT SCORES

	Competitive	Friendly
1-0	2	1
2-0	4	1
2-1	-	8
3-0	2	-
3-1	1	-
3-2	-	-
4-0	-	1
4-1	-	-
4-2	-	-
4-3	-	-
0-0	-	1
1-1	4	1
2-2	-	1
3-3	-	1
4-4	-	-
0-1	1	-
0-2	2	3
1-2	1	1
0-3	1	-
1-3	1	-
2-3	-	-
0-4	-	1
1-4	-	-
2-4	-	-
3-4	-	-
Other	1	1

Since Euro 2012

HALF-TIME/FULL-TIME DOUBLE RESULTS

Win/Win	7	35%
Draw/Win	3	15%
Lose/Win	0	0%
Win/Draw	1	5%
Draw/Draw	3	15%
Lose/Draw	0	0%
Win/Lose	0	0%
Draw/Lose	2	10%
Lose/Lose	4	20%

Win 1st half	8	40%
Win 2nd half	8	40%
Win both halves	5	25%
Goal both halves	12	60%

Overall
- Win 50%
- Draw 20%
- Lose 30%

WIN 50%

Overall: W10, D4, L6 in 20 competitive games since Euro 2012

CLEAN SHEETS

9 (45%) **Clean sheets** 11 (55%)
✓ ■■■■■■■■■ .... ✗

9 (45%) **Win to nil** 11 (55%)
✓ ■■■■■■■■■ .... ✗

4 (20%) **Fail to score** 16 (80%)
✓ ■■■■ .... ✗

4 (20%) **Lose to nil** 16 (80%)
✓ ■■■■ .... ✗

UNDER & OVER GOALS

17 (85%) **Over 1.5** 3 (15%)
✓ ■■■■■■■■■■■■■■■■■ ... ✗

7 (35%) **Over 2.5** 13 (65%)
✓ ■■■■■■■ .... ✗

3 (15%) **Over 3.5** 17 (85%)
✓ ■■■ .... ✗

1 (5%) **Over 4.5** 19 (95%)
✓ ■ .... ✗

BOTH TEAMS TO SCORE

7 (35%) **Both score** 13 (65%)
✓ ■■■■■■■ .... ✗

1 (5%) **& win** 19 (95%)
✓ ■ .... ✗

2 (10%) **& lose** 18 (90%)
✓ ■■ .... ✗

In 20 competitive games since Euro 2012

GOAL TIMES

● GOALS FOR ● GOALS AGAINST

Total match goals by half

14 (70%) **1st half** 6 (30%)
F ■■■■■■■■■■■■■■ ■■■■■■ A

16 (57%) **2nd half** 12 (43%)
F ■■■■■■■■■■■■■■■■ ■■■■■■■■■■■■ A

Goals for & against by half

14 (47%) **For** 16 (53%)
1st ■■■■■■■■ ■■■■■■■■■■■■ 2nd

6 (33%) **Against** 12 (67%)
1st ■■■■■■ ■■■■■■■■■■■■ 2nd

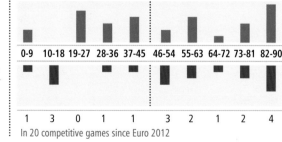

	0-9	10-18	19-27	28-36	37-45	46-54	55-63	64-72	73-81	82-90
For	2	0	5	3	4	2	4	1	3	6
Against	1	3	0	1	1	3	2	1	2	4

In 20 competitive games since Euro 2012

IF TURKEY SCORE FIRST

They win	10	■■■■■■■■■■■■■	63%
Draw	4	■■■■■	25%
They lose	2	■■■	13%

In 20 competitive games since Euro 2012

IF TURKEY CONCEDE FIRST

They win	0		0%
Draw	0		0%
They lose	4	■■■■■■■■■■■■■■■■■■■■	100%

Burak Yilmaz (17) scored in both of Turkey's qualifiers against Holland

GOALSCORERS IN QUALIFYING ● FIRST GOALS

	Goals		1st		Anytime		Percentage of team goals	
B Yilmaz	4	●●●●	2	50%	3	50%		29%
S Inan	3	●●●	3	100%	3	33%		21%
A Turan	2	●●	1	50%	2	22%		14%
U Bulut	1	●	1	100%	1	16%		7%
S Aziz	1	●	0	0%	1	14%		7%
O Ozyakup	1	●	1	100%	1	20%		7%
B Kisa	1	●	1	100%	1	100%		7%
H Calhanoglu	1	●	0	0%	1	14%		7%

In Euro 2016 qualifying

BOOKINGS

Matches played	10	☐21	▮ 2
Average make-up (☐10 ▮25)			26

In Euro 2016 qualifying

CORNERS

Avg F	3.9		48%
Avg A	4.3		52%

In Euro 2016 qualifying. Avg match total 8.2

CROATIA

Thousands lined the streets of Zagreb to welcome home Croatia's handball team after they took bronze in this year's European Championship, showing how important sport is to the country, but a section of their football supporters nearly cost them a spot at Euro 2016. Croatia are good enough to reach the latter stages – as long as the self-destruct button is not pressed.

How they qualified

Croatia beat Norway to second place by a point in their qualifying group but it should never have been so close after a blistering start saw them win four of their first five matches and draw the other away to table-topping Italy.

But a draw in the return fixture with Italy was followed by a stalemate with Azerbaijan and a loss to Norway. That saw Niko Kovac sacked and replaced by Ante Cacic, who steered the side to victories against Bulgaria and Malta in the final two games to secure qualification after a controversial campaign.

Croatian supporters got their team into trouble three times. First, flares were thrown on to the pitch in Milan. Second, they were found guilty of racist behaviour against Norway. Finally, after being ordered to play the return match against Italy behind closed doors, a swastika, visible during the game, had been marked on the pitch.

Croatia were docked a point and needed a letter from prime minister Zoran Milanovic begging Uefa not to kick them out of Euro 2016.

The Croatian football federation took matters into their own hands, banning fans from travelling to the final two away matches, but they will be back again in France.

The manager

Cacic has had a long and unspectacular career and is seen in some quarters as a yes man for a federation that is not particularly popular, but Kovac was walking on dangerous ground from the moment he fell out with star man Luka Modric.

FACTFILE

FA founded 1912
www hns-cff.hr
Head coach Ante Cacic
National league Prva Liga
Date qualified October 13, 2015

Typical starting XI (4-2-3-1) Subasic; Srna, Corluka, Vida, Pranjic; Modric, Brozovic; Perisic, Rakitic, Pjaca; Mandzukic

Strengths
☑ There is plenty of world-class talent in the midfield
☑ Mandzukic is a proven forward at this level

Weaknesses
☒ Coach Cacic lacks experience at the top level
☒ The full-backs are vulnerable defensively

Star rating ★★★☆☆

Fixtures
1 Turkey, 2pm June 12, Paris
2 Czech Rep, 5pm June 17, Saint-Etienne
3 Spain, 8pm June 21, Bordeaux
Base Coeur Cote Fleurie/Deauville

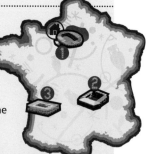

Luka Modric stars in Croatia's supremely talented midfield

Match winners

Real Madrid's Modric is capable of winning matches and he forms part of one of the most talented midfields in the tournament.

Barcelona's Ivan Rakitic plays alongside Modric and the area is so strong that one of Inter's Marcelo Brozovic and Real's Mateo Kovacic is unlikely to be selected in the starting XI. Fiorentina's Milan Badelj is another who may have to sit on the substitutes bench.

Ivan Perisic, a team-mate of Brozovic in Milan, is a massive goal threat from wide and Juventus striker Mario Mandzukic is a proven international-class forward.

Question marks

Croatia conceded just five goals in qualifying but the weakness is still at the back where Darijo Srna, who will be 34 by the time the tournament starts, is on a downward spiral and Cacic has looked at a 3-5-2 formation in the friendly win over Israel.

Centre-back Domagoj Vida was tried out at left-back as Cacic reverted to a four-man defence in the draw away to Hungary as the managers attempts to protect the rearguard.

There is nothing on Cacic's cv to suggest he is up to the task and that is arguably the biggest handicap to Croatia having an extended run in France this summer.

How to back them

The draw has been cruel and if Croatia finish second to Spain, their path to the final could feature the likes of Belgium, Germany and France. However, should they top Group E things could really open up for Cacic's men. The importance of finishing in first place cannot be overstated.

If you are a punter looking to oppose Spain in this tournament, an each-way wager on Croatia could be the best bet. The teams' meeting in the final group game in Bordeaux on June 21 could be absolutely pivotal for both nations.

EUROPEAN CHAMPIONSHIP RECORD

1960*	P	W	D	L	GF	GA
● Runners-up	2	1	0	1	6	6
Qualifying	4	2	1	1	9	4

1964*	P	W	D	L	GF	GA
Did not qualify	-	-	-	-	-	-
Qualifying	4	2	1	1	6	5

1968*	P	W	D	L	GF	GA
● Runners up	3	1	1	1	2	3
Qualifying	6	4	1	1	14	5

1972*	P	W	D	L	GF	GA
Did not qualify	-	-	-	-	-	-
Qualifying	8	3	4	1	7	5

1976*	P	W	D	L	GF	GA
● Fourth	2	0	0	2	4	7
Qualifying	8	6	1	1	15	5

1980*	P	W	D	L	GF	GA
Did not qualify	-	-	-	-	-	-
Qualifying	6	4	0	2	14	6

1984*	P	W	D	L	GF	GA
Group stage	3	0	0	3	2	10
Qualifying	6	3	2	1	12	11

1988*	P	W	D	L	GF	GA
Did not qualify	-	-	-	-	-	-
Qualifying	6	4	0	2	13	9

1992*	P	W	D	L	GF	GA
Suspended	-	-	-	-	-	-
Qualifying	8	7	0	1	24	4

1996	P	W	D	L	GF	GA
Quarter-finals	4	2	0	2	5	5
Qualifying	10	7	2	1	22	5

2000	P	W	D	L	GF	GA
Did not qualify	-	-	-	-	-	-
Qualifying	8	4	3	1	13	9

2004	P	W	D	L	GF	GA
Group stage	3	0	2	1	4	6
Qualifying	10	6	2	2	14	5

2008	P	W	D	L	GF	GA
Quarter-finals	4	3	1	0	5	2
Qualifying	12	9	2	1	28	8

2012	P	W	D	L	GF	GA
Group stage	3	1	1	1	4	3
Qualifying	12	8	2	2	21	7

Totals	P	W	D	L	GF	GA
Finals	24	8	5	11	32	42
Qualifying	108	69	21	18	212	88

* Results & goals include extra time. Competed as part of Yugoslavia 1960-1992

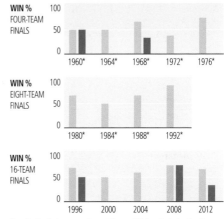

| WIN % FOUR-TEAM FINALS | 1960* | 1964* | 1968* | 1972* | 1976* |

| WIN % EIGHT-TEAM FINALS | 1980* | 1984* | 1988* | 1992* |

| WIN % 16-TEAM FINALS | 1996 | 2000 | 2004 | 2008 | 2012 |

Results include extra time. ▌ in qualifying ▌ at the finals.
* Competed as part of Yugoslavia 1960-1992

LEGENDARY PLAYER

Davor Suker scored 12 of Croatia's goals as they qualified for their first tournament as an independent nation, and then got one of the goals of the tournament at Euro 96 with a sublime chip over Peter Schmeichel in a 3-0 win over Denmark.

DAVOR SUKER LEGEND

WORLD CUP RECORD

Year	Point of exit	Year	Point of exit
1930*	● Fourth	1978*	Did not qualify
1934*	Did not qualify	1982*	Group stage
1938*	Did not qualify	1986*	Did not qualify
1950*	Group stage	1990*	Quarter-finals
1954*	Quarter-finals	1994	Did not enter
1958*	Quarter-finals	1998	● Third
1962*	● Fourth	2002	Group stage
1966*	Did not qualify	2006	Group stage
1970*	Did not qualify	2010	Did not qualify
1974*	Second round	2014	Group stage

* Competed as part of Yugoslavia between 1930-1990

DID YOU KNOW?

In January, Luka Modric became the first Croatian to be named in the Fifa/FIFPro World XI

GROUP D

HOW THEY QUALIFIED

Group H	P	W	D	L	F	A	GD	Pts
Italy	10	7	3	0	16	7	+9	24
Croatia	10	6	3	1	20	5	+15	20
Norway	10	6	1	3	13	10	+3	19
Bulgaria	10	3	2	5	9	12	-3	11
Azerbaijan	10	1	3	6	7	18	-11	6
Malta	10	0	2	8	3	16	-13	2

Croatia deducted 1pt

Match stats in qualifying

Possession	▐▐▐▐▐▐▐▐▐▐▐	60%
Shots on target	▐▐▐▐▐▐▐▐▐▐▐	67%
Shots off target	▐▐▐▐▐▐▐▐▐▐▐	70%
Corners	▐▐▐▐▐▐▐▐▐▐▐	67%

Averages of match totals in qualifying. See pages 228-254 for full qualifying results

Results & prices

	W	D	L
Croatia......(0) 2-0 (0).........Malta	1-14	14-1	45-1
Bulgaria....(0) 0-1 (1) ...... Croatia	13-10	9-4	27-10
Croatia......(4) 6-0 (0) .Azerbaijan	1-6	7-1	22-1
Italy ....(1) 1-1 (1) ...... Croatia	3-1	9-4	5-4
Croatia......(1) 5-1 (0) ..... Norway	1-2	7-2	8-1
Croatia......(1) 1-1 (1) ....Italy	7-5	21-10	12-5
Azerbaijan (0) 0-0 (0) ...... Croatia	4-11	4-1	10-1
Norway.....(0) 2-0 (0) ...... Croatia	6-5	12-5	29-10
Croatia......(2) 3-0 (0) .....Bulgaria	1-3	9-2	13-1
Malta........(0) 0-1 (1) ...... Croatia	1-10	12-1	33-1

Profit & loss in qualifying   -1.53 1.35 -6.10

Figures based on a £1 level stake using best odds in the Racing Post on day of match. W shows win price, whether home or away, L the price of the opposition

PLAYERS USED IN QUALIFYING

Pos		Club	Age	CAREER		QUALIFYING			
				P	G	P	G		
GK	Danijel Subasic	Monaco	31	19	-	10	-	-	-
DEF	Gordon Schildenfeld	Din Zagreb	31	25	1	2	1	-	-
DEF	Dejan Lovren	Liverpool	26	31	2	1	-	-	-
DEF	Vedran Corluka	Loko Moscow	30	87	4	9	-	1	1
DEF	Marin Leovac	PAOK Salonika	27	3	-	1	-	-	-
DEF	Dario Srna	Shakhtar	34	129	21	9	-	1	1
DEF	Hrvoje Milic	Hajduk Split	27	6	-	1	-	-	-
DEF	Domagoj Vida	Dynamo Kiev	27	36	1	9	-	2	-
DEF	Sime Vrsaljko	Sassuolo	24	17	-	3	-	1	-
DEF	Danijel Pranjic	Panathinaikos	34	58	1	6	1	-	-
DEF	Josip Pivaric	Din Zagreb	27	5	-	2	-	-	-
MID	Ivan Rakitic	Barcelona	28	75	10	10	1	1	-
MID	Luka Modric	Real Madrid	30	89	10	8	2	1	-
MID	Alen Halilovic	Sp. Gijon	19	8	-	2	-	-	-
MID	Marcelo Brozovic	Inter	23	16	4	9	2	2	-
MID	Mateo Kovacic	Real Madrid	22	26	1	8	-	3	-
MID	Milan Badelj	Fiorentina	27	18	1	5	-	1	-
MID	Ivan Perisic	Inter	27	45	12	9	6	3	-
MID	Marko Pjaca	Din Zagreb	21	6	-	4	-	-	-
ATT	Ante Rebic	Verona	22	10	1	1	-	1	-
ATT	Nikola Kalinic	Fiorentina	28	27	8	4	1	-	-
ATT	Mario Mandzukic	Juventus	30	65	21	8	1	2	-
ATT	Andrej Kramaric	Hoffenheim	24	9	3	6	2	-	-
ATT	Ivica Olic	Hamburg	36	104	20	8	1	3	-
ATT	Duje Cop	Malaga	26	3	-	1	-	-	1
ATT	Nikica Jelavic	Beijing Renhe	30	36	6	1	-	-	-

CROATIA

CORRECT SCORES

	Competitive	Friendly
1-0	3	1
2-0	4	2
2-1	2	3
3-0	1	-
3-1	-	1
3-2	-	1
4-0	1	2
4-1	-	-
4-2	-	-
4-3	-	-
0-0	2	-
1-1	4	1
2-2	-	1
3-3	-	-
4-4	-	-
0-1	1	1
0-2	2	-
1-2	1	1
0-3	-	-
1-3	2	-
2-3	-	-
0-4	-	-
1-4	-	-
2-4	-	1
3-4	-	-
Other	2	-

Since Euro 2012

HALF-TIME/FULL-TIME DOUBLE RESULTS

Win/Win	9	36%
Draw/Win	3	12%
Lose/Win	1	4%
Win/Draw	0	0%
Draw/Draw	6	24%
Lose/Draw	0	0%
Win/Lose	0	0%
Draw/Lose	3	12%
Lose/Lose	3	12%

Win 1st half	9	36%
Win 2nd half	11	44%
Win both halves	6	24%
Goal both halves	11	44%

Overall
- Win 52%
- Draw 24%
- Lose 24%

WIN 52%

Overall: W13, D6, L6 in 25 competitive games since Euro 2012

CLEAN SHEETS

12 (48%) **Clean sheets** 13 (52%) ✓ ✗

10 (40%) **Win to nil** 15 (60%) ✓ ✗

5 (20%) **Fail to score** 20 (80%) ✓ ✗

3 (12%) **Lose to nil** 22 (88%) ✓ ✗

UNDER & OVER GOALS

19 (76%) **Over 1.5** 6 (24%) ✓ ✗

9 (36%) **Over 2.5** 16 (64%) ✓ ✗

5 (20%) **Over 3.5** 20 (80%) ✓ ✗

2 (8%) **Over 4.5** 23 (92%) ✓ ✗

BOTH TEAMS TO SCORE

10 (40%) **Both score** 15 (60%) ✓ ✗

3 (12%) **& win** 22 (88%) ✓ ✗

3 (12%) **& lose** 22 (88%) ✓ ✗

In 25 competitive games since Euro 2012

GOAL TIMES

● GOALS FOR ● GOALS AGAINST

Total match goals by half

19 (66%) **1st half** 10 (34%)
F ▮▮▮▮▮▮▮▮▮ A

21 (68%) **2nd half** 10 (32%)
F ▮▮▮▮▮▮▮▮▮ A

Goals for & against by half

19 (48%) **For** 21 (53%)
1st ▮▮▮▮▮▮▮▮▮ 2nd

10 (50%) **Against** 10 (50%)
1st ▮▮▮▮▮▮▮▮▮ 2nd

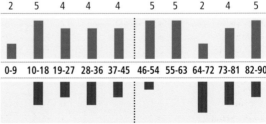

0-9	10-18	19-27	28-36	37-45	46-54	55-63	64-72	73-81	82-90
2	5	4	4	4	5	5	2	4	5
0	3	2	3	2	1	0	4	3	2

In 25 competitive games since Euro 2012

IF CROATIA SCORE FIRST

They win	11		73%
Draw	3		20%
They lose	1		7%

In 25 competitive games since Euro 2012

IF CROATIA CONCEDE FIRST

They win	2		25%
Draw	1		13%
They lose	5		63%

GROUP D

Top scorer
Ivan Perisic

GOALSCORERS IN QUALIFYING ● FIRST GOALS

	Goals		1st		Anytime		Percentage of team goals	
I Perisic	6	●●●●●●	2	33%	5	55%	▮▮▮▮▮▮	30%
L Modric	2	●●	1	50%	2	25%	▮▮	10%
A Kramaric	2	●●	1	50%	2	33%	▮▮	10%
M Brozovic	2	●●	1	50%	2	22%	▮▮	10%
I Olic	1	●	0	0%	1	12%	▮	5%
D Pranjic	1	●	0	0%	1	16%	▮	5%
I Rakitic	1	●	0	0%	1	10%	▮	5%
M Mandzukic	1	●	1	100%	1	12%	▮	5%
N Kalinic	1	●	0	0%	1	25%	▮	5%
G Schildenfeld	1	●	0	0%	1	50%	▮	5%

In Euro 2016 qualifying

BOOKINGS

Matches played	10	☐ 21	▮ 3
Average make-up (☐ 10 ▮ 25)			28.5

In Euro 2016 qualifying

CORNERS

Avg F	6.7	▮▮▮▮▮▮▮▮▮▮▮▮▮	67%
Avg A	3.3	▮▮▮▮▮▮▮	33%

In Euro 2016 qualifying. Avg match total 10

Big hitters can prove there is little depth in the group of death

Many observers have dubbed this section the group of death but **Belgium** and **Italy** can show there is not too much depth to the pool by coming through as automatic qualifiers.

The two big hitters meet in Lyon on June 13 in the highlight of the first-round matches and there is a fair chance one of them will be left in a difficult position, but games against Ireland and Sweden give them decent prospects of recovering the situation.

Belgium are strong in all departments and could be fighting it out in the latter stages as their young side looks to build on the quarter-final appearance in Brazil in 2014.

Thibaut Courtois is a top stopper, Vincent Kompany's influence at Manchester City is obvious and Belgium's strong Tottenham contingent, led by Toby Alderweireld, have had fine seasons.

Their many forward options include Eden Hazard and Kevin De Bruyne – exceptional creative talents – although it could be argued that finishing second in Group E and potentially avoiding France and Germany until the final would be best for Belgium's long-term ambitions.

Italy crashed out at the first hurdle in major tournaments in 2004, 2010 and 2014 but they are better equipped than Sweden and Ireland to claim a place in the top two.

Antonio Conte's team were unbeaten in qualifying and have bags of experience with a core group from beaten 2015 Champions League finalists Juventus.

Sweden, who took only two points against Austria and Russia in qualifying, are reliant on 34-year-old Zlatan Ibrahimovic and for all Ireland's miraculous four-point haul against Germany in qualifying, this is a side who took just two points off Poland and Scotland.

Those games against Germany saw Ireland lose the shot count 26-5, shots on target 11-3 and the corners 20-5, while enjoying an average of just 35 per cent possession compared to Germany's 65. It was heroic stuff but ultimately required much luck.

In qualification terms, much will depend on how Martin O'Neill's side fare against Sweden.

Recommended bet

€€€€ Belgium-Italy dual forecast

TO WIN THE GROUP

	bet365	BetBright	Betfair	Betfred	Betway	Boyles	Coral	Hills	Lads	Power	Sky Bet
Belgium	Evs	11-10	**5-4**	Evs	11-10	11-10	11-10	Evs	Evs	11-10	6-5
Italy	13-8	13-8	**7-4**	6-4	**7-4**	13-8	13-8	13-8	**7-4**	13-8	**7-4**
Sweden	6	6	6	6	11-2	11-2	6	11-2	5	5	5
Ireland	12	10	7	12	8	10	9	10	12	10	8

Win only. Prices correct March 31

Belgium v Italy is the key game in Group E and one of the pair could be left in an tight spot

TO QUALIFY

	bet365	BetBright	Betfair	Betfred	Betway	Boyles	Coral	Hills	Lads	Power	Sky Bet
Belgium	1-10	1-10	**1-6**	1-8	1-8	1-10	1-10	1-8	1-9	1-10	1-7
Italy	1-6	1-7	**2-9**	1-6	1-6	1-6	1-6	1-7	2-11	1-6	**2-9**
Sweden	4-6	8-13	8-11	8-11	4-6	4-7	**4-5**	4-7	3-5	8-13	8-11
Ireland	**13-8**	6-4	Evs	11-8	**13-8**	6-5	5-4	5-4	11-8	6-5	5-4

Win only. Prices correct March 31

5PM JUNE 13 – IRELAND V SWEDEN

	bet365	Betfair	Betfred	Betway	Boyles	Coral	Hills	Lads	Power	Sky Bet
Sweden	7-5	29-20	7-5	7-5	7-5	7-5	**6-4**	7-5	7-5	11-8
Draw	21-10	21-10	21-10	21-10	21-10	2	2	2	**11-5**	**11-5**
Ireland	21-10	9-5	21-10	**11-5**	2	19-10	9-5	21-10	2	2

Best prices as decimal odds: Sweden 2.5 , draw 3.2, Ireland 3.2. 103%. Prices correct March 31

8PM JUNE 13 – BELGIUM V ITALY

	bet365	Betfair	Betfred	Betway	Boyles	Coral	Hills	Lads	Power	Sky Bet
Belgium	**8-5**	7-5	6-4	6-4	29-20	7-5	29-20	7-5	7-5	3-2
Draw	2	21-10	21-10	21-10	2	2	19-10	21-10	**11-5**	**11-5**
Italy	19-10	15-8	2	2	**21-10**	19-10	2	2	15-8	15-8

Belgium 2.6, draw 3.2, Italy 3.1. 102%

2PM JUNE 17 – ITALY V SWEDEN

	Betfair	Betfred	Power
Italy	**19-20**	**19-20**	**19-20**
Draw	9-4	23-10	9-4
Sweden	3	3	3

Italy 1.95, draw 3.3, Sweden 4. 107%

2PM JUNE 18 – BELGIUM V IRELAND

	Betfair	Betfred	Power
Belgium	1-2	**4-7**	1-2
Draw	3	16-5	3
Ireland	9-2	9-2	9-2

Belgium 1.57, draw 4.2, Rep Of Ireland 5.5. 106%

8PM JUNE 22 – SWEDEN V BELGIUM

	Betfair	Betfred	Power
Belgium	**7-10**	4-6	**7-10**
Draw	5-2	13-5	5-2
Sweden	19-5	9-2	19-5

Belgium 1.7, draw 3.6, Sweden 5.5. 105%

8PM JUNE 22 – ITALY V IRELAND

	Betfair	Betfred	Power
Italy	4-6	8-11	4-6
Draw	5-2	13-5	5-2
Ireland	7-2	19-5	7-2

Italy 1.73, draw 3.6, Rep of Ireland 4.8. 107%

Ciaran Clark scored in a recent friendly for Ireland

HOW THEY PERFORMED IN QUALIFYING

	Group/Pos		P	Home			Away			F	A	GD	Pts	Home Pos%	Shots On	Off
				W	D	L	W	D	L							
Italy	Group H	1st	10	4	1	0	3	2	0	16	7	+9	24	55.6	25	43
Belgium	Group B	1st	10	4	1	0	3	1	1	24	5	+19	23	68.4	39	38
Ireland	Group D	3rd	10	3	2	0	2	1	2	19	7	+12	18	50.8	33	22
Sweden	Group G	3rd	10	3	1	1	2	2	1	15	9	+6	18	56.8	28	28

Pos% percentage of total possession, **Shots on/off** shots on and off target, **Shots On%** percentage of shots on target (accuracy), **Shots%** percentage of total match shots

If you backed them P/L figures based on a £1 level stake using best odds in the Racing Post on day of match. Percentages represent probablility of victory implied by the win odds. 75%+ matches where the best price

Read ↓ then →	Belgium					Italy					Ireland					Sweden				
	W	D	L	F	A	W	D	L	F	A	W	D	L	F	A	W	D	L	F	A
Belgium						-	-	-	-	-	-	-	-	-	-	1	0	0	2	0
						1	0	1	4	4	-	-	-	-	-					
Italy	-	-	-	-	-						1	2	0	5	3	0	1	0	1	1
	1	0	1	4	4						1	1	1	2	3	1	0	0	1	0
Ireland	-	-	-	-	-	0	2	1	3	5						0	1	1	1	2
	-	-	-	-	-	1	1	1	3	2						1	0	0	3	0
Sweden	-	-	-	-	-	0	1	0	1	1	1	1	0	2	1					
	0	0	1	0	2	0	0	1	0	1	0	0	1	0	3					

Includes all European Championship and World Cup matches since the 2002 World Cup. 90-minute results only. Competitive results above friendly results (in grey)

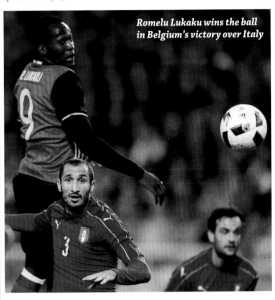

Romelu Lukaku wins the ball in Belgium's victory over Italy

Euro 2004 group stage
June 18, 2004
Italy............... (1) 1-1 (0) ....Sweden

Friendly
August 17, 2005
Ireland .... (1) 1-2 (2) .... Italy

March 1, 2006
Ireland .... (1) 3-0 (0) ....Sweden

May 30, 2008
Italy............... (2) 3-1 (0) .... Belgium

World Cup 2010 qualifying
April 1, 2009
Italy............... (1) 1-1 (0) ....Ireland

October 10, 2009
Ireland .... (1) 2-2 (1)................Italy

Friendly
November 18, 2009
Italy............... (1) 1-0 (0) ....Sweden

June 7, 2011
Italy............... (0) 0-2 (1)............Ireland

Euro 2012 group stage
June 18, 2012
Italy............... (1) 2-0 (0) ....Ireland

World Cup 2014 qualifying
March 22, 2013
Sweden .... (0) 0-0 (0) ....Ireland

September 6, 2013
Ireland .... (1) 1-2 (1)..........Sweden

Friendly
May 31, 2014
Italy............... (0) 0-0 (0) ....Ireland

June 1, 2014
Sweden .... (0) 0-2 (1).......... Belgium

November 13, 2015
Belgium.......... (1) 3-1 (1)................Italy

Away Pos%	Shots On	Off	Shots overall On%	Shots%	If you backed them P 75%+		P 50-75%		P 25-50%		P <25%	
60.0	26	33	40.2	70.9	4	+0.52	4	+1.20	2	-2.00	0	0.00
64.6	30	37	47.9	73.5	4	-0.82	5	+0.75	1	-1.00	0	0.00
47.6	19	17	57.1	56.5	2	+0.05	1	+0.53	4	-1.62	3	+4.50
55.0	23	25	49.0	58.8	3	+0.37	2	+0.94	5	-5.00	0	0.00

was 1-3 or shorter **50-75%** matches where the best price was longer than 1-3 and no bigger than Evens **75-25%** matches where the best price was longer than Evens and no bigger than 3-1 **<25%** matches where the best price was longer than 3-1

Only completed matches are included. See pages 228-254 for full qualifying results

BELGIUM

F ifa's rankings are much-maligned – often rightly so – but they can help to identify improving sides and Belgium have improved in each of the last seven years. After finishing 2009 in 66th spot, they were 57th in 2010, 41st in 2011, 21st in 2012, 11th in 2013 and fourth in 2014 before being ranked number one at the end of 2015. Now it is up to the Red Devils to prove Fifa's number crunchers right.

How they qualified

Belgium's shot ratio against opponents who finished in the top three was 63 per cent and bettered only by England, Portugal and Germany, as they finished two points clear of Wales in Group B.

However, it was not entirely convincing and much of the qualification campaign was a bit of a slog. Marc Wilmots' side took only one point from six against Wales and were held to a 1-1 draw by third-placed Bosnia.

Kevin De Bruyne and Eden Hazard excelled with five goals each in qualifying, while fellow attacking midfielder Marouane Fellaini chipped in with four, but the forwards failed to fire. Christian Benteke bagged once in four starts and Romelu Lukaku failed to notch in three.

A friendly demolition of France in Paris – it finished 4-3 but the hosts scored twice after the 89th minute – was far superior to anything witnessed in the qualifying campaign.

The manager

The results have been good under Wilmots but there is a feeling that the Belgians should be capable of more. They were fairly direct during the run to the World Cup quarter-finals, when Argentina beat them 1-0 in a tight contest.

Four of Belgium's six goals at the World Cup were scored by substitutes so Wilmots has earned a reputation in some quarters as a man who can change games from the sidelines but that may be exaggerating the situation – Belgium just have incredible depth to their squad.

FACTFILE

FA founded 1895
www belgianfootball.be
Head coach Marc Wilmots
National league Pro League
Date qualified October 10, 2015

Typical starting XI (4-2-3-1) Courtois; Alderweireld, Kompany, Lombaerts, Vertonghen; Witsel, Nainggolan; De Bruyne, Fellaini, Hazard; Benteke

Strengths
☑ The depth of the squad is sensational
☑ Hazard and De Bruyne are magical match winners

Weaknesses
☒ The full-back berths are occupied by centre-backs
☒ Potentially a tough draw for the Red Devils

Star rating ★★★★☆

Fixtures
1 Italy, 8pm June 13, Lyon
2 Ireland, 2pm June 18, Bordeaux
3 Sweden, 8pm June 22, Nice
Base Bordeaux

*Eden Hazard
starts the party*

Match winners

This is a side of outrageous talent. Belgium are led by the brilliant De Bruyne and Hazard and there is quality in just about every position.

Goalkeeper Thibaut Courtois is world class, centre-back Vincent Kompany's influence on the side is huge and Radja Nainggolan and Axel Witsel provide a strong platform in midfield. The list of potential match winners is endless and being able to rotate excellent players in midfield and attack should be a plus as the tournament progresses.

Question marks

Wilmots is still to work out who the ideal man is to lead the forward line and the full-back positions are occupied by Tottenham centre-backs Toby Alderweireld and Jan Vertonghen, who would presumably prefer to play in their normal roles.

Kompany and De Bruyne have both endured injury setbacks this season for Manchester City.

How to back them

This is a side who should improve for their World Cup run given only one player over the age of 29 went to Brazil in 2014. However, the draw has been brutal. Should they top their group, Belgium face likely matches against Germany and France before the final.

Finishing second could even be seen as an advantage so it may be wise to avoid lumping on Belgium to hit the summit, because they play in the final match of the group stage and will know exactly how the knockout draw has worked out before facing Sweden.

Before the draw they were an extremely attractive bet, but the play now is to split stakes on De Bruyne and Hazard to top the scoring charts. On qualifying form they should be much closer to Lukaku and Benteke in the betting.

EUROPEAN CHAMPIONSHIP RECORD

1960	P	W	D	L	GF	GA
Did not enter	-	-	-	-	-	-
Qualifying	-	-	-	-	-	-

1964	P	W	D	L	GF	GA
Did not qualify	-	-	-	-	-	-
Qualifying	2	0	0	2	2	4

1968	P	W	D	L	GF	GA
Did not qualify	-	-	-	-	-	-
Qualifying	6	3	1	2	14	9

1972	P	W	D	L	GF	GA
● Third	2	1	0	1	3	3
Qualifying	8	5	2	1	13	4

1976	P	W	D	L	GF	GA
Did not qualify	-	-	-	-	-	-
Qualifying	8	3	2	3	7	10

1980	P	W	D	L	GF	GA
● Runners-up	4	1	2	1	4	4
Qualifying	8	4	4	0	12	5

1984	P	W	D	L	GF	GA
Group stage	3	1	0	2	4	8
Qualifying	6	4	1	1	12	8

1988	P	W	D	L	GF	GA
Did not qualify	-	-	-	-	-	-
Qualifying	8	3	3	2	16	8

1992	P	W	D	L	GF	GA
Did not qualify	-	-	-	-	-	-
Qualifying	6	2	1	3	7	6

1996	P	W	D	L	GF	GA
Did not qualify	-	-	-	-	-	-
Qualifying	10	4	3	3	17	13

2000	P	W	D	L	GF	GA
Group stage	3	1	0	2	2	5
Qualifying	-	-	-	-	-	-

2004	P	W	D	L	GF	GA
Did not qualify	-	-	-	-	-	-
Qualifying	8	5	1	2	11	9

2008	P	W	D	L	GF	GA
Did not qualify	-	-	-	-	-	-
Qualifying	14	5	3	6	14	16

2012	P	W	D	L	GF	GA
Did not qualify	-	-	-	-	-	-
Qualifying	10	4	3	3	21	15

Totals	P	W	D	L	GF	GA
Finals	12	4	2	6	13	20
Qualifying	94	42	24	28	146	107

Results & goals include extra time

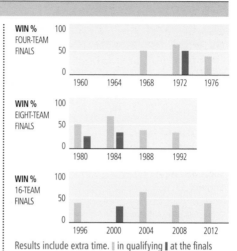

WIN % FOUR-TEAM FINALS — 1960, 1964, 1968, 1972, 1976

WIN % EIGHT-TEAM FINALS — 1980, 1984, 1988, 1992

WIN % 16-TEAM FINALS — 1996, 2000, 2004, 2008, 2012

Results include extra time. ▌ in qualifying ▌ at the finals

LEGENDARY PLAYER

Jan Ceulemans is Belgium's most capped player and his international career coincided with the Red Devils' best ever spell, as they reached the final of Euro 1980 and finished fourth at Mexico 86, where he wore the captain's armband.

JAN CEULEMANS LEGEND

WORLD CUP RECORD

Year	Point of exit	Year	Point of exit
1930	Group stage	1978	Did not qualify
1934	First round	1982	Second round
1938	First round	1986	● Fourth
1950	Did not enter	1990	Round of 16
1954	Group stage	1994	Round of 16
1958	Did not qualify	1998	Group stage
1962	Did not qualify	2002	Round of 16
1966	Did not qualify	2006	Did not qualify
1970	Group stage	2010	Did not qualify
1974	Did not qualify	2014	Quarter-finals

DID YOU KNOW?

Before finishing as runners-up at Euro 1980, Belgium had only ever won two games at the World Cup and European Championship finals

GROUP E

HOW THEY QUALIFIED

Group B	P	W	D	L	F	A	GD	Pts
Belgium	10	7	2	1	24	5	+19	23
Wales	10	6	3	1	11	4	+7	21
Bosnia-Hz.	10	5	2	3	17	12	+5	17
Israel	10	4	1	5	16	14	+2	13
Cyprus	10	4	0	6	16	17	-1	12
Andorra	10	0	0	10	4	36	-32	0

Match stats in qualifying

Possession	▮▮▮▮▮▮▮▮▮▮▮	67%
Shots on target	▮▮▮▮▮▮▮▮▮▮▮▮	73%
Shots off target	▮▮▮▮▮▮▮▮▮▮▮▮	74%
Corners	▮▮▮▮▮▮▮▮▮▮▮	72%

Averages of match totals in qualifying. See pages 228-254 for full qualifying results

Results & prices

	W	D	L
Belgium ....(3) 6-0 (0) .....Andorra	1-100	28-1	66-1
Bosnia-Hz. (1) 1-1 (0) .....Belgium	5-4	12-5	5-2
Belgium ....(0) 0-0 (0) ....Wales	3-10	5-1	12-1
Belgium ....(2) 5-0 (0) ....Cyprus	2-13	8-1	28-1
Israel ....(0) 0-1 (1) .....Belgium	8-15	10-3	13-2
Wales ....(1) 1-0 (0) .....Belgium	4-5	11-4	17-4
Belgium ....(2) 3-1 (1) .Bosnia-Hz.	1-2	7-2	7-1
Cyprus ......(0) 0-1 (0) .....Belgium	4-11	17-4	11-1
Andorra ....(0) 1-4 (2) .....Belgium	1-50	33-1	100-1
Belgium ....(0) 3-1 (0) ....Israel	4-11	9-2	9-1

Profit & loss in qualifying   -1.07 -0.60 -4.75

Figures based on a £1 level stake using best odds in the Racing Post on day of match. W shows win price, whether home or away, L the price of the opposition

PLAYERS USED IN QUALIFYING

Pos		Club	Age	CAREER P	G	QUALIFYING P	G		
GK	Thibaut Courtois	Chelsea	23	34	-	8	-	-	-
GK	Simon Mignolet	Liverpool	27	18	-	2	-	-	-
DEF	Jordan Lukaku	Oostende	21	2	-	1	-	1	-
DEF	Thomas Vermaelen	Barcelona	29	52	1	2	-	-	-
DEF	Sebastien Pocognoli	West Brom	28	13	-	1	-	-	-
DEF	Jan Vertonghen	Tottenham	28	74	6	10	-	2	-
DEF	Anthony Vanden Borre	Anderlecht	28	28	1	1	-	-	-
DEF	Thomas Meunier	Club Brugge	24	5	-	2	-	-	-
DEF	Vincent Kompany	Man City	29	70	4	7	-	3	1
DEF	Nicolas Lombaerts	Zenit	30	39	3	7	-	2	-
DEF	Toby Alderweireld	Tottenham	26	53	1	10	-	1	-
DEF	Jason Denayer	Galatasaray	20	5	-	2	-	-	-
DEF	Luis Pedro Cavanda	Trabzonspor	25	2	-	1	-	-	-
MID	Dries Mertens	Napoli	28	43	8	9	3	-	-
MID	Nacer Chadli	Tottenham	26	32	4	4	1	-	-
MID	Kevin De Bruyne	Man City	24	38	12	10	5	1	-
MID	Steven Defour	Anderlecht	27	46	2	2	-	-	-
MID	Marouane Fellaini	Man Utd	27	67	15	8	4	-	-
MID	Eden Hazard	Chelsea	24	62	12	9	5	-	-
MID	Adnan Januzaj	Man Utd	20	6	-	1	-	-	-
MID	Radja Nainggolan	Roma	27	18	4	9	2	-	-
MID	Axel Witsel	Zenit	26	66	6	8	-	-	-
MID	Yannick Carrasco	Atl Madrid	22	4	-	2	-	-	-
MID	Zakaria Bakkali	Valencia	19	2	-	1	-	-	-
ATT	Laurent Depoitre	Gent	26	1	1	1	1	1	-
ATT	Michy Batshuayi	Marseille	22	3	2	1	1	-	-
ATT	Christian Benteke	Liverpool	24	24	6	5	1	-	-
ATT	Divock Origi	Liverpool	20	16	3	7	1	-	-
ATT	Romelu Lukaku	Everton	22	43	12	5	-	-	-

BELGIUM

CORRECT SCORES

	Competitive	Friendly
1-0	5	1
2-0	4	2
2-1	3	1
3-0	1	-
3-1	2	2
3-2	-	-
4-0	-	-
4-1	1	-
4-2	-	2
4-3	-	1
0-0	2	1
1-1	3	-
2-2	-	1
3-3	-	-
4-4	-	-
0-1	2	-
0-2	-	1
1-2	-	2
0-3	-	-
1-3	-	-
2-3	-	1
0-4	-	-
1-4	-	-
2-4	-	-
3-4	-	-
Other	2	1

Since Euro 2012

HALF-TIME/FULL-TIME DOUBLE RESULTS

Win/Win	11	44%
Draw/Win	6	24%
Lose/Win	1	4%
Win/Draw	0	0%
Draw/Draw	4	16%
Lose/Draw	1	4%
Win/Lose	0	0%
Draw/Lose	0	0%
Lose/Lose	2	8%

Win 1st half	11	44%
Win 2nd half	16	64%
Win both halves	8	32%
Goal both halves	12	48%

Overall
- Win 72%
- Draw 20%
- Lose 8%

WIN 72%

Overall: W18, D5, L2 in 25 competitive games since Euro 2012

CLEAN SHEETS

14 (56%) **Clean sheets** 11 (44%)

4 (16%) **Fail to score** 21 (84%)

12 (48%) **Win to nil** 13 (52%)

2 (8%) **Lose to nil** 23 (92%)

UNDER & OVER GOALS

16 (64%) **Over 1.5** 9 (36%)

9 (36%) **Over 2.5** 16 (64%)

5 (20%) **Over 3.5** 20 (80%)

3 (12%) **Over 4.5** 22 (88%)

BOTH TEAMS TO SCORE

9 (36%) **Both score** 16 (64%)

6 (24%) **& win** 19 (76%)

0 (0%) **& lose** 25 (100%)

In 25 competitive games since Euro 2012

GOAL TIMES

● GOALS FOR ● GOALS AGAINST

Total match goals by half

18 (75%) **1st half** 6 (25%)
F ■■■■■■■■■■■■■■■ ■■■ A

30 (83%) **2nd half** 6 (17%)
F ■■■■■■■■■■■■■■■■ ■■■ A

Goals for & against by half

18 (38%) **For** 30 (63%)
1st ■■■■■■■ ■■■■■■■■■■■ 2nd

6 (50%) **Against** 6 (50%)
1st ■■■■■■■■■ ■■■■■■■■■ 2nd

	1	2	4	4	7	1	5	11	5	8
	0-9	10-18	19-27	28-36	37-45	46-54	55-63	64-72	73-81	82-90
	2	1	2	1	0	1	0	0	0	5

In 25 competitive games since Euro 2012

IF BELGIUM SCORE FIRST

They win	16	■■■■■■■■■■■■■■■■	94%
They draw	1	■	6%
They lose	0		0%

In 25 competitive games since 2012 World Cup

IF BELGIUM CONCEDE FIRST

They win	2	■■■■■■	33%
They draw	2	■■■■■■	33%
They lose	2	■■■■■■	33%

Kevin De Bruyne

GOALSCORERS IN QUALIFYING

● FIRST GOALS

	Goals		1st		Anytime		Percentage of team goals	
E Hazard	5	●●●●●	1	20%	5	55%		21%
K De Bruyne	5	●●●●●	1	20%	4	40%		21%
M Fellaini	4	●●●●	2	50%	3	37%		17%
D Mertens	3	●●●	1	33%	2	22%		13%
R Nainggolan	2	●●	1	50%	2	22%		8%
N Chadli	1	●	0	0%	1	25%		4%
C Benteke	1	●	0	0%	1	20%		4%
M Batshuayi	1	●	0	0%	1	100%		4%
D Origi	1	●	0	0%	1	14%		4%
L Depoitre	1	●	0	0%	1	100%		4%

In Euro 2016 qualifying

BOOKINGS

Matches played	10	☐ 11		▮ 1
Average make-up (☐ 10 ▮ 25)				13.5

In Euro 2016 qualifying

CORNERS

Avg F	7.5		72%
Avg A	2.9		28%

In Euro 2016 qualifying. Avg match total 10.4

ITALY

L et Italy coach Antonio Conte describe what to expect: "We are not the favourites, but in France we will cause problems for anyone we face. I want a Nazionale that makes Italians proud. That doesn't mean you have to win, but rather see good football at an intense tempo. I hope to be given the chance to work after the Serie A season ends and prepare a small war machine."

GROUP E

How they qualified

Rarely can an unbeaten campaign have been so readily dismissed but Italian supporters were not impressed despite their team making it to the finals comfortably.

No table-topper in the groups with six teams scored fewer goals than Italy, who found the net just 16 times – the same as Northern Ireland – and they were dominated in a 1-1 home draw with Croatia in which the visitors had 62 per cent possession, won the shot count 15-5, shots on target 9-2 and corners 5-0.

One-nil wins over Malta home and away did little to raise expectations, although Conte claimed it was only normal to expect problems with the squad in the process of regeneration after Italy's disappointing exit at the group stage of the last World Cup.

Conte started with a three-man defence but switched to a four during the campaign and used 34 players. No team who qualified selected more.

The manager

Conte led Juventus to a hat-trick of Serie A titles and is one of the highest-paid international managers.

A portion of his astronomical wages comes from sponsor Puma, which is one of many controversial aspects to Conte's role. The outspoken gaffer was the subject of death threats from Juve supporters after Claudio Marchisio was injured on international duty, with many suggesting that the players were worked too hard in training.

Conte's attempts to schedule a mid-season get-together were vetoed by the clubs and he

FACTFILE

FA founded 1898
www figc.it
Head coach Antonio Conte
National league Serie A
Date qualified October 10, 2015

....

Typical starting XI (4-1-2-3) Buffon; Darmian, Bonucci, Chiellini, De Sciglio; Verratti; Florenzi, Marchisio; Candreva, Pelle, Immobile

....

Strengths
- ☑ Centre-backs are superb and vastly experienced
- ☑ Italy are flexible in terms of tactics and formations

Weaknesses
- ☒ Ageing stars remain influential
- ☒ The Azzurri lack a genuine goalscoring threat

Star rating ★★★☆☆

Fixtures
1 Belgium, 8pm June 13, Lyon
2 Sweden, 2pm June 17, Toulouse
3 Ireland, 8pm June 22, Lille
Base Montpellier/Grammot

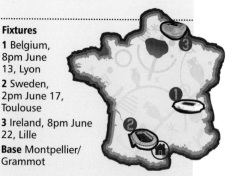

Marco Verratti is starting to live to his billing as the new Pirlo

was further frustrated when the Coppa Italia final was arranged for a date after the end of the Serie A season.

Given the constant running battles it is no surprise that he is leaving his post after the tournament and it is widely reported that Conte will be Chelsea's next manager.

Match winners

Even at 38, keeper Gigi Buffon is exceptional and the all-Juventus defensive backbone is completed by Giorgio Chiellini, Leonardo Bonucci and Andrea Barzagli.

Marco Verratti is beginning to live up to the hype as the new Andrea Pirlo and, Lorenzo Insigne, who has settled his differences with Conte, could be exactly what the Azzurri are missing. The winger has been in exceptional form for Napoli and is the one Italy player who can potentially turn a game.

Question marks

Pirlo, who will be 37 when the tournament begins, is now playing in New York and was dropped for the March friendlies, while the full-back options are average. That is a concern as Conte has hinted he would prefer to use a four-man defence in France.

None of the forward options – and Conte has tried plenty – are proven at anything like this level and the manager's demands for a tenacious, hard-pressing approach may be difficult at the end of a long club season.

How to back them

Italy have qualified for every European Championship since the tournament was extended to 16 teams in 1996 but their group-stage record is relatively poor. They won exactly one match in four of those five championships. The exception came in 2000, when they took nine points in the first round and went all the way to the final.

Their group, containing Ireland, Belgium and Sweden, is finely balanced and in four of their previous five tournaments they collected exactly four or five points. Those look the best bets again.

ITALY

EUROPEAN CHAMPIONSHIP RECORD

1960	P	W	D	L	GF	GA
Did not enter	-	-	-	-	-	-
Qualifying	-	-	-	-	-	-

1964	P	W	D	L	GF	GA
Did not qualify	-	-	-	-	-	-
Qualifying	4	2	1	1	8	3

1968	P	W	D	L	GF	GA
● Winners	3	1	2	0	3	1
Qualifying	8	6	1	1	21	6

1972	P	W	D	L	GF	GA
Did not qualify	-	-	-	-	-	-
Qualifying	8	4	3	1	13	6

1976	P	W	D	L	GF	GA
Did not qualify	-	-	-	-	-	-
Qualifying	6	2	3	1	3	3

1980	P	W	D	L	GF	GA
● Fourth	4	1	3	0	2	1
Qualifying	-	-	-	-	-	-

1984	P	W	D	L	GF	GA
Did not qualify	-	-	-	-	-	-
Qualifying	8	1	3	4	6	12

1988	P	W	D	L	GF	GA
● Semi-finals	4	2	1	1	4	3
Qualifying	8	6	1	1	16	4

1992	P	W	D	L	GF	GA
Did not qualify	-	-	-	-	-	-
Qualifying	8	3	4	1	12	5

1996	P	W	D	L	GF	GA
Group stage	3	1	1	1	3	3
Qualifying	10	7	2	1	20	6

2000	P	W	D	L	GF	GA
● Runners-up	6	4	1	1	9	4
Qualifying	8	4	3	1	13	5

2004	P	W	D	L	GF	GA
Group stage	3	1	2	0	3	2
Qualifying	8	5	2	1	17	4

2008	P	W	D	L	GF	GA
Quarter-finals	4	1	2	1	3	4
Qualifying	12	9	2	1	22	9

2012	P	W	D	L	GF	GA
● Runners-up	6	2	3	1	6	7
Qualifying	9	7	2	0	17	2

Totals	P	W	D	L	GF	GA
Finals	33	13	15	5	33	25
Qualifying	97	56	27	14	168	65

Results & goals include extra time

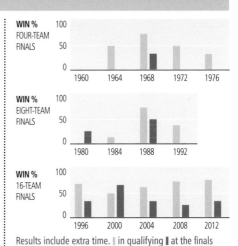

WIN % FOUR-TEAM FINALS — 1960, 1964, 1968, 1972, 1976

WIN % EIGHT-TEAM FINALS — 1980, 1984, 1988, 1992

WIN % 16-TEAM FINALS — 1996, 2000, 2004, 2008, 2012

Results include extra time. ▌ in qualifying ▌ at the finals

LEGENDARY PLAYER

Italy's record scorer **Luigi Riva** was recovering from a broken leg when Italy hosted the 1968 European Championships and he missed their semi-final and the final, but he was there for the replay to open the scoring in the Azzurri's 2-0 win over Yugoslavia.

LUIGI RIVA — LEGEND

WORLD CUP RECORD

Year	Point of exit	Year	Point of exit
1930	Did not enter	1978	● Fourth
1934	● Winners	1982	● Winners
1938	● Winners	1986	Round of 16
1950	Group stage	1990	● Third
1954	Group stage	1994	● Runners-up
1958	Did not qualify	1998	Quarter-finals
1962	Group stage	2002	Round of 16
1966	Group stage	2006	● Winners
1970	● Runners-up	2010	Group stage
1974	Group stage	2014	Group stage

DID YOU KNOW?

Along with USSR (1960), Italy are one of only two nations to have been behind at half-time in the final and gone on to lift the trophy, after a replay in 1968

GROUP E

HOW THEY QUALIFIED

Group H	P	W	D	L	F	A	GD	Pts
Italy	**10**	**7**	**3**	**0**	**16**	**7**	**+9**	**24**
Croatia	**10**	**6**	**3**	**1**	**20**	**5**	**+15**	**20**
Norway	10	6	1	3	13	10	+3	19
Bulgaria	10	3	2	5	9	12	-3	11
Azerbaijan	10	1	3	6	7	18	-11	6
Malta	10	0	2	8	3	16	-13	2

Croatia deducted 1pt

Match stats in qualifying

Possession	58%
Shots on target	66%
Shots off target	75%
Corners	75%

Averages of match totals in qualifying. See pages 228-254 for full qualifying results

Results & prices	W	D	L
Norway.....(0) 0-2 (1)...........Italy	4-5	27-10	9-2
Italy..........(1) 2-1 (0).Azerbaijan	1-10	9-1	28-1
Malta........(0) 0-1 (1)...........Italy	1-14	14-1	50-1
Italy..........(1) 1-1 (1)...... Croatia	5-4	9-4	3-1
Bulgaria....(2) 2-2 (1)...........Italy	10-11	12-5	4-1
Croatia......(1) 1-1 (1)...........Italy	12-5	21-10	7-5
Italy..........(0) 1-0 (0).........Malta	1-20	25-1	80-1
Italy..........(1) 1-0 (0).....Bulgaria	1-2	10-3	15-2
Azerbaijan (1) 1-3 (2)...........Italy	3-10	17-4	16-1
Italy..........(0) 2-1 (1)..... Norway	9-10	11-4	15-4
Profit & loss in qualifying	-0.28	-0.25	-10

Figures based on a £1 level stake using best odds in the Racing Post on day of match. W shows win price, whether home or away, L the price of the opposition

PLAYERS USED IN QUALIFYING

Pos		Club	CAREER Age	P	G	QUALIFYING P	G	□	■
GK	Salvatore Sirigu	Paris St-Germain	29	15	-	2	-	-	-
GK	Gianluigi Buffon	Juventus	38	156	-	9	-	1	-
DEF	Andrea Barzagli	Juventus	35	54	-	2	-	-	-
DEF	Luca Antonelli	Milan	29	12	-	1	-	-	-
DEF	Lorenzo De Silvestri	Sampdoria	28	6	-	1	-	-	-
DEF	Matteo Darmian	Man Utd	26	21	1	10	1	2	-
DEF	Giorgio Chiellini	Juventus	31	82	6	8	2	-	-
DEF	Manuel Pasqual	Fiorentina	34	11	-	4	-	-	-
DEF	Mattia De Sciglio	Milan	23	22	-	7	-	-	-
DEF	Andrea Ranocchia	Sampdoria	28	21	-	4	-	-	-
DEF	Angelo Ogbonna	West Ham	28	10	-	1	-	-	-
DEF	Leonardo Bonucci	Juventus	29	55	3	9	1	-	1
DEF	Davide Astori	Fiorentina	29	11	1	2	-	1	-
MID	Emanuele Giaccherini	Bologna	31	23	3	1	-	-	-
MID	Daniele De Rossi	Roma	32	101	17	3	1	-	1
MID	Alessandro Florenzi	Roma	25	15	2	6	1	1	-
MID	Marco Parolo	Lazio	31	18	-	4	-	1	-
MID	Marco Verratti	Paris St-Germain	23	15	1	5	-	-	-
MID	Andrea Poli	Milan	26	5	1	1	-	-	-
MID	Andrea Bertolacci	Milan	25	5	-	3	-	-	-
MID	Roberto Soriano	Sampdoria	25	8	-	4	-	1	-
MID	Antonio Candreva	Lazio	29	36	3	9	2	1	-
MID	Claudio Marchisio	Juventus	29	54	5	4	-	1	-
MID	Alberto Aquilani	Sporting Lisbon	31	38	5	2	-	-	-
MID	Andrea Pirlo	New York City	37	116	13	3	-	1	-
MID	Riccardo Montolivo	Milan	31	62	2	2	-	-	-
ATT	Manolo Gabbiadini	Napoli	24	6	1	2	-	-	-
ATT	Eder	Inter	29	9	2	5	2	-	-
ATT	Graziano Pelle	Southampton	30	11	4	7	3	-	-
ATT	Simone Zaza	Juventus	24	9	1	5	1	1	-
ATT	Ciro Immobile	Torino	26	12	1	5	-	2	-
ATT	Sebastian Giovinco	Toronto	29	23	1	4	-	-	-
ATT	Stephan El Shaarawy	Roma	23	18	3	4	1	-	-
ATT	Mattia Destro	Bologna	25	8	1	1	-	-	-

CORRECT SCORES

	Competitive	Friendly
1-0	4	1
2-0	3	1
2-1	5	-
3-0	-	-
3-1	3	-
3-2	-	-
4-0	-	1
4-1	-	-
4-2	-	-
4-3	1	-
0-0	2	1
1-1	2	5
2-2	5	4
3-3	-	-
4-4	-	-
0-1	2	2
0-2	-	-
1-2	-	3
0-3	-	-
1-3	-	1
2-3	-	-
0-4	-	-
1-4	-	1
2-4	1	-
3-4	-	-
Other	-	-

Since Euro 2012

HALF-TIME/FULL-TIME DOUBLE RESULTS

Win/Win	9	32%	Win 1st half	11	39%
Draw/Win	4	14%	Win 2nd half	12	43%
Lose/Win	3	11%	Win both halves	4	14%
Win/Draw	2	7%	Goal both halves	17	61%
Draw/Draw	6	21%			
Lose/Draw	1	4%	**Overall**		
Win/Lose	0	0%	● Win	57%	
Draw/Lose	1	4%	● Draw	32%	
Lose/Lose	2	7%	● Lose	11%	

WIN 57%

Overall: W16, D9, L3 in 28 competitive games since Euro 2012

CLEAN SHEETS

9 (32%)   **Clean sheets**   19 (68%)

4 (14%)   **Fail to score**   24 (86%)

7 (25%)   **Win to nil**   21 (75%)

2 (7%)   **Lose to nil**   26 (93%)

UNDER & OVER GOALS

20 (71%)   **Over 1.5**   8 (29%)

15 (54%)   **Over 2.5**   13 (46%)

10 (36%)   **Over 3.5**   18 (64%)

2 (7%)   **Over 4.5**   26 (93%)

BOTH TEAMS TO SCORE

17 (61%)   **Both score**   11 (39%)

9 (32%)   **& win**   19 (68%)

1 (4%)   **& lose**   27 (96%)

In 28 competitive games since Euro 2012

GOAL TIMES

● GOALS FOR ● GOALS AGAINST

Total match goals by half

24 (57%)   **1st half**   18 (43%)
F   A

23 (68%)   **2nd half**   11 (32%)
F   A

Goals for & against by half

24 (51%)   **For**   23 (49%)
1st   2nd

18 (62%)   **Against**   11 (38%)
1st   2nd

	0-9	10-18	19-27	28-36	37-45	46-54	55-63	64-72	73-81	82-90
Goals for	4	4	4	5	7	7	1	4	4	7
Goals against	1	4	4	4	5	0	2	4	4	1

In 28 competitive games since Euro 2012

IF ITALY SCORE FIRST

They win	13		76%
Draw	4		24%
They lose	0		0%

In 28 competitive games since Euro 2012

IF ITALY CONCEDE FIRST

They win	3		33%
Draw	3		33%
They lose	3		33%

GROUP F

Graziano Pelle was top scorer in qualifying

GOALSCORERS IN QUALIFYING ● FIRST GOALS

	Goals		1st		Anytime	Percentage of team goals	
G Pelle	3	●●●	2	66%	3 42%	▌▌▌▌	19%
G Chiellini	2	●●	1	50%	1 12%	▌▌▌	13%
Eder	2	●●	1	50%	2 40%	▌▌▌	13%
A Candreva	2	●●	1	50%	2 22%	▌▌▌	13%
D De Rossi	1	●	1	100%	1 33%	▌	6%
M Darmian	1	●	0	0%	1 10%	▌	6%
L Bonucci	1	●	0	0%	1 11%	▌	6%
S El Shaarawy	1	●	0	0%	1 25%	▌	6%
S Zaza	1	●	1	100%	1 20%	▌	6%
A Florenzi	1	●	0	0%	1 16%	▌	6%

In Euro 2016 qualifying

BOOKINGS

Matches played 10 ☐13 ▊2
Average make-up (☐10 ▊25) 18

In Euro 2016 qualifying

CORNERS

Avg F 6.9 ▊▊▊▊▊▊▊▊▊▊▊▊▊▊ 75%
Avg A 2.3 ▊▊▊▊▊ 25%

In Euro 2016 qualifying. Avg match total 9.2

IRELAND

[handwritten: 1-1 R Keane 1st 15/2 5/1 3=18]

[handwritten: Ireland v Swed 1-1 R ✓]

Twice Ireland have qualified for the European Championships and twice they have fallen at the first hurdle after being given incredibly tough draws. It's deja vu in France, with Belgium, Italy and Sweden lying in wait. Ireland finished third in a group that contained both finalists, Holland and USSR, in 1988, and got a similar draw in 2012 with Italy and Spain.

How they qualified

Qualification was a rollercoaster. Four of Ireland's five wins were against the bottom two, Georgia and Gibraltar, and they picked up only two of a possible 12 points against direct qualification rivals Poland and Scotland.

The decisive factor was the superhuman effort against Germany. Ireland drew 1-1 away to the world champions then beat them 1-0 in Dublin to set up a two-legged playoff against Bosnia, which Martin O'Neill's men won 3-1 on aggregate.

Ireland's average age in qualifying was the highest on the continent at 28 and more than two years above the average, while their shot ratio in matches against sides who also finished in the top three was a paltry 32 per cent. Only Albania, with 26 per cent, qualified with a lower figure.

The manager

O'Neill, as you would expect from a player who won the European Cup with Nottingham Forest, revels in the underdog tag.

As a manager, he took Wycombe into the Football League, helped Leicester earn promotion to the Premier League and win a couple of League Cups, and guided Celtic to multiple trophies as well as a Uefa Cup final, which they lost to Porto.

O'Neill is not attempting to reinvent the wheel and keeps things fairly basic. His teams have a hard-working ethos – everyone in the side is asked to defend and, while the football is not pretty, it does the job.

Match winners

O'Neill does not much care for stars, which

FACTFILE

FA founded 1921
www fai.ie
Head coach Martin O'Neill
National league Premier Division
Date qualified November 16, 2015

Typical starting XI (4-4-1-1) Given; Coleman, O'Shea, Keogh, Brady; Hendrick, McCarthy, Whelan, McClean; Hoolahan; Walters

Strengths
- ☑ A never-say-die spirit saw them battle through qualifying
- ☑ All the players buy into the game plan

Weaknesses
- ☒ A number of the squad are not first-team regulars in the top flight
- ☒ Ireland turn possession over to opponents too frequently

Star rating ★☆☆☆☆

Fixtures
1 Sweden, 5pm June 13, Saint-Denis
2 Belgium, 2pm June 18, Bordeaux
3 Italy, 8pm June 22, Lille
Base Versailles

GROUP E

Shane Long scores against world champions Germany

is just as well because there are not too many in the Irish ranks now that record goalscorer Robbie Keane's career is in the final furlong.

With Keane expected to be used as an impact sub, Jonathan Walters and Shane Long will have to take up the scoring mantle, while Wes Hoolahan is the one player given licence to create.

James McCarthy and Seamus Coleman are proven Premier League performers for Everton and Robbie Brady's set-pieces could be a useful weapon this summer.

Question marks

The goalkeeping situation is far from ideal with the two prime candidates, Shay Given and Darren Randolph, only substitutes for Stoke and West Ham. Rob Elliot of Newcastle was ruled out because of a knee injury.

There are also problems across the defence. John O'Shea has struggled for Sunderland, Marc Wilson doesn't play regularly for Stoke

and the same is true of Ciaran Clark at Aston Villa. Stephen Ward and Richard Keogh are only in the Championship and when used at left-back, Brady sometimes neglects his defensive responsibilities so O'Neill will have to protect the rearguard with a safety-in-numbers approach.

How to back them

Everything depends on the opener against Sweden in Paris. Win and qualification is on, but anything else and O'Neill's men will need to beat one of either Italy or Belgium, so expect fireworks in the Stade de France.

Ireland were excellent under pressure in the playoff against Bosnia and at home to Germany and they could be overpriced at 11-5 to beat the Swedes.

More adventurous punters could consider a last-16 exit at around 15-8 but either way, Ireland can outperform bookmakers' expectations of bottom spot.

IRELAND

EUROPEAN CHAMPIONSHIP RECORD

1960	P	W	D	L	GF	GA
Did not qualify	-	-	-	-	-	-
Qualifying	2	1	0	1	2	4

1964	P	W	D	L	GF	GA
Did not qualify	-	-	-	-	-	-
Qualifying	6	2	2	2	9	12

1968	P	W	D	L	GF	GA
Did not qualify	-	-	-	-	-	-
Qualifying	6	2	1	3	5	8

1972	P	W	D	L	GF	GA
Did not qualify	-	-	-	-	-	-
Qualifying	6	0	1	5	3	17

1976	P	W	D	L	GF	GA
Did not qualify	-	-	-	-	-	-
Qualifying	6	3	1	2	11	5

1980	P	W	D	L	GF	GA
Did not qualify	-	-	-	-	-	-
Qualifying	8	2	3	3	9	8

1984	P	W	D	L	GF	GA
Did not qualify	-	-	-	-	-	-
Qualifying	8	4	1	3	20	10

1988	P	W	D	L	GF	GA
Group stage	3	1	1	1	2	2
Qualifying	8	4	3	1	10	5

1992	P	W	D	L	GF	GA
Did not qualify	-	-	-	-	-	-
Qualifying	6	2	4	0	13	6

1996	P	W	D	L	GF	GA
Did not qualify	-	-	-	-	-	-
Qualifying	11	5	2	4	17	13

2000	P	W	D	L	GF	GA
Did not qualify	-	-	-	-	-	-
Qualifying	10	5	3	2	15	7

2004	P	W	D	L	GF	GA
Did not qualify	-	-	-	-	-	-
Qualifying	8	3	2	3	10	11

2008	P	W	D	L	GF	GA
Did not qualify	-	-	-	-	-	-
Qualifying	12	4	5	3	17	14

2012	P	W	D	L	GF	GA
Group stage	3	0	0	3	1	9
Qualifying	12	7	4	1	20	8

Totals	P	W	D	L	GF	GA
Finals	6	1	1	4	3	11
Qualifying	109	44	32	33	161	128

Results & goals include extra time

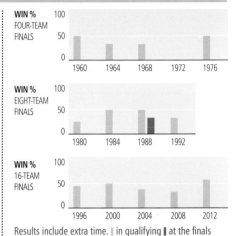

WIN % FOUR-TEAM FINALS — bar chart: 1960, 1964, 1968, 1972, 1976

WIN % EIGHT-TEAM FINALS — bar chart: 1980, 1984, 1988, 1992

WIN % 16-TEAM FINALS — bar chart: 1996, 2000, 2004, 2008, 2012

Results include extra time. ▌ in qualifying ▐ at the finals

LEGENDARY PLAYER

His achievements for Ireland are overshadowed by the notorious Saipan incident. But on the way to the 2002 World Cup, tenacious midfielder **Roy Keane** played a vital role, scoring a key goal against Portugal. He was outstanding at USA 94 too.

ROY KEANE LEGEND

WORLD CUP RECORD

Year	Point of exit	Year	Point of exit
1930	Did not enter	1978	Did not qualify
1934	Did not qualify	1982	Did not qualify
1938	Did not qualify	1986	Did not qualify
1950	Did not qualify	1990	Quarter-finals
1954	Did not qualify	1994	Round of 16
1958	Did not qualify	1998	Did not qualify
1962	Did not qualify	2002	Round of 16
1966	Did not qualify	2006	Did not qualify
1970	Did not qualify	2010	Did not qualify
1974	Did not qualify	2014	Did not qualify

DID YOU KNOW?

Only Poland and England managed to get a higher proportion of their shots on target in qualifying than Ireland's 55.4 per cent

GROUP E

HOW THEY QUALIFIED

Group D	P	W	D	L	F	A	GD	Pts
Germany	10	7	1	2	24	9	+15	22
Poland	10	6	3	1	33	10	+23	21
Ireland	10	5	3	2	19	7	+12	18
Scotland	10	4	3	3	22	12	+10	15
Georgia	10	3	0	7	10	16	-6	9
Gibraltar	10	0	0	10	2	56	-54	0

Match stats in qualifying

Possession	▮▮▮▮▮▮▮▮	47%
Shots on target	▮▮▮▮▮▮▮▮▮▮▮	64%
Shots off target	▮▮▮▮▮▮▮▮	47%
Corners	▮▮▮▮▮▮▮▮▮▮	58%

Averages of match totals in qualifying. See pages 228-254 for full qualifying results

Results & prices

	W	D	L
Georgia ....(1) 1-2 (1) ....Ireland	11-8	9-4	12-5
Ireland......(3) 7-0 (0) ....Gibraltar	1-50	33-1	66-1
Germany...(0) 1-1 (0) ....Ireland	14-1	21-4	2-7
Scotland ...(0) 1-0 (0) ....Ireland	5-2	9-4	7-5
Ireland......(0) 1-1 (1) ....Poland	13-8	9-4	21-10
Ireland......(1) 1-1 (0) .....Scotland	7-5	11-5	5-2
Gibraltar...(0) 0-4 (1) ....Ireland	1-33	25-1	66-1
Ireland......(0) 1-0 (0) .....Georgia	8-15	10-3	7-1
Ireland......(0) 1-0 (0)...Germany	13-2	7-2	8-15
Poland......(2) 2-1 (1) ....Ireland	15-4	5-2	9-10
Bosnia-Hz. (0) 1-1 (0) ....Ireland	10-3	12-5	21-20
Ireland......(1) 2-0 (0) . Bosnia-Hz.	6-4	11-5	23-10

Profit & loss in qualifying   3.96   4.1   -7.69

Figures based on a £1 level stake using best odds in the Racing Post on day of match. W shows win price, whether home or away, L the price of the opposition

PLAYERS USED IN QUALIFYING

Pos		Club	Age	CAREER P	CAREER G	QUALIFYING P	QUALIFYING G	▯	▮
GK	Shay Given	Stoke	40	133	-	5	-	-	-
GK	David Forde	Millwall	36	23	-	4	-	-	-
GK	Darren Randolph	West Ham	29	8	-	4	-	-	-
DEF	Ciaran Clark	Aston Villa	26	18	2	4	-	-	-
DEF	Cyrus Christie	Derby	23	4	1	2	1	-	-
DEF	Richard Keogh	Derby	29	11	1	5	-	-	-
DEF	Marc Wilson	Stoke	28	24	1	6	-	2	-
DEF	John O'Shea	Sunderland	35	110	3	11	1	2	1
DEF	Seamus Coleman	Everton	27	33	-	8	-	2	-
DEF	Stephen Ward	Burnley	30	32	2	6	-	1	-
MID	David Meyler	Hull	27	14	-	4	-	-	-
MID	Darron Gibson	Everton	28	25	1	3	-	-	-
MID	Glenn Whelan	Stoke	32	71	2	9	-	4	-
MID	Robbie Brady	Norwich	24	23	4	11	1	-	-
MID	Wes Hoolahan	Norwich	34	29	2	10	1	2	-
MID	Aiden McGeady	Sheffield Wednesday	30	81	5	8	2	1	-
MID	Stephen Quinn	Reading	30	13	-	4	-	1	-
MID	Jeff Hendrick	Derby	24	20	-	10	-	1	-
MID	James McClean	West Brom	27	33	5	9	2	4	-
MID	James McCarthy	Everton	25	35	-	9	-	2	-
ATT	Kevin Doyle	Colorado	32	62	14	1	-	-	-
ATT	Robbie Keane	LA Galaxy	35	143	67	9	5	-	-
ATT	Jonathan Walters	Stoke	32	38	10	10	5	3	-
ATT	Shane Long	Southampton	29	61	15	9	3	-	-
ATT	Daryl Murphy	Ipswich	33	20	-	5	-	-	-

SOCCERBASE.COM

IRELAND

CORRECT SCORES

	Competitive	Friendly
1-0	2	1
2-0	1	2
2-1	2	-
3-0	1	1
3-1	1	-
3-2	-	-
4-0	1	1
4-1	1	2
4-2	-	-
4-3	-	-
0-0	1	5
1-1	4	2
2-2	1	1
3-3	-	-
4-4	-	-
0-1	2	1
0-2	-	1
1-2	2	2
0-3	1	-
1-3	-	-
2-3	-	-
0-4	-	-
1-4	-	-
2-4	-	-
3-4	-	-
Other	2	1

Since Euro 2012

HALF-TIME/FULL-TIME DOUBLE RESULTS

Win/Win	5	23%
Draw/Win	4	18%
Lose/Win	1	5%
Win/Draw	2	9%
Draw/Draw	3	14%
Lose/Draw	1	5%
Win/Lose	0	0%
Draw/Lose	3	14%
Lose/Lose	3	14%

Overall: W10, D6, L6 in 22 competitive games since Euro 2012

Win 1st half	7	32%
Win 2nd half	11	50%
Win both halves	5	23%
Goal both halves	13	59%

Overall
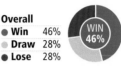
- Win 46%
- Draw 28%
- Lose 28%

CLEAN SHEETS

| 7 (32%) | Clean sheets | 15 (68%) |
| 6 (27%) | Win to nil | 16 (73%) |

| 4 (18%) | Fail to score | 18 (82%) |
| 3 (14%) | Lose to nil | 19 (86%) |

UNDER & OVER GOALS

17 (77%)	Over 1.5	5 (23%)
12 (55%)	Over 2.5	10 (45%)
6 (27%)	Over 3.5	16 (73%)
3 (14%)	Over 4.5	19 (86%)

BOTH TEAMS TO SCORE

12 (55%)	Both score	10 (45%)
4 (18%)	& win	18 (82%)
3 (14%)	& lose	19 (86%)

In 22 competitive games since Euro 2012

GOAL TIMES

Total match goals by half

14 (56%)	1st half	11 (44%)
F		A
24 (63%)	2nd half	14 (37%)
F		A

Goals for & against by half

14 (37%)	For	24 (63%)
1st		2nd
11 (44%)	Against	14 (56%)
1st		2nd

● GOALS FOR ● GOALS AGAINST

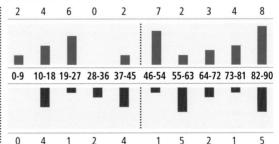

In 22 competitive games since Euro 2012

IF IRELAND SCORE FIRST

They win	8		73%
Draw	2		18%
They lose	1		9%

In 22 competitive games since Euro 2012

IF IRELAND CONCEDE FIRST

They win	2		20%
Draw	3		30%
They lose	5		50%

Jonathan Walters scored twice against Bosnia in the playoffs

GOALSCORERS IN QUALIFYING ● FIRST GOALS

	Goals		1st		Anytime	Percentage of team goals	
R Keane	5	●●●●●	1	20%	2 22%		23%
J Walters	5	●●●●●●	3	60%	4 40%		23%
S Long	3	●●●	1	33%	3 33%		14%
A McGeady	2	●●	1	50%	1 12%		9%
J McClean	2	●●	0	0%	1 11%		9%
J O'Shea	1	●	0	0%	1 9%		5%
W Hoolahan	1	●	0	0%	1 10%		5%
C Christie	1	●	1	100%	1 50%		5%
R Brady	1	●	1	100%	1 9%		5%

In Euro 2016 qualifying

BOOKINGS

Matches played	10	☐25	▮ 1
Average make-up (☐10 ▮25)			27.5

In Euro 2016 qualifying

CORNERS

Avg F	6		58%
Avg A	4.4		42%

In Euro 2016 qualifying. Avg match total 10.4

SWEDEN

Irland v Swed 1-1 R ✓

A fter Sweden missed out on Brazil 2014, Zlatan Ibrahimovic modestly said: "One thing is for sure, a World Cup without me is nothing to watch." At least the Euros will be worth watching in what seems sure to be Ibrahimovic's last major tournament appearance, but a difficult draw means it could be three and out for Sweden's 34-year-old talisman.

How they qualified

A solid start suggested Sweden would qualify automatically but the campaign turned after a shoddy September, when a 1-0 loss in Russia was followed by a humbling 4-1 home defeat by Austria. That sent the Swedes into an all-Scandinavian playoff against Denmark.

It was then that Ibrahimovic, who scored 11 of Sweden's 19 goals in qualifying, really came to the party, notching three of their goals in a 4-3 aggregate success.

The free kick that essentially won the tie in Copenhagen was breathtaking and silenced those who believe Ibrahimovic is a flat-track bully who fails to show up on the big occasion.

The manager

Erik Hamren, who replaced Lars Lagerback in 2009, has announced he will be stepping down after the European Championship and his approach is more progressive than his predecessor's.

Eyebrows were raised at this year's Ballon d'Or vote when Hamren picked Ibrahimovic as the world's best player ahead of Cristiano Ronaldo and Lionel Messi but massaging the ego of his captain comes with the territory of being Sweden's manager.

Match winners

Ibrahimovic was voted as Sweden's second-greatest sportsman last year, behind 11-time Grand Slam winner Bjorn Borg, but he was not overjoyed with silver.

"Thank you but to finish second is like finishing last," he responded.

"On that list I would have been number

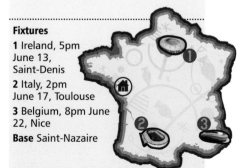

Sweden celebrate after beating Denmark in the playoffs

one, two, three, four and five, with due respect to the others."

In terms of Sweden's best footballers at Euro 2016 he is the only standout performer, with 33-year-old midfielder Kim Kallstrom one of the few fit to lace Ibra's boots.

Question marks

The main problem is what happens if the opposition successfully nullify Ibrahimovic. It's easier said than done but there are few others ready to step up and make themselves a hero.

Even though Sweden won last year's European Under-21 Championship, not too many of those youngsters are pushing for starting berths. Sweden are an average side with one exceptional individual talent and Hamren is forced to build his whole gameplan around Ibrahimovic.

Bizarrely Hamren has three decent left-backs – Martin Olsson, Oscar Wendt and Pierre Bengtsson – which must be frustrating, as normally only one of those would start.

However, Bengtsson has been used as right-back, which brings greater quality into the side albeit at the cost of balance.

How to back them

Ibrahimovic is a worthy odds-on favourite to be Sweden's top goalscorer but it will probably work out better value just to back him to score in the three individual matches against Ireland, Italy and Belgium.

Interestingly, though, he has failed to notch in his three appearances against Ireland.

While they are lucky to have such a remarkable player, aside of Ibrahimovic this looks to be a relatively weak squad who failed to win five of their six matches against Austria, Russia and Denmark during the qualifying campaign.

Even allowing for the brilliance of Ibra, Sweden could be overpriced to finish bottom of a competitive section in which their fate could be sealed in the must-win opener against Ireland.

EUROPEAN CHAMPIONSHIP RECORD

1960	P	W	D	L	GF	GA
Did not enter	-	-	-	-	-	-
Qualifying	-	-	-	-	-	-

1964	P	W	D	L	GF	GA
Did not qualify	-	-	-	-	-	-
Qualifying	6	2	3	1	8	7

1968	P	W	D	L	GF	GA
Did not qualify	-	-	-	-	-	-
Qualifying	6	2	1	3	9	12

1972	P	W	D	L	GF	GA
Did not qualify	-	-	-	-	-	-
Qualifying	6	2	2	2	3	5

1976	P	W	D	L	GF	GA
Did not qualify	-	-	-	-	-	-
Qualifying	6	3	0	3	8	9

1980	P	W	D	L	GF	GA
Did not qualify	-	-	-	-	-	-
Qualifying	6	1	2	3	9	13

1984	P	W	D	L	GF	GA
Did not qualify	-	-	-	-	-	-
Qualifying	8	5	1	2	14	5

1988	P	W	D	L	GF	GA
Did not qualify	-	-	-	-	-	-
Qualifying	8	4	2	2	12	5

1992	P	W	D	L	GF	GA
● Semi-finals	4	2	1	1	6	5
Qualifying	-	-	-	-	-	-

1996	P	W	D	L	GF	GA
Did not qualify	-	-	-	-	-	-
Qualifying	8	2	3	3	9	10

2000	P	W	D	L	GF	GA
Group stage	3	0	1	2	2	4
Qualifying	8	7	1	0	10	1

2004	P	W	D	L	GF	GA
Quarter-finals	4	1	3	0	8	3
Qualifying	8	5	2	1	19	3

2008	P	W	D	L	GF	GA
Group stage	3	1	0	2	3	4
Qualifying	11	7	2	2	20	9

2012	P	W	D	L	GF	GA
Group stage	3	1	0	2	5	5
Qualifying	10	8	0	2	31	11

Totals	P	W	D	L	GF	GA
Finals	17	5	5	7	24	21
Qualifying	91	48	19	24	152	90

Results & goals include extra time

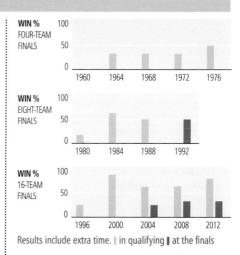

WIN % FOUR-TEAM FINALS
100 / 50 / 0
1960 1964 1968 1972 1976

WIN % EIGHT-TEAM FINALS
100 / 50 / 0
1980 1984 1988 1992

WIN % 16-TEAM FINALS
100 / 50 / 0
1996 2000 2004 2008 2012

Results include extra time. ▌ in qualifying ▌ at the finals

LEGENDARY PLAYER

Tomas Brolin flopped in the Premier League but was part of the Swedish team that reached the semi-finals at Euro 92 – his three goals included a beauty against England – and he got another three as they went on to finish third at USA 94.

TOMAS BROLIN LEGEND

WORLD CUP RECORD

Year	Point of exit		Year	Point of exit
1930	Did not enter		1978	Group stage
1934	Quarter-finals		1982	Did not qualify
1938	● Fourth		1986	Did not qualify
1950	● Third		1990	Group stage
1954	Did not qualify		1994	● Third
1958	● Runners-up		1998	Did not qualify
1962	Did not qualify		2002	Round of 16
1966	Did not qualify		2006	Round of 16
1970	Group stage		2010	Did not qualify
1974	Second round		2014	Did not qualify

DID YOU KNOW?

He's never been further than the group stage, but only Michel Platini and Alan Shearer have scored more goals at the Euros than Zlatan Ibrahimovic

HOW THEY QUALIFIED

Group G	P	W	D	L	F	A	GD	Pts
Austria	10	9	1	0	22	5	+17	28
Russia	10	6	2	2	21	5	+16	20
Sweden	10	5	3	2	15	9	+6	18
Montenegro	10	3	2	5	10	13	-3	11
Liechtenstein	10	1	2	7	2	26	-24	5
Moldova	10	0	2	8	4	16	-12	2

Match stats in qualifying

Possession	▮▮▮▮▮▮▮▮▮▮	53%
Shots on target	▮▮▮▮▮▮▮▮▮▮	56%
Shots off target	▮▮▮▮▮▮▮▮▮▮	55%
Corners	▮▮▮▮▮▮▮▮▮▮	54%

Averages of match totals in qualifying. See pages 228-254 for full qualifying results

Results & prices		W	D	L
Austria......(1) 1-1 (1) ..... Sweden		11-5	23-10	6-4
Sweden......(0) 1-1 (1) ....Russia		33-20	9-4	2-1
Sweden......(1) 2-0 (0)Liechtenstein		1-25	14-1	66-1
Montenegro(0)1-1 (1) ..... Sweden		7-5	9-4	23-10
Moldova...(0) 0-2 (0) ..... Sweden		4-9	15-4	9-1
Sweden......(3) 3-1 (0)Montenegro		1-2	7-2	8-1
Russia........(1) 1-0 (0) ..... Sweden		3-1	9-4	23-20
Sweden......(0) 1-4 (2) ....Austria		5-4	5-2	13-5
Liechtenstein(0)0-2 (1) ..... Sweden		1-8	10-1	33-1
Sweden......(1) 2-0 (0) ....Moldova		1-5	13-2	20-1
Sweden......(1) 2-0 (0) ....Denmark		7-5	9-4	5-2
Profit & loss in qualifying	**-3.29**	**1.3**	**-6.25**

Figures based on a £1 level stake using best odds in the Racing Post on day of match. W shows win price, whether home or away, L the price of the opposition

PLAYERS USED IN QUALIFYING

				CAREER		QUALIFYING			
Pos		Club	Age	P	G	P	G	▯	▮
GK	Andreas Isaksson	Kasimpasa	34	128	-	12	-	-	-
DEF	Anton Tinnerholm	Malmo	25	6	-	1	-	-	-
DEF	Alexander Milosevic	Hannover	24	5	-	1	-	-	-
DEF	Oscar Wendt	Mgladbach	30	25	-	2	-	-	-
DEF	Erik Johansson	Copenhagen	27	8	-	4	-	-	-
DEF	Martin Olsson	Norwich	28	34	5	10	-	1	-
DEF	Mikael Lustig	Celtic	29	50	2	5	-	1	-
DEF	Andreas Granqvist	FK Krasnodar	31	50	3	11	-	2	1
DEF	Pierre Bengtsson	Mainz	28	24	-	8	-	1	-
DEF	Mikael Antonsson	Copenhagen	35	28	-	9	-	-	-
MID	Emil Forsberg	RB Leipzig	24	15	1	8	1	2	-
MID	Erkan Zengin	Trabzonspor	30	19	3	9	3	1	-
MID	Pontus Wernbloom	CSKA Moscow	29	50	2	6	-	2	-
MID	Sebastian Larsson	Sunderland	31	82	6	11	-	2	-
MID	Kim Kallstrom	Grasshoppers	33	127	16	11	-	4	-
MID	Albin Ekdal	Hamburg	26	21	-	8	-	2	-
MID	Jimmy Durmaz	Olympiakos	27	30	2	8	1	-	-
MID	Alex Kacaniklic	Fulham	24	19	3	1	-	-	-
MID	Abdul Khalili	Mersin	24	1	-	1	-	-	-
MID	Oscar Lewicki	Malmo	23	9	-	4	-	-	-
MID	Oscar Hiljemark	Palermo	23	9	1	1	-	-	-
MID	Gustav Svensson	Guangzhou R&F	29	6	-	2	-	-	-
MID	Nabil Bahoui	Hamburg	25	8	-	2	-	-	-
ATT	Marcus Berg	Panathinaikos	29	37	10	7	2	-	-
ATT	John Guidetti	Celta Vigo	24	7	-	3	-	-	-
ATT	Isaac Kiese Thelin	Bordeaux	23	7	-	4	-	-	-
ATT	Ola Toivonen	Sunderland	29	45	9	4	1	-	-
ATT	Zlatan Ibrahimovic	Paris St-Germain	34	112	62	10	11	2	-
ATT	Branimir Hrgota	Mgladbach	23	3	-	1	-	-	-
ATT	Johan Elmander	Brondby	35	85	20	3	-	1	-

SWEDEN

CORRECT SCORES

	Competitive	Friendly
1-0	1	2
2-0	6	3
2-1	4	1
3-0	-	1
3-1	1	1
3-2	-	-
4-0	-	-
4-1	-	-
4-2	-	2
4-3	-	-
0-0	1	2
1-1	3	2
2-2	1	-
3-3	-	-
4-4	1	-
0-1	2	3
0-2	-	1
1-2	1	2
0-3	-	1
1-3	-	-
2-3	1	1
0-4	-	-
1-4	1	-
2-4	-	-
3-4	-	-
Other	1	-

Since Euro 2012

HALF-TIME/FULL-TIME DOUBLE RESULTS

Win/Win	8	33%
Draw/Win	3	13%
Lose/Win	1	4%
Win/Draw	2	8%
Draw/Draw	2	8%
Lose/Draw	2	8%
Win/Lose	1	4%
Draw/Lose	2	8%
Lose/Lose	3	13%

Win 1st half	11	46%
Win 2nd half	12	50%
Win both halves	5	21%
Goal both halves	16	67%

Overall
- ● Win 50%
- ● Draw 24%
- ● Lose 25%

WIN 50%

Overall: W12, D6, L6 in competitive 24 games since Euro 2012

CLEAN SHEETS

8 (33%) **Clean sheets** 16 (67%) ✓ ✗

7 (29%) **Win to nil** 17 (71%) ✓ ✗

3 (13%) **Fail to score** 21 (88%) ✓ ✗

2 (8%) **Lose to nil** 22 (92%) ✓ ✗

UNDER & OVER GOALS

20 (83%) **Over 1.5** 4 (17%) ✓ ✗

11 (46%) **Over 2.5** 13 (54%) ✓ ✗

6 (25%) **Over 3.5** 18 (75%) ✓ ✗

4 (17%) **Over 4.5** 20 (83%) ✓ ✗

BOTH TEAMS TO SCORE

14 (58%) **Both score** 10 (42%) ✓ ✗

5 (21%) **& win** 19 (79%) ✓ ✗

4 (17%) **& lose** 20 (83%) ✓ ✗

In 24 competitive games since Euro 2012

GOAL TIMES

Total match goals by half

16 (55%) **1st half** 13 (45%)
F A

24 (59%) **2nd half** 17 (41%)
F A

Goals for & against by half

16 (40%) **For** 24 (60%)
1st 2nd

13 (43%) **Against** 17 (57%)
1st 2nd

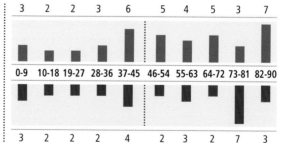

● GOALS FOR ● GOALS AGAINST

	0-9	10-18	19-27	28-36	37-45	46-54	55-63	64-72	73-81	82-90
For	3	2	2	3	6	5	4	5	3	7
Against	3	2	2	2	4	2	3	2	7	3

In 24 competitive games since Euro 2012

IF SWEDEN SCORE FIRST

They win	9		75%
Draw	2		17%
They lose	1		8%

in 24 competitive games since Euro 2012

IF SWEDEN CONCEDE FIRST

They win	3		27%
Draw	3		27%
They lose	5		45%

Stopping Zlatan is the key to stopping Sweden but it's easier said than done

GOALSCORERS IN QUALIFYING
● FIRST GOALS

	Goals		1st		Anytime		Percentage of team goals	
Z Ibrahimovic	11	●●●●●●●●●●●	4	36%	8	80%	▮▮▮▮▮▮▮▮▮▮▮▮▮	58%
E Zengin	3	●●●	1	33%	3	33%	▮▮▮	16%
M Berg	2	●●	2	100%	2	28%	▮▮	11%
O Toivonen	1	●	0	0%	1	25%	▮	5%
J Durmaz	1	●	0	0%	1	12%	▮	5%
E Forsberg	1	●	1	100%	1	12%	▮	5%

In Euro 2016 qualifying

BOOKINGS

Matches played	12	▯ 21	▮ 1
Average make-up (▯ 10 ▮ 25)			19.6

In Euro 2016 qualifying

CORNERS

Avg F	5.7	▮▮▮▮▮▮▮▮▮	54%
Avg A	4.8	▮▮▮▮▮▮▮	46%

In Euro 2016 qualifying. Avg match total 10.5

Playing the long game might be about to pay dividends for Austria

Most of the top seeds should show Uefa's rankings are spot on with dominant group displays but there could be an upset in Group F, where **Austria** possess the tools to push Portugal out of first spot.

Austria had been in the doldrums for many years but they have been investing time in building up their youngsters and have stuck with them, accepting short-term pain with the aim of long-term gain.

The payback started with a brilliant qualification campaign. Marcel Koller's side won their last nine matches and they can build on that with a fine Euro 2016.

This settled side is fast, young, dynamic and hungry. The team virtually picks itself and is the polar opposite of a Portuguese outfit who rely almost solely on Cristiano Ronaldo's individual brilliance to get them out of difficult situations.

And Austria aren't short of individual talent themselves. Bayern Munich's David Alaba is the pick of the bunch but it's much more of a team effort with a sprinkling of stardust from the inconsistent but mercurial Marko Arnautovic.

Austria looked good in qualifying but it could be argued that the likes of Leicester's Christian Fuchs and Mainz's Julian Baumgartlinger have gone on again, surpassing expectations throughout the season with their fairytale rises up the standings in England and Germany.

Portugal won seven of their eight qualifiers but scored only 11 goals. Ronaldo grabbed five of those and Joao Moutinho was the only other player to notch more than once.

They are a conservative side under former Greece boss Fernando Santos and if Ronaldo is struggling for form or fitness as he was at the World Cup, it could be a difficult few weeks for Portugal, even though Iceland and Hungary won't be expected to cause too many issues.

Both sides will put men behind the ball and that is just the sort of tactic that can nullify Portugal, particularly in their opening game against defensively sound Iceland, who beat Holland home and away in qualifying.

Recommended bet

€€€€€ Austria to win the group

TO WIN THE GROUP

	bet365	BetBright	Betfair	Betfred	Betway	Boyles	Coral	Hills	Lads	Power	Sky Bet
Portugal	5-6	5-6	5-6	4-5	10-11	5-6	Evs	4-5	19-20	5-6	10-11
Austria	9-4	9-4	2	2	9-4	11-5	15-8	9-4	15-8	11-5	2
Iceland	9-2	5	6	11-2	9-2	5	5	5	11-2	11-2	11-2
Hungary	12	12	8	12	10	12	12	10	10	9	9

Win only. Prices correct March 31

Marko Arnautovic has had a fine season for Stoke and he can help Austria enjoy a great summer

TO QUALIFY

	bet365	BetBright	Betfair	Betfred	Betway	Boyles	Coral	Hills	Lads	Power	Sky Bet
Portugal	1-10	1-12	2-25	1-10	1-10	1-12	1-10	1-12	**1-9**	1-18	1-10
Austria	**1-4**	1-5	1-6	**1-4**	1-5	1-5	1-5	1-6	2-11	**1-4**	2-9
Iceland	8-13	4-7	**4-5**	4-6	8-13	8-15	4-6	8-13	8-11	8-13	4-6
Hungary	11-8	**7-5**	Evs	5-4	11-8	**7-5**	11-8	11-8	6-5	11-10	5-4

Win only. Prices correct March 31

5PM JUNE 14 – AUSTRIA V HUNGARY

	bet365	Betfair	Betfred	Betway	Boyles	Coral	Hills	Lads	Power	Sky Bet
Austria	**5-6**	**5-6**	4-5	**5-6**	**5-6**	4-5	4-5	4-5	8-11	**5-6**
Draw	**5-2**	12-5	**5-2**	12-5	**5-2**	12-5	11-5	12-5	**5-2**	12-5
Hungary	10-3	3	18-5	**15-4**	10-3	10-3	7-2	**15-4**	**15-4**	7-2

Best prices as decimal odds: Austria 1.83, draw 3.5, Hungary 4.75. 104%. Prices correct March 31

8PM JUNE 14 – PORTUGAL V ICELAND

	bet365	Betfair	Betfred	Betway	Boyles	Coral	Hills	Lads	Power	Sky Bet
Portugal	8-13	8-13	8-13	**4-6**	8-13	8-13	13-20	8-13	8-13	**4-6**
Draw	13-5	5-2	**13-5**	5-2	5-2	5-2	23-10	5-2	12-5	**13-5**
Iceland	5	9-2	5	5	5	9-2	9-2	5	5	9-2

Portugal 1.67, draw 3.6, Iceland 6. 104%

5PM JUNE 18 – ICELAND V HUNGARY

	Betfair	Betfred	Power
Iceland	**5-4**	**5-4**	**5-4**
Hungary	21-10	**11-5**	21-10
Draw	11-5	**9-4**	11-5

Iceland 2.25, draw 3.2, Draw 3.25. 106%

8PM JUNE 18 – PORTUGAL V AUSTRIA

	Betfair	Betfred	Power
Portugal	**13-10**	**13-10**	**13-10**
Draw	21-10	**11-5**	21-10
Austria	21-10	**11-5**	21-10

Portugal 2.3, draw 3.2, Austria 3.2. 106%

5PM JUNE 22 – ICELAND V AUSTRIA

	Betfair	Betfred	Power
Austria	Evs	**21-20**	Evs
Draw	11-5	**9-4**	11-5
Iceland	**14-5**	11-4	**14-5**

Austria 2.05, draw 3.25, Iceland 3.8. 106%

5PM JUNE 22 – HUNGARY V PORTUGAL

	Betfair	Betfred	Power
Portugal	**4-7**	**4-7**	**4-7**
Draw	14-5	3	14-5
Hungary	9-2	5	9-2

Portugal 1.57, draw 4, Hungary 6. 105%

Renato Sanches is one of a decent crop of Portugal youngsters

HOW THEY PERFORMED IN QUALIFYING

				Home			Away							Home	Shots	
	Group/Pos		P	W	D	L	W	D	L	F	A	GD	Pts	Pos%	On	Off
Austria	Group G	1st	10	4	1	0	5	0	0	22	5	+17	**28**	58.4	39	36
Portugal	Group I	1st	8	3	0	1	4	0	0	11	5	+6	**21**	60.3	22	35
Iceland	Group A	2nd	10	3	2	0	3	0	2	17	6	+11	**20**	47.2	21	21
Hungary	Group F	3rd	10	2	2	1	2	2	1	11	9	+2	**16**	48.6	21	31

Pos% percentage of total possession, **Shots on/off** shots on and off target, **Shots On%** percentage of shots on target (accuracy), **Shots%** percentage of total match shots

If you backed them P/L figures based on a £1 level stake using best odds in the Racing Post on day of match. Percentages represent probablility of victory implied by the win odds. **75%+** matches where the best price

Read 1 then →	Portugal					Iceland					Austria					Hungary				
	W	D	L	F	A	W	D	L	F	A	W	D	L	F	A	W	D	L	F	A
Portugal						2	0	0	8	4	-	-	-	-	-	2	0	0	4	0
						-	-													
Iceland	0	0	2	4	8						-	-	-	-	-	0	0	2	4	6
	-	-									0	1	0	1	1	0	0	2	0	6
Austria	-	-	-	-	-	-	-	-	-	-						-	-	-	-	-
						0	1	0	1	1						0	0	1	1	2
Hungary	0	0	2	0	4	2	0	0	6	4	-	-	-	-						
	-	-				2	0	0	6	0	1	0	0	2	1					

Includes all European Championship and World Cup matches since the 2002 World Cup. 90-minute results only. Competitive results above friendly results (in grey)

Friendly September 7, 2002 Iceland .... (0) 0-2 (0) .... Hungary	World Cup 2010 qualifying September 9, 2009 Hungary .... (0) 0-1 (1) .... Portugal	Euro 2012 qualifying October 7, 2011 Portugal .... (3) 5-3 (0) .... Iceland
World Cup 2006 qualifying September 8, 2004 Hungary .... (0) 3-2 (1) .... Iceland June 4, 2005 Iceland .... (1) 2-3 (1) .... Hungary	October 10, 2009 Portugal .... (1) 3-0 (0) .... Hungary Euro 2012 qualifying October 12, 2010 Iceland .... (1) 1-3 (2) .... Portugal	Friendly May 30, 2014 Austria .... (1) 1-1 (0) .... Iceland
Friendly August 16, 2006 Austria .... (0) 1-2 (2) .... Hungary	Friendly August 10, 2011 Hungary .... (2) 4-0 (0) .... Iceland	*Iceland were unbeaten at the Laugardalsvollur National Stadium (below) in qualifying*

Away	Shots		Shots overall		If you backed them							
Pos%	On	Off	On%	Shots%	P	75%+	P	50-75%	P	25-50%	P	<25%
56.0	40	33	53.4	69.5	3	+0.46	2	+1.70	4	+5.20	1	+3.75
44.8	18	20	42.1	61.3	2	-0.78	4	+2.58	2	+3.65	0	0.00
47.8	18	29	43.8	47.3	1	-1.00	2	-0.05	2	+3.08	5	+15.20
45.6	24	24	45.0	58.1	2	+0.63	1	-1.00	6	-0.30	1	-1.00

was 1-3 or shorter **50-75%** matches where the best price was longer than 1-3 and no bigger than Evens **75-25%** matches where the best price was longer than Evens and no bigger than 3-1 **<25%** matches where the best price was longer than 3-1

Only completed matches are included. See pages 228-254 for full qualifying results

PORTUGAL

T he one thing missing from Cristiano Ronaldo's glittering career is international honours with Portugal and the 31-year-old won't get many more opportunities to put that right. But he should be comforted by Portugal's excellent championship record – they have qualified for the Euros on six occasions, reaching at least the quarter-finals every time and the semi-finals four times.

How they qualified

After their group-stage exit at the World Cup, Portugal started slowly, and boss Paulo Bento was sacked after they lost their opening game 1-0 at home to Albania.

Crucially, Ronaldo was absent for that contest but the Real Madrid star was Portugal's talisman thereafter as they won all seven matches, despite scoring only 11 goals. Every victory was by one goal.

Ronaldo notched five times and was so often the difference-maker, scoring the only goal on 95 minutes in Denmark and a 72nd-minute winner at home to Armenia, before grabbing a hat-trick in the 3-2 return success in Yerevan.

Dominating matches came easy to Portugal and their shot ratio in games against sides who finished in the top three was 73 per cent, second only to Germany. Finishing off opponents proved difficult, however, despite a soft group made easier by Serbia's self-destruction.

Group I had the fewest teams in qualifying so all of those involved played home and away friendlies with hosts France and Portugal lost both times.

The manager

Fernando Santos, who has worked at each of Portugal's big-three club sides – Porto, Sporting and Benfica – replaced Bento after a respectable spell in charge of Greece. The football was never pretty but he led the Euro 2004 winners to the knockout stages of Euro 2012 and the last World Cup.

Santos was banned by Fifa for eight matches after comments made following

FACTFILE

FA founded 1914
www fpf.pt
Head coach Fernando Santos
National league Primeira Liga
Date qualified October 8, 2015

Typical starting XI (4-2-3-1) Patricio; Vieirinha, Carvalho, Pepe, Eliseu; Moutinho, Tiago; Silva, Danny, Nani; Ronaldo

Strengths
☑ Ronaldo remains a world-class operator
☑ Plenty of midfield options

Weaknesses
☒ A number of key men are past their best
☒ No natural number nine

Star rating ★★☆☆☆

Fixtures

1 Iceland, 8pm June 14, Saint-Etienne

2 Austria, 8pm June 18, Paris

3 Hungary, 5pm June 22, Lyon

Base Linas-Marcoussis

PARIS

World class: Cristiano Ronaldo

Greece's World Cup exit to Costa Rica, but the duration of his punishment was halved on appeal.

Match winners

There is no point looking past Ronaldo. Some have suggested his influence is on the wane at Real Madrid but he still scored a record 11 goals in the Champions League group stage this season and was second only to Lionel Messi at the Fifa Ballon d'Or gala in January.

Joao Moutinho and Danny are technically gifted and it will be fascinating to see whether Santos is brave enough to call up some of their fabulously talented youngsters such as Andre Gomes, Bernardo Silva, Ruben Neves, Renato Sanches and Goncalo Guedes.

Question marks

It's the age-old problem of a central striker and Ronaldo could end up doing that job. The likes of Nelson Oliveira and Lucas Joao are plying their trade in England's Championship, while Eder, the only natural striker named in the squad for the March friendlies, was a reserve at Swansea so moved to Lille in the hope of impressing.

Centre-backs Ricardo Carvalho (38) and Pepe (32) will have a combined age of 70 come the start of the tournament.

There is a suggestion that the more mature players, including Ronaldo, are on the downgrade and one of the old heads, Tiago, is set to miss out because of injury.

How to back them

A group that also contains Iceland and Hungary should mean Portugal progress but they may be vulnerable to Austria and a straight forecast with the favourites finishing second could be best.

Ronaldo is seen as a good thing to be Portugal's top goalscorer but punters should bear in mind that in six tournament appearances, only once (at Euro 2012) has he finished on his own as their leading scorer.

PORTUGAL

EUROPEAN CHAMPIONSHIP RECORD

1960	P	W	D	L	GF	GA
Did not qualify	-	-	-	-	-	-
Qualifying	4	3	0	1	8	8

1964	P	W	D	L	GF	GA
Did not qualify	-	-	-	-	-	-
Qualifying	2	1	0	1	4	4

1968	P	W	D	L	GF	GA
Did not qualify	-	-	-	-	-	-
Qualifying	6	2	2	2	6	6

1972	P	W	D	L	GF	GA
Did not qualify	-	-	-	-	-	-
Qualifying	6	3	1	2	10	6

1976	P	W	D	L	GF	GA
Did not qualify	-	-	-	-	-	-
Qualifying	6	2	3	1	5	7

1980	P	W	D	L	GF	GA
Did not qualify	-	-	-	-	-	-
Qualifying	8	4	1	3	10	11

1984	P	W	D	L	GF	GA
Semi-finals	4	1	2	1	4	4
Qualifying	6	5	0	1	11	6

1988	P	W	D	L	GF	GA
Did not qualify	-	-	-	-	-	-
Qualifying	8	2	4	2	6	8

1992	P	W	D	L	GF	GA
Did not qualify	-	-	-	-	-	-
Qualifying	8	5	1	2	11	4

1996	P	W	D	L	GF	GA
Quarter-finals	4	2	1	1	5	2
Qualifying	10	7	2	1	29	7

2000	P	W	D	L	GF	GA
Semi-finals	5	4	0	1	10	4
Qualifying	10	7	2	1	32	4

2004	P	W	D	L	GF	GA
Runners-up	6	3	1	2	8	6
Qualifying	-	-	-	-	-	-

2008	P	W	D	L	GF	GA
Quarter-finals	4	2	0	2	7	6
Qualifying	14	7	6	1	24	10

2012	P	W	D	L	GF	GA
Semi-finals	5	3	1	1	6	4
Qualifying	10	6	2	2	27	14

Totals	P	W	D	L	GF	GA
Finals	28	15	5	8	40	26
Qualifying	98	54	24	20	183	95

Results & goals include extra time

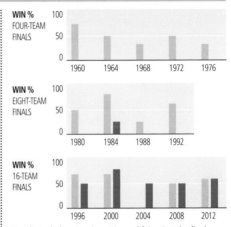

WIN % FOUR-TEAM FINALS — 1960, 1964, 1968, 1972, 1976

WIN % EIGHT-TEAM FINALS — 1980, 1984, 1988, 1992

WIN % 16-TEAM FINALS — 1996, 2000, 2004, 2008, 2012

Results include extra time. ▌ in qualifying ▌ at the finals

LEGENDARY PLAYER

Luis Figo was the best player of Portugal's golden generation. He won everything there is to win at club level and appeared a record 127 times for his country, playing in the final of Euro 2004 and the semi-finals of the 2006 World Cup.

LUIS FIGO   LEGEND

WORLD CUP RECORD

Year	Point of exit		Year	Point of exit
1930	Did not enter		1978	Did not qualify
1934	Did not qualify		1982	Did not qualify
1938	Did not qualify		1986	Group stage
1950	Did not qualify		1990	Did not qualify
1954	Did not qualify		1994	Did not qualify
1958	Did not qualify		1998	Did not qualify
1962	Did not qualify		2002	Group stage
1966	Third		2006	Fourth
1970	Did not qualify		2010	Round of 16
1974	Did not qualify		2014	Group stage

DID YOU KNOW?

Cristiano Ronaldo is two games off equalling Lilian Thuram's record of 16 appearances by an outfield player at the European Championship finals

HOW THEY QUALIFIED

Group I	P	W	D	L	F	A	GD	Pts
Portugal	**8**	**7**	**0**	**1**	**11**	**5**	**+6**	**21**
Albania	**8**	**4**	**2**	**2**	**10**	**5**	**+5**	**14**
Denmark	8	3	3	2	8	5	+3	12
Serbia	8	2	1	5	8	13	-5	4
Armenia	8	0	2	6	5	14	-9	2

Serbia deducted 3pts

Match stats in qualifying

Possession	53%
Shots on target	63%
Shots off target	60%
Corners	61%

Averages of match totals in qualifying. See pages 228-254 for full qualifying results

Results & prices	W	D	L
Portugal ...(0) 0-1 (0)......Albania	2-7	5-1	12-1
Denmark...(0) 0-1 (0).... Portugal	7-5	23-10	23-10
Portugal ...(0) 1-0 (0).... Armenia	2-9	13-2	16-1
Portugal ...(1) 2-1 (0)........Serbia	6-10	3-1	6-1
Armenia....(1) 2-3 (1).... Portugal	1-2	7-2	15-2
Albania.....(0) 0-1 (0).... Portugal	8-11	13-5	5-1
Portugal ...(0) 1-0 (0)....Denmark	3-4	11-4	9-2
Serbia.......(0) 1-2 (1).... Portugal	9-4	9-4	6-4
Profit & loss in qualifying	**5.45**	**-8**	**5**

Figures based on a £1 level stake using best odds in the Racing Post on day of match. W shows win price, whether home or away, L the price of the opposition. See pages 228-254 for full qualifying results

PLAYERS USED IN QUALIFYING

Pos		Club	Age	CAREER P	CAREER G	QUALIFYING P	QUALIFYING G		
GK	Rui Patricio	Sporting Lisbon	28	43	-	8	-	2	-
DEF	Eliseu	Benfica	32	14	1	5	-	-	-
DEF	Nelson Semedo	Benfica	22	1	-	1	-	1	-
DEF	Pepe	Real Madrid	33	70	3	4	-	1	-
DEF	Vieirinha	Wolfsburg	30	19	1	3	-	-	-
DEF	Bruno Alves	Fenerbahce	34	84	10	4	-	-	-
DEF	Cedric	Southampton	24	9	-	3	-	-	-
DEF	Fabio Coentrao	Monaco	28	51	5	4	1	1	-
DEF	Joao Pereira	Sporting Lisbon	32	40	-	1	-	-	-
DEF	Jose Bosingwa	Trabzonspor	33	27	-	2	-	-	-
DEF	Jose Fonte	Southampton	32	9	-	4	-	-	-
DEF	Luis Neto	Zenit	28	11	-	1	-	-	-
DEF	Ricardo Carvalho	Monaco	38	83	5	6	1	1	-
DEF	Ricardo Costa	Granada	35	22	1	1	-	-	-
DEF	Raphael Guerreiro	Lorient	22	5	1	1	-	-	-
MID	Adrien Silva	Sporting Lisbon	27	7	-	1	-	-	-
MID	Andre Andre	Porto	26	4	1	1	-	1	-
MID	Andre Gomes	Valencia	22	5	-	1	-	-	-
MID	Tiago	Atl Madrid	35	66	3	5	-	2	1
MID	Bernardo Silva	Monaco	21	6	-	2	-	-	-
MID	Danilo	Porto	24	9	-	3	-	2	-
MID	Joao Mario	Sporting Lisbon	23	8	-	1	-	-	-
MID	Joao Moutinho	Monaco	29	81	4	7	2	1	-
MID	Miguel Veloso	Dynamo Kiev	30	56	3	3	1	-	-
MID	Ricardo Quaresma	Besiktas	32	47	4	6	-	-	-
MID	William Carvalho	Sporting Lisbon	24	17	-	5	-	1	-
MID	Danny	Zenit	32	38	4	7	-	2	-
MID	Nani	Fenerbahce	29	94	18	8	1	3	-
MID	Ricardo Horta	Malaga	21	1	-	1	-	-	-
ATT	Eder	Swansea	28	23	1	5	-	-	-
ATT	Cristiano Ronaldo	Real Madrid	31	125	56	6	5	1	-
ATT	Helder Postiga	Rio Ave	33	71	27	1	-	-	-
ATT	Ivan Cavaleiro	Monaco	22	2	-	1	-	-	-

CORRECT SCORES

	Competitive	Friendly
1-0	6	4
2-0	1	2
2-1	4	1
3-0	2	-
3-1	-	-
3-2	2	-
4-0	-	-
4-1	-	-
4-2	1	-
4-3	-	-
0-0	-	1
1-1	2	1
2-2	1	1
3-3	1	-
4-4	-	-
0-1	2	3
0-2	-	1
1-2	-	1
0-3	-	-
1-3	-	1
2-3	-	1
0-4	1	-
1-4	-	-
2-4	-	-
3-4	-	-
Other	-	2

Since Euro 2012

HALF-TIME/FULL-TIME DOUBLE RESULTS

Win/Win	5	22%
Draw/Win	11	48%
Lose/Win	0	0%
Win/Draw	2	9%
Draw/Draw	0	0%
Lose/Draw	2	9%
Win/Lose	0	0%
Draw/Lose	1	4%
Lose/Lose	2	9%

Win 1st half	7	30%
Win 2nd half	14	61%
Win both halves	1	4%
Goal both halves	12	52%

Overall
- Win 69%
- Draw 18%
- Lose 13%

WIN 69%

Overall: W16, D4, L3 in 23 competitive games since Euro 2012

CLEAN SHEETS

9 (39%) **Clean sheets** 14 (61%) ✓ ✗

9 (39%) **Win to nil** 14 (61%) ✓ ✗

3 (13%) **Fail to score** 20 (87%) ✓ ✗

3 (13%) **Lose to nil** 20 (87%) ✓ ✗

UNDER & OVER GOALS

15 (65%) **Over 1.5** 8 (35%) ✓ ✗

12 (52%) **Over 2.5** 11 (48%) ✓ ✗

6 (26%) **Over 3.5** 17 (74%) ✓ ✗

5 (22%) **Over 4.5** 18 (78%) ✓ ✗

BOTH TEAMS TO SCORE

11 (48%) **Both score** 12 (52%) ✓ ✗

7 (30%) **& win** 16 (70%) ✓ ✗

0 (0%) **& lose** 23 (100%) ✓ ✗

In 23 competitive games since Euro 2012

GOAL TIMES

Total match goals by half

12 (55%) **1st half** 10 (45%)
F A

27 (68%) **2nd half** 13 (33%)
F A

Goals for & against by half

12 (31%) **For** 27 (69%)
1st 2nd

10 (43%) **Against** 13 (57%)
1st 2nd

● GOALS FOR ● GOALS AGAINST

	0-9	10-18	19-27	28-36	37-45	46-54	55-63	64-72	73-81	82-90
For	4	1	1	6	0	2	5	4	8	8
Against	1	3	1	3	2	2	2	6	2	1

In 23 competitive games since Euro 2012

IF PORTUGAL SCORE FIRST

They win	14		82%
Draw	3		18%
They lose	0		0%

In 23 competitive games since Euro 2012

IF PORTUGAL CONCEDE FIRST

They win	2		33%
Draw	1		17%
They lose	3		50%

Joao Moutinho's two goals made him Portugal's top scorer in qualifying after Ronaldo

GOALSCORERS IN QUALIFYING

● FIRST GOALS

	Goals		1st		Anytime		Percentage of team goals	
C Ronaldo	5	●●●●●	2	40%	3	50%		45%
J Moutinho	2	●●	1	50%	2	28%		18%
R Carvalho	1	●	1	100%	1	16%		9%
Nani	1	●	1	100%	1	12%		9%
M Veloso	1	●	1	100%	1	33%		9%
F Coentrao	1	●	0	0%	1	25%		9%

In Euro 2016 qualifying

BOOKINGS

Matches played	8	☐ 19	▮ 1
Average make-up (☐ 10 ▮ 25)			26.9

In Euro 2016 qualifying

CORNERS

Avg F	5.8		61%
Avg A	3.6		39%

In Euro 2016 qualifying. Avg match total 9.4

ICELAND

B igger is not always better. Iceland has a population of around 330,000, roughly the same as the West Yorkshire city of Wakefield, which makes them the smallest country ever to reach the European Championships. Their years of hard work recruiting youth coaches and investing in indoor football facilities has been rewarded in spectacular fashion.

How they qualified

Iceland booked their ticket for France with ease, qualifying with two matches to spare after starting with six wins in seven, a run that included a double over World Cup semi-finalists Holland.

They probably would have finished top of the section but eased up when the job was done, drawing with Kazakhstan and Latvia before losing 1-0 to Turkey.

Continuity in team selection was key and Iceland used the joint-fewest players in qualifying (20). That point was emphasised as the same XI started the opening four group matches in the basic 4-4-2 formation that was the shape throughout.

The manager

They are under the dual management of Lars Lagerback and Heimir Hallgrimsson, who is currently still working part-time as a dentist but will give up the day job to become full-time boss when Lagerback retires at the end of Euro 2016.

Lagerback, who was involved in various Swedish national teams from 1990 to 2009 (including the top job for the last nine years), is the main man in the partnership but refuses to take much credit for the rise of Icelandic football.

Structure over style is Lagerback's way and Hallgrimsson told the Guardian: "We win on unity and hard work and organisation. We have to be better than everyone else in these areas."

Possession means little in Lagerback's philosophy and they had just 35 per cent of the ball in the 1-0 win away to Holland

FACTFILE

FA founded 1947

www ksi.is

Head coach Lars Lagerback & Heimir Hallgrimsson

National league Urvalsdeild

Date qualified September 6, 2015

Typical starting XI (4-4-2) Halldorsson; Saevarsson, Arnason, R Sigurdsson, Skulason; Gudmundsson, Gunnarsson, G Sigurdsson, B Bjarnason; Sigthorsson, Bodvarsson

Strengths
☑ Superb team unity and organisation
☑ A real threat from set-pieces

Weaknesses
☒ Iceland boast very little quality outside of the starting XI
☒ Poor in possession

Star rating ★☆☆☆☆

Fixtures

1 Portugal, 8pm June 14, Saint-Etienne

2 Hungary, 5pm June 18, Marseille

3 Austria, 5pm June 22, Saint-Denis

Base Annecy-le-Vieux

Kolbeinn Sigthorsson scores against Latvia

despite the Dutch being reduced to ten men in the first half. In the reverse fixture Iceland had 26 per cent possession and ran out 2-0 winners.

Match winners

The way Iceland play is all about the team being greater than any single individual. The side is full of grafters and together they are greater than the sum of their parts.

That said, Gylfi Sigurdsson scored six times during qualifying and is absolutely lethal from dead-ball situations, while long throws from Cardiff's Aron Gunnarsson will also cause problems.

Nantes striker Kolbeinn Sigthorsson is one of many who seems to up his game for the national team.

Question marks

There is very little in the way of depth and some of those who could feature from the bench, such as Eidur Gudjohnsen (Molde)

and Aron Sigurdarson (Tromso), joined Norwegian clubs in 2016 to enhance their claims of making the finals.

Man for man Iceland are among the weakest teams in the competition so it will be interesting to see just how far team unity can take a side, particularly if confidence is dented by a meeting with Cristiano Ronaldo's Portugal in their opening game.

Centre-back Kari Arnason won't be looking forward to tackling Ronaldo – the Malmo man called him "unstoppable" after the Swedish side were beaten 8-0 by Real Madrid in this season's Champions League.

How to back them

The group draw could have been much worse, but Iceland still don't have the individual talent to stick with Austria and Portugal. However, they are not totally out of the running to qualify and deserve to be favourites in the betting to finish third ahead of Hungary.

ICELAND

EUROPEAN CHAMPIONSHIP RECORD

1960	P	W	D	L	GF	GA
Did not enter	-	-	-	-	-	-
Qualifying	-	-	-	-	-	-

1964	P	W	D	L	GF	GA
Did not qualify	-	-	-	-	-	-
Qualifying	2	0	1	1	3	5

1968	P	W	D	L	GF	GA
Did not enter	-	-	-	-	-	-
Qualifying	-	-	-	-	-	-

1972	P	W	D	L	GF	GA
Did not enter	-	-	-	-	-	-
Qualifying	-	-	-	-	-	-

1976	P	W	D	L	GF	GA
Did not qualify	-	-	-	-	-	-
Qualifying	6	1	2	3	3	8

1980	P	W	D	L	GF	GA
Did not qualify	-	-	-	-	-	-
Qualifying	8	0	0	8	2	21

1984	P	W	D	L	GF	GA
Did not qualify	-	-	-	-	-	-
Qualifying	8	1	1	6	3	13

1988	P	W	D	L	GF	GA
Did not qualify	-	-	-	-	-	-
Qualifying	8	2	2	4	4	14

1992	P	W	D	L	GF	GA
Did not qualify	-	-	-	-	-	-
Qualifying	8	2	0	6	7	10

1996	P	W	D	L	GF	GA
Did not qualify	-	-	-	-	-	-
Qualifying	8	1	2	5	3	12

2000	P	W	D	L	GF	GA
Did not qualify	-	-	-	-	-	-
Qualifying	10	4	3	3	12	7

2004	P	W	D	L	GF	GA
Did not qualify	-	-	-	-	-	-
Qualifying	8	4	1	3	11	9

2008	P	W	D	L	GF	GA
Did not qualify	-	-	-	-	-	-
Qualifying	12	2	2	8	10	27

2012	P	W	D	L	GF	GA
Did not qualify	-	-	-	-	-	-
Qualifying	8	1	1	6	6	14

Totals	P	W	D	L	GF	GA
Finals	-	-	-	-	-	-
Qualifying	86	18	15	53	64	140

Results & goals include extra time

WIN %
FOUR-TEAM FINALS
100 — 50 — 0
1960 1964 1968 1972 1976

WIN %
EIGHT-TEAM FINALS
100 — 50 — 0
1980 1984 1988 1992

WIN %
16-TEAM FINALS
100 — 50 — 0
1996 2000 2004 2008 2012

Results include extra time. █ in qualifying █ at the finals

LEGENDARY PLAYER

EIDUR GUDJOHNSEN LEGEND

Eidur Gudjohnsen is approaching the end of his career, but Iceland's record scorer, who has won titles in Holland, England and Spain, as well as the Champions League with Barcelona, played his part in getting his country to their first ever finals.

WORLD CUP RECORD

Year	Point of exit	Year	Point of exit
1930	Did not enter	1978	Did not qualify
1934	Did not enter	1982	Did not qualify
1938	Did not enter	1986	Did not qualify
1950	Did not enter	1990	Did not qualify
1954	Did not enter	1994	Did not qualify
1958	Did not qualify	1998	Did not qualify
1962	Did not enter	2002	Did not qualify
1966	Did not enter	2006	Did not qualify
1970	Did not enter	2010	Did not qualify
1974	Did not qualify	2014	Did not qualify

DID YOU KNOW?

Arnor and Eidur Gudjohnsen became the first father and son to play in the same international team when they lined up against Estonia in 1996

HOW THEY QUALIFIED

Group A	P	W	D	L	F	A	GD	Pts
Czech Rep	10	7	1	2	19	14	+5	22
Iceland	10	6	2	2	17	6	+11	20
Turkey	10	5	3	2	14	9	+5	18
Holland	10	4	1	5	17	14	+3	13
Kazakhstan	10	1	2	7	7	18	-11	5
Latvia	10	0	5	5	6	19	-13	5

Match stats in qualifying

Possession	▌▌▌▌▌▌▌▌▌	48%
Shots on target	▌▌▌▌▌▌▌▌▌	49%
Shots off target	▌▌▌▌▌▌▌▌	46%
Corners	▌▌▌▌▌▌▌▌▌	50%

Averages of match totals in qualifying. See pages 228-254 for full qualifying results

Results & prices

	W	D	L
Iceland......(1) 3-0 (0) ....Turkey	16-5	12-5	11-10
Latvia ....(0) 0-3 (0) ...... Iceland	6-5	12-5	14-5
Iceland......(2) 2-0 (0) .....Holland	5-1	3-1	4-6
Czech Rep.(1) 2-1 (1) ...... Iceland	9-2	11-4	4-5
Kazakhstan(0) 0-3 (2) ...... Iceland	20-21	12-5	18-5
Iceland......(0) 2-1 (0) . Czech Rep	15-8	11-5	13-8
Holland......(0) 0-1 (0) ...... Iceland	9-1	17-4	4-11
Iceland......(0) 0-0 (0) Kazakhstan	1-3	5-1	11-1
Iceland......(2) 2-2 (0) ....Latvia	9-20	18-5	8-1
Turkey.......(0) 1-0 (0) ...... Iceland	7-1	16-5	4-7

Profit & loss in qualifying   17.23 0.60 -6.63

Figures based on a £1 level stake using best odds in the Racing Post on day of match. W shows win price, whether home or away, L the price of the opposition

PLAYERS USED IN QUALIFYING

				CAREER		QUALIFYING			
Pos		Club	Age	P	G	P	G	▯	■
GK	Ogmundur Kristinsson	Hammarby	26	10	-	1	-	-	-
GK	Hannes Halldorsson	NEC Nijmegen	32	33	-	9	-	-	-
DEF	Birkir Saevarsson	Hammarby	31	56	-	8	-	1	-
DEF	Ragnar Sigurdsson	FK Krasnodar	29	54	1	10	1	2	-
DEF	Solvi Ottesen	Wuhan Zall	32	28	-	1	-	-	-
DEF	Ari Skulason	OB Odense	29	37	-	10	-	2	-
DEF	Kari Arnason	Malmo	33	48	2	10	-	1	-
MID	Theodor E Bjarnason	Aarhus	29	26	-	4	-	1	-
MID	Aron Gunnarsson	Cardiff	27	57	2	9	2	1	1
MID	Birkir Bjarnason	Basel	28	45	6	10	2	-	-
MID	Emil Hallfredsson	Udinese	31	52	1	7	-	-	-
MID	Gylfi Sigurdsson	Swansea	26	37	12	10	6	1	-
MID	Johann Gudmundsson	Charlton	25	45	5	7	-	2	-
MID	Olafur Ingi Skulason	Genclerbirligi	33	26	1	3	-	-	-
MID	Rurik Gislason	Nuremberg	28	37	3	5	1	1	-
ATT	Alfred Finnbogason	Augsburg	27	32	7	5	-	1	-
ATT	Eidur Gudjohnsen	Molde	37	84	25	3	1	-	-
ATT	Jon Bodvarsson	Kaiserslautern	24	20	1	9	1	-	-
ATT	Kolbeinn Sigthorsson	Nantes	26	37	19	10	3	2	-
ATT	Vidar Kjartansson	Malmo	26	9	1	3	-	-	-

ICELAND

CORRECT SCORES

	Competitive	Friendly
1-0	1	3
2-0	3	2
2-1	4	1
3-0	3	-
3-1	-	-
3-2	-	1
4-0	-	-
4-1	-	-
4-2	-	-
4-3	-	-
0-0	2	-
1-1	1	3
2-2	1	-
3-3	-	-
4-4	1	-
0-1	2	-
0-2	2	2
1-2	1	2
0-3	-	-
1-3	-	3
2-3	-	1
0-4	-	-
1-4	-	-
2-4	1	1
3-4	-	-
Other	-	-

Since Euro 2012

HALF-TIME/FULL-TIME DOUBLE RESULTS

Win/Win	4	18%	Win 1st half	5	23%
Draw/Win	6	27%	Win 2nd half	11	50%
Lose/Win	1	5%	Win both halves	3	14%
Win/Draw	1	5%	Goal both halves	11	50%
Draw/Draw	3	14%			
Lose/Draw	1	5%	**Overall**		
Win/Lose	0	0%	● Win	50%	
Draw/Lose	5	23%	● Draw	23%	
Lose/Lose	1	5%	● Lose	27%	

WIN 50%

Overall: W11, D5, L6 in 22 competitive games since Euro 2012

CLEAN SHEETS

9 (41%) **Clean sheets** 13 (59%)
✓ ❌

7 (32%) **Win to nil** 15 (68%)
✓ ❌

6 (27%) **Fail to score** 16 (73%)
✓ ❌

4 (18%) **Lose to nil** 18 (82%)
✓ ❌

UNDER & OVER GOALS

17 (77%) **Over 1.5** 5 (23%)
✓ ❌

11 (50%) **Over 2.5** 11 (50%)
✓ ❌

4 (18%) **Over 3.5** 18 (82%)
✓ ❌

2 (9%) **Over 4.5** 20 (91%)
✓ ❌

BOTH TEAMS TO SCORE

9 (41%) **Both score** 13 (59%)
✓ ❌

3 (14%) **& win** 19 (86%)
✓ ❌

3 (14%) **& lose** 19 (86%)
✓ ❌

In 22 competitive games since Euro 2012

GOAL TIMES

Total match goals by half

15 (58%) **1st half** 11 (42%)
F A

19 (61%) **2nd half** 12 (39%)
F A

Goals for & against by half

15 (44%) **For** 19 (56%)
1st 2nd

11 (48%) **Against** 12 (52%)
1st 2nd

● GOALS FOR ● GOALS AGAINST

	0-9	10-18	19-27	28-36	37-45	46-54	55-63	64-72	73-81	82-90
For	3	4	6	1	1	2	4	2	8	3
Against	1	2	2	5	1	3	4	2	1	2

In 22 competitive games since Euro 2012

IF ICELAND SCORE FIRST

They win	8		67%
Draw	3		25%
They lose	1		8%

In 22 competitive games since Euro 2012

IF ICELAND CONCEDE FIRST

They win	3		37%
Draw	0		0%
They lose	5		63%

Gylfi Sigurdsson has scored ten goals in Iceland's last two qualifying campaigns

GOALSCORERS IN QUALIFYING ● FIRST GOALS

	Goals		1st		Anytime		Percentage of team goals	
G Sigurdsson	6	●●●●●●	3	50%	5	50%	▆▆▆▆▆▆▆	35%
K Sigthorsson	3	●●●	1	33%	3	30%	▆▆▆▆	18%
A Gunnarsson	2	●●	0	0%	2	22%	▆▆	12%
B Bjarnason	2	●●	0	0%	1	10%	▆▆	12%
E Gudjohnsen	1	●	1	100%	1	33%	▆	6%
R Gislason	1	●	0	0%	1	20%	▆	6%
R Sigurdsson	1	●	1	100%	1	10%	▆	6%
J Bodvarsson	1	●	1	100%	1	11%	▆	6%

In Euro 2016 qualifying

BOOKINGS

Matches played	10	☐15	▮ 1
Average make-up (☐10 ▮25)			17.5

In Euro 2016 qualifying

CORNERS

Avg F	3.9	▆▆▆▆▆▆▆▆▆	50%
Avg A	3.9	▆▆▆▆▆▆▆▆▆	50%

In Euro 2016 qualifying. Avg match total 7.8

AUSTRIA

Aust ✓ Hungray

A ustrian football fans have had little to shout about since beating arch-enemies West Germany in 1978, when Hans Krankl scored one of the great World Cup goals, but that is about to change. Their last knockout match at a finals was in 1954, but this is Austria's best side in nearly 40 years and Marcel Koller's men could be the dark horses of Euro 2016.

How they qualified

Koller has had Austria going the right way for a while and it all came together beautifully in qualifying. They managed nine straight wins and their only dropped points came in a 1-1 draw with Sweden on matchday one. Only England (30) could better Austria's haul of 28 points.

Three results stand out above all others – the 4-1 success in Sweden, because of the quality of the opposition, and the two 1-0 victories against Russia which were both achieved without star man David Alaba.

Goalkeeper Robert Almer broke the national team record after going 603 minutes without conceding and this is a settled side – nine of the players started at least nine of the qualifiers.

The manager

Koller was unpopular when given the job in 2011 but he has since won over even his harshest critics and the Swiss-born coach has turned down the opportunity to manage his home nation, as well as rumoured interest from Borussia Monchengladbach, to finish off his good work with Austria.

He believes in a varied backroom staff that includes experts in psychology, physiology and performance data, and has spent much of his time getting into the brains of the Austrian squad to demand more from a nation of stereotypically relaxed people.

On his style of play, Koller gave an excellent interview to The Blizzard in which he said: "I like my team to be active, not to sit back and wait for a mistake. We want to try to get possession back as quickly as possible

FACTFILE

FA founded 1904
www oefb.at
Head coach Marcel Koller
National league Bundesliga
Date qualified September 8, 2015

Typical starting XI (4-2-3-1) Almer; Klein, Dragovic, Prodl, Fuchs; Baumgartinger, Alaba; Harnik, Junuzovic, Arnautovic; Janko

Strengths
☑ Austria have a young, dynamic team
☑ They seem guaranteed to score goals
Weaknesses
☒ There is a lack of depth in several positions
☒ Virtually no tournament pedigree
Star rating ★★★☆☆

Fixtures
1 Hungary, 5pm June 14, Bordeaux
2 Portugal, 8pm June 18, Paris
3 Iceland, 5pm June 22, Saint-Denis
Base Mallemort

Expect fireworks from Austria

and, when we have the ball, I want us to play football with a lot of technique, running and intensity."

Match winners

The versatile Alaba was described by Pep Guardiola as Bayern Munich's "God". One of the world's most blessed footballers, he is capable of playing almost any outfield position from centre-back to the number ten. With Austria, Alaba is the midfield dynamo.

Inconsistent attacking trio Marko Arnautovic, Zlatko Junuzovic and Martin Harnik are capable of moments of magic and supply lone forward Marc Janko with decent opportunities.

Question marks

There is plenty of depth in the centre of Austria's defence, where Sebastian Prodl, Martin Hinteregger or Kevin Wimmer could partner the highly rated Aleksandar Dragovic, but elsewhere there is not a great deal in the way of cover. Expectations are high, which could be an issue for a country not used to international success.

How to back them

This group gives them a chance to grow into the tournament and should they top the section, the path to the finals would read something like Italy-Spain-England.

If Austria finish second, the market anticipates a last-16 tie with Russia, before a meeting with hosts France in the quarter-finals.

It's worth chucking a few quid on them each-way and also having a small play on the spreads, where you can win decent money if Austria reach the quarter-finals and not do too much damage if they exit at the last-16 stage.

Stronger fancies include Austria to win Group F, a dual forecast with Portugal, Austria to reach the quarter-finals, and the nap, to beat Hungary at 5-6 on June 14.

AUSTRIA

EUROPEAN CHAMPIONSHIP RECORD

1960	P	W	D	L	GF	GA
Did not qualify	-	-	-	-	-	-
Qualifying	4	2	0	2	10	11

1964	P	W	D	L	GF	GA
Did not qualify	-	-	-	-	-	-
Qualifying	2	0	1	1	2	3

1968	P	W	D	L	GF	GA
Did not qualify	-	-	-	-	-	-
Qualifying	6	2	2	2	8	10

1972	P	W	D	L	GF	GA
Did not qualify	-	-	-	-	-	-
Qualifying	6	3	1	2	14	6

1976	P	W	D	L	GF	GA
Did not qualify	-	-	-	-	-	-
Qualifying	6	3	1	2	11	7

1980	P	W	D	L	GF	GA
Did not qualify	-	-	-	-	-	-
Qualifying	8	4	3	1	14	7

1984	P	W	D	L	GF	GA
Did not qualify	-	-	-	-	-	-
Qualifying	8	4	1	3	15	10

1988	P	W	D	L	GF	GA
Did not qualify	-	-	-	-	-	-
Qualifying	6	2	1	3	6	9

1992	P	W	D	L	GF	GA
Did not qualify	-	-	-	-	-	-
Qualifying	8	1	1	6	6	14

1996	P	W	D	L	GF	GA
Did not qualify	-	-	-	-	-	-
Qualifying	10	5	1	4	29	14

2000	P	W	D	L	GF	GA
Did not qualify	-	-	-	-	-	-
Qualifying	8	4	1	3	19	20

2004	P	W	D	L	GF	GA
Did not qualify	-	-	-	-	-	-
Qualifying	8	3	0	5	12	14

2008	P	W	D	L	GF	GA
Group stage	3	0	1	2	1	3
Qualifying	-	-	-	-	-	-

2012	P	W	D	L	GF	GA
Did not qualify	-	-	-	-	-	-
Qualifying	10	3	3	4	16	17

Totals	P	W	D	L	GF	GA
Finals	3	0	1	2	1	3
Qualifying	90	36	16	38	162	142

Results & goals include extra time

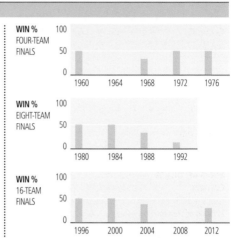

WIN % FOUR-TEAM FINALS — 1960, 1964, 1968, 1972, 1976

WIN % EIGHT-TEAM FINALS — 1980, 1984, 1988, 1992

WIN % 16-TEAM FINALS — 1996, 2000, 2004, 2008, 2012

Results include extra time. ▯ in qualifying ▮ at the finals

LEGENDARY PLAYER

He never got to play at the European Championships but **Hans Krankl** represented Austria at the 1978 and 1982 World Cups, scoring two superb goals in their shock 3-2 win over West Germany in the second group stage at Argentina 78.

HANS KRANKL — LEGEND

WORLD CUP RECORD

Year	Point of exit	Year	Point of exit
1930	Did not enter	1978	Second round
1934	● Fourth	1982	Second round
1938	Withdrew	1986	Did not qualify
1950	Withdrew	1990	Group stage
1954	● Third	1994	Did not qualify
1958	Group stage	1998	Group stage
1962	Withdrew	2002	Did not qualify
1966	Did not qualify	2006	Did not qualify
1970	Did not qualify	2010	Did not qualify
1974	Did not qualify	2014	Did not qualify

DID YOU KNOW?

Austria slumped to their worst ever position in the Fifa rankings after Euro 2008; they ended 2015 in their best ever position

HOW THEY QUALIFIED

Group G	P	W	D	L	F	A	GD	Pts
Austria	10	9	1	0	22	5	+17	28
Russia	10	6	2	2	21	5	+16	20
Sweden	10	5	3	2	15	9	+6	18
Montenegro	10	3	2	5	10	13	-3	11
Liechtenstein	10	1	2	7	2	26	-24	5
Moldova	10	0	2	8	4	16	-12	2

Match stats in qualifying

Possession	▮▮▮▮▮▮▮▮▮▮▮	57%
Shots on target	▮▮▮▮▮▮▮▮▮▮▮▮▮▮	75%
Shots off target	▮▮▮▮▮▮▮▮▮▮▮▮	64%
Corners	▮▮▮▮▮▮▮▮▮▮▮▮	65%

Averages of match totals in qualifying. See pages 228-254 for full qualifying results

Results & prices	W	D	L
Austria......(1) 1-1 (1) ..... Sweden	6-4	23-10	11-5
Moldova ... (1) 1-2 (1) ....Austria	7-10	11-4	19-4
Austria......(1) 1-0 (0)Montenegro	Evs	5-2	10-3
Austria......(0) 1-0 (0) ....Russia	19-10	11-5	9-5
Liechtenstein(0) 0-5 (2) .....Austria	1-5	13-2	20-1
Russia.......(0) 0-1 (1) ....Austria	15-4	12-5	20-21
Austria......(0) 1-0 (0) ....Moldova	1-5	15-2	20-1
Sweden.....(0) 1-4 (2) ....Austria	13-5	5-2	5-4
Montenegro(1)2-3 (0) ....Austria	17-10	23-10	2-1
Austria......(1) 3-0 (0)Liechtenstein	1-16	15-1	66-1

Profit & loss in qualifying   11.11 -6.70 -10

Figures based on a £1 level stake using best odds in the Racing Post on day of match. W shows win price, whether home or away, L the price of the opposition

PLAYERS USED IN QUALIFYING

Pos		Club	Age	CAREER P	G	QUALIFYING P	G	▯	▮
GK	Robert Almer	Austria Vienna	32	27	-	10	-	-	-
DEF	Aleksandar Dragovic	Dynamo Kiev	25	45	1	10	-	2	-
DEF	Christian Fuchs	Leicester	30	74	1	10	-	-	-
DEF	Florian Klein	Stuttgart	29	35	-	10	-	2	-
DEF	Martin Hinteregger	RB Salzburg	23	12	-	5	-	1	-
DEF	Sebastien Prodl	Watford	28	56	4	7	-	2	-
MID	David Alaba	Bayern Munich	23	44	11	8	4	-	-
MID	Christoph Leitgeb	RB Salzburg	31	41	-	3	-	-	-
MID	Jakob Jantscher	Lucerne	27	21	1	3	-	-	-
MID	Julian Baumgartlinger	Mainz	28	43	1	9	-	2	-
MID	Martin Harnik	Stuttgart	29	56	14	10	3	-	-
MID	Stefan Ilsanker	RB Leipzig	27	14	-	7	-	1	-
MID	Valentino Lazaro	RB Salzburg	20	4	-	2	-	-	-
MID	Zlatko Junuzovic	W Bremen	28	46	7	10	2	2	-
MID	Marko Arnautovic	Stoke	27	50	10	10	3	-	-
ATT	Lukas Hinterseer	Ingolstadt	24	8	-	2	-	-	-
ATT	Marc Janko	Basel	32	52	26	9	7	1	1
ATT	Marcel Sabitzer	RB Leipzig	22	16	3	7	1	-	-
ATT	Marco Djuricin	Brentford	23	2	-	1	-	-	-
ATT	Rubin Okotie	1860 Munich	29	16	2	7	2	1	-

AUSTRIA

CORRECT SCORES

	Competitive	Friendly
1-0	5	1
2-0	-	1
2-1	2	2
3-0	2	-
3-1	-	-
3-2	1	-
4-0	1	-
4-1	1	-
4-2	-	-
4-3	-	-
0-0	1	-
1-1	1	3
2-2	1	-
3-3	-	-
4-4	-	-
0-1	-	-
0-2	-	1
1-2	2	4
0-3	1	1
1-3	-	-
2-3	-	-
0-4	-	-
1-4	-	-
2-4	-	-
3-4	-	-
Other	2	-

Since Euro 2012

HALF-TIME/FULL-TIME DOUBLE RESULTS

Win/Win	9	45%
Draw/Win	4	20%
Lose/Win	1	5%
Win/Draw	0	0%
Draw/Draw	2	10%
Lose/Draw	1	5%
Win/Lose	1	5%
Draw/Lose	0	0%
Lose/Lose	2	10%

Win 1st half	10	50%
Win 2nd half	12	60%
Win both halves	6	30%
Goal both halves	13	65%

Overall
- **Win** 70%
- **Draw** 15%
- **Lose** 15%

WIN 70%

Overall: W14, D3, L3 in 20 competitive games since Euro 2012

CLEAN SHEETS

11 (55%) **Clean sheets** 9 (45%)
✓ ▓▓▓▓▓▓▓▓▓░░░░░░░░ ✗

10 (50%) **Win to nil** 10 (50%)
✓ ▓▓▓▓▓▓▓▓░░░░░░░░░ ✗

2 (10%) **Fail to score** 18 (90%)
✓ ▓▓░░░░░░░░░░░░░░░ ✗

1 (5%) **Lose to nil** 19 (95%)
✓ ▓░░░░░░░░░░░░░░░░ ✗

UNDER & OVER GOALS

14 (70%) **Over 1.5** 6 (30%)
✓ ▓▓▓▓▓▓▓▓▓▓▓▓░░░░░ ✗

13 (65%) **Over 2.5** 7 (35%)
✓ ▓▓▓▓▓▓▓▓▓▓▓░░░░░░ ✗

6 (30%) **Over 3.5** 14 (70%)
✓ ▓▓▓▓▓░░░░░░░░░░░░ ✗

4 (20%) **Over 4.5** 16 (80%)
✓ ▓▓▓▓░░░░░░░░░░░░░ ✗

BOTH TEAMS TO SCORE

8 (40%) **Both score** 12 (60%)
✓ ▓▓▓▓▓▓▓░░░░░░░░░░ ✗

4 (20%) **& win** 16 (80%)
✓ ▓▓▓▓░░░░░░░░░░░░░ ✗

2 (10%) **& lose** 18 (90%)
✓ ▓▓░░░░░░░░░░░░░░░ ✗

In 20 competitive games since Euro 2012

GOAL TIMES

● GOALS FOR ● GOALS AGAINST

Total match goals by half

18 (72%) **1st half** 7 (28%)
F ▓▓▓▓▓▓▓▓▓▓▓▓▓░░░░░ A

24 (75%) **2nd half** 8 (25%)
F ▓▓▓▓▓▓▓▓▓▓▓▓▓▓░░░░ A

Goals for & against by half

18 (43%) **For** 24 (57%)
1st ▓▓▓▓▓▓▓▓░░░░░░░░ 2nd

7 (47%) **Against** 8 (53%)
1st ▓▓▓▓▓▓▓░░░░░░░░ 2nd

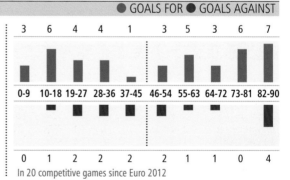

	0-9	10-18	19-27	28-36	37-45	46-54	55-63	64-72	73-81	82-90
Goals for	3	6	4	4	1	3	5	3	6	7
Goals against	0	1	2	2	2	2	1	1	0	4

In 20 competitive games since Euro 2012

IF AUSTRIA SCORE FIRST

They win	13	▓▓▓▓▓▓▓▓▓▓▓▓▓░░	81%
Draw	2	▓▓▓░░░░░░░░░░░░	13%
They lose	1	▓░░░░░░░░░░░░░░	6%

In 20 competitive games since Euro 2012

IF AUSTRIA CONCEDE FIRST

They win	1	▓▓▓▓▓░░░░░░░░░░	33%
Draw	0	░░░░░░░░░░░░░░░	0%
They lose	2	▓▓▓▓▓▓▓▓▓▓░░░░░	67%

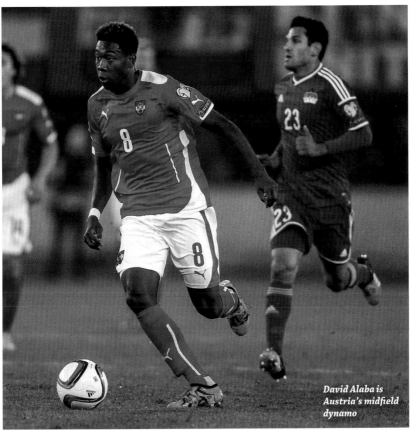

David Alaba is Austria's midfield dynamo

GOALSCORERS IN QUALIFYING   ● FIRST GOALS

	Goals		1st		Anytime		Percentage of team goals	
M Janko	7	●●●●●●●	1	14%	6	66%	▌▌▌▌▌▌	32%
D Alaba	4	●●●●	3	75%	4	50%	▌▌▌▌	18%
M Harnik	3	●●●	1	33%	2	20%	▌▌▌	14%
M Arnautovic	3	●●●	1	33%	3	30%	▌▌▌	14%
Z Junuzovic	2	●●	1	50%	2	20%	▌▌	9%
R Okotie	2	●●	2	100%	2	28%	▌▌	9%
M Sabitzer	1	●	0	0%	1	14%	▌	5%

In Euro 2016 qualifying

BOOKINGS

Matches played	10	☐14	▐ 1
Average make-up (☐10 ▐25)			16.5

In Euro 2016 qualifying

CORNERS

Avg F	6.8	▌▌▌▌▌▌▌▌▌▌▌	65%
Avg A	3.6	▌▌▌▌▌▌	35%

In Euro 2016 qualifying. Avg match total 10.4

HUNGARY

Austria v Hungary (handwritten)

Hun v Port (handwritten)

L ooking back to the end of qualifying for Brazil 2014 it would have taken a brave – or foolish – punter to predict Hungary could recover from the humiliation of losing 8-1 to Holland to reach the Euros. Not much will be expected of the Magyars in France but for this football-loving nation, this is about being back in the big time, mixing it with the best for the first time since 1986.

How they qualified

Reaching the finals is a big deal but it would be wrong to go overboard about the way Hungary did it. They qualified in third spot behind Romania and Northern Ireland before beating Norway, one of the weaker teams in the playoffs.

Despite overcoming Norway 3-1 on aggregate, Hungary averaged 35 per cent possession over the two legs, lost the shot count 25-15 and the corners battle 25-4. It remains a mystery quite how Norway, who hit the woodwork twice, lost the first leg 1-0.

No team came through a six-team group with fewer points than Hungary's tally of 16, and their goal difference of +2 was also the worst of any qualifier.

Before the playoffs, Hungary's only wins came against Finland and the Faroe Islands. Even then, three of those were 1-0 victories in a campaign that saw the Magyars employ three different managers.

Attila Pinter was booted out after the defeat to Northern Ireland and his successor, Pal Dardai, was in control of Hungary and Hertha Berlin before he decided to concentrate solely on Bundesliga matters. That left German Bernd Storck to see them over the line.

The manager

Storck made his managerial name in Kazakhstan but had predominantly worked as an assistant or with youth teams, including Hungary, where he was promoted from the Under-20 side. Many bemoaned the football association going with the cheap option.

However, Storck won over the doubters

FACTFILE

FA founded 1901
www mlsz.hu
Head coach Bernd Storck
National league Nemzeti Bajnoksag I
Date qualified November 15, 2015

Typical starting XI (4-2-3-1) Kiraly; Fiola, Juhasz, Guzmics, Kadar; Elek, Tozser; Lovrencsics, Gera, Dzsudzsak; Szalai

Strengths
☑ Kiraly was brilliant in the playoff win over Norway
☑ A few different options up front
Weaknesses
☒ Key men are now in latter stages of their careers
☒ Few players are involved at the highest level of club football
Star rating ★☆☆☆☆

Fixtures
1 Austria, 5pm June 14, Bordeaux
2 Iceland, 5pm June 18, Marseille
3 Portugal, 5pm June 22, Lyon
Base Tourrettes

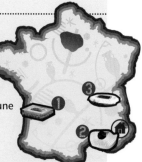

(handwritten margin notes) Hun v Port · 3-1 · 2-1 b · 5pm · wed 22 16/1 · 17/2

Bernd Stock celebrates Hungary's qualification with Tamas Kadar

thanks to his side's playoff victory over Norway and he is more than happy to blood the younger players he worked with in his previous role.

Storck, who recently extended his contract, caused a scene by taking apart Dardai's backroom staff and among those to come in was World Cup and European Championship winner Andreas Moller.

Match winners

Their tracksuit bottom-wearing veteran goalkeeper Gabor Kiraly was outstanding against Norway and will doubtless be working overtime during the tournament, while Zoltan Gera remains a pivotal playmaker and Balazs Dzsudzsak has long been seen as Hungary's most talented individual.

It will be interesting to see just how many of the youngsters Storck will introduce into the squad for the finals – Laszlo Kleinheisler made his debut for the senior team against Norway and scored after 26 minutes, which helped him earn a January move to Bundesliga side Werder Bremen.

Adam Nagy is another pushing for a spot and Storck could be tempted to give a chance to a few of the other players who helped Hungary reach the last 16 of the Under-20 World Cup last year.

Question marks

At the time of writing not one of Hungary's squad is a regular starter in Europe's elite leagues so there is an obvious issue over the quality of the side.

Age is a factor for some of the key players too. Kiraly is 40, Gera will be 37 by the time Euro 2016 starts and key centre-back Roland Juhasz will turn 33 before it is over.

How to back them

Odds-on punters are pointed towards Hungary not to qualify from Group F even though a section containing Portugal, Austria and Iceland could have been stronger.

Even if Hungary win their easiest match against Iceland – and that is no gimme – qualification is a tall order for a team with obvious weaknesses all over the pitch.

HUNGARY

EUROPEAN CHAMPIONSHIP RECORD

1960	P	W	D	L	GF	GA
Did not qualify	-	-	-	-	-	-
Qualifying	2	0	0	2	1	4

1964	P	W	D	L	GF	GA
● Third	2	1	0	1	4	3
Qualifying	6	4	2	0	14	8

1968	P	W	D	L	GF	GA
Did not qualify	-	-	-	-	-	-
Qualifying	8	5	1	2	17	8

1972	P	W	D	L	GF	GA
● Fourth	2	0	0	2	1	3
Qualifying	9	5	3	1	17	9

1976	P	W	D	L	GF	GA
Did not qualify	-	-	-	-	-	-
Qualifying	6	3	1	2	15	8

1980	P	W	D	L	GF	GA
Did not qualify	-	-	-	-	-	-
Qualifying	6	2	2	2	9	9

1984	P	W	D	L	GF	GA
Did not qualify	-	-	-	-	-	-
Qualifying	8	3	1	4	18	17

1988	P	W	D	L	GF	GA
Did not qualify	-	-	-	-	-	-
Qualifying	8	4	0	4	13	11

1992	P	W	D	L	GF	GA
Did not qualify	-	-	-	-	-	-
Qualifying	8	2	4	2	10	9

1996	P	W	D	L	GF	GA
Did not qualify	-	-	-	-	-	-
Qualifying	8	2	2	4	7	13

2000	P	W	D	L	GF	GA
Did not qualify	-	-	-	-	-	-
Qualifying	10	3	3	4	14	10

2004	P	W	D	L	GF	GA
Did not qualify	-	-	-	-	-	-
Qualifying	8	3	2	3	15	9

2008	P	W	D	L	GF	GA
Did not qualify	-	-	-	-	-	-
Qualifying	12	4	0	8	11	22

2012	P	W	D	L	GF	GA
Did not qualify	-	-	-	-	-	-
Qualifying	10	6	1	3	22	14

Totals	P	W	D	L	GF	GA
Finals	4	1	0	3	5	6
Qualifying	109	46	22	41	183	151

Results & goals include extra time

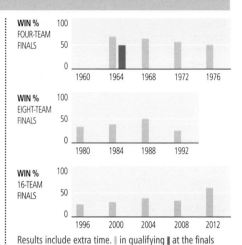

WIN %
FOUR-TEAM FINALS — 100 / 50 / 0
1960 1964 1968 1972 1976

WIN %
EIGHT-TEAM FINALS — 100 / 50 / 0
1980 1984 1988 1992

WIN %
16-TEAM FINALS — 100 / 50 / 0
1996 2000 2004 2008 2012

Results include extra time. ▌ in qualifying ▌ at the finals

LEGENDARY PLAYER

Part of the Mighty Magyars side that made it to the World Cup final in 1954 and, after the Hungarian uprising of 1956, a member of the Real Madrid team that dominated Europe, **Ferenc Puskas** had outrageous skill and a formidable scoring record.

FERENC PUSKAS · LEGEND

WORLD CUP RECORD

Year	Point of exit	Year	Point of exit
1930	Did not enter	1978	Group stage
1934	Quarter-finals	1982	Group stage
1938	● Runners-up	1986	Group stage
1950	Did not enter	1990	Did not qualify
1954	● Runners-up	1994	Did not qualify
1958	Group stage	1998	Did not qualify
1962	Quarter-finals	2002	Did not qualify
1966	Quarter-finals	2006	Did not qualify
1970	Did not qualify	2010	Did not qualify
1974	Did not qualify	2014	Did not qualify

DID YOU KNOW?

Hungary's players were shown more yellow cards – 38 – than any other team in qualifying, but none were sent off

HOW THEY QUALIFIED

Group F	P	W	D	L	F	A	GD	Pts
N Ireland	10	6	3	1	16	8	+8	21
Romania	10	5	5	0	11	2	+9	20
Hungary	10	4	4	2	11	9	+2	16
Finland	10	3	3	4	9	10	-1	12
Faroe Islands	10	2	0	8	6	17	-11	6
Greece	10	1	3	6	7	14	-7	6

Match stats in qualifying

Possession	▮▮▮▮▮▮▮▮▮	45%
Shots on target	▮▮▮▮▮▮▮▮▮▮▮	59%
Shots off target	▮▮▮▮▮▮▮▮▮▮	51%
Corners	▮▮▮▮▮▮▮▮▮	44%

Averages of match totals in qualifying. See pages 228-254 for full qualifying results

Results & prices

	W	D	L
Hungary....(0) 1-2 (0) ... N Ireland	1-2	10-3	7-1
Romania ... (1) 1-1 (0) .... Hungary	19-4	13-5	4-5
Faroes......(0) 0-1 (1) .... Hungary	1-3	5-1	9-1
Hungary....(0) 1-0 (0) ...... Finland	13-10	9-4	13-5
Hungary....(0) 0-0 (0) ....Greece	17-10	11-5	2-1
Finland .....(0) 0-1 (0) .... Hungary	12-5	11-5	6-4
Hungary....(0) 0-0 (0) ....Romania	2-1	21-10	9-5
N Ireland ..(0) 1-1 (0) .... Hungary	21-10	23-10	13-8
Hungary...(0) 2-1 (1) .... Faroes	3-10	9-2	14-1
Greece......(1) 4-3 (1) .... Hungary	9-4	21-10	8-5
Norway.....(0) 0-1 (1) ..... Hungary	15-4	12-5	20-21
Hungary...(1) 2-1 (0) ..... Norway	9-5	11-5	15-8

Profit & loss in qualifying 3.88 1.2 -1.4

Figures based on a £1 level stake using best odds in the Racing Post on day of match. W shows win price, whether home or away, L the price of the opposition

PLAYERS USED IN QUALIFYING

				CAREER		QUALIFYING			
Pos		Club	Age	P	G	P	G	▯	▮
GK	Denes Dibusz	Ferencvaros	25	4	-	1	-	-	-
GK	Peter Gulacsi	RB Leipzig	26	2	-	1	-	-	-
GK	Gabor Kiraly	Szom. Haladas	40	101	-	10	-	1	-
DEF	Attila Fiola	Puskas Akademia	26	13	-	10	-	1	-
DEF	Tamas Kadar	Lech Poznan	26	28	-	11	-	1	-
DEF	Gyula Forro	Puskas Akademia	28	3	-	1	-	-	-
DEF	Adam Pinter	Ferencvaros	27	19	-	2	-	1	-
DEF	Leandro Almeida	Ferencvaros	34	16	-	4	-	3	-
DEF	Richard Guzmics	Wisla Krakow	29	13	1	5	1	2	-
DEF	Mihaly Korhut	Debrecen	27	4	-	1	-	-	-
DEF	Zsolt Korcsmar	Vasa	27	24	-	1	-	1	-
DEF	Roland Juhasz	Videoton	32	90	6	9	-	3	-
DEF	Adam Lang	Videoton	23	9	-	4	-	1	-
DEF	Zoltan Liptak	Diosgyor	31	17	1	1	-	-	-
DEF	Vilmos Vanczak	FC Sion	32	80	4	2	-	1	-
MID	Balazs Balogh	Ujpest Dozsa	25	1	-	1	-	-	-
MID	Istvan Kovacs	Videoton	24	5	-	1	-	-	-
MID	Balazs Dzsudzsak	Bursaspor	29	76	18	12	1	2	-
MID	Daniel Tozser	QPR	31	31	1	8	-	3	-
MID	Zsolt Kalmar	FSV Frankfurt	21	7	-	3	-	-	-
MID	Jozsef Varga	Debrecen	28	31	-	3	-	1	-
MID	Akos Elek	Diosgyor	27	38	1	8	-	4	-
MID	Zoltan Stieber	Nuremberg	27	11	2	4	1	1	-
MID	Adam Bodi	Debrecen	25	1	-	1	-	-	-
MID	Adam Nagy	Ferencvaros	20	6	-	5	-	1	-
MID	Laszlo Kleinheisler	W Bremen	22	3	1	2	1	-	-
MID	Adam Simon	Videoton	26	3	-	1	-	-	-
MID	Zoltan Gera	Ferencvaros	37	87	24	9	1	5	-
MID	Gergo Lovrencsics	Lech Poznan	27	11	1	6	1	-	-
MID	Adam Gyurcso	Pogon Szczecin	25	13	1	7	1	-	-
ATT	Krisztian Simon	1860 Munich	25	4	-	1	-	-	-
ATT	Daniel Bode	Ferencvaros	29	11	4	3	2	2	-
ATT	Adam Szalai	Hannoer	28	30	8	8	1	1	-
ATT	Gergely Rudolf	Videoton	31	28	10	1	-	-	-
ATT	Krisztian Nemeth	Al-Gharafa	27	24	3	7	2	2	-
ATT	Nemanja Nikolic	Legia Warsaw	28	17	3	10	-	-	-
ATT	Tamas Priskin	Slovan Bratislava	29	55	17	8	2	1	-

HUNGARY

CORRECT SCORES

	Competitive	Friendly
1-0	5	2
2-0	1	-
2-1	2	-
3-0	-	1
3-1	1	-
3-2	-	-
4-0	-	1
4-1	-	-
4-2	-	-
4-3	-	-
0-0	2	-
1-1	3	4
2-2	1	1
3-3	-	-
4-4	-	-
0-1	-	-
0-2	-	1
1-2	1	2
0-3	1	-
1-3	-	-
2-3	-	-
0-4	-	-
1-4	1	-
2-4	-	-
3-4	1	-
Other	3	-

Since Euro 2012

HALF-TIME/FULL-TIME DOUBLE RESULTS

Win/Win	5	23%
Draw/Win	5	23%
Lose/Win	1	5%
Win/Draw	1	5%
Draw/Draw	4	18%
Lose/Draw	1	5%
Win/Lose	0	0%
Draw/Lose	2	9%
Lose/Lose	3	14%

Win 1st half	6	27%
Win 2nd half	9	41%
Win both halves	2	9%
Goal both halves	11	50%

Overall
- Win 50%
- Draw 27%
- Lose 23%

WIN 50%

Overall: W11, D6, L5 in 22 competitive games since Euro 2012

CLEAN SHEETS

9 (41%) **Clean sheets** 13 (59%)

7 (32%) **Win to nil** 15 (68%)

3 (14%) **Fail to score** 19 (86%)

1 (5%) **Lose to nil** 21 (95%)

UNDER & OVER GOALS

15 (68%) **Over 1.5** 7 (32%)

11 (50%) **Over 2.5** 11 (50%)

7 (32%) **Over 3.5** 15 (68%)

5 (23%) **Over 4.5** 17 (77%)

BOTH TEAMS TO SCORE

12 (55%) **Both score** 10 (45%)

4 (18%) **& win** 18 (82%)

4 (18%) **& lose** 18 (82%)

In 22 competitive games since Euro 2012

GOAL TIMES

Total match goals by half

12 (50%) **1st half** 12 (50%)
F ▮▮▮▮▮▮▮▮▮▮ ▮▮▮▮▮▮▮▮▮▮ A

23 (56%) **2nd half** 18 (44%)
F ▮▮▮▮▮▮▮▮▮▮▮▮ ▮▮▮▮▮▮▮▮▮ A

Goals for & against by half

12 (34%) **For** 23 (66%)
1st ▮▮▮▮▮▮▮ ▮▮▮▮▮▮▮▮▮▮▮▮▮ 2nd

12 (40%) **Against** 18 (60%)
1st ▮▮▮▮▮▮▮ ▮▮▮▮▮▮▮▮▮▮▮▮ 2nd

● GOALS FOR ● GOALS AGAINST

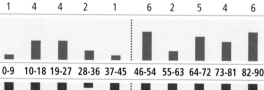

1	4	4	2	1	6	2	5	4	6
0-9	10-18	19-27	28-36	37-45	46-54	55-63	64-72	73-81	82-90
3	2	3	1	3	3	2	2	3	8

In 22 competitive games since Euro 2012

IF HUNGARY SCORE FIRST

They win	9	75%
Draw	2	17%
They lose	1	8%

In 22 competitive games since Euro 2012

IF HUNGARY CONCEDE FIRST

They win	2	25%
Draw	2	25%
They lose	4	50%

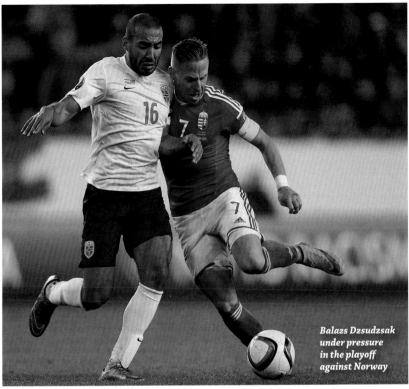

Balazs Dzsudzsak under pressure in the playoff against Norway

GOALSCORERS IN QUALIFYING

● FIRST GOALS

	Goals		1st		Anytime		Percentage of team goals	
T Priskin	2	●●	2	100%	2	25%	▮▮▮	14%
K Nemeth	2	●●	0	0%	1	14%	▮▮▮	14%
D Bode	2	●●	0	0%	1	33%	▮▮▮	14%
Z Gera	1	●	1	100%	1	11%	▮	7%
B Dzsudzsak	1	●	0	0%	1	8%	▮	7%
Z Stieber	1	●	1	100%	1	25%	▮	7%
A Szalai	1	●	1	100%	1	12%	▮	7%
G Lovrencsics	1	●	0	0%	1	16%	▮	7%
R Guzmics	1	●	1	100%	1	20%	▮	7%
L Kleinheisler	1	●	1	100%	1	50%	▮	7%

In Euro 2016 qualifying

BOOKINGS

Matches played	12	☐38	▮ 0
Average make-up (☐10 ▮25)			31.7

In Euro 2016 qualifying

CORNERS

Avg F	4.2	▮▮▮▮▮▮▮▮	44%
Avg A	5.3	▮▮▮▮▮▮▮▮▮▮	56%

In Euro 2016 qualifying. Avg match total 9.4

THE MEN IN THE MIDDLE

Numerous academic studies suggest that, as you would expect, referees have a profound impact on the result of a football match, as well as the numbers of goals, penalties and cards, writes Paul Charlton.

But the first dismissal at the European Championship finals had little impact on the match result, with Spanish referee Jose Maria Ortiz sending off England's Alan Mullery in the 89th minute of their 1968 semi-final against Yugoslavia. England were already trailing 1-0 to Dragan Dzajic's goal, scored just three minutes earlier. Mullery, famously, was the first ever England player to be sent off in their 424th international, but there was little time for Sir Alf Ramsey's side to get back into that particular game.

Czechoslovakia's 3-1 win over Holland in the 1976 tournament opener can perhaps lay claim to be the dirtiest match at the finals. Both teams were reduced to ten men by the hour mark and Dutch substitute Wim van Hanegem was sent off by Clive Thomas in the second half of extra time. Given there were only four games at the final tournament, that match alone made Euro 1976 the dirtiest, if the average red cards per game is the yardstick. Thomas also showed four yellow cards, still a relatively new innovation, during the 120 minutes of play.

In the modern 16-team era, Spain's group-stage draw with Bulgaria at Euro 96 saw Piero Ceccarini issue seven yellow cards and two reds. Nobody likes to see that, unless you've bought bookings – it made up 120.

The 18 referee appointments were announced in December, followed by the names of their assistants in February. There are a number of familiar faces on the list and

this group of referees are no strangers to the big occasion – between the moment Howard Webb blew the final whistle at the 2010 World Cup final and the end of 2015, they had been in charge of four out of five Europa League finals, four Champions League finals, five out of six Uefa Super Cups, one Fifa Club World Cup final, and, thanks to Nicola Rizzi, the final of the last World Cup.

Since the initial announcement, the officials have undergone a number of training courses but despite Uefa's best efforts, there are bound to be some controversies, and the impact of a refereeing decision can have ramifications later in the tournament – or even beyond.

A player who is booked in two separate matches will be suspended for the next match in the tournament, although yellow cards picked up during the finals will expire after the quarter-finals have been completed, reducing the likelihood of a player missing out on the final. A red card means a one-match suspension but this can be increased at Uefa's discretion for serious offences, including extending a ban into other competitions.

As for who might referee the final, Gottfried Dienst, the ref at Wembley in 1966, was the last final arbiter to have already officiated at a World Cup final, although Vojtech Christov, the ref in 1984, had run the line at the final in Spain two years earlier.

Pedro Proenca, the ref in the final in 2012, is the only man to have been in charge of the Champions League final in the same year and only the second ref since 1988 to have previously taken charge of Europe's biggest club match.

Nicola Rizzoli in charge of the World Cup final

RECENT INTERNATIONAL RECORDS OF EURO 2016 REFEREES

		Euro 2012				Brazil 2014				Euro 2016 qualifying					Avg
		G	🟨	🟨🟥	🟥	G	🟨	🟨🟥	🟥	Rank	G	🟨	🟨🟥	🟥	make-up
Cuneyt Cakir	TUR	3	16	1	0	3	11	0	0	16	6	27	2	1	57.5
William Collum	SCO	-	-	-	-	-	-	-	-	22	5	25	0	1	55.0
Mark Clattenburg	ENG	-	-	-	-	-	-	-	-	23	7	33	2	0	54.3
Milorad Mazic	SRB	-	-	-	-	2	3	0	1	26	6	25	1	1	50.0
Martin Atkinson	ENG	-	-	-	-	-	-	-	-	30	6	27	1	0	49.2
Pavel Kralovec	CZE	-	-	-	-	-	-	-	-	34	5	24	0	0	48.0
Bjorn Kuipers	NED	2	8	0	0	3	5	0	0	36	6	28	0	0	46.7
Jonas Eriksson	SWE	2	9	0	0	3	8	0	0	41	5	22	0	0	44.0
Damir Skomina	SVN	3	9	0	0	-	-	-	-	42	4	15	0	1	43.8
Sergey Karasev	RUS	-	-	-	-	-	-	-	-	44	3	8	0	2	43.3
Clement Turpin	FRA	-	-	-	-	-	-	-	-	50	3	12	0	0	40.0
Nicola Rizzoli	ITA	3	8	0	0	4	13	0	0	54	6	24	0	0	40.0
Carlos Velasco Carballo	ESP	2	3	1	1	3	8	0	0	61	6	21	1	0	39.2
Ovidiu Alin Hategan	ROU	-	-	-	-	-	-	-	-	62	4	10	0	2	37.5
Szymon Marciniak	POL	-	-	-	-	-	-	-	-	63	4	12	1	0	36.3
Svein Oddvar Moen	NOR	-	-	-	-	-	-	-	-	68	5	15	1	0	35.0
Viktor Kassai	HUN	2	12	0	0	-	-	-	-	71	3	10	0	0	33.3
Felix Brych	DEU	-	-	-	-	2	6	0	1	87	7	18	0	0	25.7

Tournament finals records do not include cards shown in extra time. Officials ranked by average bookings make-up in Euro 2016 qualification (highest first, 97 referees used in total). Make-ups 🟨 10pts 🟥 25pts, max 35pts per player

MARTIN ATKINSON (ENGLAND)   GAMES 6   ☐27 ▉1 ▉0   AVG MAKE-UP 49.2

Group I October 14, 2014
Serbia .... (0) 3-3 (0) .... Albania
................................Make-up 0

Group G November 15, 2014
Austria......... (0) 1-0 (0).......... Russia
▉▉▉3 ....Make-up 30

Group H June 12, 2015
Croatia......... (1) 1-1 (1)............... Italy
▉▉▉▉▉▉▉▉8 ▉1 ....Make-up 105

Group C September 8, 2015
Slovakia.......... (0) 0-0 (0).......... Ukraine
▉▉▉▉▉5 ....Make-up 50

Group A October 10, 2015
Czech Rep..... (0) 0-2 (0)............Turkey
▉▉▉▉▉▉6 ....Make-up 60

Playoffs November 17, 2015
Denmark....... (0) 2-2 (1).........Sweden
▉▉▉▉▉5 ....Make-up 50

FELIX BRYCH (GERMANY)   GAMES 7   ☐18 ▉0 ▉0   AVG MAKE-UP 25.7

Group I October 14, 2014
Denmark....... (0) 0-1 (0)........Portugal
▉1 ....Make-up 10

Group E November 15, 2014
San Marino... (0) 0-0 (0)..........Estonia
▉▉▉▉▉5 ....Make-up 50

Group A March 28, 2015
Holland......... (0) 1-1 (1)............Turkey
▉▉2 ....Make-up 20

Group B June 12, 2015
Wales............ (1) 1-0 (0)........ Belgium
▉▉2 ....Make-up 20

Group F September 4, 2015
Hungary .... (0) 0-0 (0)....... Romania
▉▉▉▉▉▉▉7 ....Make-up 70

Group H October 13, 2015
Italy .... (0) 2-1 (1)..........Norway
................................Make-up 0

Playoffs November 13, 2015
Bosnia-Hz..... (0) 1-1 (0)........... Ireland
▉1 ....Make-up 10

CUNEYT CAKIR (TURKEY)   GAMES 6   ☐27 ▉2 ▉1   AVG MAKE-UP 57.5

Group E September 8, 2014
Switzerland.. (0) 0-2 (0)........ England
▉▉2 ....Make-up 20

Group I November 14, 2014
Serbia .... (1) 1-3 (0)........Denmark
▉▉▉3 ....Make-up 30

Group C March 27, 2015
Spain .... (1) 1-0 (0).......... Ukraine
▉▉▉▉4 ....Make-up 40

Group F September 7, 2015
N Ireland ...... (0) 1-1 (0)........Hungary
▉▉▉▉▉▉▉7 ▉1 ....Make-up 95

Group D October 11, 2015
Poland .... (2) 2-1 (1)........... Ireland
▉▉▉▉▉5 ▉1 ....Make-up 75

Playoffs November 17, 2015
Slovenia........ (1) 1-1 (0).......... Ukraine
▉▉▉▉▉▉6 ▉1 ....Make-up 85

MARK CLATTENBURG (ENGLAND)   GAMES 7   ☐33 ▉2 ▉0   AVG MAKE-UP 54.3

Group F September 7, 2014
Greece .... (0) 0-1 (1)....... Romania
▉▉▉▉▉▉▉▉8 ▉1 ....Make-up 105

Group B November 16, 2014
Cyprus .... (3) 5-0 (0)........ Andorra
▉▉2 ....Make-up 20

Group B March 31, 2015
Israel .... (0) 0-1 (1)........ Belgium
▉▉▉▉▉▉6 ▉1 ....Make-up 85

Group G September 5, 2015
Russia............ (1) 1-0 (0)..........Sweden
▉▉▉▉4 ....Make-up 40

Group I October 8, 2015
Portugal .... (0) 1-0 (0)....... Denmark
▉▉▉▉▉5 ....Make-up 50

Group H October 13, 2015
Malta............ (0) 0-1 (1)..........Croatia
▉▉▉3 ....Make-up 30

Playoffs November 12, 2015
Norway......... (0) 0-1 (1)........Hungary
▉▉▉▉▉5 ....Make-up 50

WILLIAM COLLUM (SCOTLAND)   GAMES 5   ☐25 ▣0 ▮1   AVG MAKE-UP 55

Group F October 11, 2014
Romania ...... (1) 1-1 (0)........Hungary
▯▯▯▯▯▯▯▯▯▯▯ 12 .....Make-up 120

Group G November 15, 2014
Montenegro. (0) 1-1 (1).........Sweden
▯▯▯▯ 4 ....Make-up 40

Group A June 12, 2015
Iceland.......... (0) 2-1 (0)......Czech Rep
▯▯ 2 ....Make-up 20

Group I September 4, 2015
Denmark....... (0) 0-0 (0).........Albania
▯▯▯▯▯ 6 ....Make-up 60

Group H October 10, 2015
Azerbaijan.... (1) 1-3 (2)............... Italy
▯1 ▮1 ....Make-up 35

JONAS ERIKSSON (SWEDEN)   GAMES 5   ☐22 ▣0 ▮0   AVG MAKE-UP 44

Group A October 10, 2014
Turkey........... (1) 1-2 (1).....Czech Rep
▯1 ....Make-up 10

Group F November 14, 2014
Romania ...... (0) 2-0 (0).......N Ireland
▯▯▯▯▯ 5 ....Make-up 50

Group D March 29, 2015
Ireland.......... (0) 1-1 (1).......... Poland
▯▯▯▯▯▯▯▯ 8 ....Make-up 80

Group I September 7, 2015
Albania.......... (0) 0-1 (0).........Portugal
▯▯▯ 3 ....Make-up 30

Playoffs November 14, 2015
Ukraine.......... (1) 2-0 (0).......Slovenia
▯▯▯▯▯ 5 ....Make-up 50

OVIDIU ALIN HATEGAN (ROMANIA)   GAMES 4   ☐10 ▣0 ▮2   AVG MAKE-UP 37.5

Group H October 13, 2014
Malta............. (0) 0-1 (1)............... Italy
▯▯ 2 ▮▮ 2 ....Make-up 70

Group B March 28, 2015
Belgium .... (2) 5-0 (0)...........Cyprus
....Make-up 0

Group D September 4, 2015
Georgia .... (1) 1-0 (0)....... Scotland
▯▯▯ 3 ....Make-up 30

Group C October 9, 2015
Macedonia ... (0) 0-2 (0)......... Ukraine
▯▯▯▯▯ 5 ....Make-up 50

SERGEY KARASEV (RUSSIA)   GAMES 3   ☐8 ▣0 ▮2   AVG MAKE-UP 43.3

Group F March 29, 2015
Hungary .... (0) 0-0 (0).......... Greece
▯▯▯▯▯ 5 ....Make-up 50

Group H September 6, 2015
Italy .... (1) 1-0 (0)........Bulgaria
▯▯▯ 3 ▮▮ 2 ....Make-up 80

Group F October 11, 2015
Finland .... (0) 1-1 (1).......N Ireland
....Make-up 0

Referee's records in Euro 2016 qualifying. Bookings make-ups ☐ 10pts ▮ 25pts, maximum 35pts per player

BIGGEST BOOKINGS MAKE-UPS IN EURO 2016 QUALIFICATION

Match	Referee	Group	Date	☐	▣	▮	MU
Serbia .... (0) 1-2 (1)..... Portugal	David Fernandez Borbalan	Group I	Oct 11, 2015	8	1	1	130
Romania ... (1) 1-1 (0) .... Hungary	William Collum	Group F	Oct 11, 2014	12	0	0	120
Wales........ (2) 2-1 (1)........ Cyprus	Manual Grafe	Group B	Oct 13, 2014	9	0	1	115
Wales........ (0) 2-0 (0) .....Andorra	Kevin Blom	Group B	Oct 13, 2015	11	0	0	110
Lithuania .. (1) 2-1 (0) San Marino	Clayton Pisani	Group E	Sept 8, 2015	6	1	1	110
Croatia...... (1) 1-1 (1)............Italy	Martin Atkinson	Group H	Jun 12, 2015	8	1	0	105
Greece ...... (0) 0-1 (1)..... Romania	Mark Clattenburg	Group F	Sept 7, 2014	8	1	0	105
Bosnia-Hz. (3) 3-0 (0) .....Andorra	Arnold Hunter	Group B	Sept 6, 2015	5	0	2	100
Macedonia (1) 1-2 (1)....... Belarus	Anthony Taylor	Group C	Mar 27, 2015	10	0	0	100

VIKTOR KASSAI (HUNGARY) GAMES 3 ☐10 ☐0 ☐0 AVG MAKE-UP 33.3

Group I October 11, 2014
Albania......... (1) 1-1 (0)........Denmark
....Make-up 0

Group H September 6, 2015
Norway......... (0) 2-0 (0)..........Croatia
☐☐☐☐☐6 ....Make-up 60

Group D October 8, 2015
Scotland ...... (1) 2-2 (1).......... Poland
☐☐☐☐4 ....Make-up 40

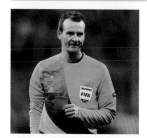

PAVEL KRALOVEC (CZECH REP) GAMES 5 ☐24 ☐0 ☐0 AVG MAKE-UP 48

Group G September 8, 2014
Austria........... (1) 1-1 (1)..........Sweden
☐☐☐☐4 ....Make-up 40

Group B November 16, 2014
Belgium .... (0) 0-0 (0)............Wales
☐☐☐☐4 ....Make-up 40

Group E March 27, 2015
England .... (2) 4-0 (0)....... Lithuania
☐☐☐3 ....Make-up 30

Group E September 5, 2015
Switzerland.. (0) 3-2 (1)........Slovenia
☐☐☐☐☐☐☐9 ....Make-up 90

Group D October 11, 2015
Germany....... (0) 2-1 (0)..........Georgia
☐☐☐4 ....Make-up 40

BJORN KUIPERS (HOLLAND) GAMES 6 ☐28 ☐0 ☐0 AVG MAKE-UP 46.7

Group C October 9, 2014
Slovakia........ (1) 2-1 (0).............Spain
☐☐☐☐☐☐☐7 ....Make-up 70

Group H November 16, 2014
Italy .... (1) 1-1 (1)..........Croatia
☐☐☐3 ....Make-up 30

Group I June 13, 2015
Denmark....... (1) 2-0 (0)............ Serbia
☐☐☐3 ....Make-up 30

Group D September 7, 2015
Scotland .... (2) 2-3 (2).......Germany
☐☐2 ....Make-up 20

Group E October 9, 2015
Slovenia........ (1) 1-1 (0)...... Lithuania
☐☐☐☐☐6 ....Make-up 60

Playoffs November 16, 2015
Ireland.......... (1) 2-0 (0)..... Bosnia-Hz.
☐☐☐☐☐☐☐7 ....Make-up 70

SZYMON MARCINIAK (POLAND) GAMES 4 ☐12 ☐1 ☐0 AVG MAKE-UP 36.3

Group E September 8, 2014
Estonia .... (0) 1-0 (0)........Slovenia
☐☐2 ☐1 ....Make-up 45

Group F March 29, 2015
N Ireland ...... (2) 2-1 (0)...........Finland
☐☐☐☐4 ....Make-up 40

Group B September 3, 2015
Cyprus .... (0) 0-1 (0)............Wales
....Make-up 0

Group I October 11, 2015
Armenia........ (0) 0-3 (2)...........Albania
☐☐☐☐☐6 ....Make-up 60

MILORAD MAZIC (SERBIA) GAMES 6 ☐25 ☐1 ☐1 AVG MAKE-UP 50

Group H September 9, 2014
Norway......... (0) 0-2 (1)............... Italy
☐☐☐☐4 ....Make-up 40

Group D November 14, 2014
Scotland ...... (0) 1-0 (0)............Ireland
☐☐☐☐☐6 ....Make-up 60

Group B March 28, 2015
Israel .... (0) 0-3 (1)............Wales
☐☐2 ☐1 ....Make-up 45

Group G June 14, 2015
Russia .... (0) 0-1 (1)..........Austria
☐☐2 ....Make-up 20

Group A September 3, 2015
Holland......... (0) 0-1 (0)..........Iceland
☐☐☐☐5 ☐1 ....Make-up 75

Group C October 12, 2015
Ukraine......... (0) 0-1 (1)..............Spain
☐☐☐☐☐6 ....Make-up 60

SVEIN ODDVAR MOEN (NORWAY)   GAMES 5 ☐15 ☖1 ■0 AVG MAKE-UP 35

Group D September 7, 2014

Germany....... (1) 2-1 (0)........ Scotland
☐☐☐☐☐5 ☖1 ....Make-up 75

Group E November 15, 2014

Switzerland.. (0) 4-0 (0)....... Lithuania
☐☐☐3 ....Make-up 30

Group A June 12, 2015

Latvia .... (0) 0-2 (0)..........Holland
☐☐2 ....Make-up 20

Group I September 7, 2015

Armenia........ (0) 0-0 (0).......Denmark
☐☐☐☐4 ....Make-up 40

Group G October 12, 2015

Russia .... (2) 2-0 (0).. Montenegro
☐1 ....Make-up 10

NICOLA RIZZOLI (ITALY)   GAMES 6 ☐24 ☖0 ■0 AVG MAKE-UP 40

Group G October 9, 2014

Sweden......... (0) 1-1 (1)............ Russia
☐☐☐☐☐5 ....Make-up 50

Group F November 14, 2014

Greece .... (0) 0-1 (0).Faroe Islands
☐☐☐☐4 ....Make-up 40

Group D June 13, 2015

Ireland.......... (1) 1-1 (0)....... Scotland
☐☐☐☐4 ....Make-up 40

Group D September 4, 2015

Germany....... (2) 3-1 (1).......... Poland
☐☐☐☐4 ....Make-up 40

Group I October 8, 2015

Albania......... (0) 0-2 (0)........... Serbia
☐☐☐☐☐5 ....Make-up 50

Playoffs November 14, 2015

Sweden......... (1) 2-1 (0).......Denmark
☐☐2 ....Make-up 20

DAMIR SKOMINA (SLOVENIA)   GAMES 4 ☐15 ☖0 ■1 AVG MAKE-UP 43.8

Group D October 14, 2014

Germany....... (0) 1-1 (0)...........Ireland
☐☐☐3 ....Make-up 30

Group H March 28, 2015

Bulgaria........ (2) 2-2 (1)............... Italy
☐☐☐☐4 ....Make-up 40

Group C September 5, 2015

Spain .... (2) 2-0 (0)........Slovakia
☐☐2 ....Make-up 20

Group A October 13, 2015

Holland......... (0) 2-3 (2).....Czech Rep
☐☐☐☐☐☐6 ■1 ....Make-up 85

CLEMENT TURPIN (FRANCE)   GAMES 3 ☐12 ☖0 ■0 AVG MAKE-UP 40

Group F November 14, 2014

Hungary .... (0) 1-0 (0)..........Finland
☐☐☐☐4 ....Make-up 40

Group D March 29, 2015

Georgia .... (0) 0-2 (2)........Germany
☐☐☐☐4 ....Make-up 40

Group A October 10, 2015

Kazakhstan .. (0) 1-2 (1)..........Holland
☐☐☐☐4 ....Make-up 40

CARLOS VELASCO CARBALLO (SPAIN)   GAMES 6 ☐21 ☖1 ■0 AVG MAKE-UP 39.2

Group A October 13, 2014

Iceland.......... (2) 2-0 (0)..........Holland
☐1 ....Make-up 10

Group H March 28, 2015

Croatia.......... (1) 5-1 (0).........Norway
☐☐☐☐☐☐6 ☖1 ....Make-up 85

Group F June 13, 2015

N Ireland ...... (0) 0-0 (0)....... Romania
☐☐☐☐4 ....Make-up 40

Group G September 8, 2015

Sweden......... (0) 1-4 (2)...........Austria
☐☐☐☐4 ....Make-up 40

Group D October 8, 2015

Ireland.......... (0) 1-0 (0).......Germany
☐☐2 ....Make-up 20

Playoffs November 15, 2015

Hungary .... (1) 2-1 (0)..........Norway
☐☐☐☐4 ....Make-up 40

TOURNAMENT TRENDS

Paul Charlton looks at what punters can learn from past tournaments

Hosts France celebrate with the trophy in 1984

Home advantage

Historically, the hosts can boast a 21 per cent strike-rate in the European Championships, with three winners and a beaten finalist in the 14 editions so far.

Of course, that includes the first five tournaments, in which the hosts were one of only four teams at the finals, but even after the format changed to eight teams in 1980 and then 16 in 1996, the hosts or co-hosts of seven tournaments in succession reached at least the semi-finals.

However, that run came to an end eight years ago, with co-hosts Austria and Switzerland both going out in the group stage in 2008, and Poland and Ukraine following suit four years later. While the co-hosts were among the weakest sides in the two tournaments, for all four teams, those early exits represented their best performances at the finals – and for Ukraine and Austria, their tournament debuts. Overall, five of the ten hosts or co-hosts, excluding tournament debutants, at least matched their previous best performance at the finals.

Portugal, in 2004, were the last hosts to reach the final. And the last hosts to win it? France in 1984.

EUROPEAN CHAMPIONSHIP HOSTS

	Hosts	Teams	Performance
1960	**France***	4	Semi-finalists
1964	**Spain***	4	**Winners**
1968	**Italy***	4	**Winners**
1972	**Belgium***	4	Semi-finalists
1976	**Yugoslavia**	4	Semi-finalists
1980	**Italy**	8	Semi-finalists
1984	**France**	8	**Winners**
1988	**West Germany**	8	Semi-finalists
1992	**Sweden***	8	Semi-finalists
1996	**England**	16	Semi-finalists
2000	**Belgium**	16	Group stage
	Holland		Semi-finalists
2004	**Portugal**	16	Beaten finalists
2008	**Austria***	16	Group stage
	Switzerland		Group stage
2012	**Poland**	16	Group stage
	Ukraine*	16	Group stage

*Finals debut

Performance at previous tournament

In 1984, the second European Championship finals with eight teams, winners France had failed to qualify for the previous tournament

EUROPEAN CHAMPIONSHIP FINALISTS AT PREVIOUS TOURNAMENT

	Winners	Previous Euros	Runners-up	Previous Euros
1964	Spain	Did not qualify	USSR	Winners
1968	Italy	Did not qualify	Yugslovia	Did not qualify
1972	West Germany	Did not qualify	USSR	Semi-finals
1976	Czechoslovakia	Did not qualify	West Germany	Winners
1980	West Germany	Beaten finalists	Belgium	Did not qualify
1984	France	Did not qualify	Spain	Group stage
1988	Holland	Did not qualify	USSR	Did not qualify
1992	Denmark	Group stage	Germany	Semi-finals
1996	Germany	Beaten finalists	Czech Republic	Did not qualify
2000	France	Semi-finals	Italy	Group stage
2004	Greece	Did not qualify	Portugal	Semi-finals
2008	Spain	Group stage	Germany	Group stage
2012	Spain	Winners	Italy	Quarter-finals

EUROPEAN CHAMPIONSHIP FINALISTS AT PREVIOUS WORLD CUP

	Winners	Previous World Cup	Runners-up	Previous World Cup
1960	USSR	Quarter-finals	Yugoslavia	Quarter-finals
1964	Spain	Group stage	USSR	Quarter-finals
1968	Italy	Group stage	Yugslovia	Did not qualify
1972	West Germany	Third place	USSR	Quarter-finals
1976	Czechoslovakia	Did not qualify	West Germany	Winners
1980	West Germany	Second group stage	Belgium	Did not qualify
1984	France	Fourth place	Spain	Second group stage
1988	Holland	Did not qualify	USSR	Round of 16
1992	Denmark	Did not qualify	Germany	Winners*
1996	Germany	Quarter-finals	Czech Republic	Did not qualify
2000	France	Winners	Italy	Quarter-finals
2004	Greece	Did not qualify	Portugal	Group stage
2008	Spain	Round of 16	Germany	Third place
2012	Spain	Winners	Italy	Group stage

*As West Germany

and runners-up Spain had gone out in the group stage with just one point. Four years later, neither of the two finalists, Holland and USSR, had qualified for Euro 84.

Since then, Czech Republic, runners-up in 1996, and Greece, winners in 2004, have reached the final without taking part in the previous tournament while Denmark, Italy, Spain and Germany have all reached the final after going out in the group stage four years earlier. Spain are the only team to have retained the trophy and Germany are the only other team to have reached the final two tournaments running since the four-team format was ditched for Euro 1980.

Performance at previous World Cup

Coming just two years before the European Championships, the World Cup should be a decent yardstick. Of the seven defending world champions to contest the Euros, there have been two winners, France in 2000 and Spain in 2012, and two beaten finalists, West Germany in 1976 and the newly unified Germany in 1992, who had won the World Cup as West Germany in 1990.

WORLD CUP WINNERS AT THE EUROS

	World Cup winners	Performance at subsequent Euros
1966	England	Third
1974	West Germany	Beaten finalists
1982	Italy	Did not qualify
1990	West Germany	Beaten finalists*
1998	France	Winners
2006	Italy	Quarter-finals
2010	Spain	Winners

*As Germany

But against that, seven of the 28 European finalists since 1960 – most recently Greece in 2004 – had failed to qualify for the World Cup and two of the last three beaten finalists had gone out of the previous World Cup in the group stage.

Performance in qualifying

Since Euro 96, the first 16-team final tournament, 14 nations have qualified via a playoff – one in 1996, four in 2000 and 2012, and five in 2004. Nine of those teams went out in the group stage, three went out in the quarter-finals – the first of the knockout rounds – and two went as far as the semi-finals, with one of those, Portugal, knocking out their fellow playoff winners, Czech Republic, in the last 16 four years ago.

The Czechs were the only team in the five 16-team final tournaments to qualify via the playoffs and win their group but even then it was a relatively easy section containing Greece, Russia and co-hosts Poland, and they were able to top the table with a negative goal difference.

Spain and Germany took maximum points in qualifying for Euro 2012 – Spain won it and Germany reached the semis – but the best performers in terms of average points per game in qualifying have not always translated that dominance into a strong showing at the finals.

Czech Republic and Greece went out in the group stages of Euro 2000 and Euro 2008, while Spain and Russia, joint-best qualifiers for Euro 96 went out in the quarter-finals and group stage respectively. The Czechs took maximum points from their Euro 2000 qualifying group as did France ahead of Euro 2004, but the defending champions went no further than the quarters.

Germany in 1996 and Spain in 2012 were the only winners of a 16-team Euros to have qualified with an average of 2.5 points a

HOW THE WINNERS QUALIFIED

Winner	Pos	P	W	D	L	F	A	GD	Pts	Avg
1996 Germany	1	10	8	1	1	27	10	+17	25	2.50
'00 France	1	10	6	3	1	17	10	+7	21	2.10
'04 Greece	1	8	6	0	2	8	4	+4	18	2.25
'08 Spain	1	12	9	1	2	23	8	+15	28	2.33
'12 Spain	1	8	8	0	0	26	6	+20	24	3.00

Avg average points per game

game or greater but it's worth noting that each of the last five winners topped their qualifying group.

Top scorers

Fernando Torres won the Golden Boot at Euro 2012 but the key fact for punters was that six players dead-heated for top scorer honours. Three of the five 16-team final tournaments since Euro 96 saw a player finish alone as top scorer and all three played for teams that got at least as far as the semi-finals.

The format is different this time and there might be less chance of your top scorer bet ending in a disappointing draw. In the three World Cups that used the Euro 2016 format, Gary Lineker and Toto Schillaci top-scored in isolation in 1986 and 1990, with Hristo Stoichkov and Oleg Salenko sharing the honours at USA 94. Russia didn't even get out of the group stage and Salenko got five of his six goals in their game against Cameroon so that can probably be dismissed as a freak occurrence. Bulgaria and Italy reached the semi-finals and England reached the last eight in 1986.

An extra round of knockout matches – potentially an extra 120 minutes for every striker involved to score – should help reduce the chances of a dead-heat and, with the addition of eight extra teams, some of them weaker than the usual high-class field that makes up the group stage, there should be more opportunities for the top strikers.

Overall at the last five tournament finals, 31 of the 42 goals (74 per cent) scored by the 11 players who top-scored or dead-heated for top-scorer came in the group stage, with only three of those getting more than a single goal in the knockout rounds.

And don't read too much into goals scored in qualification as that hasn't been much of a guide in recent years. None of the top scorers in qualifying for the five tournaments since Euro 96 have finished as top scorer at the finals, with Davor Suker, who tied for second at Euro 96 after top-scoring with 12 goals in qualifying, coming closest.

Klaas-Jan Huntelaar was top scorer with 12 goals in qualifying for Euro 2012 but drew a blank at the finals, and of the six players who dead-heated in Poland and Ukraine, Cristiano Ronaldo did best in the build up

	Top scorer	Country	Goals		Finish	Club	League	Goals	Top scorer?
1996	**Alan Shearer**	England	5	●●●●●	SF	Blackburn	England	31	✓
2000	**Savo Milosevic**	Yugoslavia	5	●●●●●	QF	Real Zaragoza	Spain	21	✗
	Patrick Kluivert	Holland	5	●●●●●	SF	Barcelona	Spain	15	✗
2004	**Milan Baros**	Czech Rep	5	●●●●●	SF	Liverpool	England	1	✗
2008	**David Villa**	Spain	4	●●●●	W	Barcelona	Spain	18	✗
2012	**Cristiano Ronaldo**	Portugal	3	●●●	SF	Real Madrid	Spain	46	✗
	Mario Gomez	Germany	3	●●●	SF	Bayern Munich	Germany	26	✗
	Mario Balotelli	Italy	3	●●●	F	Manchester City	England	13	✗
	Mario Mandzukic	Croatia	3	●●●	GS	Wolfsburg	Germany	12	✗
	Fernando Torres	Spain	3	●●●	W	Chelsea	England	6	✗
	Alan Dzagoev	Russia	3	●●●	GS	CSKA Moscow	Russia	5	✗

Clubs and league goals in season preceding European Championship finals. Finish shows point of exit from Euros. **GS** group stage, **QF** quarter-finals, **SF** semi-finals, **F** beaten finalists, **W** winners

as one of four players on seven goals. David Villa, top scorer at Euro 2008, got seven in qualifying – six players scored more – while Milan Baros got three in qualifying for Euro 2004, two fewer than he grabbed at the finals. Savo Milosevic and Patrick Kluivert, who each got five goals at Euro 2000, only managed four between them in qualifying – and with Holland co-hosting, Milosevic got them all. Like Kluivert, Alan Shearer, the top scorer at Euro 96, was playing for the hosts so took no part in the qualifiers.

Note too, that Shearer was the last player to be top scorer both at the Euros and in his domestic league. He notched 31 goals in 1995-96, a record that still has not been beaten in a 38-game Premier League season.

Milosevic, Mario Gomez and Ronaldo all put in very respectable league campaigns ahead of the European Championships where they were top scorers or joint-top scorers – Ronaldo got 46 in Spain in 2011-12 only to be beaten by Lionel Messi – but Baros only scored once ahead of Euro 2004, while Alan Dzagoev and Torres got 11 league goals between them in Russia and England in the season before Euro 2012.

Seeded in group stage

Being seeded for the group-stage draw has not been such an advantage at recent European Championships, partly due to some weak hosts and co-hosts and the sheer strength in depth of the field.

Only one of the four teams in Pot One at the draw made it out of the group stage at

Euro 2008 and Euro 2012, and Euro 2004 is the only 16-team final tournament to see all four seeds win their groups.

However, all 18 seeded teams at the three World Cups to use the new format qualified for the knockout rounds, albeit with six of those – including four of the six seeds at USA 94 – getting through in third place. Five of the six World Cup finalists and two of the three winners at those tournaments were seeded for the group-stage draw.

The seeds for the Euro 2016 draw were France (as hosts), Spain, Germany, England, Portugal and Belgium.

Position in group stage

The new format for the final tournament is the same as that used for the 1986, 1990 and 1994 World Cups (minus the third-place match), with the four best third-placed teams qualifying from the group stage.

In each of those World Cups, three of the four third-placed sides went out in the first knockout round but, of the three teams that did get past the last 16, two, Argentina in 1990 and Italy in 1994, made it to the final.

Euro 96 winners Germany and beaten finalists Czech Republic finished first and second in Group C, runners-up Italy won their group in 2000 but winners France finished second behind Holland, runners-up Portugal finished ahead of winners Greece in Group A in 2004, defending champions Spain won their groups in both 2008 and 2012, with Germany, beaten finalists in 2008, finishing second in their section in

*Alan Shearer
at Euro 96*

2008 and Italy finishing second behind Spain in Group C four years ago.

Spain in 2008 were the only winners in the last five editions to take maximum points in the group stage.

Total goals

In the five 16-team European Championships, goals have become more scarce as the tournament has progressed. The group stages of Euro 96 to Euro 2012 have averaged 2.51 goals a game, with the quarter-finals, semi-finals and finals averaging 2.0, 1.8 and 2.0 goals in 90 minutes.

The three 24-team World Cups to use the format for Euro 2016 have followed a similar pattern, averaging 2.4 goals in the group stage, 2.5 in the last 16 and then, as the remaining runners get stronger and the

stakes get higher, 2.17 in the quarters, 2.0 in the semis and 2.0 in the final. Again, these figures do not include extra time.

TOURNAMENT GOALS AT THE EUROS

	1996	'00	'04	'08	'12	Avg
Group stage	55	65	64	57	60	2.51
Quarter-finals	4	14	6	7	9	2.00
Semi-finals	2	2	3	8	3	1.80
Final	2	2	1	1	4	2.00

TOURNAMENT GOALS – WORLD CUP

	1986	1990	1994	Avg
Group stage	84	82	93	2.40
Round of 16	23	13	24	2.50
Quarter-finals	7	6	13	2.17
Semi-finals	4	4	4	2.00
Final	5	1	0	2.00

Avg average goals per game

NO MIDDLE GROUND

The history of betting on the Euros

Feast or famine – that's the story of past European Championship outright markets for punters and bookmakers alike, writes Mark Langdon.

History suggests that finding the middle ground in Euro 2016 is about as likely as finding one of the locals wearing a jersey in support of hated Tour de France champion Chris Froome.

Greece's 100-1 triumph has gone down as one of sport's greatest shocks, but the European Championship has thrown up its fair share of surprises since football betting gained popularity among punters.

At Euro 88, Holland reigned supreme, while the leaders of the eight-team market, favourites West Germany and 5-1 shots England, fell short.

Denmark, 18-1 and seventh of eight nations in the Euro 92 betting, were victorious despite only being parachuted into the tournament at short notice to replace disqualified Yugoslavia.

And at Euro 96, each-way punters could have taken 80-1 about beaten finalists Czech Republic. In fact, the Czechs drifted to 150-1 with a couple of firms after losing their opening game, but the tournament was won by favourites Germany and bookmakers had to wait another eight years before they could celebrate the most ridiculous of underdog triumphs.

Ladbrokes reckoned at the time that Greece's win was "their best ever tournament result" and Coral said they had "scooped the lot" although William Hill did report one Woking-based punter had £4,000 on the Greeks at 50-1 during the tournament and another £8,000 five days later.

One Betfair punter managed to secure £2 at 499-1 about Greece lifting the trophy in Lisbon, while bookmakers were trembling at the prospect of a monster payout on

Greek celebrations in 2004

England before their quarter-final exit on penalties to hosts Portugal.

It wasn't all a bookmakers' benefit, with Milan Baros a relatively well-backed 66-1 Golden Boot winner, but the matches were generally a shocker, all started by Greece's defeat of 8-13 shots Portugal in the first match of the competition.

The Greeks were still 5-2 pokes going into the final, and 2004 will always be known as the year of the underdog by football punters, who were still reeling from Porto's 66-1 success in the Champions League final against 125-1 rags Monaco.

However, in between the Greek tragedy and great Danes bringing home the bacon, punters have also dished some heavy punishments and bookies are still scarred by the battering they received in 2000 when Racing Post Sport's heavily supported outright selection France obliged at 13-2.

Les Bleus needed an injury-time equaliser and a golden goal to do the World Cup-European Championship double, and it was a tournament in which a whopping 18 match favourites won.

Sportingbet's veteran PR man Russ Wiseman could still recall the pain when he spoke to the Racing Post 14 years later.

"It was a shocker", he said. "A real disaster zone for us at Bet Direct at the time and I know other firms were even worse off."

Coral alone lost 40 per cent of its annual profits through its then internet site Eurobet, who had dipped their toes into the foreign world of Asian handicaps and those firms who were beaten black and blue were fortunate that football turnover was just beginning to take off.

By 2008 it was all the rage and business was booming, despite England's absence from the finals in Austria and Switzerland. If anything, British punters were eager to bet so they could have a team to follow through the tournament, and Spain's star-studded squad, which included English-based quartet Cesc Fabregas, Fernando Torres, Xabi Alonso and Pepe Reina, ticked all the boxes at 11-2.

Bet365's Steve Freeth called the tournament "carnage" and added "the final was the worst football result in our history" as a tremendously well-backed Torres scored the only goal in a 1-0 success over Germany and was named man of the match to the delight of those who followed him in just about every market possible.

Hills reported a £50,000 bet on La Roja at 11-2 ante-post and Ladbrokes a £30,000 punt at 4-1, but there were streams of other smaller wagers. Coral's industry-estimated losses of upwards of £5m seemed on the low side at the time considering Paddy Power and BoyleSports both reckoned their losses were each in excess of £1m on their own.

Spain then repeated the trick as 3-1 joint-favourites four years ago with a demolition job on Italy in the final to continue the feast or famine theme.

So that's that then. Feast or famine. Split the stakes on France and Northern Ireland...

The idea for a European football championship was first mooted in 1927 by Henri Delaunay, the secretary of the French FA, but it was more than 30 years later that the first ball was kicked.

The inaugural Uefa European Nations Cup got off to a low-key start with Europe's two World Cup-winning nations, Italy and West Germany, opting out, along with Sweden, the beaten finalists in 1958, and all four of the Home Nations.

That left 17 teams for the qualifying rounds and although Ireland contested a preliminary stage – they were knocked out by Czechoslovakia – it was USSR's Anatoli Ilyin who had the honour of scoring the first goal in a 3-1 win over Hungary in the first round.

But qualifying didn't go entirely smoothly. The Soviet Union were drawn with Spain for the quarter-finals, the last round of games before the four-team final tournament, but USSR were refused entry into Spain by General Franco and received a bye into the finals.

France were selected as hosts, but without Just Fontaine – scorer of 13 goals in the 1958 World Cup and Europe's top scorer with five goals during qualification – they were swiftly eliminated by Yugoslavia in a 5-4 thriller.

In the final, Yugoslavia met USSR, who had beaten Czechoslovakia 3-0 in the other semi. Milan Galic, who had netted first against the French, opened the scoring for Yugoslavia with a glancing near-post header just before half-time, but Slava Metreveli equalised soon after the break, tapping in after Blagoje Vidinic spilled a save. Viktor Ponedelnik headed the USSR's winner in extra time.

CLUBS IN WINNING SQUADS

18	Bayern Munich
15	Barcelona
13	Real Madrid
9	B M'gladbach, Bordeaux
8	Dortmund
7	Inter, Milan, Monaco, Slovan Bratislava, Valencia
6	Juventus, Zaragoza, Panathinaikos,
5	AEK Athens, Ajax, Arsenal, Chelsea, Cologne, Liverpool, PSV, Werder Bremen

Top 20 clubs with most players in winning squads (all time). Source: Wikipedia

Michel Platini's record tally of goals at Euro 84

HOME-BASED WINNERS

USSR (1960), Italy (1968), West Germany (1972), Czechoslovakia (1976)

TOURNAMENT SUMMARY

Winners USSR **Runners-up** Yugoslavia

Total entries 17   **Finals debutants** Czechoslovakia, France, USSR, Yugoslavia

Top scorers Galic (Yugoslavia), Heutte (France), Ivanov (USSR), Jerkovic (Yugoslavia), Ponedelnik (USSR) **all 2 goals**

Overs % by round · BTTS % by round · Goals at the finals · Overs 50% · BTTS 50%

	Total games	Total goals	Avg goals	Over 2.5 goals		Both score	
Final	1	2	2	0	0%	1	100%
Third place	1	2	2	0	0%	0	0%
Semi-finals	2	12	6	2	100%	1	50%
Totals	4	16	4	2	50%	2	50%
Qualifying	24	91	3.79	15	63%	13	54%

Only goals scored in normal time are counted (except goalscorers)

Semi-finals
USSR .... (1) 3-0 (0) . Czechoslovakia
France .... (1) 4-5 (1) .... Yugoslavia

3rd/4th place playoff
France .... (0) 0-2 (0) . Czechoslovakia

Final
USSR .... (0) 2-1 (1) .... Yugoslavia
AET. 1-1 after 90 mins

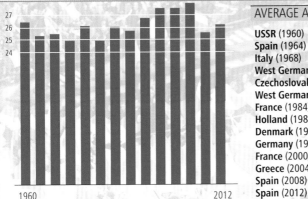

AVERAGE AGES OF WINNING SQUADS

USSR (1960)	26 years 170 days
Spain (1964)	25 years 137 days
Italy (1968)	25 years 192 days
West Germany (1972)	24 years 342 days
Czechoslovakia (1976)	26 years 55 days
West Germany (1980)	24 years 346 days
France (1984)	26 years 21 days
Holland (1988)	25 years 264 days
Denmark (1992)	26 years 284 days
Germany (1996)	27 years 201 days
France (2000)	27 years 192 days
Greece (2004)	27 years 347 days
Spain (2008)	25 years 219 days
Spain (2012)	26 years 91 days

Overall average 26 years 85 days. Ages of outfield players on the opening day of the tournament. Source: Wikipedia

95% France (1984), **91%** West Germany (1980), Germany (1996), **90%** Spain (1964), **78%** Spain (2008, 2012), **75%** Holland (1988), **65%** Denmark (1992), Greece (2004), **32%** France (2000)

Percentage of squad members playing in national league of winning nation. Source: Wikipedia

---

SPAIN 1964

There were 29 teams involved in 1964 but the format stayed the same – home and away knockout rounds leading to a four-team final tournament. England made their first appearance, losing 6-3 on aggregate to France in the preliminary round of qualifying. But the Dutch endured the greatest shame, losing 3-2 on aggregate to Luxembourg, despite both legs being played in Holland.

Spain were selected to host with Hungary, Denmark – conquerors of the mighty Luxembourg – and USSR making up the final four.

This time the Soviets were allowed in. The defending champions blitzed the Danes 3-0 while the hosts needed extra-time to beat the Magyars and set up the match that should have happened four years earlier.

Both sides scored within the first eight minutes, Spain taking the lead through Jesus Pereda's close-range strike and Galimzian Khusainov levelling from a free-kick two minutes later. It remained level until Real Zaragoza striker Marcelino buried a stooping header for the hosts six minutes from time.

TOURNAMENT SUMMARY

Winners Spain **Runners-up** USSR

Total entries 29   **Finals debutants** Denmark, Hungary, Spain

Top scorers Bene (Hungary), Novak (Hungary), Pereda (Spain) **all 2 goals**

Overs % by round   BTTS % by round   Goals at the finals

Q SF 3rd F   Q SF 3rd F   Overs 50%   BTTS 75%

	Total games	Total goals	Avg goals	Over 2.5 goals		Both score	
Final	1	3	3	1	100%	1	100%
Third place	1	2	2	0	0%	1	100%
Semi-finals	2	5	2.5	1	50%	1	50%
Totals	**4**	**10**	**2.5**	**2**	**50%**	**3**	**75%**
Qualifying	48	156	3.25	26	54%	33	69%

Only goals scored in normal time are counted (except goalscorers)

Semi-finals
Spain.............. (1) 2-1 (0) ....Hungary
AET. 1-1 after 90 mins
USSR .... (2) 3-0 (0) ....Denmark

3rd/4th place playoff
Hungary......... (1) 3-1 (0) ....Denmark
AET. 1-1 after 90 mins

Final
Spain.............. (1) 2-1 (1)...............USSR

There was a new qualifying format in 1968 and a new name, as the Uefa European Championship adopted its current title.

West Germany, World Cup finalists in 1966, made their tournament debut in the new qualifying groups, but failed to reach the two-legged quarter-finals that preceded the four-team final tournament after finishing second in qualifying to Yugoslavia. A 1-0 defeat in Belgrade and a 0-0 draw away to pointless Albania saw them eliminated early.

England reached the quarters ahead of Scotland, Wales and Northern Ireland in a group that used the results of the Home Championships, and the World Cup holders knocked out European champions Spain 3-1 on aggregate, thanks to goals from Bobby Charlton, Martin Peters and Norman Hunter. However, like the Germans, England fell foul of Yugoslavia in the semi-finals.

Yugoslavia's opponents in the final were hosts Italy, who were making their debut appearance and had a lucky coin toss to thank for their passage past the Soviet Union after their semi-final finished goalless.

The final, at Rome's Stadio Olimpico, was also tight. Dragan Dzajic opened the scoring shortly before the break and Angelo Domenghini nearly produced an almost instant response, a thunderous shot crashing off the woodwork. But he hit the target with ten minutes to go,

his low free-kick somehow finding its way through the Yugoslavian wall.

Italy bossed the replay two days later, with Luigi Riva finding the net on 13 minutes and Pietro Anastasi grabbing the second with a stunning turn and volley shortly after the half-hour mark to wrap things up.

Semi-finals
Yugoslavia ..... (0) 1-0 (0) .... England
Italy .... (0) 0-0 (0) .... USSR
AET – result decided by coin toss

3rd/4th place playoff
England.......... (1) 2-0 (0) .... USSR

Final
Italy .... (0) 1-1 (1) .... Yugoslavia
AET. 1-1 after 90 mins

Final replay
Italy .... (2) 2-0 (0) ...... Yugoslavia

The Italian team pose after beating Yugoslavia in the replay

TOURNAMENT SUMMARY

Winners Italy **Runners-up** Yugoslavia

Total entries 31   **Finals debutants** England, Italy

Top scorer Dzajic (Yugoslavia) **2 goals**

Overs % by round	BTTS % by round	Goals at the finals
Q PO SF 3rd F	Q PO SF 3rd F	Overs 0% BTTS 20%

	Total games	Total goals	Avg goals	Over 2.5 goals	Both score
Final	2	4	2	0	0%	1	50%
Third place	1	2	2	0	0%	0	0%
Semi-finals	2	1	0.5	0	0%	0	0%
Totals	5	7	1.4	0	0%	1	20%
Playoffs	8	24	3	4	50%	4	50%
Qualifying	90	282	3.13	53	59%	45	50%

Only goals scored in normal time are counted (except goalscorers)

Franz Beckenbauer takes the trophy

West Germany and hosts Belgium were debutants at the four-team final tournament, Belgium having knocked out defending champions Italy in their two-legged quarter-final and the Germans seeing off England 3-1 on aggregate with the help of two late goals in the first leg at Wembley.

They faced each other in the semi-finals, with Odilon Polleunis's late goal scant consolation after Gerd Muller had bagged a brace.

The Soviet Union beat Hungary in the other semi, but despite reaching their third final in four tournaments, USSR were no match for the Germans.

Franz Beckenbauer, who went on to win Uefa's European Footballer of the Year award, was impeccable in the sweeper role and Muller, who was on the way

Semi-finals
Belgium.......... (0) 1-2 (1)..... W Germany
USSR .... (0) 1-0 (0) ....Hungary

3rd/4th place playoff
Belgium.......... (1) 2-1 (0) ....Hungary

Final
W Germany.... (1) 3-0 (0) ....USSR

to scoring 85 goals in the calendar year – a record that stood until Lionel Messi broke it in 2012 – netted another double either side of Herbert Wimmer's precise finish.

TOURNAMENT SUMMARY

Winners West Germany **Runners-up** USSR

Total entries 32   **Finals debutants** Belgium, West Germany

Top scorer G Muller (West Germany) **4 goals**

Overs % by round   **BTTS % by round**   **Goals at the finals**

Q PO SF 3rd F   Q PO SF 3rd F   Overs 75%   BTTS 50%

	Total games	Total goals	Avg goals	Over 2.5 goals		Both score	
Final	1	3	3	1	100%	0	0%
Third place	1	3	3	1	100%	1	100%
Semi-finals	2	4	2	1	50%	1	50%
Totals	4	10	2.5	3	75%	2	50%
Playoffs	9	19	2.11	5	55.56%	5	55.56%
Qualifying	96	263	2.74	50	52.08%	37	38.54%

Only goals scored in normal time are counted (except goalscorers)

Wales went closest of the home nations to reaching the last of the four-team tournaments but, trailing 2-0 from the first leg against Yugoslavia in Zagreb, a harsh penalty decision at Ninian Park left the Dragons needing three goals to take the tie to extra time.

Ian Evans got one back before half time but Wales's luck was out. John Toshack had two efforts disallowed, and Terry Yorath missed a penalty.

The victors went on to host a tournament which opened with Czechoslovakia taking on Johan Cruyff's Holland in a downpour in the first semi-final in Zagreb.

TOURNAMENT SUMMARY

Winners Czechoslovakia **Runners-up** West Germany

Total entries 32   **Finals debutants** Holland

Top scorers D Muller (West Germany) **4 goals**

Overs % by round

Q PO SF 3rd F

BTTS % by round

Q PO SF 3rd F

Goals at the finals

Overs 75%   BTTS 100%

	Total games	Total goals	Avg goals	Over 2.5 goals		Both score	
Final	1	4	4	1	100%	1	100%
Third place	1	4	4	1	100%	1	100%
Semi-finals	2	6	3	1	50%	2	100%
Totals	4	14	3.5	3	75%	4	100%
Playoffs	8	22	2.75	3	38%	4	50%
Qualifying	96	267	2.78	54	56%	48	50%

Only goals scored in normal time are counted (except goalscorers)

HISTORY

John Toshack's diving header against Yugoslavia was disallowed

The Czechs needed extra time to get past the Dutch, with Anton Ondrus opening the scoring with a header in the first half and then levelling the match with 13 minutes to go with a spectacular volley into his own net. Zdenek Nehoda and Frantisek Vesely spared the Slovan Bratislava defender's blushes with goals deep into extra time.

Meanwhile, Germany, the defending world and European champions, had been paired with the hosts, and they needed 120 minutes to get the job done after Danilo Popivoda and Dragan Dzajic had put Yugoslavia two up in the first half hour. Heinz Flohe got one back and then it was

Muller to the rescue.

Gerd Muller had retired from international football after scoring the winner in the 1974 World Cup final, but Dieter Muller – no relation – matched Der Bomber's 1972 championship record by also netting four goals at the finals, starting with a hat-trick against Yugoslavia. He levelled with eight minutes to go then put his side two clear in the final five minutes of extra time.

In the final, Germany again quickly found themselves two goals down, Jan Svehlik and Karol Dobias punishing some slack German defending, before Muller responded. Bernd Holzenbein's headed equaliser in the dying seconds sent the match to

extra time but the score remained level and, for the first time, penalties were needed to decide a major international final.

The first seven spot kicks all went in but then Uli Hoeness sent his penalty over the bar, setting the stage for Antonin Panenka to coolly chip the ball over German keeper Sepp Maier.

Semi-finals
Czechoslovakia. (1) 3-1 (0) ....Holland
AET. 1-1 after 90 mins
W Germany.... (0) 4-2 (2) ......Yugoslavia
AET. 2-2 after 90 mins

3rd/4th place playoff
Holland .... (2) 3-2 (1).......Yugoslavia
AET. 2-2 after 90 mins

Final
Czechoslovakia. (2) 2-2 (1)..... W Germany
AET. 2-2 after 90 mins. Czechoslovakia
won 5-3 on penalties

There were two major changes to the format for 1980 – for the first time, the hosts, Italy, did not need to qualify, and the final tournament was expanded to eight teams. That meant two groups of four, with the winners going straight to the final and the runners-up playing off for third place.

Kevin Keegan, European Footballer of the Year in 1978 and 1979, had top-scored in qualifying with seven goals, but England were disappointing. They finished third in Group B after claiming just one point from their opening two games; a draw against group winners Belgium followed with defeat by Italy.

West Germany won the other group. They beat defending champions Czechoslovakia 1-0 thanks to Karl-Heinz Rummenigge's goal, while Klaus Allofs' hat-trick against Holland in their second match was enough to see him finish the tournament as top scorer.

Horst Hrubesch, a late call-up after Klaus Fischer broke his leg, scored both of Germany's goals in the final, controlling Bernd Schuster's neat chip on his chest before firing in the opener – his first in international football – from just outside the Belgian box with ten minutes gone.

The Red Devils equalised through Rene Vandereycken's penalty with 15 minutes to go, but Hrubesch was on hand to finish it off in dramatic fashion, heading home a Rummenigge corner with a minute to go.

A happy Horst Hrubesch

Group A	P	W	D	L	F	A	GD	Pts
W Germany	3	2	1	0	4	2	2	5
Czechoslovakia	3	1	1	1	4	3	1	3
Holland	3	1	1	1	4	4	0	3
Greece	3	0	1	2	1	4	-3	1

W Germany.... (0) 1-0 (0) . Czechoslovakia
Holland .... (0) 1-0 (0) .... Greece
W Germany.... (1) 3-2 (0) .... Holland
Czechoslovakia. (2) 3-1 (1)............. Greece
Holland .... (0) 1-1 (1).. Czechoslovakia
W Germany.... (0) 0-0 (0) .... Greece

Group B	P	W	D	L	F	A	GD	Pts
Belgium	3	1	2	0	3	2	1	4
Italy	3	1	2	0	1	0	1	4
England	3	1	1	1	3	3	0	3
Spain	3	0	1	2	2	4	-2	1

Belgium.......... (1) 1-1 (1).......... England
Spain............. (0) 0-0 (0) .... Italy
Spain............. (1) 1-2 (1).......... Belgium
Italy............... (0) 1-0 (0) .... England
Italy............... (0) 0-0 (0) .... Belgium
England.......... (1) 2-1 (0) .... Spain

3rd/4th place playoff
Italy............... (0) 1-1 (0) . Czechoslovakia
AET. 1-1 after 90 mins – Czechoslovakia won 9-8 on penalties

Final
W Germany.... (1) 2-1 (0) .... Belgium

TOURNAMENT SUMMARY

Winners West Germany **Runners-up** Belgium

Total entries 32   **Finals debutants** Greece

Top scorer Allofs (West Germany) **3 goals**

Overs % by round   **BTTS % by round**   **Goals at the finals**

Q   GS   3rd   F   Q   GS   3rd   F   Overs 36%   BTTS 57%

	Total games	Total goals	Avg goals	Over 2.5 goals		Both score	
Final	1	3	3	1	100%	1	100%
Third place	1	2	2	0	0%	1	100%
Group stage	12	22	1.83	4	33%	6	50%
Totals	14	27	1.93	5	36%	8	57%
Qualifying	108	327	3.03	61	56%	49	45%

Only goals scored in normal time are counted (except goalscorers)

There were some notable absentees at the finals in 1984, with England having been pipped to top spot in qualifying Group 3 by Denmark, reigning world champions Italy finishing fourth, only ahead of Cyprus, in Group 5, and Poland, World Cup semi-finalists in 1982, finishing third of four in Group 2.

France, the other beaten semi-finalists in Spain, hosted the tournament and it was Michel Platini's time to shine. He made the perfect start, scoring the winner against Denmark in France's opener, and followed up with hat-tricks against both Belgium and Yugoslavia in the two remaining group games.

There were upsets in both groups. West Germany, who had contested the last three finals, were held to a goalless draw in their opener by debutants Portugal. The holders ended up third while Portugal progressed.

Denmark, making their first finals appearance in 20 years, beat 1980 runners-up Belgium in their final group-stage match. It sealed second place for the Danes, who followed France into the semi-finals.

Both the unfancied teams fought hard in the semis. Spain needed penalties to see off Denmark, while Portugal took France to extratime, with Platini scoring the winner on 119 minutes, slotting home Jean Tigana's cutback from six yards, after Rui Jordao had scored twice for the Portuguese.

Inevitably, Platini opened the scoring in the final, Luis Arconada fumbling his low free-kick over the line, before Bruno Bellone put matters beyond doubt in the final minute.

TOURNAMENT SUMMARY

Winners France **Runners-up** Spain

Total entries 34   **Finals debutants** Portugal, Romania

Top scorer Platini (France) **9 goals**

Overs % by round   **BTTS % by round**   **Goals at the finals**

Q GS SF F   Q GS SF F   Overs 33%   BTTS 47%

	Total games	Total goals	Avg goals	Over 2.5 goals	Both score
Final	1	2	2	0	0%	0	0%
Semi-finals	2	4	2	0	0%	2	100%
Group stage	12	32	2.67	5	42%	5	42%
Totals	15	38	2.53	5	33%	7	47%
Qualifying	116	339	2.92	59	51%	49	42%

Only goals scored in normal time are counted (except goalscorers)

Group A	P	W	D	L	F	A	GD	Pts
France	3	3	0	0	9	2	7	6
Denmark	3	2	0	1	8	3	5	4
Belgium	3	1	0	2	4	8	-4	2
Yugoslavia	3	0	0	3	2	10	-8	0

Group B	P	W	D	L	F	A	GD	Pts
Spain	3	1	2	0	3	2	1	4
Portugal	3	1	2	0	2	1	1	4
W Germany	3	1	1	1	2	2	0	3
Romania	3	0	1	2	2	4	-2	1

France .... (0) 1-0 (0) .... Denmark
Belgium .... (2) 2-0 (0) ...... Yugoslavia
France .... (3) 5-0 (0) .... Belgium
Denmark .... (2) 5-0 (0) ...... Yugoslavia
Denmark .... (1) 3-2 (2) .... Belgium
France .... (0) 3-2 (1) ...... Yugoslavia

W Germany.... (0) 0-0 (0) .... Portugal
Spain .... (1) 1-1 (1) .... Romania
W Germany.... (1) 2-1 (0) .... Romania
Spain .... (0) 1-1 (0) .... Portugal
Portugal .... (0) 1-0 (0) .... Romania
W Germany.... (0) 0-1 (0) .... Spain

Semi-finals
France .... (1) 3-2 (0) .... Portugal
AET. 1-1 after 90 mins

Denmark .... (1) 1-1 (0) .... Spain
AET. 1-1 after 90 mins. Spain won 5-4 pens

Final
France .... (0) 2-0 (0) .... Spain

Holders France failed to qualify for Euro 88, finishing third in their group behind USSR and East Germany – and only ahead of Iceland on goal difference – but England had no such problems.

Bobby Robson's side qualified superbly, winning five of their six matches without conceding a single goal until the 80th minute of their final game. However, in Germany the Three Lions lost their opening game 1-0 to debutants Ireland – Gary Lineker and Glenn Hoddle both hit the woodwork – and were undone by a Marco van Basten hat-trick in a 3-1 loss to Holland that ended their involvement after two games.

Ireland's 1-1 draw with the Soviet Union in their second match, courtesy of Ronnie Whelan's spectacular volley, meant they only needed to draw their final group game against the Dutch to reach the semi-finals. Paul McGrath hit the post for Jack Charlton's side, but Wim Kieft's header put the Dutch through as runners-up behind USSR.

Holland took on the hosts, West Germany, in the first semi-final. The game was heading for extra time after each side had scored from the penalty spot, but then Van Basten tucked the ball away with two minutes left.

There was another upset in the other semi, with the Soviet Union beating Italy 2-0, Hennadiy Lytovchenko and Oleg Protasov scoring in a four-minute second-half blitz.

USSR had beaten Holland in their opening group game

but the Dutch got the result when it mattered, Ruud Gullit heading the first before Van Basten's famous volley sealed it.

Group A	P	W	D	L	F	A	GD	Pts
W Germany	3	2	1	0	5	1	4	5
Italy	3	2	1	0	4	1	3	5
Spain	3	1	0	2	3	5	-2	2
Denmark	3	0	0	3	2	7	-5	0

W Germany.... (0) 1-1 (0) .... Italy
Spain............. (1) 3-2 (1)..........Denmark
W Germany.... (1) 2-0 (0) ....Denmark
Italy................(0) 1-0 (0) .... Spain
Italy................(0) 2-0 (0) ....Denmark
W Germany.... (1) 2-0 (0) .... Spain

Group B	P	W	D	L	F	A	GD	Pts
USSR	3	2	1	0	5	2	3	5
Holland	3	2	0	1	4	2	2	4
Rep of Ireland	3	1	1	1	2	2	0	3
England	3	0	0	3	2	7	-5	0

England.......... (0) 0-1 (1)..Rep of Ireland
Holland .... (0) 0-1 (0) .... USSR
Rep of Ireland (1) 1-1 (0) .... USSR
Holland .... (1) 3-1 (0) .... England
England.......... (1) 1-3 (2) .... USSR
Holland .... (0) 1-0 (0) .Rep of Ireland

Semi-finals
W Germany.... (0) 1-2 (0) ....Holland
USSR .... (0) 2-0 (0) .... Italy

Final
Holland .... (1) 2-0 (0) .... USSR

Marco van Basten gets the first goal of a hat-trick against England

TOURNAMENT SUMMARY

Winners Holland **Runners-up** USSR

Total entries 33   **Finals debutants** Republic of Ireland

Top scorer Van Basten (Holland) **5 goals**

Overs % by round	BTTS % by round	Goals at the finals
Q GS SF F	Q GS SF F	Overs 20% BTTS 33%

	Total games	Total goals	Avg goals	Over 2.5 goals		Both score	
Final	1	2	2	0	0%	0	0%
Semi-finals	2	2	1	0	0%	0	0%
Group stage	12	27	2.25	3	25%	5	42%
Totals	**15**	**31**	**2.07**	**3**	**20%**	**5**	**33%**
Qualifying	116	279	2.41	46	40%	37	32%

Only goals scored in normal time are counted (except goalscorers)

TOURNAMENT SUMMARY

Winners Denmark **Runners-up** Germany

Total entries 34 **Finals debutants** CIS, Germany, Scotland, Sweden

Top scorers Bergkamp (Holland),Brolin (Sweden), Larsen (Denmark), Riedle (Germany) **all 3 goals**

Overs % by round **BTTS % by round** **Goals at the finals**

Overs 33% BTTS 47%

	Total games	Total goals	Avg goals	Over 2.5 goals		Both score	
Final	1	2	2	0	0%	0	0%
Semi-finals	2	6	3	1	50%	2	100%
Group stage	12	21	1.75	4	33%	5	42%
Totals	15	29	1.93	5	33%	7	47%
Qualifying	123	333	2.71	58	47%	47	38%

Only goals scored in normal time are counted (except goalscorers)

Group 1	P	W	D	L	F	A	GD	Pts
Sweden	3	2	1	0	4	2	2	5
Denmark	3	1	1	1	2	2	0	3
France	3	0	2	1	2	3	-1	2
England	3	0	2	1	1	2	-1	2

Sweden .... (1) 1-1 (0) ....France
Denmark .... (0) 0-0 (0) ....England
Sweden .... (0) 1-0 (0) ....Denmark
England .... (0) 0-0 (0) ....France
Sweden .... (0) 2-1 (1)..........England
Denmark .... (1) 2-1 (0) ....France

Group 2	P	W	D	L	F	A	GD	Pts
Holland	3	2	1	0	4	1	3	5
Germany	3	1	1	1	4	4	0	3
Scotland	3	1	0	2	3	3	0	2
CIS	3	0	2	1	1	4	-3	2

CIS.................. (0) 1-1 (0) ....Germany
Holland .... (0) 1-0 (0) .... Scotland
Scotland.......... (0) 0-2 (1)........Germany
Holland.......... (0) 0-0 (0) .... CIS
Scotland........ (2) 3-0 (0) .... CIS
Holland .... (2) 3-1 (0) ....Germany

Semi-finals
Sweden .... (0) 2-3 (1)........Germany
Denmark .... (2) 2-2 (1)..........Holland
AET. 2-2 after 90 mins – Denmark won
5-4 on penalties

Final
Denmark .... (1) 2-0 (0) ....Germany

Denmark celebrate John Jensen's opener in the final

The fall of the Berlin Wall in 1989 was symbolic of change across Central and Eastern Europe and that was reflected at Euro 92.

It was the first tournament for the reunified Germany and the dissolved Soviet Union competed as CIS, the Commonwealth of Independent States. But the biggest impact was Fifa's decision to ban Yugoslavia from international football, in response to United Nations sanctions imposed after the outbreak of war in Bosnia-Herzegovina.

Yugoslavia had gone out of the 1990 World Cup only on penalties to Argentina in the quarter-finals and had finished their qualifying group a point ahead of Denmark.

The Danes were the beneficiaries and while legend has it that they were dragged from the beach to take part, they were all aware that the back door might be about to open.

Denmark's first game was a goalless draw with England and a 1-0 loss to hosts Sweden left Richard Moller's side needing to beat France to qualify for the semis. Goals from Henrik Larsen and Lars Elstrup either side of Jean-Pierre Papin's equaliser for the French did the job.

They met defending champions Holland in the semis and, thanks to two more goals from Larsen, took the Dutch to extra time and penalties. Holland's hero in 1988, Marco van Basten, saw his spot kick saved by Peter Schmeichel and the Danes

were through.

Germany, who won the World Cup as West Germany two years earlier, had knocked out Sweden in the other semi-final, but they

couldn't overcome Denmark in the final. John Jensen and Kim Vilfort scored in either half and Schmeichel proved unbeatable in the Danish goal.

Euro 96 saw the tournament double in size to 16 teams and six teams make their debuts, albeit some of them were old faces competing under new names. One of those – Czech Republic – would make a big impression.

The tournamant was hosted by England, for whom striker Alan Shearer had gone 12 games without a goal. But he ended the drought with the first goal of the game against debutants Switzerland. However, a late equaliser from the penalty spot meant the first game ended in disappointment for the hosts.

It was against Scotland that England's party got started. Shearer opened the scoring again but when Tony Adams fouled Gordon Durie in the box, it looked as if history might be about to repeat itself. However, David Seaman saved Gary McAllister's spot kick and a minute later, Paul Gascoigne latched on to Darren Anderton's inch-perfect pass, flicked the ball over Colin Hendry's head and volleyed past Andy Goram to put the game beyond doubt.

A superb 4-1 win over Holland, in which Shearer scored two more, saw England go through as group winners and the Dutch edge out Scotland on goal difference.

The Three Lions edged past Spain on penalties in the quarter-finals. Spain got the ball in the net twice and had a good penalty appeal turned down, but luck was with England and Stuart Pearce's celebration after burying his

kick in the shootout provided one of the tournament's iconic moments as he laid the ghost of Italia 90 to rest.

But it all went wrong against the Germans in the semi-finals as England were beaten on penalties.

Shearer struck just three minutes in, but Stefan Kuntz equalised 13 minutes later. In extra time, Anderton hit the post and Gascoigne was millimetres away from connecting with Shearer's cross to score a golden goal. In the end, after the first ten penalties went in, Gareth Southgate missed,

Andreas Muller didn't and the tournament was over for Terry Venables's side.

In the final, Germany met Czech Republic, who they had already beaten 2-0 in their opening group game.

Since then, though, the Czechs had beaten Italy and drawn with Russia in the group stage to reach the quarter-finals, where Karel Poborsky's sublime chip was enough to see off Portugal. A goalless draw with France in the semis and victory on penalties gave them the chance to beat the Germans when it really mattered.

HISTORY

Winners Germany **Runners-up** Czech Republic

Total entries 48   **Finals debutants** Bulgaria, Croatia, Czech Republic, Russia, Switzerland, Turkey

Top scorer Shearer (England) **5 goals**

Overs % by round   BTTS % by round   Goals at the finals

Q PO GS QF SF F   Q PO GS QF SF F   Overs 35%   BTTS 42%

	Total games	Total goals	Avg goals	Over 2.5 goals		Both score	
Final	1	2	2	0	0%	1	100%
Semi-finals	2	2	1	0	0%	1	50%
Quarter-finals	4	4	1	1	25%	1	25%
Group stage	24	55	2.29	10	42%	10	42%
Totals	31	63	2.03	11	35%	13	42%
Playoffs	1	2	2	0	0%	0	0%
Qualifying	230	678	2.95	123	53%	92	40%

Only goals scored in normal time are counted (except goalscorers)

Group A	P	W	D	L	F	A	GD	Pts
England	3	2	1	0	7	2	5	7
Holland	3	1	1	1	3	4	-1	4
Scotland	3	1	1	1	1	2	-1	4
Switzerland	3	0	1	2	1	4	-3	1

England.......... (1) 1-1 (0) .... Switzerland
Holland .... (0) 0-0 (0) .... Scotland
Holland .... (0) 2-0 (0) .... Switzerland
England.......... (0) 2-0 (0) .... Scotland
England.......... (1) 4-1 (0) ....Holland
Scotland.......... (1) 1-0 (0) .... Switzerland

Group B	P	W	D	L	F	A	GD	Pts
France	3	2	1	0	5	2	3	7
Spain	3	1	2	0	4	3	1	5
Bulgaria	3	1	1	1	3	4	-1	4
Romania	3	0	0	3	1	4	-3	0

Spain.............. (0) 1-1 (0) ....Bulgaria
Romania.......... (0) 0-1 (1)..............France
Bulgaria .... (1) 1-0 (0) .... Romania
France .... (0) 1-1 (0) .... Spain
Romania.......... (1) 1-2 (1)................. Spain
France .... (1) 3-1 (0) ....Bulgaria

Group C	P	W	D	L	F	A	GD	Pts
Germany	3	2	1	0	5	0	5	7
Czech Rep	3	1	1	1	5	6	-1	4
Italy	3	1	1	1	3	3	0	4
Russia	3	0	1	2	4	8	-4	1

Germany .... (2) 2-0 (0) ....Czech Rep
Italy.............. (1) 2-1 (1)..............Russia

Czech Rep ...... (2) 2-1 (1)................Italy
Russia .... (0) 0-3 (0) ....Germany
Italy.............. (0) 0-0 (0) ....Germany
Russia .... (0) 3-3 (2) ....Czech Rep

Group D	P	W	D	L	F	A	GD	Pts
Portugal	3	2	1	0	5	1	4	7
Croatia	3	2	0	1	4	3	1	6
Denmark	3	1	1	1	4	4	0	4
Turkey	3	0	0	3	0	5	-5	0

Denmark .... (1) 1-1 (0) .... Portugal
Turkey .... (0) 0-1 (0) ....Croatia
Portugal.......... (0) 1-0 (0) ....Turkey
Croatia .... (0) 3-0 (0) ....Denmark
Croatia .... (0) 0-3 (2) .... Portugal
Turkey .... (0) 0-3 (0) ....Denmark

Quarter-finals
England.......... (0) 0-0 (0) .... Spain
AET. England won 4-2 on penalties
France .... (0) 0-0 (0) ....Holland
AET. France won 5-4 on penalties
Germany .... (1) 2-1 (0) ....Croatia
Portugal.......... (0) 0-1 (0) ......Czech Rep

Semi-finals
England.......... (1) 1-1 (1)..........Germany
AET. 1-1 90 mins – Germany won 6-5 on penalties
France .... (0) 0-0 (0) ......Czech Rep
AET. Czech Rep won 6-5 on penalties

Final
Germany .... (0) 2-1 (0) ....Czech Rep
AET. 1-1 after 90 mins – Germany won by golden goal

Patrik Berger gave the Czechs the lead from the penalty spot just before the hour mark, but there would be no upset.

Berti Vogts brought Oliver Bierhoff off the bench, and he equalised within four minutes of joining the action, heading in from Christian Ziege's free-kick. Five minutes into extra time, Bierhoff struck again, settling the final with a golden goal.

He picked up Jurgen Klinsmann's cross with his back to goal, and Petr Kouba could only palm Bierhoff's deflected shot into the net.

For the first time, the finals were hosted by two countries, Holland and Belgium, and the tournament also saw the introduction of a fourth official to assist the referee.

England, Ireland and Scotland all ended up in the qualification playoffs, where Ireland lost to Turkey on away goals and England beat Scotland 2-1, Paul Scholes scoring twice at Hampden Park and Don Hutchison finding the net for the Scots in a 1-0 win at Wembley.

Norway made their debut at the finals, but the surprise qualifiers were Slovenia, with Zlatko Zahovic's nine goals only bettered by Spain's Raul.

At the finals, England bowed out at the group stage. However, Kevin Keegan's men could take some consolation from a first competitive win over Germany since 1966, as the defending champions finished bottom of Group A with a single point.

Portugal topped the table with nine points and a Nuno Gomes brace saw them beat ten-man Turkey to set up a semi-final against World Cup holders France. Gomes struck again but Thierry Henry's second-half equaliser and Zinedine Zidane's golden goal penalty got the French through.

In the final France met an Italian side who had run up a perfect nine points in the group stage and had shown real grit to get past Holland in their semi-final.

They were reduced to ten men when Gianluca Zambrotta was shown a second yellow with just 34

Didier Deschamps lifts the trophy as France complete back-to-back World Cup and European Championship victories

minutes gone, and survived two penalties in the opening 90 minutes, Francesco Toldo saving Frank de Boer's spot kick and Patrick Kluivert hitting the post, to take the match to extra time.

Toldo saved again from De Boer in the shootout, Jaap Stam blazed over and Toldo's save from Paul Bosvelt put the Italians through as 3-1

winners of the shootout.

The final also turned into a tense affair, despite both sides creating plenty of chances. It took until the 55th minute for Italy to open the scoring, Marco Delvecchio volleying in Gianluca Pessotto's cross from six yards.

Roger Lemerre responded by sending on Sylvain Wiltord and, later, David Trezeguet,

TOURNAMENT SUMMARY

Winners France **Runners-up** Italy

Total entries 51   **Finals debutants** Norway, Slovenia

Top scorers Milosevic (Yugoslavia), Kluivert (Holland) **both 5 goals**

Overs % by round	BTTS % by round	Goals at the finals

Q PO GS QF SF F   Q PO GS QF SF F   Overs 48%   BTTS 48%

	Total games	Total goals	Avg goals	Over 2.5 goals		Both score	
Final	1	2	2	0	0%	1	100%
Semi-finals	2	2	1	0	0%	1	50%
Quarter-finals	4	14	3.5	2	50%	2	50%
Group stage	24	65	2.71	13	54 %	11	46%
Totals	31	83	2.68	15	48%	15	48%
Playoffs	8	18	2.25	3	38%	3	38%
Qualifying	220	634	2.88	120	55%	86	39%

Only goals scored in normal time are counted (except goalscorers)

Group A	P	W	D	L	F	A	GD	Pts
Portugal	**3**	**3**	**0**	**0**	**7**	**2**	**5**	**9**
Romania	**3**	**1**	**1**	**1**	**4**	**4**	**0**	**4**
England	3	1	0	2	5	6	-1	3
Germany	3	0	1	2	1	5	-4	1

Germany .... (1) 1-1 (1) .... Romania
Portugal .... (2) 3-2 (2) .... England
England .... (0) 1-0 (0) .... Germany
Romania .... (0) 0-1 (0) .... Portugal
England .... (2) 2-3 (1) .... Romania
Portugal .... (1) 3-0 (0) .... Germany

Group B	P	W	D	L	F	A	GD	Pts
Italy	**3**	**3**	**0**	**0**	**6**	**2**	**4**	**9**
Turkey	**3**	**1**	**1**	**1**	**3**	**2**	**1**	**4**
Belgium	3	1	0	2	2	5	-3	3
Sweden	3	0	1	2	2	4	-2	1

Belgium.......... (1) 2-1 (0) .... Sweden
Turkey .... (0) 1-2 (0) .... Italy
Belgium.......... (0) 0-2 (1) .... Italy
Sweden .... (0) 0-0 (0) .... Turkey
Italy................ (1) 2-1 (0) .... Sweden
Belgium.......... (0) 0-2 (1) .... Turkey

Group C	P	W	D	L	F	A	GD	Pts
Spain	**3**	**2**	**0**	**1**	**6**	**5**	**1**	**6**
Yugoslavia	**3**	**1**	**1**	**1**	**7**	**7**	**0**	**4**
Norway	3	1	1	1	1	1	0	4
Slovenia	3	0	2	1	4	5	-1	2

Yugoslavia ..... (0) 3-3 (1) .... Slovenia
Spain .... (0) 0-1 (0) .... Norway

Slovenia .... (0) 1-2 (1) .... Spain
Norway .... (0) 0-1 (1) ...... Yugoslavia
Yugoslavia ..... (1) 3-4 (1) .... Spain
Slovenia .... (0) 0-0 (0) .... Norway

Group D	P	W	D	L	F	A	GD	Pts
Holland	**3**	**3**	**0**	**0**	**7**	**2**	**5**	**9**
France	**3**	**2**	**0**	**1**	**7**	**4**	**3**	**6**
Czech Rep	3	1	0	2	3	3	0	3
Denmark	3	0	0	3	0	8	-8	0

Holland .... (0) 1-0 (0) ...... Czech Rep
France .... (1) 3-0 (0) .... Denmark
Czech Rep ...... (1) 1-2 (1) .... France
Holland .... (0) 3-0 (0) .... Denmark
Holland .... (1) 3-2 (2) .... France
Denmark .... (0) 0-2 (0) ...... Czech Rep

Quarter-finals
Turkey .... (0) 0-2 (1) .... Portugal
Romania .... (0) 0-2 (2) .... Italy
Spain .... (1) 1-2 (1) .... France
Holland .... (2) 6-1 (0) ..... Yugoslavia

Semi-finals
Portugal .... (1) 1-2 (0) .... France
AET. 1-1 after 90 mins – France won by golden goal
Holland .... (0) 0-0 (0) .... Italy
AET. Italy won 3-1 on penalties

Final
Italy................ (0) 1-2 (0) .... France
AET. 1-1 after 90 mins – France won by golden goal

but as the clocked ticked into injury time, it looked as if the match was slipping away from the French.

However, Wiltord levelled it with a low drive from a tight angle and in extra time, Trezeguet gave Toldo no chance as he blasted Roberto Pires's cutback into the roof of the Italian net to score the golden goal.

Euro 2004 saw one of the biggest upsets in sporting history as unfancied Greece grafted their way to glory.

The Greeks had qualified well. After losing their first two matches, to Spain and Ukraine, they won the next six without conceding to finish top of Group 6. But Otto Rehhagel's side were still considered rank outsiders to win the tournament.

Greece met Portugal in the opening game. The hosts were coached by Luiz Felipe Scolari, who had led Brazil to their fifth World Cup victory two years earlier, and they could boast some major talent in their ranks in the form of Luis Figo, Rui Costa and a young Cristiano Ronaldo.

However, the first surprise of the tournament came early on, as goals from Giorgos Karagounis and Angelos Basinas meant Ronaldo's first international goal, scored in the third minute of added time, was mere consolation.

A point from the next two group games was enough to see Greece through to a quarter-final against defending champions France and Angelos Charisteas's second-half header proved the difference between the two sides.

In the other half of the draw, Portugal were making steady progress. Despite losing to Greece, they won the group and faced England in the quarter-finals.

Michael Owen opened the scoring after just three minutes, finishing cleverly after David James's punt found its way through to the

Angelos Charisteas scores the winner in the final

Group A	P	W	D	L	F	A	GD	Pts
Portugal	3	2	0	1	4	2	2	6
Greece	3	1	1	1	4	4	0	4
Spain	3	1	1	1	2	2	0	4
Russia	3	1	0	2	2	4	-2	3

Portugal........ (0) 1-2 (1)............ Greece
Spain............. (0) 1-0 (0) .... Russia
Greece........... (0) 1-1 (1)............. Spain
Portugal........ (1) 2-0 (0) .... Russia
Portugal........ (0) 1-0 (0) .... Spain
Russia .... (2) 2-1 (1)........... Greece

Group B	P	W	D	L	F	A	GD	Pts
France	3	2	1	0	7	4	3	7
England	3	2	0	1	8	4	4	6
Croatia	3	0	2	1	4	6	-2	2
Switzerland	3	0	1	2	1	6	-5	1

Switzerland.... (0) 0-0 (0) ....Croatia
France .... (0) 2-1 (1).......... England
Croatia .... (0) 2-2 (1)...........France
England.......... (1) 3-0 (0) .... Switzerland
Croatia .... (1) 2-4 (2) .... England
Switzerland.... (1) 1-3 (1)............France

Group C	P	W	D	L	F	A	GD	Pts
Sweden	3	1	2	0	8	3	5	5
Denmark	3	1	2	0	4	2	2	5
Italy	3	1	2	0	3	2	1	5
Bulgaria	3	0	0	3	1	9	-8	0

Denmark .... (0) 0-0 (0) .... Italy
Sweden.......... (1) 5-0 (0) ....Bulgaria
Italy................ (1) 1-1 (0) ....Sweden
Bulgaria .... (0) 0-2 (1).......Denmark
Italy................ (0) 2-1 (1).........Bulgaria
Denmark .... (1) 2-2 (0) ....Sweden

Group D	P	W	D	L	F	A	GD	Pts
Czech Rep	3	3	0	0	7	4	3	9
Holland	3	1	1	1	6	4	2	4
Germany	3	0	2	1	2	3	-1	2
Latvia	3	0	1	2	1	5	-4	1

Czech Rep ...... (0) 2-1 (1)............... Latvia
Germany .... (1) 1-1 (0) ....Holland
Latvia............. (0) 0-0 (1) ....Germany
Holland .... (2) 2-3 (1).......Czech Rep
Germany .... (1) 1-2 (1).......Czech Rep
Holland .... (2) 3-0 (0) .... Latvia

Liverpool striker. However, less than 25 minutes later, Wayne Rooney, who had lit up the group stage with four goals, limped off with a broken metatarsal.

The Portuguese piled on the pressure and, with just seven minutes to go, Helder Postiga finally levelled the match.

Rui Costa put the hosts ahead in the second half of extra time, firing an unstoppable shot into the England net after carrying the ball all the way to the edge of the box from the centre circle, but a Frank Lampard goal sent the match to penalties.

David Beckham, who had missed his last two penalties for England, blasted his spot kick over the bar, as did Rui Costa. That set things up for Portugal keeper Ricardo to play the hero, saving from Darius Vassell before scoring the winning penalty.

Portugal beat Holland 2-1 to book their place in the final, Ronaldo scoring first and Maniche doubling their lead with a stunning strike from the corner of the Dutch penalty area.

Meanwhile, Greece were grinding their way to the final, soaking up pressure against Czech Republic to force their semi-final to extra time, before Traianos Dellas connected with Vasilis Tsiartas's corner at the near post for a silver-goal winner.

Portugal were expected to beat the Greeks when it mattered most but they couldn't break the deadlock.

Instead, Charisteas got the only goal of the game, heading in Basinas's corner as the game headed towards the hour mark, and with Antonios Nikopolidis in inspired form in the Greek goal, the hosts ended the night disappointed.

Disappointment for Ronaldo

TOURNAMENT SUMMARY

Winners Greece **Runners-up** Portugal

Total entries 51   **Finals debutants** Latvia

Top scorer Baros (Czech Republic) **5 goals**

Overs % by round   **BTTS % by round**   **Goals at the finals**

Q PO GS QF SF F   Q PO GS QF SF F   Overs 52%   BTTS 52%

	Total games	Total goals	Avg goals	Over 2.5 goals		Both score	
Final	1	1	1	0	0%	0	0%
Semi-finals	2	3	1.5	1	50%	1	50%
Quarter-finals	4	6	1.5	1	25%	1	25%
Group stage	24	64	2.67	14	58%	14	58%
Totals	**31**	**74**	**2.39**	**16**	**52%**	**16**	**52%**
Playoffs	10	22	2.2	4	40%	3	30%
Qualifying	200	544	2.72	104	52%	76	38%

Only goals scored in normal time are counted (except goalscorers)

Euro 2008 marked the beginning of a glorious era for Spain, as they won their first major trophy since Marcelino's header in the Bernabeu turned the European Championship final in their favour in 1964.

None of the home nations qualified, although Northern Ireland's David Healy was top scorer in qualifying. The Republic of Ireland missed out too, finishing third behind Czech Republic and Germany in their group.

Both co-hosts, Austria and Switzerland, went out in the group stage, along with defending champions Greece, who were the only team in the tournament not to take a point, their only goal coming against Spain.

Along with Croatia and Holland, Luis Aragones's side took maximum points from the group stage, and that goal against Greece was the last that Spain conceded in the tournament.

They beat Italy on penalties after a goalless draw in the quarter-finals and thrashed Russia, who they had already beaten 4-1 in the group stage, 3-0 in the semis.

They met Germany in the final. Joachim Low's team had beaten both Portugal and Turkey 3-2, but they couldn't find the net against the Spanish.

Spain were without the tournament's leading scorer, David Villa, but Fernando Torres proved the difference, showing pace and power to get to Xavi's through ball ahead of Philipp Lahm and dink the ball over a diving Jens Lehmann.

Winners Spain **Runners-up** Germany

Total entries 52 **Finals debutants** Austria, Poland

Top scorer Villa (Spain) **4 goals**

Overs % by round	BTTS % by round	Goals at the finals
Q GS QF SF F	Q GS QF SF F	Overs 39% BTTS 42%

	Total games	Total goals	Avg goals	Over 2.5 goals		Both score	
Final	1	1	1	0	0%	0	0%
Semi-finals	2	8	4	2	100%	1	50%
Quarter-finals	4	7	1.75	1	25%	2	50%
Group stage	24	57	2.38	9	38%	10	42 %
Totals	31	73	2.35	12	39%	13	42%
Qualifying	305	833	2.73	157	51%	117	38%

Only goals scored in normal time are counted (except goalscorers)

Group A	P	W	D	L	F	A	GD	Pts
Portugal	3	2	0	1	5	3	2	6
Turkey	3	2	0	1	5	5	0	6
Czech Rep	3	1	0	2	4	6	-2	3
Switzerland	3	1	0	2	3	3	0	3

Switzerland.... (0) 0-1 (0) ......Czech Rep
Portugal .... (0) 2-0 (0) ....Turkey
Czech Rep ...... (1) 1-3 (1)......... Portugal
Switzerland.... (1) 1-2 (0) ....Turkey
Turkey .... (0) 3-2 (1).......Czech Rep
Switzerland.... (0) 2-0 (0) .... Portugal

Group B	P	W	D	L	F	A	GD	Pts
Croatia	3	3	0	0	4	1	3	9
Germany	3	2	0	1	4	2	2	6
Austria	3	0	1	2	1	3	-2	1
Poland	3	0	1	2	1	4	-3	1

Austria .... (0) 0-1 (1)...........Croatia
Germany .... (1) 2-0 (0) ....Poland
Austria .... (0) 1-1 (1)...........Poland
Croatia .... (1) 2-1 (0) ....Germany
Austria .... (0) 0-1 (0) ....Germany
Poland............ (0) 0-1 (0) ....Croatia

Group C	P	W	D	L	F	A	GD	Pts
Holland	3	3	0	0	9	1	8	9
Italy	3	1	1	1	3	4	-1	4
Romania	3	0	2	1	1	3	-2	2
France	3	0	1	2	1	6	-5	1

Holland .... (2) 3-0 (0) ....Italy

Romania........ (0) 0-0 (0) ....France
Holland ....(1) 4-1 (0) ....France
Italy................ (0) 1-1 (0) .... Romania
France .... (0) 0-2 (1)................. Italy
Holland .... (0) 2-0 (0) .... Romania

Group D	P	W	D	L	F	A	GD	Pts
Spain	3	3	0	0	8	3	5	9
Russia	3	2	0	1	4	4	0	6
Sweden	3	1	0	2	3	4	-1	3
Greece	3	0	0	3	1	5	-4	0

Greece............ (0) 0-2 (0) ....Sweden
Spain.............. (2) 4-1 (0) ....Russia
Greece............ (0) 0-1 (1)............Russia
Sweden.......... (1) 1-2 (1).............. Spain
Greece............ (1) 1-2 (0) .... Spain
Russia .... (1) 2-0 (0) ....Sweden

Quarter-finals
Portugal .... (1) 2-3 (2) ....Germany
Croatia .... (0) 1-1 (0) ....Turkey
AET. 0-0 after 90 mins – Turkey won
3-1 on penalties
Holland .... (0) 1-3 (0) ....Russia
AET.1-1 after 90 minutes
Spain.............. (0) 0-0 (0) ....Italy
AET. Spain won 4-2 on penalties

Semi-finals
Germany .... (1) 3-2 (1)............Turkey
Russia .... (0) 0-3 (0) .... Spain

Final
Germany .... (0) 0-1 (1)............... Spain

*Fernando Torres puts
Spain ahead in the final*

At Euro 2012, Spain became the first team to win back-to-back European Championships, and after Antonio Di Natale's goal in their opening 1-1 draw with Italy, they did it without conceding.

Co-hosts Poland and Ukraine both went out in the group stage, as did Holland, who Spain had beaten in the final of the 2010 World Cup. Like the Dutch, Ireland also failed to pick up any group-stage points, losing to Croatia, Spain and Italy.

England finished top of their section ahead of France but were outplayed by Italy in the quarter-finals and were beaten on penalties after the match finished goalless.

Spain beat the French 2-0 in the other half of the draw thanks to a double from Xabi Alonso to set up a semi-final against Portugal.

Cristiano Ronaldo had scored three times in Portugal's two previous games – a group-stage win over Holland and a quarter-final victory against Czech Republic – but he couldn't find the net in a nervy semi-final. After 120 minutes without a goal, Spain won the penalty shootout.

Mario Balotelli scored twice for Italy in their semi-final victory over Germany, setting up a rematch of Italy's group-stage draw with Spain.

There was no doubt who was the better side in the

The Spanish team celebrate at the final whistle

TOURNAMENT SUMMARY

Winners Spain **Runners-up** Italy

Total entries 53   **Finals debutants** Ukraine

Top scorers Balotelli (Italy), Dzagoev (Russia), Gomez (Germany), Mandzukic (Croatia), Ronaldo (Portugal), Torres (Spain) **all 3 goals**

Overs % by round   **BTTS % by round**   **Goals at the finals**

Q PO GS QF SF F   Q PO GS QF SF F   Overs 42%   BTTS 52%

	Total games	Total goals	Avg goals	Over 2.5 Goals		Both score	
Final	1	4	4	1	100%	0	0%
Semi-finals	2	3	1.5	1	50%	1	50%
Quarter-finals	4	9	2.25	1	25%	1	25%
Group stage	24	60	2.5	10	42%	14	58%
Totals	31	76	2.45	13	42%	16	52%
Playoffs	8	20	2.5	3	38%	2	25%
Qualifying	239	645	2.7	115	48%	99	42%

Only goals scored in normal time are counted (except goalscorers)

Group A	P	W	D	L	F	A	GD	Pts
Czech Rep	3	2	0	1	4	5	-1	6
Greece	3	1	1	1	3	3	0	4
Russia	3	1	1	1	5	3	2	4
Poland	3	0	2	1	2	3	-1	2

Poland............ (1) 1-1 (0) .... Greece
Russia .... (2) 4-1 (0) ......Czech Rep
Greece............ (0) 1-2 (2) ......Czech Rep
Poland............ (0) 1-1 (1)............ Russia
Greece............ (1) 1-0 (0) .... Russia
Czech Rep ...... (0) 1-0 (0) .... Poland

Group B	P	W	D	L	F	A	GD	Pts
Germany	3	3	0	0	5	2	3	9
Portugal	3	2	0	1	5	4	1	6
Denmark	3	1	0	2	4	5	-1	3
Holland	3	0	0	3	2	5	-3	0

Germany .... (0) 1-0 (0) .... Portugal
Holland .... (0) 0-1 (1).........Denmark
Denmark .... (1) 2-3 (2) .... Portugal
Holland .... (0) 1-2 (2) .... Germany
Portugal.......... (1) 2-1 (1).........Holland
Denmark .... (1) 1-2 (1) .... Germany

Group C	P	W	D	L	F	A	GD	Pts
Spain	3	2	1	0	6	1	5	7
Italy	3	1	2	0	4	2	2	5
Croatia	3	1	1	1	4	3	1	4
Rep of Ireland	3	0	0	3	1	9	-8	0

Rep of Ireland. (1) 1-3 (2) ....Croatia
Spain.............. (0) 1-1 (0) ....Italy
Italy................ (1) 1-1 (0) ....Croatia
Spain.............. (1) 4-0 (0) . Rep of Ireland
Italy................ (1) 2-0 (0) . Rep of Ireland
Croatia .... (0) 0-1 (0) .... Spain

Group D	P	W	D	L	F	A	GD	Pts
England	3	2	1	0	5	3	2	7
France	3	1	1	1	3	3	0	4
Ukraine	3	1	0	2	2	4	-2	3
Sweden	3	1	0	2	5	5	0	3

France .... (1) 1-1 (1).........England
Ukraine .... (0) 2-1 (0) ....Sweden
Ukraine .... (0) 0-2 (0) ....France
Sweden .... (0) 2-3 (1)..........England
Sweden .... (0) 2-0 (0) ....France
England........... (0) 1-0 (0) ....Ukraine

Quarter-finals
Czech Rep ...... (0) 0-1 (0) ...... Portugal
Germany .... (1) 4-2 (0) .... Greece
Spain.............. (1) 2-0 (0) ....France
England........... (0) 0-0 (0) .... Italy
AET. Italy won 4-2 on penalties

Semi-finals
Portugal .... (0) 0-0 (0) .... Spain
AET. Spain won 4-2 on penalties
Germany .... (0) 1-2 (2) .... Italy

Final
Spain.............. (2) 4-0 (0) .... Italy

final. David Silva opened the scoring after 14 minutes, heading in Cesc Fabregas's cutback, and Jordi Alba latched on to Xavi's inch-perfect through ball to put La Roja two up before the break. With Italy having used all their substitutions, an injury to Thiago Motta meant they were forced to play the final half hour with ten men. And there was no way back as Fernando Torres and Juan Mata piled on the hurt in the final six minutes.

MINNOWS EARN THEIR MOMENT IN THE SUN

Cast your mind back to February 23, 2014 when the qualifying draw was made for Euro 2016, writes James Milton.

Future England star Dele Alli was at MK Dons, preparing for a trip to Oldham in League One. Gibraltar – soon to become one of the most feared teams in Europe – was just a small blob off the coast of Spain, populated by bookies. And the men running world football were universally regarded as unimpeachable paragons of humility and integrity.

Perhaps my memory is playing tricks on me with that last one.

Critics claimed that the expansion of the European Championships to 24 teams would dilute the quality of the finals and render the qualifying campaign even more meaningless than usual.

Euro 2016, they said, would be easier to qualify for than a payday loan from an unscrupulous short-term lender offering 3,000 per cent APR.

So let's start this review of the qualifiers by saluting a couple of absent friends who achieved what many regarded as an impossible task – failing to reach the finals in France.

Holland, third in the 2014 World Cup, were just 2-7 to win Group A, but a miserable haul of one point from six games against Iceland, Czech Republic and Turkey condemned them to fourth place in the section.

Iceland did the double over the Dutch, landing odds of 5-1 at home and 9-1 away to finish with a level-stakes profit of +17.23.

Reaching their first major tournament is a remarkable feat given that the country's population is smaller than the cast of Keeping Up With The Kardashians.

Holland's performances were horrible, but the performances of 2004 champions Greece were even grimmer. The 11-10 Group F favourites finished bottom, losing at home and away to the Faroe Islands. Coach Claudio Ranieri was sacked after the home defeat to the Faroes. Whatever happened to Ranieri eh? He'll never work again, that's for sure.

In ten games, Greece scored only seven goals, four of which came in their final match against a Hungary side so desperate for a win that they ended up playing with a rush goalie. The poor old Greeks couldn't even blame it on a tough draw.

One way for punters to judge the standard of a qualifying group is to look at the list of top goalscorers. Wayne Rooney, Cristiano Ronaldo and Zlatan Ibrahimovic all finished top or joint-top of their group's scoring charts. Edin Dzeko and Gareth Bale stole the show in Group B while Group D was dominated by Robert Lewandowski and Thomas Muller.

In Greece's group, though, only one player scored more goals than Northern Ireland centre-back Gareth McAuley, who notched a handsome tally of three. That's your each-way bet for the Golden Boot sorted.

Northern Ireland qualified for their first European Championships in fine style, as the 33-1 ante-post shots won Group F by a point from Romania, whose rock-solid defence

Fans at Euro qualifiers – spot the odd one out

conceded only two goals in ten games.

Don't expect tiki-taka from Michael O'Neill's men – they had only 44 per cent of possession in their matches – but they're quite happy to sit back and wait for a moment of magic from the prolific McAuley.

Possession isn't everything, of course. Andorra had only 18 per cent of the ball in their Group B games yet still ended up with, er, no points. Gibraltar also drew a blank in their first ever qualifying campaign but they certainly laid down a marker with their impressive goal difference of minus 54.

Bale's Wales reached their first Euros and the other tournament debutants in France are Iceland, Albania and corner-shy Slovakia, who claimed only 37 per cent of the flag-kicks in their games. If you can't make money out of that statistical nugget, you may as well give up betting.

The Republic of Ireland came through a tricky playoff clash against Bosnia-Herzegovina, having already caused a huge shock in Group D by beating world champions Germany 1-0. That result was quite literally a Long shot as Shane Long scored Ireland's late winner, delighting connoisseurs of rubbish puns.

England's victory in Switzerland on matchday one effectively ended Group E as a contest, but Roy Hodgson's men kept their focus admirably to win ten out of ten in qualifying.

The Three Lions weren't given much of a scare by any opponents. In ten matches they allowed only 12 shots on target, leaving Hodgson with an unusual selection conundrum – should he even bother taking a goalkeeper to the finals? I suppose it's a nice problem to have.

Even the spectre of the penalty shootout shouldn't worry Roy's boys as Rooney rattled in four spot-kicks in qualifying. If he can hold his nerve in front of a raucous crowd of 4,378 away at San Marino, then slotting home the decisive penalty in the final in Paris should be a piece of tarte tatin.

GROUP A

	P	W	D	L	F	A	W	D	L	F	A	GD	Pts
			HOME						AWAY				
Czech Rep	10	3	1	1	7	6	4	0	1	12	8	+5	22
Iceland	10	3	2	0	9	3	3	0	2	8	3	+11	20
Turkey	10	3	1	1	9	4	2	2	1	5	5	+5	18
Holland	10	2	1	2	12	6	2	0	3	5	8	+3	13
Kazakhstan	10	0	1	4	3	10	1	1	3	4	8	-11	5
Latvia	10	0	1	4	2	9	0	4	1	4	10	-13	5

BEST ANTE-POST ODDS

Holland	2-7
Turkey	13-2
Czech Republic	8-1
Iceland	50-1
Latvia	250-1
Kazakhstan	1,000-1

Best win odds in the Racing Post

Matchday One
September 9, 2014

Czech Rep..... (1) 2-1 (0)..........**Holland**
HOME 10-3 DRAW 13-5 AWAY 1-1
POS 32/68
SH ON 4/3
SH OFF 4/4
CRN 6/5
SCORERS **Czech Rep:** Dockal (22) Pilar (90) **Holland:** de Vrij (55)
CARDS **Czech Rep:** Prochazka Limbersky **Holland:** Martins Indi

Iceland.......... (1) 3-0 (0)............**Turkey**
HOME 16-5 DRAW 12-5 AWAY 11-10
POS 45/55
SH ON 5/5
SH OFF 7/7
CRN 6/5
SCORERS **Iceland:** Bodvarsson (18) Sigurdsson (75) Sigthorsson (77)
CARDS **Iceland:** Skulason Sigurdsson **Turkey:** Gonul Toprak Turan

Kazakhstan .. (0) 0-0 (0)............**Latvia**
HOME 7-5 DRAW 9-4 AWAY 5-2
POS 57/43
SH ON 2/1
SH OFF 4/3
CRN 9/1
CARDS **Latvia:** Sabala Gorkss Zjuzins

Matchday Two
October 10, 2014

Holland......... (0) 3-1 (1)....**Kazakhstan**
HOME 1-12 DRAW 11-1 AWAY 40-1
POS 85/15
SH ON 9/2
SH OFF 12/1
CRN 8/1
SCORERS **Holland:** Huntelaar (61) Afellay (82) van Persie (pen 89) **Kazakhstan:** Abdulin (17)
CARDS **Kazakhstan:** Abdulin Dmitrenko Shomko Dzolchiev

Latvia .... (0) 0-3 (0)............**Iceland**
HOME 14-5 DRAW 12-5 AWAY 6-5
POS 30/70
SH ON 2/5
SH OFF 5/12
CRN 1/5
SCORERS **Iceland:** Sigurdsson (66) Gunnarsson (76) Gislason (90)
CARDS **Latvia:** Rudnevs Bulvitis Fertovs

Turkey........... (1) 1-2 (1)......**Czech Rep**
HOME 13-10 DRAW 23-10 AWAY 5-2
POS 60/40
SH ON 6/3
SH OFF 7/3
CRN 4/1
SCORERS **Turkey:** Bulut (8) **Czech Rep:** Sivok (15) Dockal (58)
CARDS **Turkey:** Ozyakup

Matchday Three
October 13, 2014

Iceland.......... (2) 2-0 (0)..........**Holland**
HOME 5-1 DRAW 3-1 AWAY 4-6
POS 26/74
SH ON 3/2
SH OFF 2/5
CRN 2/5
SCORERS **Iceland:** Sigurdsson (pen 10, 42)
CARDS **Holland:** de Jong

Kazakhstan .. (0) 2-4 (2)......**Czech Rep**
HOME 7-1 DRAW 15-4 AWAY 9-20
POS 47/53
SH ON 5/5
SH OFF 9/2
CRN 2/2
SCORERS **Kazakhstan:** Logvinenko (84, 90) **Czech Rep:** Dockal (13) Lafata (44) Krejci (56) Necid (87)
CARDS **Kazakhstan:** Tagybergen Nusserbayev **Czech Rep:** Kolar Darida

Latvia .... (0) 1-1 (0)............**Turkey**
HOME 21-4 DRAW 29-10 AWAY 4-6
POS 30/70
SH ON 4/6
SH OFF 3/9
CRN 3/6
SCORERS **Latvia:** Sabala (pen 54) **Turkey:** Bilal Kisa (47)
CARDS **Latvia:** Sabala Visnakovs Freimanis **Turkey:** Turan Tore Bilal Kisa Altintop

Matchday Four
November 16, 2014

Czech Rep..... (1) 2-1 (1)..........**Iceland**
HOME 4-5 DRAW 11-4 AWAY 9-2
POS 61/39
SH ON 4/3
SH OFF 11/2
CRN 8/3
SCORERS **Czech Rep:** Kaderabek (45) Bodvarsson (61 og) **Iceland:** Sigurdsson (9)
CARDS **Czech Rep:** Dockal **Iceland:** Sigurdsson Bjarnason Gislason Sigthorsson

Holland........ (3) 6-0 (0)............**Latvia**
HOME 1-6 DRAW 7-1 AWAY 20-1
POS 77/23
SH ON 13/2
SH OFF 8/5
CRN 14/2
SCORERS **Holland:** van Persie (6) Robben (35, 82) Huntelaar (42, 89) Bruma (77)
CARDS **Holland:** de Vrij **Latvia:** Zjuzins Kurakins Laizans

Turkey........... (2) 3-1 (0)....**Kazakhstan**
HOME 1-4 DRAW 11-2 AWAY 18-1
POS 66/34
SH ON 7/3
SH OFF 10/2
CRN 4/6
SCORERS **Turkey:** Burak Yilmaz (pen 26, 29) Aziz (82) **Kazakhstan:** Smakov (pen 87)
CARDS **Turkey:** Burak Yilmaz Mehmet Topal Turan **Kazakhstan:** Nurgaliev

Matchday Five
March 28, 2015

Czech Rep..... (0) 1-1 (1)............**Latvia**
HOME 1-4 DRAW 11-2 AWAY 18-1
POS 73/27
SH ON 6/3
SH OFF 8/4
CRN 12/5
SCORERS **Czech Rep:** Pilar (90) **Latvia:** Visnakovs (30)
CARDS **Czech Rep:** Limbersky Dockal **Latvia:** Gorkss Freimanis

Holland........ (0) 1-1 (1)............**Turkey**
HOME 4-7 DRAW 10-3 AWAY 6-1
POS 70/30
SH ON 8/2
SH OFF 7/5
CRN 5/0
SCORERS **Holland:** Huntelaar (90) **Turkey:** Burak Yilmaz (37)
CARDS **Holland:** van der Wiel **Turkey:** Tore

Kazakhstan .. (0) 0-3 (2)..........**Iceland**
HOME 18-5 DRAW 12-5 AWAY 20-21
POS 50/50
SH ON 3/7
SH OFF 4/6
CRN 3/3
SCORERS **Iceland:** Gudjohnsen (20) Bjarnason (32, 90)
CARDS **Kazakhstan:** Nurgaliev Kuantayev **Iceland:** Skulason

Iceland......... (0) **2-1** (0).....**Czech Rep**
HOME 15-8   DRAW 11-5   AWAY 13-8
POS   52/48
SH ON 4/3
SH OFF 3/6
CRN   4/4
SCORERS **Iceland**: Gunnarsson (60)
Sigthorsson (76) **Czech Rep**: Dockal (55)
CARDS **Czech Rep**: Rosicky Krejci

Kazakhstan .. (0) **0-1** (0)...........**Turkey**
HOME 15-2   DRAW 7-2   AWAY 1-2
POS   41/59
SH ON 1/5
SH OFF 3/11
CRN   3/7
SCORERS **Turkey**: Turan (83)
CARDS **Kazakhstan**: Schmidtgal
Abdulin Shomko

Latvia .... (0) **0-2** (0).........**Holland**
HOME 20-1   DRAW 11-2   AWAY 1-5
POS   32/68
SH ON 0/10
SH OFF 3/11
CRN   0/8
SCORERS **Holland**: Wijnaldum (67)
Narsingh (71)
CARDS **Latvia**: Rakels **Holland**:
Martins Indi

Czech Rep..... (0) **2-1** (1)....**Kazakhstan**
HOME 1-5   DRAW 13-2   AWAY 18-1
POS   68/32
SH ON 2/1
SH OFF 11/5
CRN   11/1
SCORERS **Czech Rep**: Skoda (74, 86)
Kazakhstan: Logvinenko (21)
CARDS **Kazakhstan**: Shomko

Holland......... (0) **0-1** (0)...........**Iceland**
HOME 4-11   DRAW 17-4   AWAY 9-1

GROUP A TOP SCORERS

POS   65/35
SH ON 9/3
SH OFF 5/5
CRN   7/2
SCORERS **Iceland**: Sigurdsson (pen 51)
CARDS **Holland**: van der Wiel
Sneijder Martins Indi **Iceland**:
Sigthorsson Arnason Saevarsson

Turkey.......... (0) **1-1** (0)...........**Latvia**
HOME 1-4   DRAW 11-2   AWAY 17-1
POS   70/30
SH ON 12/4
SH OFF 6/5
CRN   8/4
SCORERS **Turkey**: Inan (77) **Latvia**:
Sabala (90)
CARDS **Turkey**: Tufan
Latvia: Tarasovs Vanins Visnakovs

Iceland......... (0) **0-0** (0)....**Kazakhstan**
HOME 1-3   DRAW 5-1   AWAY 11-1
POS   55/45
SH ON 2/1
SH OFF 5/2
CRN   7/0
CARDS **Iceland**: Gudmundsson
Gunnarsson **Kazakhstan**: Dzolchiev
Suyumbayev Logvinenko Merkel

Latvia .... (0) **1-2** (2).....**Czech Rep**
HOME 6-1   DRAW 16-5   AWAY 6-10
POS   42/58
SH ON 3/8
SH OFF 4/2
CRN   3/4
SCORERS **Latvia**: Zjuzins (73) **Czech
Rep**: Limbersky (13) Darida (25)
CARDS **Latvia**: Maksimenko Dubra

Turkey.......... (2) **3-0** (0).........**Holland**
HOME 5-2   DRAW 5-2   AWAY 5-4
POS   32/68
SH ON 4/4
SH OFF 3/6
CRN   2/5
SCORERS **Turkey**: Ozyakup (8) Turan
(26) Burak Yilmaz (85)

CARDS **Turkey**: Turan Ozbayrakli
Balta Ozyakup Tufan
Holland: van Persie van der Wiel

Czech Rep..... (0) **0-2** (0)...........**Turkey**
HOME 7-4   DRAW 23-10   AWAY 9-5
POS   62/38
SH ON 2/3
SH OFF 7/6
CRN   6/1
SCORERS **Turkey**: Inan (pen 62)
Calhanoglu (79)
CARDS **Czech Rep**: Krejci Dockal
Pavelka Novak **Turkey**: Ozbayrakli
Volkan Sen

Iceland......... (2) **2-2** (0)...........**Latvia**
HOME 9-20   DRAW 18-5   AWAY 8-1
POS   58/42
SH ON 7/7
SH OFF 4/10
CRN   3/4
SCORERS **Iceland**: Sigthorsson (5)
Sigurdsson (27) **Latvia**: Cauna (49)
Sabala (68)
CARDS **Iceland**: Finnbogason
Sigurdsson **Latvia**: Tarasovs
Maksimenko

Kazakhstan .. (0) **1-2** (1).........**Holland**
HOME 14-1   DRAW 11-2   AWAY 2-7
POS   40/60
SH ON 2/7
SH OFF 6/6
CRN   3/3
SCORERS **Kazakhstan**: Kuat (90)
Holland: Wijnaldum (33) Sneijder (50)
CARDS **Kazakhstan**: Logvinenko
Holland: Blind Bruma El Ghazi

Holland........ (0) **2-3** (2)......**Czech Rep**
HOME 4-9   DRAW 4-1   AWAY 8-1
POS   60/40
SH ON 4/3
SH OFF 6/4
CRN   6/5
SCORERS **Holland**: Huntelaar (70) van
Persie (83) **Czech Rep**: Kaderabek (24)
Sural (35) van Persie (66 og)
CARDS **Holland**: Huntelaar Blind
van Persie Sneijder **Czech Rep**:
Skalak Gebre Selassie Suchy

Latvia .... (0) **0-1** (0)....**Kazakhstan**
HOME 5-4   DRAW 23-10   AWAY 11-4
POS   55/45
SH ON 1/8
SH OFF 4/4
CRN   7/1
SCORERS **Kazakhstan**: Kuat (65)
CARDS **Latvia**: Karasausks
Kazakhstan: Kuat

Turkey.......... (0) **1-0** (0)...........**Iceland**
HOME 4-7   DRAW 16-5   AWAY 7-1
POS   55/45
SH ON 4/0
SH OFF 4/4
CRN   2/4
SCORERS **Turkey**: Inan (89)
CARDS **Turkey**: Tosun Tore
Iceland: Gudmundsson

	P	Goals	
G Sigurdsson (Iceland)	10	6	●●●●●●
K-J Huntelaar (Holland)	8	5	●●●●●
B Yilmaz (Turkey)	6	4	●●●●
B Dockal (Czech Rep)	9	4	●●●●
R van Persie (Holland)	8	4	●●●●
S Inan (Turkey)	9	3	●●●
V Sabala (Latvia)	9	3	●●●
Y Logvinenko (Kazakhstan)	9	3	●●●
K Sigthorsson (Iceland)	10	3	●●●

Players scoring three goals or more in this group

WORLD CUP 2018 EUROPEAN QUALIFYING DRAW

Group A Holland, France, Sweden, Bulgaria, Belarus, Luxembourg **Group B** Portugal, Switzerland, Hungary, Faroe Islands, Latvia, Andorra **Group C** Germany, Czech Rep, N Ireland, Norway, Azerbaijan, San Marino **Group E** Romania, Denmark, Poland, Montenegro, Armenia, Kazakhstan **Group I** Croatia, Iceland, Ukraine, Turkey, Finland

Hosts Russia and nine group winners qualify. Eight best runners-up go to playoffs

	P	W	D	L	F	A	W	D	L	F	A	GD	Pts
			HOME						AWAY				
Belgium	10	4	1	0	17	2	3	1	1	7	3	+19	23
Wales	10	3	2	0	5	1	3	1	1	6	3	+7	21
Bosnia-Hz.	10	3	1	1	10	4	2	1	2	7	8	+5	17
Israel	10	2	0	3	8	6	2	1	2	8	8	+2	13
Cyprus	10	1	0	4	8	7	3	0	2	8	10	-1	12
Andorra	10	0	0	5	4	16	0	0	5	0	20	-32	0

BEST ANTE-POST ODDS

Belgium	4-9
Bosnia-Hz	3-1
Israel	25-1
Wales	33-1
Cyprus	200-1
Andorra	5,000-1

Best win odds in the Racing Post

Matchday One
September 9, 2014

Andorra .... (1) 1-2 (1) .... Wales
HOME 25-1   DRAW 10-1   AWAY 1-6
POS   24/76
SH ON   1/5
SH OFF   1/4
CRN   0/8
SCORERS **Andorra:** Lima (pen 6)
Wales: Bale (22, 81)
CARDS **Andorra:** Peppe ▌ Lorenzo ▌
Maneiro ▌ Vieira ▌ Riera ▌ Vales ▌
Wales: Allen ▌ Church ▌

Bosnia-Hz. .... (1) 1-2 (1) .... Cyprus
HOME 2-9   DRAW 13-2   AWAY 16-1
POS   69/31
SH ON   5/4
SH OFF   15/1
CRN   7/4
SCORERS **Bosnia-Hz.:** Ibisevic (6)
Cyprus: Christofi (45, 73)
CARDS **Bosnia-Hz.:** Prcic ▌ Dzeko ▌
Cyprus: Efrem ▌ Laban ▌

Matchday Two
October 10, 2014

Belgium .... (3) 6-0 (0) .... Andorra
HOME 1-100 DRAW 28-1   AWAY 66-1
POS   83/17
SH ON   8/0
SH OFF   11/1
CRN   12/0
SCORERS **Belgium:** De Bruyne (pen
30, 34) Chadli (37) Origi (58) Mertens
(65, 68)
CARDS **Andorra:** Vieira ▌ Ayala ▌
Lorenzo ▌ San Nicolas ▌

Cyprus .... (0) 1-2 (2) .... Israel
HOME 11-4   DRAW 23-10   AWAY 6-5
POS   57/43
SH ON   3/5
SH OFF   2/10
CRN   9/2
SCORERS **Cyprus:** Makrides (67)
Israel: Damari (38) Ben Haim (45)
CARDS **Cyprus:** Laban ▌
Israel: Meshumar ▌ Martziano ▌ Ben
Haim ▌ Rafaelov ▌

Wales............ (0) 0-0 (0) ..... Bosnia-Hz.
HOME 13-5   DRAW 12-5   AWAY 5-4
POS   40/60
SH ON   2/8
SH OFF   8/4
CRN   6/6
CARDS **Wales:** Taylor ▌ Chester ▌
Williams ▌ **Bosnia-Hz.:** Hadzic ▌
Pjanic ▌ Dzeko ▌

Matchday Three
October 13, 2014

Andorra .... (1) 1-4 (2) .... Israel
HOME 45-1   DRAW 14-1   AWAY 1-14
POS   20/80
SH ON   3/11
SH OFF   0/8
CRN   1/12
SCORERS **Andorra:** Lima (pen 14)
Israel: Damari (3, 41, 82) Hemed
(pen 90)
CARDS **Andorra:** Rubio ▌ Martinez Alejo
▌ **Israel:** Vermouth ▌

Bosnia-Hz. .... (1) 1-1 (1) .... Belgium
HOME 5-2   DRAW 12-5   AWAY 5-4
POS   38/62
SH ON   4/7
SH OFF   5/8
CRN   6/6
SCORERS **Bosnia-Hz.:** Dzeko (28)
Belgium: Nainggolan (51)
CARDS **Belgium:** Kompany ▌

Wales............ (2) 2-1 (1) .... Cyprus
HOME 4-9   DRAW 7-2   AWAY 8-1
POS   39/61
SH ON   8/2
SH OFF   5/5
CRN   8/1
SCORERS **Wales:** Cotterill (13) Robson-
Kanu (23) **Cyprus:** Laban (36)
CARDS **Wales:** Ledley ▌ Cotterill ▌
Bale ▌ Edwards ▌ King ▌
Cyprus: Nicolaou ▌ A Charalambous ▌
Sotiriou ▌ Kyriakou ▌ Merkis ▌

Matchday Four
November 16, 2014

Belgium .... (0) 0-0 (0) .... Wales
HOME 3-10   DRAW 5-1   AWAY 12-1
POS   60/40
SH ON   5/4
SH OFF   7/3
CRN   8/3
CARDS **Wales:** Ledley ▌ Allen ▌
Williams ▌ Hennessey ▌

Cyprus .... (3) 5-0 (0) .... Andorra
HOME 1-6   DRAW 8-1   AWAY 25-1
POS   83/17
SH ON   9/0
SH OFF   7/2
CRN   3/0
SCORERS **Cyprus:** Merkis (9) Efrem
(31, 42, 60) Christofi (pen 87)
CARDS **Andorra:** Martinez Alejo ▌
Pujol ▌

Israel .... (2) 3-0 (0) ..... Bosnia-Hz.
HOME 7-4   DRAW 23-10   AWAY 2-1
POS   61/39
SH ON   9/3
SH OFF   4/8
CRN   2/3
SCORERS **Israel:** Vermouth (36)
Damari (45) Zahavi (70)
CARDS **Israel:** Ben-Haim ▌ Yeini ▌
Biton ▌ **Bosnia-Hz.:** Spahic ▌ Kvrzic ▌
Sunjic ▌

Matchday Five
March 28, 2015

Andorra .... (0) 0-3 (1) ..... Bosnia-Hz.
HOME 40-1   DRAW 14-1   AWAY 1-11
POS   17/83
SH ON   0/5
SH OFF   3/12
CRN   0/6
SCORERS **Bosnia-Hz.:** Dzeko (13,
49, 62)
CARDS **Andorra:** Vieira ▌ Clemente ▌
Bosnia-Hz.: Vranjes ▌

Belgium .... (2) 5-0 (0) .... Cyprus
HOME 2-13   DRAW 8-1   AWAY 28-1
POS   67/33
SH ON   11/0
SH OFF   6/1
CRN   10/1
SCORERS **Belgium:** Fellaini (21, 66)
Benteke (35) Hazard (67) Batshuayi (80)

Israel .... (0) 0-3 (1) .... Wales
HOME 13-10 DRAW 23-10   AWAY 14-5
POS   47/53
SH ON   3/5
SH OFF   1/7
CRN   2/3
SCORERS **Wales:** Ramsey (45) Bale
(50, 77)
CARDS **Israel:** Rafaelov ▌ Tibi ▌▌

March 31, 2015

Israel .... (0) 0-1 (1) .... Belgium
HOME 13-2   DRAW 10-3   AWAY 8-15
POS   44/56
SH ON   5/7
SH OFF   3/9
CRN   5/5
SCORERS **Belgium:** Fellaini (9)
CARDS **Israel:** Dgani ▌ Yeini ▌
Rafaelov ▌ **Belgium:** Kompany ▌▌
Alderweireld ▌ Lombaerts ▌

Matchday Six
June 12, 2015

Andorra .... (1) 1-3 (2) .... Cyprus
HOME 14-1   DRAW 5-1   AWAY 1-4
POS   25/75
SH ON   2/5
SH OFF   4/2
CRN   3/8

SCORERS **Andorra:** Dosa Junior (2 og)
Cyprus: Mitides (14, 45, 53)
CARDS **Andorra:** Rubio ▌ Ayala ▌
Rebes ▌ Garcia ▌ **Cyprus:** Laban ▌

Bosnia-Hz. .... (2) 3-1 (1) ....Israel
HOME 8-11   DRAW 11-4   AWAY 9-2
POS   53/47
SH ON   6/4
SH OFF 8/4
CRN   7/1
SCORERS **Bosnia-Hz.:** Visca (42, 75)
Dzeko (pen 45) **Israel:** Ben Haim (41)
CARDS **Bosnia-Hz.:** Medunjanin ▌
Israel: Yeini ▌ Ben Harush ▌ Ben-Haim ▌

Wales............ (1) 1-0 (0) .... Belgium
HOME 17-4   DRAW 11-4   AWAY 4-5
POS   35/65
SH ON   2/1
SH OFF 3/8
CRN   1/9
SCORERS **Wales:** Bale (25)
CARDS **Wales:** Allen ▌
Belgium: Lombaerts ▌

Matchday Seven
September 3, 2015

Belgium .... (2) 3-1 (1) ..... Bosnia-Hz.
HOME 1-2   DRAW 7-2   AWAY 7-1
POS   67/33
SH ON   6/5
SH OFF 4/1
CRN   4/6
SCORERS **Belgium:** Fellaini (23) De
Bruyne (43) Hazard (pen 78)
Bosnia-Hz.: Dzeko (15)
CARDS **Bosnia-Hz.:** Kolasinac ▌
Sunjic ▌ Lulic ▌

Cyprus .... (0) 0-1 (0) ....Wales
HOME 9-2   DRAW 13-5   AWAY 5-6
POS   53/47
SH ON   1/5
SH OFF 7/1
CRN   3/3
SCORERS **Wales:** Bale (82)

Israel .... (4) 4-0 (0) .... Andorra
HOME 1-14   DRAW 14-1   AWAY 45-1
POS   84/16
SH ON   13/0
SH OFF 9/2
CRN   14/2
SCORERS **Israel:** Zahavi (3) Biton (22)
Hemed (pen 26) Dabour (38)
CARDS **Israel:** Hemed ▌ **Andorra:**
Vieira ▌ San Nicolas ▌ Rubio ▌

Matchday Eight
September 6, 2015

Bosnia-Hz. .... (3) 3-0 (0) .... Andorra
HOME 1-50   DRAW 28-1   AWAY 70-1
POS   89/11
SH ON   7/1
SH OFF 12/2
CRN   7/0
SCORERS **Bosnia-Hz.:** Bicakcic (14)
Dzeko (30) Lulic (45)
CARDS **Bosnia-Hz.:** Ibisevic ▌ Hadzic ▌
Besic ▌ **Andorra:** Martinez Alejo ▌
Ayala ▌ Rebes ▌ Rodriguez Soria ▌

Cyprus .... (0) 0-1 (0) .... Belgium
HOME 11-1   DRAW 17-4   AWAY 4-11
POS   46/54
SH ON   1/8
SH OFF 6/8
CRN   5/6
SCORERS **Belgium:** Hazard (86)
CARDS **Cyprus:** Antoniades ▌
Demetriou ▌ Economides ▌
Belgium: Kompany ▌

Wales............ (0) 0-0 (0) ....Israel
HOME 10-11   DRAW 13-5   AWAY 4-1
POS   62/38
SH ON   7/1
SH OFF 7/1
CRN   11/1
CARDS **Wales:** Richards ▌
Robson-Kanu ▌ **Israel:** Dabour ▌ Dasa ▌
Natcho ▌ Dgani ▌ Biton ▌

Matchday Nine
October 10, 2015

Andorra .... (0) 1-4 (2) .... Belgium
HOME 100-1   DRAW 33-1   AWAY 1-50
POS   14/86
SH ON   2/7
SH OFF 2/4
CRN   0/8
SCORERS **Andorra:** Lima (pen 51)
Belgium: Nainggolan (19) De Bruyne
(42) Hazard (pen 56) Depoitre (64)
CARDS **Andorra:** Rebes ▌ Sonejee ▌
Riera ▌ Garcia ▌ **Belgium:** Lukaku ▌
Vertonghen ▌ Depoitre ▌

Bosnia-Hz. .... (0) 2-0 (0) ....Wales
HOME 19-20   DRAW 13-5   AWAY 7-2
POS   57/43
SH ON   2/2
SH OFF 4/6
CRN   2/2
SCORERS **Bosnia-Hz.:** Djuric (71)
Ibisevic (90)
CARDS **Bosnia-Hz.:** Spahic ▌ Begovic ▌
Sunjic ▌ **Wales:** Taylor ▌

Israel .... (0) 1-2 (0) ....Cyprus
HOME 11-20   DRAW 10-3   AWAY 13-2
POS   64/36
SH ON   5/5
SH OFF 12/1
CRN   5/3
SCORERS **Israel:** Biton (76) **Cyprus:**
Dosa Junior (58) Demetriou (80)
CARDS **Israel:** Biton ▌ Ben Haim ▌
Cyprus: Antoniades ▌ Dosa Junior ▌

Matchday Ten
October 13, 2015

Belgium .... (0) 3-1 (0) ....Israel
HOME 4-11   DRAW 9-2   AWAY 9-1
POS   65/35
SH ON   9/2
SH OFF 10/2
CRN   7/2
SCORERS **Belgium:** Mertens (64)
De Bruyne (78) Hazard (84) **Israel:**
Hemed (88)
CARDS **Belgium:** De Bruyne ▌
Vertonghen ▌ **Israel:** Rikan ▌

Cyprus .... (2) 2-3 (2) ..... Bosnia-Hz.
HOME 18-5   DRAW 27-10   AWAY 9-10
POS   56/44
SH ON   4/3
SH OFF 4/6
CRN   11/2
SCORERS **Cyprus:** Charalampidis (32)
Mitides (41) **Bosnia-Hz.:** Medunjanin
(13, 44) Djuric (67)
CARDS **Cyprus:** Nikolaou ▌ Dosa Junior ▌
Bosnia-Hz.: Begovic ▌ Pjanic ▌ Djuric
▌ Mujdza ▌

Wales............ (0) 2-0 (0) .... Andorra
HOME 1-20   DRAW 20-1   AWAY 80-1
POS   81/19
SH ON   11/0
SH OFF 15/1
CRN   13/1
SCORERS **Wales:** Ramsey (50) Bale (86)
CARDS **Wales:** Vaughan ▌ Williams ▌
Gunter ▌ **Andorra:** Lima ▌ Lorenzo ▌
Vieira ▌ Pol ▌ Rodrigues ▌ Ayala ▌
Sanchez ▌

WORLD CUP 2018 EUROPEAN QUALIFYING DRAW

Group B Portugal, Switzerland, Hungary, Faroe Islands, Latvia, Andorra **Group D** Wales, Austria, Serbia, Ireland, Moldova, Georgia **Group G** Spain, Italy, Albania, Israel, Macedonia, Liechtenstein **Group H** Belgium, Bosnia-Hz., Greece, Estonia, Cyprus

Hosts Russia and nine group winners qualify. Eight best runners-up go to playoffs

GROUP B TOP SCORERS

	P	Goals
E Dzeko (Bosnia-Hz.)	7	7 ●●●●●●●
G Bale (Wales)	10	7 ●●●●●●●
O Damari (Israel)	6	5 ●●●●●
E Hazard (Belgium)	9	5 ●●●●●
K De Bruyne (Belgium)	10	5 ●●●●●
N Mytidis (Cyprus)	7	4 ●●●●
M Fellaini (Belgium)	8	4 ●●●●
D Christofi (Cyprus)	5	3 ●●●
G Efrem (Cyprus)	6	3 ●●●
T Hemed (Israel)	7	3 ●●●
D Mertens (Belgium)	9	3 ●●●
I Lima (Andorra)	10	3 ●●●

Players scoring three goals or more in this group

	P	W	D	L	F	A	W	D	L	F	A	GD	Pts
Spain	10	5	0	0	15	1	4	0	1	8	2	+20	27
Slovakia	10	3	1	1	7	3	4	0	1	10	5	+9	22
Ukraine	10	3	0	2	7	3	3	1	1	7	1	+10	19
Belarus	10	1	1	3	3	6	2	1	2	5	8	-6	11
Luxembourg	10	1	1	3	4	12	0	0	5	2	15	-21	4
Macedonia	10	1	0	4	4	9	0	1	4	2	9	-12	4

BEST ANTE-POST ODDS

Spain	1-12
Ukraine	9-1
Slovakia	25-1
Belarus	250-1
Macedonia	500-1
Luxembourg	5,000-1

Best win odds in the Racing Post

Matchday One
September 8, 2014

Luxembourg. (1) 1-1 (0)..........Belarus
HOME 7-1   DRAW 14-5   AWAY 4-7
POS   36/64
SH ON   2/7
SH OFF 6/12
CRN   3/7

SCORERS **Luxembourg:** Krogh Gerson (42) **Belarus:** Dragun (78)

CARDS **Luxembourg:** Martins Pereira ▌ Philipps ▌ Krogh Gerson ▌ Da Mota ▌ Payal ▌ **Belarus:** Olekhnovich ▌ Martynovich ▌

Spain .... (3) 5-1 (1).....Macedonia
HOME 1-12   DRAW 12-1   AWAY 33-1
POS   67/33
SH ON   8/7
SH OFF 8/2
CRN   8/5

SCORERS **Spain:** Ramos (pen 15) Alcacer (17) Busquets (45) Silva (50) Pedro (90) **Macedonia:** Ibraimi (pen 28)

CARDS **Spain:** Koke ▌ Fabregas ▌ **Macedonia:** Ristovski ▌ Abdurahimi ▌

Ukraine......... (0) 0-1 (1)........Slovakia
HOME 7-10   DRAW 29-10   AWAY 5-1
POS   60/40
SH ON   2/2
SH OFF 14/3
CRN   4/1

SCORERS **Slovakia:** Mak (17)

CARDS **Ukraine:** Stepanenko ▌ Rakitskiy ▌ Bezus ▌ Fedetskyy ▌ Edmar ▌ **Slovakia:** Kucka ▌ Durica ▌ Nemec ▌ Kiss ▌

Matchday Two
October 9, 2014

Belarus .... (0) 0-2 (0).........Ukraine
HOME 13-5   DRAW 11-5   AWAY 11-8
POS   34/66
SH ON   2/1
SH OFF 2/4
CRN   6/6

SCORERS **Ukraine:** Martynovich (82 og) Sydorchuk (90)

CARDS **Belarus:** Polyakov ▌ **Ukraine:** Kucher ▌ Zozulya ▌

Macedonia ... (1) 3-2 (2).. Luxembourg
HOME 4-9   DRAW 15-4   AWAY 9-1
POS   52/48
SH ON   3/4
SH OFF 11/6
CRN   4/5

SCORERS **Macedonia:** Trajkovski (20) Jahovic (pen 66) Abdurahimi (90) **Luxembourg:** Bensi (39) Turpel (44)

CARDS **Macedonia:** Mojsov ▌ Ristevski ▌ Sikov ▌ **Luxembourg:** Turpel ▌ Mutsch ▌ Janisch ▌ Laterza ▌ Philipps ▌

Slovakia........ (1) 2-1 (0)..............Spain
HOME 9-1   DRAW 15-4   AWAY 2-5
POS   27/73
SH ON   4/7
SH OFF 1/7
CRN   3/19

SCORERS **Slovakia:** Kucka (17) Stoch (87) **Spain:** Alcacer (82)

CARDS **Slovakia:** Kucka ▌ Hubocan ▌ Stoch ▌ Gyomber ▌ **Spain:** Silva ▌ Cazorla ▌ Costa ▌

Matchday Three
October 12, 2014

Belarus .... (0) 1-3 (0)........Slovakia
HOME 5-2   DRAW 12-5   AWAY 13-10
POS   54/46
SH ON   3/7
SH OFF 7/7
CRN   6/3

SCORERS **Belarus:** Kalachev (79) **Slovakia:** Hamsik (65, 83) Sestak (90)

CARDS **Belarus:** Verkhovtsov ▌ Shitov ▌ **Slovakia:** Gyomber ▌

Luxembourg. (0) 0-4 (2)..............Spain
HOME 66-1   DRAW 20-1   AWAY 1-25
POS   31/69
SH ON   2/7
SH OFF 2/6
CRN   4/6

SCORERS **Spain:** Silva (26) Alcacer (42) Costa (69) Bernat (88)

CARDS **Luxembourg:** Holter ▌ Jans ▌ **Spain:** Costa ▌ Pique ▌

Ukraine......... (1) 1-0 (0).....Macedonia
HOME 2-5   DRAW 15-4   AWAY 9-1
POS   65/35
SH ON   4/3
SH OFF 11/5
CRN   3/11

SCORERS **Ukraine:** Sydorchuk (45)

CARDS **Ukraine:** Fedetskyy ▌ Sydorchuk ▌ Rotan ▌ Budkivsky ▌ **Macedonia:** Jahovic ▌ Damcevski ▌ Trajkovski ▌ Abdurahimi ▌ Velkoski ▌

Matchday Four
November 15, 2014

Luxembourg. (0) 0-3 (1)..........Ukraine
HOME 16-1   DRAW 5-1   AWAY 1-4
POS   40/60
SH ON   3/6
SH OFF 4/8
CRN   3/6

SCORERS **Ukraine:** Yarmolenko (33, 53, 56)

CARDS **Luxembourg:** Martins Pereira ▌ **Ukraine:** Sydorchuk ▌ Khacheridi ▌

Macedonia ... (0) 0-2 (2)........Slovakia
HOME 18-5   DRAW 12-5   AWAY 1-1
POS   55/45
SH ON   4/3
SH OFF 12/5
CRN   5/5

SCORERS **Slovakia:** Kucka (25) Nemec (38)

CARDS **Macedonia:** Kostovski ▌ **Slovakia:** Skrtel ▌

Spain .... (2) 3-0 (0)..........Belarus
HOME 1-10   DRAW 12-1   AWAY 40-1
POS   75/25
SH ON   4/1
SH OFF 3/4
CRN   2/5

SCORERS **Spain:** Isco (18) Busquets (19) Pedro (55)

CARDS **Spain:** Busquets ▌ **Belarus:** Kalachev ▌ Balanovich ▌ Bardachow ▌

Matchday Five
March 27, 2015

Macedonia ... (1) 1-2 (1)..........Belarus
HOME 21-10   DRAW 9-4   AWAY 13-8
POS   44/56
SH ON   2/9
SH OFF 6/6
CRN   3/3

SCORERS **Macedonia:** Trajkovski (9) **Belarus:** Kalachev (44) Kornilenko (81)

CARDS **Macedonia:** Sikov ▌ Markoski ▌ Georgievski ▌ Trajkovski ▌ **Belarus:** Martynovich ▌ Kalachev ▌ Kislyak ▌ Shitov ▌ Stasevich ▌ Bardachow ▌

Slovakia......... (3) 3-0 (0).. Luxembourg
HOME 1-7   DRAW 9-1   AWAY 25-1
POS   62/38
SH ON   5/1
SH OFF 2/0
CRN   5/3

SCORERS **Slovakia:** Nemec (10) Weiss (21) Pekarik (39)

CARDS **Slovakia:** Pekarik ▌ Skrtel ▌ **Luxembourg:** Deville ▌ Holter ▌ Mutsch ▌

Spain .... (1) 1-0 (0).........Ukraine
HOME 3-10   DRAW 9-2   AWAY 13-1
POS   67/33
SH ON   3/2
SH OFF 8/7
CRN   2/5

SCORERS **Spain:** Morata (28)

CARDS **Spain:** Ramos ▌ **Ukraine:** Fedetskyy ▌ Kravets ▌ Kucher ▌

Belarus .... (0) 0-1 (1) ....**Spain**
HOME 11-1   DRAW 9-2   AWAY 1-3
POS   31/69
SH ON   2/10
SH OFF   2/10
CRN   1/9
SCORERS **Spain:** Silva (45)
CARDS **Belarus:** Bardachow
Nekhajchik **Spain:** Morata
Pedro Silva

Slovakia .... (2) 2-1 (0) .....**Macedonia**
HOME 2-7   DRAW 5-1   AWAY 15-1
POS   55/45
SH ON   6/3
SH OFF   3/2
CRN   2/2
SCORERS **Slovakia:** Salata (8) Hamsik
(38) **Macedonia:** Ademi (69)
CARDS **Slovakia:** Kucka Skrtel
Weiss **Macedonia:** Hasani

Ukraine .... (0) 3-0 (0) .. **Luxembourg**
HOME 1-8   DRAW 17-2   AWAY 25-1
POS   72/28
SH ON   6/1
SH OFF   7/2
CRN   10/1
SCORERS **Ukraine:** Kravets (49)
Harmash (57) Konoplyanka (86)
CARDS **Luxembourg:** Da Mota
Mutsch Bensi Payal

Luxembourg. (0) 1-0 (0) .....**Macedonia**
HOME 7-2   DRAW 12-5   AWAY 11-10
POS   48/52
SH ON   2/4
SH OFF   6/2
CRN   4/5
SCORERS **Luxembourg:** Thill (90)
CARDS **Luxembourg:** Martins Pereira
Macedonia: Zuta Ristovski
Abdurahimi Ristevski

Spain .... (2) 2-0 (0) ....**Slovakia**
HOME 1-3   DRAW 11-2   AWAY 14-1
POS   79/21
SH ON   3/2
SH OFF   10/3
CRN   9/3
SCORERS **Spain:** Alba (5) Iniesta
(pen 30)
CARDS **Slovakia:** Kozacik Tesak

Ukraine .... (3) 3-1 (0) ....**Belarus**
HOME 1-2   DRAW 7-2   AWAY 17-2
POS   51/49
SH ON   9/2
SH OFF   8/3
CRN   6/1
SCORERS **Ukraine:** Kravets (7)
Yarmolenko (30) Konoplyanka (pen 40)
Belarus: Kornilenko (pen 62)
CARDS **Ukraine:** Harmash
Khacheridi Rotan
Belarus: Sivakov Martynovich

Belarus .... (1) 2-0 (0).. **Luxembourg**
HOME 4-11   DRAW 9-2   AWAY 10-1
POS   62/38
SH ON   3/1
SH OFF   7/5
CRN   5/3
SCORERS **Belarus:** Gordejchuk (34, 62)
CARDS **Luxembourg:** Philipps

Macedonia ... (0) 0-1 (1) ....**Spain**
HOME 25-1   DRAW 7-1   AWAY 1-6
POS   26/74
SH ON   0/1
SH OFF   2/5
CRN   1/6
SCORERS **Spain:** Pacovski (8 og)
CARDS **Macedonia:** Petrovic **Spain:**
Costa Busquets

Slovakia .... (0) 0-0 (0) ....**Ukraine**
HOME 13-8   DRAW 11-5   AWAY 21-10
POS   38/62
SH ON   2/1
SH OFF   7/6
CRN   5/5
CARDS **Slovakia:** Hamsik Gyomber
Ukraine: Rybalka Konoplyanka
Stepanenko

Macedonia ... (0) 0-2 (0) ....**Ukraine**
HOME 9-1   DRAW 10-3   AWAY 1-2
POS   30/70
SH ON   2/7
SH OFF   1/8
CRN   2/13
SCORERS **Ukraine:** Seleznev (pen 59)
Kravets (87)
CARDS **Macedonia:** Brdarovski Zuta
Ukraine: Fedetskyy Khacheridi
Sydorchuk

Slovakia .... (0) 0-1 (1) ....**Belarus**
HOME 3-5   DRAW 16-5   AWAY 6-1
POS   59/41
SH ON   6/1
SH OFF   7/3
CRN   6/3

SCORERS **Belarus:** Dragun (34)
CARDS **Slovakia:** Skrtel
Belarus: Stasevich Martynovich
Gordejchuk Polyakov

Spain .... (1) 4-0 (0).. **Luxembourg**
HOME 1-50   DRAW 40-1   AWAY 80-1
POS   74/26
SH ON   9/1
SH OFF   10/4
CRN   8/2
SCORERS **Spain:** Cazorla (42, 85)
Alcacer (67, 80)
CARDS **Spain:** Pedro **Luxembourg:**
Bensi Malget Da Mota

Belarus .... (0) 0-0 (0) .....**Macedonia**
HOME 5-6   DRAW 13-5   AWAY 4-1
POS   54/46
SH ON   4/2
SH OFF   7/3
CRN   6/2
CARDS **Belarus:** Dragun Kislyak
Macedonia: Zuta

Luxembourg. (0) 2-4 (3) ....**Slovakia**
HOME 11-1   DRAW 9-2   AWAY 1-3
POS   47/53
SH ON   3/6
SH OFF   7/7
CRN   6/4
SCORERS **Luxembourg:** Mutsch (61)
Krogh Gerson (pen 65) **Slovakia:**
Hamsik (24, 90) Nemec (29) Mak (30)
CARDS **Luxembourg:** Mutsch
Philipps Payal Jans **Slovakia:**
Kucka Sestak Skrtel

Ukraine .... (0) 0-1 (1) ....**Spain**
HOME 21-10 DRAW 23-10   AWAY 13-8
POS   39/61
SH ON   10/7
SH OFF   11/3
CRN   8/5
SCORERS **Spain:** Mario (21)
CARDS **Ukraine:** Kucher
Stepanenko Fedetskyy
Spain: Alcantara San Jose de Gea

GROUP C TOP SCORERS

	P	Goals	
P Alcacer (Spain)	8	5	●●●●●
M Hamsik (Slovakia)	10	5	●●●●●
A Yarmolenko (Ukraine)	10	4	●●●●
A Kravets (Ukraine)	6	3	●●●
A Nemec (Slovakia)	7	3	●●●
D Silva (Spain)	8	3	●●●

Players scoring three goals or more in this group

WORLD CUP 2018 EUROPEAN QUALIFYING DRAW

Group A Holland, France, Sweden, Bulgaria, Belarus, Luxembourg
Group F England, Slovakia, Scotland, Slovenia, Lithuania, Malta **Group G** Spain, Italy, Albania, Israel, Macedonia, Liechtenstein **Group I** Croatia, Iceland, Ukraine, Turkey, Finland

Hosts Russia and nine group winners qualify. Eight best runners-up go to playoffs

GROUP D

		HOME					AWAY					
	P	W	D	L	F	A	W	D	L	F	A	GD	Pts
Germany	10	4	1	0	12	4	3	0	2	12	5	+15	22
Poland	10	4	1	0	18	4	2	2	1	15	6	+23	21
Ireland	10	3	2	0	11	2	2	1	2	8	5	+12	18
Scotland	10	3	1	1	12	6	1	2	2	10	6	+10	15
Georgia	10	2	0	3	6	8	1	0	4	4	8	-6	9
Gibraltar	10	0	0	5	0	27	0	0	5	2	29	-54	0

BEST ANTE-POST ODDS

Germany	1-8
Poland	10-1
Ireland	16-1
Scotland	40-1
Georgia	500-1
Gibraltar	10,000-1

Best win odds in the Racing Post

Matchday One
September 7, 2014

Georgia .... (1) 1-2 (1) .... Ireland
HOME 12-5   DRAW 9-4   AWAY 11-8
POS   45/55
SH ON   2/3
SH OFF   2/3
CRN   4/4
SCORERS **Georgia:** Okriashvili (38)
Ireland: McGeady (23, 90)
CARDS **Georgia:** Kvirkvelia ▌ Khubutia ▌ Daushvili ▌ **Ireland:** Walters ▌

Germany ...... (1) 2-1 (0) ...... Scotland
HOME 1-6   DRAW 15-2   AWAY 18-1
POS   69/31
SH ON   9/3
SH OFF   11/4
CRN   12/1
SCORERS **Germany:** Muller (18, 70)
Scotland: Anya (66)
CARDS **Germany:** Durm ▌ Muller ▌ **Scotland:** Hanley ▌ Morrison ▌ Mulgrew ▌

Gibraltar ...... (0) 0-7 (1) .... Poland
HOME 30-1   DRAW 14-1   AWAY 1-12
POS   32/68
SH ON   1/15
SH OFF   3/9
CRN   3/9
SCORERS **Poland:** Grosicki (10, 48) Lewandowski (50, 53, 86, 90) Szukala (58)
CARDS **Gibraltar:** Artell ▌ **Poland:** Klich ▌ Glik ▌

Matchday Two
October 11, 2014

Ireland .... (3) 7-0 (0) .... Gibraltar
HOME 1-50   DRAW 33-1   AWAY 66-1
POS   67/33
SH ON   16/2
SH OFF   6/1
CRN   10/4
SCORERS **Ireland:** Keane (6, 14, pen 18) McClean (46, 53) Perez (51 og) Hoolahan (56)

Poland .... (0) 2-0 (0) .... Germany
HOME 6-1   DRAW 10-3   AWAY 8-15
POS   33/67
SH ON   3/9
SH OFF   2/10
CRN   0/6
SCORERS **Poland:** Milik (51) Mila (88)
CARDS **Poland:** Szukala ▌ Lewandowski ▌ Piszczek ▌ **Germany:** Boateng ▌ Bellarabi ▌

Scotland .... (1) 1-0 (0) .... Georgia
HOME 8-11   DRAW 11-4   AWAY 5-1

POS   63/37
SH ON   5/0
SH OFF   9/4
CRN   9/3
SCORERS **Scotland:** Khubutia (28 og)
CARDS **Scotland:** Morrison ▌ Maloney ▌ **Georgia:** Grigalava ▌ Daushvili ▌

Matchday Three
October 14, 2014

Germany ...... (0) 1-1 (0) .... Ireland
HOME 2-7   DRAW 21-4   AWAY 14-1
POS   65/35
SH ON   8/1
SH OFF   7/0
CRN   9/1
SCORERS **Germany:** Kroos (71)
Ireland: O'Shea (90)
CARDS **Germany:** Hummels ▌ **Ireland:** Whelan ▌ Wilson ▌

Gibraltar ...... (0) 0-3 (2) ....Georgia
HOME 20-1   DRAW 7-1   AWAY 2-11
POS   29/71
SH ON   3/12
SH OFF   2/2
CRN   6/5
SCORERS **Georgia:** Gelashvili (9) Okriashvili (19) Kankava (69)
CARDS **Gibraltar:** Garcia ▌ Casciaro ▌ Chipolina ▌ **Georgia:** Dzaria ▌ Papunashvili ▌

Poland .... (1) 2-2 (1) .... Scotland
HOME 19-20   DRAW 5-2   AWAY 15-4
POS   45/55
SH ON   4/3
SH OFF   9/2
CRN   7/2
SCORERS **Poland:** Maczynski (11) Milik (76) **Scotland:** Maloney (18) Naismith (57)
CARDS **Poland:** Krychowiak ▌ Mila ▌ **Scotland:** Greer ▌

Matchday Four
November 14, 2014

Georgia .... (0) 0-4 (0) .... Poland
HOME 15-4   DRAW 12-5   AWAY 19-20
POS   44/56
SH ON   0/7
SH OFF   10/6
CRN   4/4
SCORERS **Poland:** Glik (51) Krychowiak (70) Mila (73) Milik (90)
CARDS **Georgia:** Kankava ▌ Lobjanidze ▌ **Poland:** Glik ▌ Jodlowiec ▌ Linetty ▌

Germany ...... (3) 4-0 (0) ....Gibraltar
HOME 1-100   DRAW 50-1   AWAY 200-1
POS   84/16
SH ON   7/2
SH OFF   20/0
CRN   20/2

SCORERS **Germany:** Muller (12, 29) Gotze (38) Santos (67 og)

Scotland .... (0) 1-0 (0) .... Ireland
HOME 7-5   DRAW 9-4   AWAY 5-2
POS   58/42
SH ON   2/4
SH OFF   7/1
CRN   3/8
SCORERS **Scotland:** Maloney (74)
CARDS **Scotland:** Hanley ▌ Robertson ▌ **Ireland:** McGeady ▌ Hendrick ▌ Coleman ▌ Quinn ▌

Matchday Five
March 29, 2015

Georgia .... (0) 0-2 (2) .... Germany
HOME 25-1   DRAW 9-1   AWAY 2-13
POS   24/76
SH ON   0/8
SH OFF   3/8
CRN   7/8
SCORERS **Germany:** Reus (39) Muller (44)
CARDS **Georgia:** Makharadze ▌ Kankava ▌ Chanturia ▌ **Germany:** Schweinsteiger ▌

Ireland.......... (0) 1-1 (1) .... Poland
HOME 13-8   DRAW 9-4   AWAY 21-10
POS   56/44
SH ON   3/1
SH OFF   7/5
CRN   5/1
SCORERS **Ireland:** Long (90) **Poland:** Peszko (26)
CARDS **Ireland:** Hoolahan ▌ O'Shea ▌ Coleman ▌ Wilson ▌ McCarthy ▌ **Poland:** Glik ▌ Szukala ▌ Peszko ▌

Scotland .... (4) 6-1 (1) ....Gibraltar
HOME 1-50   DRAW 40-1   AWAY 100-1
POS   73/27
SH ON   12/2
SH OFF   8/3
CRN   6/2
SCORERS **Scotland:** Maloney (pen 18, pen 34) Fletcher (29, 77, 90) Naismith (39) **Gibraltar:** Casciaro (19)

Matchday Six
June 13, 2015

Gibraltar ...... (0) 0-7 (1) .... Germany
HOME 150-1   DRAW 80-1   AWAY 1-100
POS   27/73
SH ON   7/16
SH OFF   3/7
CRN   2/6
SCORERS **Germany:** Schurrle (28, 65, 71) Kruse (47, 81) Gundogan (51) Bellarabi (57)
CARDS **Gibraltar:** Chipolina ▌ Casciaro ▌

Ireland.......... (1) 1-1 (0)........ Scotland
HOME 7-5   DRAW 11-5   AWAY 5-2
POS   52/48
SH ON   5/1
SH OFF   3/3
CRN   13/4
SCORERS Ireland: Walters (38)
Scotland: O'Shea (47 og)
CARDS Ireland: Whelan ▌ McCarthy ▌
McClean ▌ Scotland: Naismith ▌

Poland .... (0) 4-0 (0).........Georgia
HOME 3-10   DRAW 19-4   AWAY 12-1
POS   46/54
SH ON   11/3
SH OFF   6/3
CRN   9/5
SCORERS Poland: Milik (62)
Lewandowski (89, 90, 90)

Matchday Seven
September 4, 2015

Georgia .... (1) 1-0 (0)........ Scotland
HOME 15-4   DRAW 11-5   AWAY 21-20
POS   46/54
SH ON   3/0
SH OFF   4/4
CRN   5/7
SCORERS Georgia: Qazaishvili (37)
CARDS Georgia: Kashia ▌ Ananidze ▌
Navalovski ▌

Germany....... (2) 3-1 (1).......... Poland
HOME 3-10   DRAW 5-1   AWAY 10-1
POS   71/29
SH ON   10/8
SH OFF   8/3
CRN   9/2
SCORERS Germany: Muller (12) Gotze
(19, 82) Poland: Lewandowski (36)
CARDS Germany: Kroos ▌
Schweinsteiger ▌ Poland: Rybus ▌
Grosicki ▌

GROUP D TOP SCORERS

	P	Goals	
R Lewandowski (Poland)	10	13	●●●●●●●●●●●●●
T Muller (Germany)	9	9	●●●●●●●●●
S Fletcher (Scotland)	10	7	●●●●●●●
A Milik (Poland)	9	6	●●●●●●
R Keane (Ireland)	9	5	●●●●●
S Maloney (Scotland)	10	5	●●●●●
K Grosicki (Poland)	9	4	●●●●
M Kruse (Germany)	5	3	●●●
A Schurrle (Germany)	7	3	●●●
S Long (Ireland)	8	3	●●●
J Walters (Ireland)	9	3	●●●
M Gotze (Germany)	9	3	●●●
S Naismith (Scotland)	9	3	●●●
T Okriashvili (Georgia)	10	3	●●●

Players scoring three goals or more in this group

WORLD CUP 2018 EUROPEAN QUALIFYING DRAW

Group C Germany, Czech Rep, N Ireland, Norway, Azerbaijan, San Marino
Group D Wales, Austria, Serbia, Ireland, Moldova, Georgia **Group E** Romania, Denmark, Poland, Montenegro, Armenia, Kazakhstan **Group F** England, Slovakia, Scotland, Slovenia, Lithuania, Malta

Hosts Russia and nine group winners qualify. Eight best runners-up go to playoffs

Gibraltar........ (0) 0-4 (1)........... Ireland
HOME 66-1   DRAW 25-1   AWAY 1-33
POS   39/61
SH ON   2/8
SH OFF   1/11
CRN   4/12
SCORERS Ireland: Christie (26) Keane
(49, pen 51) Long (79)
CARDS Gibraltar: Casciaro ▌ Barnett ▌
Ireland: Walters ▌

Matchday Eight
September 7, 2015

Ireland.......... (0) 1-0 (0).........Georgia
HOME 8-15   DRAW 10-3   AWAY 7-1
POS   51/49
SH ON   7/2
SH OFF   4/3
CRN   6/1
SCORERS Ireland: Walters (69)
CARDS Ireland: Whelan ▌ McClean ▌

Poland .... (4) 8-1 (0)........ Gibraltar
HOME 1-100 DRAW 50-1 AWAY 150-1
POS   66/34
SH ON   16/7
SH OFF   6/2
CRN   11/5
SCORERS Poland: Grosicki (8, 15)
Lewandowski (18, 29) Milik (56, 72)
Blaszczykowski (pen 59) Kapustka (73)
Gibraltar: Gosling (87)

Scotland .... (2) 2-3 (1)........ Germany
HOME 15-2   DRAW 15-4   AWAY 4-9
POS   28/72
SH ON   2/6
SH OFF   1/3
CRN   2/2
SCORERS Scotland: Hummels (28 og)
McArthur (43) Germany: Muller (18,
34) Gundogan (54)
CARDS Scotland: Morrison ▌ Maloney ▌

Matchday Nine
October 8, 2015

Georgia .... (3) 4-0 (0)........ Gibraltar
HOME 1-20   DRAW 20-1   AWAY 55-1
POS   71/29
SH ON   11/2
SH OFF   10/1
CRN   8/1
SCORERS Georgia: Vatsadze (30, 45)
Okriashvili (pen 35) Qazaishvili (87)
CARDS Georgia: Okriashvili ▌
Gibraltar: Cabrera ▌

Ireland.......... (0) 1-0 (0)........ Germany
HOME 13-2   DRAW 7-2   AWAY 8-15
POS   28/72
SH ON   2/3
SH OFF   2/8
CRN   4/11
SCORERS Ireland: Long (70)
CARDS Ireland: Hoolahan ▌
Germany: Hummels ▌

Scotland .... (1) 2-2 (1).......... Poland
HOME 19-10 DRAW 9-4 AWAY 17-10
POS   42/58
SH ON   3/5
SH OFF   4/7
CRN   2/4
SCORERS Scotland: Ritchie (45)
Fletcher (62) Poland: Lewandowski
(3, 90)
CARDS Scotland: Brown ▌ Hutton ▌
Poland: Rybus ▌ Krychowiak ▌

Matchday Ten
October 11, 2015

Germany....... (0) 2-1 (0).........Georgia
HOME 1-16   DRAW 18-1   AWAY 66-1
POS   71/29
SH ON   13/5
SH OFF   10/3
CRN   9/3
SCORERS Germany: Muller (pen 50)
Kruse (79) Georgia: Kankava (53)
CARDS Germany: Hummels ▌
Georgia: Navalovski ▌ Revishvili ▌
Okriashvili ▌

Gibraltar........ (0) 0-6 (2)........ Scotland
HOME 66-1   DRAW 28-1   AWAY 1-25
POS   34/66
SH ON   0/14
SH OFF   4/13
CRN   0/7
SCORERS Scotland: Martin (24)
Maloney (39) Fletcher (52, 56, 85)
Naismith (90)

Poland .... (2) 2-1 (1).......... Ireland
HOME 91-100 DRAW 5-2 AWAY 15-4
POS   55/45
SH ON   5/3
SH OFF   5/2
CRN   4/4
SCORERS Poland: Krychowiak (13)
Lewandowski (42) Ireland: Walters
(pen 16)
CARDS Poland: Glik ▌ Peszko ▌
Ireland: O'Shea ▌▌ Whelan ▌ Walters ▌

BEST ANTE-POST ODDS

	P	W	D	L	F	A	W	D	L	F	A	GD	Pts
England	10	5	0	0	16	1	5	0	0	15	2	+28	30
Switzerland	10	4	0	1	17	4	3	0	2	7	4	+16	21
Slovenia	10	3	1	1	11	4	2	0	3	7	7	+7	16
Estonia	10	3	0	2	4	2	0	1	4	0	7	-5	10
Lithuania	10	2	0	3	4	8	1	1	3	3	10	-11	10
San Marino	10	0	1	4	0	14	0	0	5	1	22	-35	1

England	8-11
Switzerland	5-2
Slovenia	12-1
Estonia	150-1
Lithuania	300-1
San Marino	5,000-1

Best win odds in the Racing Post

Matchday One
September 8, 2014

Estonia .... (0) 1-0 (0) ....**Slovenia**
HOME 13-5   DRAW 23-10   AWAY 5-4
POS   39/61
SH ON   3/2
SH OFF   5/6
CRN   3/9
SCORERS **Estonia:** Purje (86)
CARDS **Estonia:** Antonov
Slovenia: Stevanovic

San Marino... (0) 0-2 (2) ....**Lithuania**
HOME 17-1   DRAW 13-2   AWAY 1-5
POS   29/71
SH ON   0/5
SH OFF   1/5
CRN   2/5
SCORERS **Lithuania:** Matulevicius (5)
Novikovas (36)
CARDS **San Marino:** Gasperoni
Battistini Cervellini
Lithuania: Vicius

Switzerland.. (0) 0-2 (0) ....**England**
HOME 13-8   DRAW 9-4   AWAY 2-1
POS   56/44
SH ON   3/5
SH OFF   6/5
CRN   5/6
SCORERS **England:** Welbeck (58, 90)
CARDS **England:** Delph Lambert

Matchday Two
October 9, 2014

England .... (2) 5-0 (0) ....**San Marino**
HOME 1-100   DRAW 40-1   AWAY 100-1
POS   78/22
SH ON   17/1
SH OFF   6/1
CRN   16/0
SCORERS **England:** Jagielka (24)
Rooney (pen 43) Welbeck (49)
Townsend (72) Della Valle (77 og)
CARDS **England:** Milner
San Marino: Selva Rinaldi

Lithuania ...... (0) 1-0 (0) ....**Estonia**
HOME 5-4   DRAW 9-4   AWAY 27-10
POS   53/47
SH ON   6/3
SH OFF   4/4
CRN   4/6
SCORERS **Lithuania:** Mikoliunas (76)
CARDS **Lithuania:** Andriuskevicius
Vaitkunas **Estonia:** Zenjov
Kallaste

Slovenia........ (0) 1-0 (0) ... **Switzerland**
HOME 23-10   DRAW 9-4   AWAY 7-5
POS   29/71
SH ON   1/5
SH OFF   6/10
CRN   2/10

SCORERS **Slovenia:** Novakovic (pen 79)
CARDS **Slovenia:** Ljubijankic
Lazarevic **Switzerland:** Djourou

Matchday Three
October 12, 2014

Estonia .... (0) 0-1 (0) .... **England**
HOME 12-1   DRAW 5-1   AWAY 2-7
POS   24/76
SH ON   1/6
SH OFF   4/10
CRN   1/5
SCORERS **England:** Rooney (73)
CARDS **Estonia:** Klavan **England:**
Baines Henderson Wilshere

Lithuania ...... (0) 0-2 (2) ....**Slovenia**
HOME 11-4   DRAW 23-10   AWAY 5-4
POS   48/52
SH ON   3/5
SH OFF   5/3
CRN   4/1
SCORERS **Slovenia:** Novakovic (33, 37)
CARDS **Lithuania:** Novikovas
Matulevicius Chvedukas Kijanskas
Slovenia: Stevanovic

October 14, 2014

San Marino... (0) 0-4 (3)... **Switzerland**
HOME 100-1   DRAW 33-1   AWAY 1-66
POS   21/79
SH ON   0/14
SH OFF   2/9
CRN   2/12
SCORERS **Switzerland:** Seferovic (10, 24) Dzemaili (30) Shaqiri (79)
CARDS **San Marino:** Gasperoni
Bonini **Switzerland:** Dzemaili

Matchday Four
November 15, 2014

England .... (0) 3-1 (0) ....**Slovenia**
HOME 4-11   DRAW 17-4   AWAY 11-1
POS   60/40
SH ON   5/0
SH OFF   6/3
CRN   9/2
SCORERS **England:** Rooney (pen 59)
Welbeck (66, 72) **Slovenia:** Henderson
(57 og)
CARDS **England:** Gibbs Clyne
Sterling Jagielka **Slovenia:** Cesar

San Marino... (0) 0-0 (0) ....**Estonia**
HOME 25-1   DRAW 8-1   AWAY 1-6
POS   29/71
SH ON   1/5
SH OFF   6/7
CRN   6/12
CARDS **San Marino:** Simoncini

Palazzi **Estonia:** Dmitrijev
Morozov Mets

Switzerland.. (0) 4-0 (0) .... **Lithuania**
HOME 1-4   DRAW 11-2   AWAY 18-1
POS   75/25
SH ON   13/0
SH OFF   12/6
CRN   9/2
SCORERS **Switzerland:** Arlauskis (66
og) Schar (68) Shaqiri (80, 90)
CARDS **Switzerland:** Moubandje
Drmic **Lithuania:** Freidgeimas

Matchday Five
March 27, 2015

England .... (2) 4-0 (0) .... **Lithuania**
HOME 1-7   DRAW 9-1   AWAY 28-1
POS   68/32
SH ON   9/0
SH OFF   6/1
CRN   8/1
SCORERS **England:** Rooney (6)
Welbeck (45) Sterling (58) Kane (73)
CARDS **England:** Sterling
Lithuania: Zaliukas Kazlauskas

Slovenia........ (1) 6-0 (0)....**San Marino**
HOME 1-28   DRAW 25-1   AWAY 66-1
POS   83/17
SH ON   17/0
SH OFF   15/1
CRN   19/1
SCORERS **Slovenia:** Ilicic (10) Kampl
(49) Struna (50) Novakovic (52)
Lazarevic (73) Ilic (88)
CARDS **San Marino:** Simoncini
Palazzi Selva

Switzerland.. (2) 3-0 (0)..........**Estonia**
HOME 2-9   DRAW 6-1   AWAY 20-1
POS   67/33
SH ON   6/0
SH OFF   7/6
CRN   2/1
SCORERS **Switzerland:** Schar (16)
Xhaka (27) Seferovic (80)
CARDS **Switzerland:** Xhaka Shaqiri
Estonia: Zenjov Dmitrijev

Matchday Six
June 14, 2015

Estonia .... (1) 2-0 (0)....**San Marino**
HOME 1-10   DRAW 9-1   AWAY 33-1
POS   74/26
SH ON   3/2
SH OFF   8/3
CRN   8/3
SCORERS **Estonia:** Zenjov (35, 63)
CARDS **San Marino:** Battistini

Ladbrokes

UP TO £50 FREE BET

Sign up bonus for new Online & Mobile customers*

Using promo code: F50

WHEN THE **FUN** STOPS **STOP**™   gambleaware.co.uk

Lithuania ...... (0) 1-2 (0)... Switzerland
HOME 10-1   DRAW 15-4   AWAY 2-5
POS   27/73
SH ON   3/8
SH OFF   3/4
CRN   2/14
SCORERS **Lithuania:** Cernych (64)
Switzerland: Drmic (69) Shaqiri (84)
CARDS **Lithuania:** Panka ▌ Cesnauskis ▌
Chvedukas ▌ Mikuckis ▌
Switzerland: Xhaka ▌

Slovenia....... (1) 2-3 (0)........ England
HOME 19-5   DRAW 13-5   AWAY 10-11
POS   42/58
SH ON   3/6
SH OFF   1/6
CRN   1/3
SCORERS **Slovenia:** Novakovic (37)
Pecnik (84) **England:** Wilshere (57, 73)
Rooney (86)
CARDS **Slovenia:** Brecko ▌ Kampl ▌

Matchday Seven
September 5, 2015

Estonia .... (0) 1-0 (0)....... Lithuania
HOME 13-10 DRAW 21-10   AWAY 3-1
POS   53/47
SH ON   2/5
SH OFF   7/4
CRN   8/2
SCORERS **Estonia:** Vassilijev (71)
CARDS **Estonia:** Purje ▌ Dmitrijev ▌
Lithuania: Matulevicius ▌ Zaliukas ▌
Cesnauskis ▌

San Marino... (0) 0-6 (2)........ England
HOME 100-1 DRAW 40-1   AWAY 1-80
POS   26/74
SH ON   1/8
SH OFF   1/8
CRN   1/7
SCORERS **England:** Rooney (pen 13)
Brolli (30 og) Barkley (46) Walcott (68,
78) Kane (77)

GROUP E TOP SCORERS

	P	Goals	
W Rooney (England)	8	7	●●●●●●●
D Welbeck (England)	5	6	●●●●●●
M Novakovic (Slovenia)	7	6	●●●●●●
X Shaqiri (Switzerland)	9	4	●●●●
T Walcott (England)	4	3	●●●
H Kane (England)	5	3	●●●
H Seferovic (Switzerland)	8	3	●●●
J Drmic (Switzerland)	9	3	●●●

Players scoring three goals or more in this group

WORLD CUP 2018 EUROPEAN QUALIFYING DRAW

Group B Portugal, Switzerland, Hungary, Faroe Islands, Latvia, Andorra
Group C Germany, Czech Rep, N Ireland, Norway, Azerbaijan, San Marino
Group F England, Slovakia, Scotland, Slovenia, Lithuania, Malta **Group H** Belgium, Bosnia-Hz., Greece, Estonia, Cyprus

Hosts Russia and nine group winners qualify. Eight best runners-up go to playoffs

Left: Wayne Rooney celebrates becoming England's record goalscorer in last September's qualifying win over Switzerland

---

CARDS **San Marino:** Berardi ▌

Switzerland.. (0) 3-2 (1).........Slovenia
HOME 8-15   DRAW 16-5   AWAY 7-1
POS   68/32
SH ON   6/4
SH OFF   6/2
CRN   6/3
SCORERS **Switzerland:** Drmic (80, 90)
Stocker (84) **Slovenia:** Novakovic (45)
Cesar (48)
CARDS **Switzerland:** Schar ▌
Lichtsteiner ▌ Behrami ▌ Dzemaili ▌
Slovenia: Kampl ▌ Novakovic ▌
Pecnik ▌ Handanovic ▌ Ilicic ▌

Matchday Eight
September 8, 2015

England .... (0) 2-0 (0)... Switzerland
HOME 4-5   DRAW 11-4   AWAY 9-2
POS   49/51
SH ON   7/1
SH OFF   5/5
CRN   3/8
SCORERS **England:** Kane (67) Rooney
(pen 84)
CARDS **England:** Milner ▌ Smalling ▌

Lithuania ...... (1) 2-1 (0)....San Marino
HOME 1-10   DRAW 11-1   AWAY 40-1
POS   71/29
SH ON   8/2
SH OFF   11/0
CRN   7/0
SCORERS **Lithuania:** Cernych (7)
Spalvis (90) **San Marino:** Vitaioli (55)
CARDS **Lithuania:** Novikovas ▌ Spalvis ▌
Arlauskis ▌ **San Marino:** Battistini ▌
Stefanelli ▌ Brolli ▌ Chiaruzzi ▌

Slovenia........ (0) 1-0 (0)...........Estonia
HOME 8-13   DRAW 14-5   AWAY 13-2
POS   68/32
SH ON   3/2
SH OFF   6/1
CRN   3/2

SCORERS **Slovenia:** Beric (63)
CARDS **Slovenia:** Kampl ▌
Estonia: Lindpere ▌ Mets ▌

Matchday Nine
October 9, 2015

England .... (1) 2-0 (0)..........Estonia
HOME 3-20   DRAW 8-1   AWAY 25-1
POS   63/37
SH ON   9/0
SH OFF   10/4
CRN   10/3
SCORERS **England:** Walcott (45)
Sterling (85)
CARDS **Estonia:** Pikk ▌

Slovenia........ (1) 1-1 (0)....... Lithuania
HOME 2-5   DRAW 15-4   AWAY 10-1
POS   68/32
SH ON   3/1
SH OFF   10/4
CRN   7/3
SCORERS **Slovenia:** Birsa (pen 45)
Lithuania: Novikovas (pen 79)
CARDS **Slovenia:** Struna ▌ Lazarevic ▌
Lithuania: Cernych ▌ Zaliukas ▌
Panka ▌ Petravicius ▌

Switzerland.. (1) 7-0 (0)....San Marino
HOME 1-100 DRAW 66-1 AWAY 100-1
POS   78/22
SH ON   14/1
SH OFF   14/1
CRN   11/1
SCORERS **Switzerland:** Lang (17)
Inler (pen 55) Mehmedi (65) Djourou
(pen 72) Kasami (75) Embolo (pen 80)
Derdiyok (89)
CARDS **San Marino:** Della Valle ▌
Tosi ▌

Matchday Ten
October 12, 2015

Estonia .... (0) 0-1 (0)... Switzerland
HOME 13-2   DRAW 16-5   AWAY 11-20
POS   40/60
SH ON   4/3
SH OFF   3/9
CRN   3/6
SCORERS **Switzerland:** Klavan (90 og)
CARDS **Estonia:** Mets ▌

Lithuania ...... (0) 0-3 (2)......... England
HOME 10-1   DRAW 4-1   AWAY 2-5
POS   38/62
SH ON   2/13
SH OFF   6/6
CRN   1/6
SCORERS **England:** Barkley (29)
Arlauskis (35 og) Oxlade-Chamberlain
(62)
CARDS **Lithuania:** Spalvis ▌ Vaitkunas ▌
England: Shelvey ▌ Vardy ▌

San Marino... (0) 0-2 (0).........Slovenia
HOME 50-1   DRAW 18-1   AWAY 1-20
POS   28/72
SH ON   1/5
SH OFF   2/7
CRN   4/12
SCORERS **Slovenia:** Cesar (54) Pecnik
(74)
CARDS **San Marino:** Gasperoni ▌
Brolli ▌ **Slovenia:** Ilicic ▌ Kurtic ▌

GROUP F

		HOME					AWAY						
	P	W	D	L	F	A	W	D	L	F	A	GD	Pts
N Ireland	10	3	2	0	8	3	3	1	1	8	5	+8	21
Romania	10	2	3	0	5	2	3	2	0	6	0	+9	20
Hungary	10	2	2	1	4	3	2	2	1	7	6	+2	16
Finland	10	1	2	2	3	5	2	1	2	6	5	-1	12
Faroe Islands	10	1	0	4	4	11	1	0	4	2	6	-11	6
Greece	10	1	0	4	4	8	0	3	2	3	6	-7	6

BEST ANTE-POST ODDS

Greece	11-10
Romania	11-4
Hungary	4-1
Finland	10-1
N Ireland	33-1
Faroe Islands	5,000-1

Best win odds in the Racing Post

Matchday One
September 7, 2014

Faroe Islands (1) 1-3 (0)...........Finland
HOME 12-1 DRAW 6-1 AWAY 2-7
POS 29/71
SH ON 4/14
SH OFF 2/9
CRN 4/9
SCORERS **Faroe Islands:** Holst (41)
Finland: Riski (52, 78) Eremenko (82)
CARDS **Faroe Islands:** Hansson Jacobsen Nattestad Edmundsson
Finland: Hetemaj

Greece.......... (0) 0-1 (1)........ Romania
HOME 11-10 DRAW 23-10 AWAY 10-3
POS 64/36
SH ON 2/3
SH OFF 5/5
CRN 3/2
SCORERS **Romania:** Marica (pen 10)
CARDS **Greece:** Samaris Manolas Torosidis Diamantakos Kone
Romania: Pintilii Marica Tatarusanu

Hungary .... (0) 1-2 (0)........N Ireland
HOME 1-2 DRAW 10-3 AWAY 7-1
POS 55/45
SH ON 5/4
SH OFF 4/4
CRN 9/2
SCORERS **Hungary:** Priskin (75)
N Ireland: McGinn (81) Lafferty (88)
CARDS **Hungary:** Vanczak
N Ireland: Norwood

Matchday Two
October 11, 2014

Finland......... (0) 1-1 (1)........... Greece
HOME 11-5 DRAW 11-5 AWAY 6-4
POS 50/50
SH ON 3/3
SH OFF 5/6
CRN 6/3
SCORERS **Finland:** Hurme (55) **Greece:** Karelis (24)
CARDS **Finland:** Hetemaj Sparv Maenpaa **Greece:** Torosidis Karelis Maniatis

N Ireland...... (2) 2-0 (0). Faroe Islands
HOME 2-7 DRAW 19-4 AWAY 14-1
POS 60/40
SH ON 8/1
SH OFF 13/2
CRN 6/4
SCORERS **N Ireland:** McAuley (6) Lafferty (20)
CARDS **N Ireland:** Ferguson
Faroe Islands: Naes

Romania....... (1) 1-1 (0).........Hungary
HOME 4-5 DRAW 13-5 AWAY 19-4
POS 63/37
SH ON 2/2
SH OFF 4/3
CRN 4/4
SCORERS **Romania:** Rusescu (44)
Hungary: Dzsudzsak (82)
CARDS **Romania:** Hoban Gardos Grigore Rat Chipciu
Hungary: Gera Varga Juhasz Elek Kiraly Tozser Korcsmar

Matchday Three
October 14, 2014

Faroe Islands (0) 0-1 (1).........Hungary
HOME 9-1 DRAW 5-1 AWAY 1-3
POS 58/42
SH ON 2/7
SH OFF 2/2
CRN 5/1
SCORERS **Hungary:** Szalai (21)
CARDS **Faroe Islands:** Gregersen Hansson Benjaminsen
Hungary: Gera

Finland......... (0) 0-2 (0)........ Romania
HOME 19-10 DRAW 9-4 AWAY 7-4
POS 48/52
SH ON 1/6
SH OFF 4/7
CRN 3/7
SCORERS **Romania:** Stancu (54, 83)
CARDS **Finland:** Ring
Romania: Tanase Stancu

Greece.......... (0) 0-2 (1)........N Ireland
HOME 8-15 DRAW 10-3 AWAY 7-1
POS 76/24
SH ON 1/4
SH OFF 8/1
CRN 2/3
SCORERS **N Ireland:** Ward (9) Lafferty (51)
CARDS **Greece:** Samaras Maniatis Samaris **N Ireland:** Lafferty

Matchday Four
November 14, 2014

Greece.......... (0) 0-1 (0). Faroe Islands
HOME 1-5 DRAW 13-2 AWAY 25-1
POS 65/35
SH ON 3/5
SH OFF 11/5
CRN 12/2
SCORERS **Faroe Islands:** Edmundsson (61)
CARDS **Greece:** Manolas
Faroe Islands: Olsen Hansson Gregersen

Hungary .... (0) 1-0 (0)...........Finland
HOME 13-10 DRAW 9-4 AWAY 13-5
POS 42/58
SH ON 3/2
SH OFF 2/6
CRN 1/5
SCORERS **Hungary:** Gera (84)
CARDS **Hungary:** Tozser Elek Dzsudzsak **Finland:** Hurme

Romania....... (0) 2-0 (0)........N Ireland
HOME 6-10 DRAW 3-1 AWAY 13-2
POS 61/39
SH ON 6/2
SH OFF 4/4
CRN 9/3
SCORERS **Romania:** Papp (74, 79)
CARDS **Romania:** Pintilii Chipciu Maxim **N Ireland:** McLaughlin Lafferty

Matchday Five
March 29, 2015

Hungary .... (0) 0-0 (0)........... Greece
HOME 17-10 DRAW 11-5 AWAY 2-1
POS 37/63
SH ON 3/3
SH OFF 6/5
CRN 6/4
CARDS **Hungary:** Almeida Elek Pinter **Greece:** Kone Fetfatzidis

N Ireland...... (2) 2-1 (0)...........Finland
HOME 9-5 DRAW 11-5 AWAY 19-10
POS 39/61
SH ON 2/5
SH OFF 1/4
CRN 7/7
SCORERS **N Ireland:** Lafferty (33, 38)
Finland: Sadik (90)
CARDS **N Ireland:** Baird Brunt
Finland: Pohjanpalo Arajuuri

Romania....... (1) 1-0 (0). Faroe Islands
HOME 2-13 DRAW 8-1 AWAY 25-1
POS 59/41
SH ON 6/1
SH OFF 10/1
CRN 1/1
SCORERS **Romania:** Keseru (21)
CARDS **Romania:** Torje Keseru
Faroe Islands: Vatnhamar

Matchday Six
June 13, 2015

Faroe Islands (1) 2-1 (0)........... Greece
HOME 17-2 DRAW 7-2 AWAY 4-9
POS 32/68
SH ON 4/8
SH OFF 4/10
CRN 7/11
SCORERS **Faroe Islands:** Hansson (32) Olsen (70) **Greece:** Papastathopoulos (84)
CARDS **Faroe Islands:** Benjaminsen Hansen Gregersen Olsen
Greece: Torosidis Karelis

Finland .... (0) 0-1 (0) ....Hungary
HOME 6-4   DRAW 11-5   AWAY 12-5
POS   45/55
SH ON   1/8
SH OFF   5/6
CRN   3/7
SCORERS Hungary: Stieber (82)
CARDS Finland: Riski ▌ Sparv ▌ Halsti ▌
Hungary: Lang ▌ Gera ▌ Juhasz ▌
Dzsudzsak ▌ Stieber ▌

N Ireland ...... (0) 0-0 (0) .... Romania
HOME 12-5   DRAW 11-5   AWAY 7-5
POS   50/50
SH ON   5/2
SH OFF   11/5
CRN   7/3
CARDS N Ireland: Brunt ▌ Romania:
Pintilii ▌ Sepsi ▌ Torje ▌

Matchday Seven
September 4, 2015

Faroe Islands (1) 1-3 (1) ....N Ireland
HOME 11-2   DRAW 3-1   AWAY 7-10
POS   44/56
SH ON   2/5
SH OFF   2/11
CRN   1/7
SCORERS Faroe Islands: Edmundsson
(36) N Ireland: McAuley (12, 71)
Lafferty (75)
CARDS Faroe Islands: Edmundsson ▌▌
Hansson ▌ N Ireland: McLaughlin ▌
Magennis ▌

Greece .... (0) 0-1 (0) ....Finland
HOME 4-5   DRAW 12-5   AWAY 5-1
POS   61/39
SH ON   3/1
SH OFF   12/2
CRN   8/2

SCORERS Finland: Pohjanpalo (75)
CARDS Greece: Aravidis ▌
Papastathopoulos ▌ Finland: Arajuuri ▌

Hungary .... (0) 0-0 (0) .... Romania
HOME 2-1   DRAW 21-10   AWAY 9-5
POS   40/60
SH ON   2/3
SH OFF   5/7
CRN   1/2
CARDS Hungary: Tozser ▌ Szalai ▌
Almeida ▌ Romania: Popa ▌
Chiriches ▌ Keseru ▌ Chipciu ▌

Matchday Eight
September 7, 2015

Finland .... (1) 1-0 (0). Faroe Islands
HOME 1-3   DRAW 5-1   AWAY 12-1
POS   55/45
SH ON   4/0
SH OFF   4/5
CRN   3/2
SCORERS Finland: Pohjanpalo (23)
CARDS Finland: Halsti ▌ Lam ▌ Sparv ▌
Faroe Islands: Benjaminsen ▌ Naes ▌
Olsen ▌ Hansson ▌ Bartalsstovu ▌

N Ireland ...... (0) 1-1 (0) ....Hungary
HOME 13-8   DRAW 23-10   AWAY 21-10
POS   48/52
SH ON   5/2
SH OFF   2/7
CRN   5/1
SCORERS N Ireland: Lafferty (90)
Hungary: Guzmics (74)
CARDS N Ireland: Lafferty ▌
McLaughlin ▌ Baird ▌▌
Hungary: Guzmics ▌ Almeida ▌
Priskin ▌ Nemeth ▌

Romania ...... (0) 0-0 (0) .... Greece
HOME 3-4   DRAW 3-1   AWAY 5-1
POS   52/48
SH ON   2/1
SH OFF   11/2
CRN   9/0
CARDS Romania: Papp ▌
Greece: Holebas ▌ Manolas ▌

Matchday Nine
October 8, 2015

Hungary .... (0) 2-1 (1). Faroe Islands
HOME 3-10   DRAW 9-2   AWAY 14-1
POS   69/31
SH ON   8/2
SH OFF   14/3
CRN   13/0
SCORERS Hungary: Bode (63, 71)
Faroe Islands: Jacobsen (11)
CARDS Hungary: Gera ▌ Faroe
Islands: Baldvinsson ▌ Gregersen ▌▌

N Ireland ...... (1) 3-1 (0) .... Greece
HOME 13-8   DRAW 19-10   AWAY 12-5
POS   33/67
SH ON   3/4
SH OFF   11/4
CRN   10/3
SCORERS N Ireland: Davis (35, 58)
Magennis (49) Greece: Aravidis (86)

Romania .... (0) 1-1 (0) ....Finland
HOME 8-11   DRAW 13-5   AWAY 5-1
POS   56/44
SH ON   9/6
SH OFF   11/3
CRN   9/4
SCORERS Romania: Hoban (90)
Finland: Pohjanpalo (66)
CARDS Romania: Hoban ▌
Finland: Pohjanpalo ▌ Halsti ▌ Toivio
▌ Hetemaj ▌

Matchday Ten
October 11, 2015

Faroe Islands (0) 0-3 (2) .... Romania
HOME 14-1   DRAW 9-2   AWAY 3-10
POS   48/52
SH ON   3/4
SH OFF   5/6
CRN   7/6
SCORERS Romania: Budescu (4, 45)
Maxim (82)
CARDS Faroe Islands: Nattestad ▌
Hansson ▌ Faero ▌ Romania: Torje ▌
Pintilii ▌

Finland .... (0) 1-1 (1) ....N Ireland
HOME 5-4   DRAW 9-4   AWAY 27-10
POS   56/44
SH ON   5/3
SH OFF   4/2
CRN   3/4
SCORERS Finland: Arajuuri (87)
N Ireland: Cathcart (31)

Greece .... (1) 4-3 (1) ....Hungary
HOME 8-5   DRAW 21-10   AWAY 9-4
POS   58/42
SH ON   4/5
SH OFF   6/6
CRN   8/3
SCORERS Greece: Stafylidis (5)
Tachtsidis (56) Mitroglou (79) Kone
(86) Hungary: Lovrencsics (26)
Nemeth (54, 75)
CARDS Greece: Holebas ▌ Moras ▌
Hungary: Juhasz ▌ Elek ▌ Nemeth ▌
Bode ▌ Fiola ▌

Gareth McAuley celebrates a goal at home to the Faroe Islands

GROUP F TOP SCORERS

	P	Goals	
K Lafferty (N Ireland)	9	7	●●●●●●●
G McAuley (N Ireland)	10	3	●●●
J Pohjanpalo (Finland)	10	3	●●●

Players scoring three goals or more in this group

WORLD CUP 2018 EUROPEAN QUALIFYING DRAW

Group B Portugal, Switzerland, Hungary, Faroe Islands, Latvia, Andorra
Group C Germany, Czech Rep, N Ireland, Norway, Azerbaijan, San Marino
Group E Romania, Denmark, Poland, Montenegro, Armenia, Kazakhstan
Group H Belgium, Bosnia-Hz., Greece, Estonia, Cyprus **Group I** Croatia, Iceland,
Ukraine, Turkey, Finland

Hosts Russia and nine group winners qualify. Eight best runners-up go to playoffs

	P	W	D	L	F	A	W	D	L	F	A	GD	Pts
		HOME					AWAY						
Austria	10	4	1	0	7	1	5	0	0	15	4	+17	28
Russia	10	3	1	1	8	2	3	1	1	13	3	+16	20
Sweden	10	3	1	1	9	6	2	2	1	6	3	+6	18
Montenegro	10	2	1	2	7	7	1	1	3	3	6	-3	11
Liechtenstein	10	0	2	3	1	15	1	0	4	1	11	-24	5
Moldova	10	0	0	5	2	9	0	2	3	2	7	-12	2

BEST ANTE-POST ODDS

Russia	6-5
Sweden	2-1
Austria	8-1
Montenegro	10-1
Moldova	750-1
Liechtenstein	5,000-1

Best win odds in the Racing Post

Matchday One
September 8, 2014

Austria.........(1) 1-1 (1).........Sweden
HOME 6-4   DRAW 23-10   AWAY 11-5
POS   58/42
SH ON   5/2
SH OFF   5/5
CRN   11/1
SCORERS **Austria:** Alaba (pen 7)
Sweden: Zengin (12)
CARDS **Austria:** Dragovic **Sweden:**
Ibrahimovic Larsson Kallstrom

Montenegro. (1) 2-0 (0).......Moldova
HOME 1-2   DRAW 7-2   AWAY 7-1
POS   59/41
SH ON   6/2
SH OFF   5/2
CRN   8/3
SCORERS **Montenegro:** Vucinic (45)
Tomasevic (73)
CARDS **Montenegro:** Volkov Vucinic
Moldova: Armas Gheorghiev

Russia...........(1) 4-0 (0).Liechtenstein
HOME 1-20   DRAW 14-1   AWAY 40-1
POS   67/33
SH ON   11/0
SH OFF   15/3
CRN   10/1
SCORERS **Russia:** Buchel (4 og)
Burgmeier (50 og) Kombarov (pen 54)
Dzyuba (65)
CARDS **Liechtenstein:** Wieser Frick

Matchday Two
October 9, 2014

Liechtenstein (0) 0-0 (0).. Montenegro
HOME 14-1   DRAW 11-2   AWAY 2-9
POS   38/62
SH ON   0/10
SH OFF   3/13
CRN   0/10
CARDS **Liechtenstein:** Buchel Frick
Bicer **Montenegro:** Simic

Moldova.......(1) 1-2 (1)..........Austria
HOME 19-4   DRAW 11-4   AWAY 7-10
POS   35/65
SH ON   3/8
SH OFF   3/3
CRN   3/5
SCORERS **Moldova:** Dedov (pen 27)
Austria: Alaba (pen 11) Janko (51)
CARDS **Moldova:** Jardan Dedov
Austria: Prodl Baumgartlinger
Dragovic Janko

Sweden........ (0) 1-1 (1)...........Russia
HOME 33-20   DRAW 9-4   AWAY 2-1
POS   40/60
SH ON   4/2
SH OFF   2/3
CRN   6/3
SCORERS **Sweden:** Toivonen (49)
Russia: Kokorin (10)
CARDS **Sweden:** Zengin Elmander
Wernbloom **Russia:** Smolnikov
Glushakov

Matchday Three
October 12, 2014

Austria..........(1) 1-0 (0).. Montenegro
HOME 1-1   DRAW 5-2   AWAY 10-3
POS   56/44
SH ON   9/2
SH OFF   6/7
CRN   9/3
SCORERS **Austria:** Okotie (24)
CARDS **Austria:** Junuzovic
Baumgartlinger **Montenegro:**
Zverotic Bozovic Simic

Russia...........(0) 1-1 (1)........Moldova
HOME 1-12   DRAW 12-1   AWAY 40-1
POS   75/25
SH ON   6/3
SH OFF   11/2
CRN   8/2
SCORERS **Russia:** Dzyuba (pen 73)
Moldova: Epureanu (74)
CARDS **Moldova:** Erhan
Golovatenco Sidorenco

Sweden........ (1) 2-0 (0).Liechtenstein
HOME 1-25   DRAW 14-1   AWAY 66-1
POS   72/28
SH ON   8/1
SH OFF   11/2
CRN   11/0
SCORERS **Sweden:** Zengin (34)
Durmaz (46)
CARDS **Liechtenstein:** Frick
Quintans

Matchday Four
November 15, 2014

Austria..........(0) 1-0 (0)........... Russia
HOME 19-10   DRAW 11-5   AWAY 9-5
POS   45/55
SH ON   4/1
SH OFF   2/7
CRN   6/4
SCORERS **Austria:** Okotie (73)
CARDS **Austria:** Hinteregger **Russia:**
Glushakov Parshivlyuk

Moldova....... (0) 0-1 (0).Liechtenstein
HOME 3-10   DRAW 19-4   AWAY 14-1
POS   71/29
SH ON   7/2
SH OFF   9/2
CRN   3/1
SCORERS **Liechtenstein:** Burgmeier (74)
CARDS **Liechtenstein:** Brandle
Salanovic

Montenegro. (0) 1-1 (1).........Sweden
HOME 23-10   DRAW 9-4   AWAY 7-5
POS   47/53
SH ON   6/3
SH OFF   7/7
CRN   7/1
SCORERS **Montenegro:** Jovetic (pen
80) **Sweden:** Ibrahimovic (9)
CARDS **Montenegro:** Bakic Basa
Sweden: Ekdal Kallstrom

Matchday Five
March 27, 2015

Liechtenstein (0) 0-5 (2)..........Austria
HOME 20-1   DRAW 13-2   AWAY 1-5
POS   35/65
SH ON   1/6
SH OFF   2/9
CRN   1/3
SCORERS **Austria:** Harnik (14)
Janko (16) Alaba (59) Junuzovic (74)
Arnautovic (90)
CARDS **Liechtenstein:** Jehle
Austria: Klein

Moldova....... (0) 0-2 (0)........Sweden
HOME 9-1   DRAW 15-4   AWAY 4-9
POS   36/64
SH ON   0/7
SH OFF   1/6
CRN   3/5
SCORERS **Sweden:** Ibrahimovic (46,
pen 84)
CARDS **Moldova:** Golovatenco Racu
Gheorghiev Gatcan **Sweden:**
Granqvist Olsson Ibrahimovic

Montenegro...   0-3   ....Russia
HOME 16-5   DRAW 23-10   AWAY 11-10
Match abandoned (67 mins) with the
score at 0-0. Russia awarded a 3-0
victory
CARDS **Montenegro:** Kascelan
Vucinic **Russia:** Shatov Denisov

Matchday Six
June 14, 2015

Liechtenstein (1) 1-1 (1)........ Moldova
HOME 16-5   DRAW 12-5   AWAY 21-20
POS   34/66
SH ON   4/7
SH OFF   3/16
CRN   2/6

Liechtenstein: Wieser (20)
Moldova: Boghiu (43)
CARDS **Liechtenstein:** Wieser ▌ Erne ▌
Moldova: Gatcan ▌

Russia .... (0) 0-1 (1) .... **Austria**
HOME 20-21   DRAW 12-5   AWAY 15-4
POS   56/44
SH ON   5/4
SH OFF 6/8
CRN   7/5
SCORERS **Austria:** Janko (33)
CARDS **Russia:** Kokorin ▌
Austria: Klein ▌

Sweden........ (3) 3-1 (0).. **Montenegro**
HOME 1-2   DRAW 7-2   AWAY 8-1
POS   53/47
SH ON   6/6
SH OFF 5/7
CRN   5/6
SCORERS **Sweden:** Berg (37)
Ibrahimovic (40, 44)
Montenegro: Damjanovic (pen 64)
CARDS **Sweden:** Kallstrom ▌ Ekdal ▌
Montenegro: Simic ▌ Tomasevic ▌
Boljevic ▌ Vukcevic ▌

Matchday Seven
September 5, 2015

Austria.......... (0) 1-0 (0)....... **Moldova**
HOME 1-5   DRAW 15-2   AWAY 20-1
POS   68/32
SH ON   7/1
SH OFF 10/1
CRN   5/2
SCORERS **Austria:** Junuzovic (52)
CARDS **Austria:** Prodl ▌
Moldova: Cebotaru ▌ Cebanu ▌

Montenegro. (1) 2-0 (0).**Liechtenstein**
HOME 2-11   DRAW 15-2   AWAY 20-1
POS   64/36
SH ON   7/0
SH OFF 9/2
CRN   6/1
SCORERS **Montenegro:** Beciraj (38)
Jovetic (56)
CARDS **Montenegro:** Marusic ▌
Liechtenstein: Frick ▌ Wieser ▌

Russia .... (1) 1-0 (0) .... **Sweden**
HOME 23-20   DRAW 9-4   AWAY 3-1
POS   53/47
SH ON   5/5
SH OFF 4/2
CRN   4/3
SCORERS **Russia:** Dzyuba (38)
CARDS **Russia:** Dzagoev ▌ Kuzmin ▌
Sweden: Wernbloom ▌ Forsberg ▌

Matchday Eight
September 8, 2015

Liechtenstein (0) 0-7 (3) .... **Russia**
HOME 33-1   DRAW 9-1   AWAY 1-7
POS   32/68
SH ON   1/14
SH OFF 2/8
CRN   2/8
SCORERS **Russia:** Dzyuba (21, 45, 73, 90) Kokorin (pen 40) Smolov (77) Dzagoev (85)
CARDS **Liechtenstein:** Kieber ▌ Polverino ▌ Kaufmann ▌

GROUP G TOP SCORERS

	P	Goals	
A Dzyuba (Russia)	8	8	●●●●●●●●
Z Ibrahimovic (Sweden)	8	8	●●●●●●●●
M Janko (Austria)	9	7	●●●●●●●
D Alaba (Austria)	8	4	●●●●
A Kokorin (Russia)	9	3	●●●
E Zengin (Sweden)	9	3	●●●
M Arnautovic (Austria)	10	3	●●●
M Harnik (Austria)	10	3	●●●

Players scoring three goals or more in this group

WORLD CUP 2018 EUROPEAN QUALIFYING DRAW

Group A Holland, France, Sweden, Bulgaria, Belarus, Luxembourg **Group D** Wales, Austria, Serbia, Ireland, Moldova, Georgia **Group E** Romania, Denmark, Poland, Montenegro, Armenia, Kazakhstan **Group G** Spain, Italy, Albania, Israel, Macedonia, Liechtenstein

Hosts Russia and nine group winners qualify. Eight best runners-up go to playoffs

Moldova ...... (0) 0-2 (1).. **Montenegro**
HOME 10-3   DRAW 5-2   AWAY 21-20
POS   54/46
SH ON   2/5
SH OFF 9/7
CRN   9/5
SCORERS **Montenegro:** Savic (9)
Racu (65 og)
CARDS **Moldova:** Gatcan ▌
Dedov ▌ Golovatenco ▌ Cojocari ▌
Montenegro: Basa ▌ Savic ▌
Vukcevic ▌

Sweden.......... (0) 1-4 (2).......... **Austria**
HOME 5-4   DRAW 5-2   AWAY 13-5
POS   57/43
SH ON   6/12
SH OFF 3/3
CRN   8/3
SCORERS **Sweden:** Ibrahimovic (90)
Austria: Alaba (pen 9) Harnik (38, 88)
Janko (76)
CARDS **Sweden:** Granqvist ▌
Austria: Junuzovic ▌ Janko ▌ Ilsanker ▌

Matchday Nine
October 9, 2015

Liechtenstein (0) 0-2 (1) .... **Sweden**
HOME 33-1   DRAW 10-1   AWAY 1-8
POS   31/69
SH ON   1/6
SH OFF 2/5
CRN   2/12
SCORERS **Sweden:** Berg (18)
Ibrahimovic (55)
CARDS **Liechtenstein:** Rechsteiner ▌
Sweden: Kallstrom ▌ Lustig ▌

Moldova ...... (0) 1-2 (0) .... **Russia**
HOME 12-1   DRAW 5-1   AWAY 3-10
POS   34/66
SH ON   1/6
SH OFF 2/7
CRN   2/7
SCORERS **Moldova:** Cebotaru (85)
Russia: Ignashevich (58) Dzyuba (78)

CARDS **Moldova:** Antoniuc ▌
Russia: Kombarov ▌ Mamaev ▌

Montenegro. (1) 2-3 (0).......... **Austria**
HOME 2-1   DRAW 23-10   AWAY 17-10
POS   37/63
SH ON   6/10
SH OFF 3/10
CRN   4/9
SCORERS **Montenegro:** Vucinic (32) Beciraj (68) **Austria:** Janko (55) Arnautovic (81) Sabitzer (90)
CARDS **Montenegro:** Poleksic ▌
Vucinic ▌

Matchday Ten
October 12, 2015

Austria.......... (1) 3-0 (0).**Liechtenstein**
HOME 1-16   DRAW 15-1   AWAY 66-1
POS   65/35
SH ON 14/0
SH OFF 13/1
CRN   13/3
SCORERS **Austria:** Arnautovic (12)
Janko (54, 57)
CARDS **Austria:** Okotie ▌
Liechtenstein: Burgmeier ▌
Polverino ▌

Russia .... (2) 2-0 (0).. **Montenegro**
HOME 1-3   DRAW 9-2   AWAY 12-1
POS   63/37
SH ON   6/0
SH OFF 8/4
CRN   5/3
SCORERS **Russia:** Kuzmin (33) Kokorin (pen 37)
CARDS **Montenegro:** Rodic ▌

Sweden.......... (1) 2-0 (0)....... **Moldova**
HOME 1-5   DRAW 13-2   AWAY 20-1
POS   62/38
SH ON   4/0
SH OFF 7/1
CRN   7/3
SCORERS **Sweden:** Ibrahimovic (24)
Zengin (47)

SOCCERBASE.COM

GROUP H

	P	W	D	L	F	A	W	D	L	F	A	GD	Pts
		HOME					**AWAY**						
Italy	10	4	1	0	7	3	3	2	0	9	4	+9	24
Croatia	10	4	1	0	17	2	2	2	1	3	3	+15	20
Norway	10	3	1	1	6	3	3	0	2	7	7	+3	19
Bulgaria	10	1	2	2	5	5	2	0	3	4	7	-3	11
Azerbaijan	10	1	1	3	4	6	0	2	3	3	12	-11	6
Malta	10	0	1	4	2	8	0	1	4	1	8	-13	2

Croatia deducted 1pt

BEST ANTE-POST ODDS

Italy	2-5
Croatia	3-1
Norway	14-1
Bulgaria	16-1
Azerbaijan	1,000-1
Malta	5,000-1

Best win odds in the Racing Post

Matchday One
September 9, 2014

Azerbaijan.... (0) 1-2 (1)........Bulgaria
HOME 3-1   DRAW 23-10 AWAY 23-20
POS   51/49
SH ON   2/5
SH OFF 3/8
CRN   4/5
SCORERS **Azerbaijan:** Nazarov (54)
Bulgaria: Micanski (14) Hristov (87)
CARDS **Azerbaijan:** Abisov ▌ Vaqif
Cavadov ▌ Abdullayev ▌ **Bulgaria:**
Gadzhev ▌

Croatia......... (0) 2-0 (0)............Malta
HOME 1-14 DRAW 14-1 AWAY 45-1
POS   76/24
SH ON   6/2
SH OFF 15/1
CRN   17/1
SCORERS **Croatia:** Modric (46)
Kramaric (81)
CARDS **Croatia:** Mandzukic ▌
Malta: Fenech ▌ Borg ▌

Norway......... (0) 0-2 (1)............. Italy
HOME 9-2   DRAW 27-10 AWAY 4-5
POS   51/49
SH ON   0/6
SH OFF 3/5
CRN   3/6
SCORERS **Italy:** Zaza (16) Bonucci (62)
CARDS **Norway:** Nordtveit ▌ Forren ▌
Italy: Florenzi ▌ Astori ▌

Matchday Two
October 10, 2014

Bulgaria........ (0) 0-1 (1)..........Croatia
HOME 27-10 DRAW 9-4 AWAY 13-10
POS   48/52
SH ON   1/1
SH OFF 4/2
CRN   9/5
SCORERS **Croatia:** Bodurov (36 og)
CARDS **Bulgaria:** Zanev ▌
Croatia: Brozovic ▌ Vida ▌ Olic ▌

Italy.............. (1) 2-1 (0).....Azerbaijan
HOME 1-10 DRAW 9-1 AWAY 28-1
POS   61/39
SH ON   4/0
SH OFF 11/2
CRN   9/1
SCORERS **Italy:** Chiellini (43, 82)
Azerbaijan: Chiellini (76 og)
CARDS **Italy:** Pirlo ▌ Zaza ▌
Azerbaijan: Dadasov ▌ Sadygov ▌

Malta............ (0) 0-3 (2).........Norway
HOME 8-1   DRAW 4-1   AWAY 2-5
POS   41/59
SH ON   2/7
SH OFF 2/4
CRN   0/4
SCORERS **Norway:** Daehli (22) King
(25, 49)
CARDS **Malta:** Agius ▌

Matchday Three
October 13, 2014

Croatia......... (4) 6-0 (0)..... Azerbaijan
HOME 1-6   DRAW 7-1   AWAY 22-1
POS   65/35
SH ON   7/0
SH OFF 11/6
CRN   4/3
SCORERS **Croatia:** Kramaric (11) Perisic
(34, 45) Brozovic (45) Modric (pen 56)
Sadygov (61 og)
CARDS **Azerbaijan:** Ramaldanov ▌
Ramazanov ▌ Allahverdiev ▌

Malta............ (0) 0-1 (1)............... Italy
HOME 50-1 DRAW 14-1 AWAY 1-14
POS   24/76
SH ON   1/5
SH OFF 3/9
CRN   2/7
SCORERS **Italy:** Pelle (23)
CARDS **Malta:** Briffa ▌ Mifsud ▌
Italy: Darmian ▌ Bonucci ▌

Norway......... (1) 2-1 (1)........Bulgaria
HOME 6-5   DRAW 5-2   AWAY 13-5
POS   46/54
SH ON   4/1
SH OFF 5/3
CRN   5/3
SCORERS **Norway:** Elyounoussi (13)
Nielsen (72) **Bulgaria:** Bodurov (43)
CARDS **Norway:** Elyounoussi ▌
Johansen ▌ **Bulgaria:** Minev ▌
Popov ▌ Minev ▌

Matchday Four
November 16, 2014

Azerbaijan.... (0) 0-1 (1).........Norway
HOME 16-5 DRAW 12-5 AWAY 11-10
POS   60/40
SH ON   0/5
SH OFF 3/7
CRN   5/4
SCORERS **Norway:** Nordtveit (25)
CARDS **Azerbaijan:** Yunuszada ▌
Nazarov ▌ **Norway:** Elyounoussi ▌
Samuelsen ▌ Soderlund ▌

Bulgaria........ (1) 1-1 (0)............ Malta
HOME 1-5   DRAW 7-1   AWAY 17-1
POS   73/27
SH ON   3/2
SH OFF 12/3
CRN   12/3
SCORERS **Bulgaria:** Galabinov (6)
Malta: Failla (pen 49)
CARDS **Bulgaria:** Minev ▌ **Malta:**
Farrugia ▌ Failla ▌ Caruana ▌ Fenech ▌

Italy.............. (1) 1-1 (1)..........Croatia
HOME 5-4   DRAW 9-4   AWAY 3-1
POS   38/62
SH ON   2/9
SH OFF 3/6
CRN   0/5
SCORERS **Italy:** Candreva (11) **Croatia:**
Perisic (15)
CARDS **Italy:** Immobile ▌
Croatia: Kovacic ▌ Perisic ▌

Matchday Five
March 28, 2015

Azerbaijan.... (2) 2-0 (0)............. Malta
HOME 8-11 DRAW 14-5 AWAY 5-1
POS   59/41
SH ON   5/3
SH OFF 5/5
CRN   3/3
SCORERS **Azerbaijan:** Huseynov (4)
Nazarov (90)
CARDS **Azerbaijan:** Amirquliyev ▌
Nazarov ▌ **Malta:** Caruana ▌

Bulgaria........ (2) 2-2 (1)............. Italy
HOME 4-1   DRAW 12-5 AWAY 10-11
POS   30/70
SH ON   3/4
SH OFF 1/9
CRN   1/17
SCORERS **Bulgaria:** Popov (11)
Micanski (17) **Italy:** Minev (4 og)
Eder (84)
CARDS **Bulgaria:** Dyakov ▌
Italy: Immobile ▌ Soriano ▌ Darmian ▌

Croatia.......... (1) 5-1 (0).........Norway
HOME 1-2   DRAW 7-2   AWAY 8-1
POS   51/49
SH ON   7/6
SH OFF 3/3
CRN   5/3
SCORERS **Croatia:** Brozovic (30) Perisic
(54) Olic (86) Schildenfeld (86) Pranjic
(90) **Norway:** Tettey (81)
CARDS **Croatia:** Corluka ▌▌
Norway: Linnes ▌ Nordtveit ▌
Elyounoussi ▌ Nyland ▌ Samuelsen ▌

Croatia.......... (1) 1-1 (1).............. Italy
HOME 7-5   DRAW 21-10   AWAY 12-5
POS   41/59
SH ON   3/4
SH OFF   5/2
CRN   3/6
SCORERS Croatia: Mandzukic (11)
Italy: Candreva (pen 36)
CARDS Croatia: Mandzukic Olic
Srna Rebic Kovacic
Italy: Buffon Parolo Marchisio

Malta........... (0) 0-1 (0)........Bulgaria
HOME 15-2   DRAW 10-3   AWAY 1-2
POS   37/63
SH ON   2/4
SH OFF   3/8
CRN   1/3
SCORERS Bulgaria: Popov (56)
CARDS Malta: Agius Camilleri
Muscat Fenech
Bulgaria: Aleksandrov Dyakov

Norway......... (0) 0-0 (0)..... Azerbaijan
HOME 1-3   DRAW 4-1   AWAY 11-1
POS   54/46
SH ON   3/3
SH OFF   9/6
CRN   7/2
CARDS Azerbaijan: Dasdamirov

Azerbaijan.... (0) 0-0 (0)..........Croatia
HOME 10-1   DRAW 4-1   AWAY 4-11
POS   34/66
SH ON   4/4
SH OFF   3/15
CRN   1/4
CARDS Azerbaijan: Qurbanov
Agayev Qarayev Croatia: Vida
Rakitic

Bulgaria........ (0) 0-1 (0).........Norway
HOME 5-4   DRAW 12-5   AWAY 11-4
POS   47/53
SH ON   1/4
SH OFF   4/2
CRN   4/6
SCORERS Norway: Forren (57)
CARDS Bulgaria: Popov Minev
Norway: Hogli Tettey Skjelbred

Italy .... (0) 1-0 (0)............. Malta
HOME 1-20   DRAW 25-1   AWAY 80-1
POS   68/32
SH ON   3/1
SH OFF   11/2
CRN   8/1
SCORERS Italy: Pelle (69)
CARDS Italy: Candreva
Malta: Fenech

Italy .... (1) 1-0 (0)........Bulgaria
HOME 1-2   DRAW 10-3   AWAY 15-2
POS   50/50
SH ON   7/2
SH OFF   10/3
CRN   3/2
SCORERS Italy: De Rossi (pen 6)

CARDS Italy: De Rossi
Bulgaria: Minev Rangelov
Dyakov Micanski

Malta........... (0) 2-2 (1)..... Azerbaijan
HOME 11-5   DRAW 9-4   AWAY 6-4
POS   28/72
SH ON   2/5
SH OFF   3/7
CRN   1/10
SCORERS Malta: Mifsud (55) Effiong
(71) Azerbaijan: Amirquliyev (36, 80)
CARDS Malta: Effiong

Norway......... (0) 2-0 (0)..........Croatia
HOME 29-10 DRAW 12-5   AWAY 6-5
POS   42/58
SH ON   3/2
SH OFF   4/5
CRN   7/5
SCORERS Norway: Berget (51) Corluka
(69 og)
CARDS Norway: Forren Soderlund
Hogli Croatia: Vrsaljko
Brozovic Olic

Azerbaijan.... (1) 1-3 (2).............. Italy
HOME 16-1   DRAW 17-4   AWAY 3-10
POS   54/46
SH ON   6/7
SH OFF   0/8
CRN   3/5
SCORERS Azerbaijan: Nazarov (31)
Italy: Eder (11) El Shaarawy (43)
Darmian (65)
CARDS Azerbaijan: Medvedev
Guseynov

Croatia.......... (2) 3-0 (0).........Bulgaria
HOME 1-3   DRAW 9-2   AWAY 13-1
POS   63/37
SH ON   5/1
SH OFF   6/4
CRN   10/1
SCORERS Croatia: Perisic (2) Rakitic
(42) Kalinic (81)
CARDS Croatia: Perisic Cop

Norway......... (1) 2-0 (0)............. Malta
HOME 1-7   DRAW 8-1   AWAY 25-1
POS   74/26
SH ON   10/1
SH OFF   8/0
CRN   17/2

SCORERS Norway: Tettey (19)
Soderlund (52)
CARDS Malta: Briffa

Bulgaria........ (1) 2-0 (0)..... Azerbaijan
HOME 4-6   DRAW 14-5   AWAY 6-1
POS   51/49
SH ON   5/2
SH OFF   6/4
CRN   4/5
SCORERS Bulgaria: Aleksandrov (20)
Rangelov (56)
CARDS Bulgaria: Ivanov Dyakov
Milanov Azerbaijan: Sadygov
Amirquliyev Qarayev

Italy .... (0) 2-1 (1).........Norway
HOME 9-10   DRAW 11-4   AWAY 15-4
POS   61/39
SH ON   9/1
SH OFF   8/1
CRN   8/2
SCORERS Italy: Florenzi (73) Pelle (82)
Norway: Tettey (23)

Malta........... (0) 0-1 (1)..........Croatia
HOME 33-1   DRAW 12-1   AWAY 1-10
POS   31/69
SH ON   1/4
SH OFF   4/11
CRN   2/9
SCORERS Croatia: Perisic (25)
CARDS Malta: Failla
Croatia: Badelj Perisic

Ivan Perisic

GROUP H TOP SCORERS

	P	Goals
I Perisic (Croatia)	9	6 ●●●●●●
G Pelle (Italy)	7	3 ●●●
A Tettey (Norway)	9	3
D Nazarov (Azerbaijan)	10	3 ●●●

Players scoring three goals or more in this group

WORLD CUP 2018 EUROPEAN QUALIFYING DRAW

Group A Holland, France, Sweden, Bulgaria, Belarus, Luxembourg **Group C**
Germany, Czech Rep, N Ireland, Norway, Azerbaijan, San Marino **Group F** England,
Slovakia, Scotland, Slovenia, Lithuania, Malta **Group G** Spain, Italy, Albania, Israel,
Macedonia, Liechtenstein **Group I** Croatia, Iceland, Ukraine, Turkey, Finland

Hosts Russia and nine group winners qualify. Eight best runners-up go to playoffs

	HOME					AWAY						
	P	W	D	L	F	A	W	D	L	F	A	GD	Pts
Portugal	8	3	0	1	4	2	4	0	0	7	3	+6	21
Albania	8	1	1	2	3	5	3	1	0	7	0	+5	14
Denmark	8	2	1	1	4	2	1	2	1	4	3	+3	12
Serbia	8	1	0	3	4	8	1	1	2	4	5	-5	4
Armenia	8	0	2	2	3	7	0	0	4	2	7	-9	2

Serbia deducted 3pts

BEST ANTE-POST ODDS

Portugal	8-13
Denmark	7-2
Serbia	5-1
Armenia	25-1
Albania	500-1

Best win odds in the Racing Post

Matchday One
September 7, 2014

Denmark....... (0) 2-1 (0) **.........Armenia**
HOME 4-9   DRAW 7-2   AWAY 8-1
POS   67/33
SH ON   5/2
SH OFF   8/4
CRN   7/2

SCORERS **Denmark:** Hojbjerg (65) Kahlenberg (80) **Armenia:** Mkhitaryan (49)

CARDS **Denmark:** Hojbjerg
Armenia: Yedigaryan

Portugal .... (0) 0-1 (0) **..........Albania**
HOME 2-7   DRAW 5-1   AWAY 12-1
POS   66/34
SH ON   5/2
SH OFF   12/0
CRN   10/2

SCORERS **Albania:** Balaj (52)

CARDS **Portugal:** Nani
Albania: Roshi Abrashi Xhaka Mavraj Kace Berisha

Matchday Two
October 11, 2014

Albania......... (1) 1-1 (0) **.......Denmark**
HOME 13-5   DRAW 23-10   AWAY 5-4
POS   32/68
SH ON   2/3
SH OFF   6/7
CRN   2/1

SCORERS **Albania:** Lenjani (38)
Denmark: Vibe (81)

Armenia....... (0) 1-1 (0) **........... Serbia**
HOME 17-4   DRAW 11-4   AWAY 4-5
POS   37/63
SH ON   5/5
SH OFF   4/7
CRN   5/5

SCORERS **Armenia:** Arzumanyan (73)
Serbia: Tosic (90)

CARDS **Armenia:** Haroyan
Serbia: Nastasic Mitrovic

Matchday Three
October 14, 2014

Denmark....... (0) 0-1 (0) **........Portugal**
HOME 23-10 DRAW 23-10   AWAY 7-5
POS   58/42
SH ON   0/5
SH OFF   6/6
CRN   4/4

SCORERS **Portugal:** Ronaldo (90)

CARDS **Portugal:** Ronaldo

Serbia............. 0-3 **...........Albania**
HOME 8-15   DRAW 3-1   AWAY 7-1
Match abandoned (41 mins) at 0-0.
Albania awarded a 3-0 victory

CARDS **Serbia:** Ivanovic
Albania: Agolli

Matchday Four
November 14, 2014

Portugal ...... (0) 1-0 (0) **........Armenia**
HOME 2-9   DRAW 13-2   AWAY 16-1
POS   69/31
SH ON   5/6
SH OFF   13/3
CRN   7/2

SCORERS **Portugal:** Ronaldo (71)

CARDS **Portugal:** Carvalho Tiago Pepe Danny Carvalho
Armenia: Yedigaryan Arzumanyan

Serbia .... (1) 1-3 (0) **.......Denmark**
HOME 6-5   DRAW 11-5   AWAY 29-10
POS   39/61
SH ON   2/7
SH OFF   4/7
CRN   3/2

SCORERS **Serbia:** Tosic (4) **Denmark:** Bendtner (60, 85) Kjaer (62)

CARDS **Denmark:** Kvist
Krohn-Dehli Jacobsen

Matchday Five
March 29, 2015

Albania......... (0) 2-1 (1) **.........Armenia**
HOME 20-21 DRAW 12-5   AWAY 15-4
POS   64/36
SH ON   6/1
SH OFF   8/6
CRN   4/3

SCORERS **Albania:** Mavraj (77) Gashi (81) **Armenia:** Mavraj (4 og)

CARDS **Albania:** Cana Kukeli Cikalleshi **Armenia:** Pizzelli Hambardzumyan Arzumanyan

Portugal .... (1) 2-1 (0) **...........Serbia**
HOME 6-10   DRAW 3-1   AWAY 6-1
POS   55/45
SH ON   5/4
SH OFF   3/4
CRN   8/5

SCORERS **Portugal:** Carvalho (10) Coentrao (63) **Serbia:** Matic (61)

CARDS **Portugal:** Coentrao Moutinho **Serbia:** Matic Ljajic Kolarov Tosic Djuricic

Matchday Six
June 13, 2015

Armenia........ (1) 2-3 (1) **........Portugal**
HOME 15-2   DRAW 7-2   AWAY 1-2
POS   55/45
SH ON   4/4
SH OFF   5/2
CRN   3/6

SCORERS **Armenia:** Pizzelli (14) Mkoyan (71) **Portugal:** Ronaldo (pen 29, 55, 58)

CARDS **Armenia:** Hovsepyan
Portugal: Tiago Rui Patricio

Denmark....... (1) 2-0 (0) **........... Serbia**
HOME 5-4   DRAW 23-10 AWAY 13-5
POS   41/59
SH ON   6/3
SH OFF   3/5
CRN   3/5

SCORERS **Denmark:** Poulsen (13) Poulsen (87)

CARDS **Denmark:** Kjaer Kvist
Serbia: Kolarov

Matchday Seven
September 4, 2015

Denmark....... (0) 0-0 (0) **..........Albania**
HOME 7-10   DRAW 11-4   AWAY 11-2
POS   60/40
SH ON   4/2
SH OFF   9/3
CRN   9/2

CARDS **Denmark:** Jacobsen Kjaer **Albania:** Agolli Ajeti Kukeli Xhaka

Serbia .... (1) 2-0 (0) **.......Armenia**
HOME 4-9   DRAW 19-5   AWAY 15-2
POS   48/52
SH ON   5/3
SH OFF   8/4
CRN   6/8

SCORERS **Serbia:** Hayrapetyan (21 og) Ljajic (53)

CARDS **Serbia:** Ivanovic Mitrovic

Matchday Eight
September 7, 2015

Albania......... (0) 0-1 (0) **........Portugal**
HOME 5-1   DRAW 13-5   AWAY 8-11
POS   48/52
SH ON   0/5
SH OFF   4/10
CRN   4/5

SCORERS **Portugal:** Veloso (90)

CARDS **Albania:** Djimsiti Abrashi
Portugal: Nani

Armenia........ (0) 0-0 (0) **........Denmark**
HOME 18-5   DRAW 13-5   AWAY 19-20
POS   43/57
SH ON   3/2
SH OFF   6/6
CRN   3/8

CARDS **Armenia:** Ghazaryan Mkrtchyan Movsisyan
Denmark: Jorgensen

Albania........ **(0) 0-2 (0)**........... **Serbia**
HOME 15-8   DRAW 2-1   AWAY 19-10
POS   51/49
SH ON   5/2
SH OFF   4/5
CRN   5/2
SCORERS **Serbia:** Kolarov (90) Ljajic (90)
CARDS **Albania:** Cana ▌ Agolli ▌

Serbia: Milivojevic ▌ Tomovic ▌

Portugal ...... **(0) 1-0 (0)**........ **Denmark**
HOME 3-4   DRAW 11-4   AWAY 9-2
POS   51/49
SH ON   7/4
SH OFF   7/5
CRN   6/7
SCORERS **Portugal:** Moutinho (66)
CARDS **Portugal:** Rui Patricio ▌ Pereira ▌
Denmark: Hojbjerg ▌ Eriksen ▌ Wass ▌

Armenia........ **(0) 0-3 (2)**........... **Albania**
HOME 5-2   DRAW 23-10   AWAY 11-8
POS   62/38
SH ON   3/6
SH OFF   8/3
CRN   2/2
SCORERS **Albania:** Hovhannisyan (9
og) Djimsiti (23) Sadiku (76)
CARDS **Armenia:** Arzumanyan ▌
Yuspashyan ▌ Andonian ▌
Albania: Aliji ▌ Djimsiti ▌ Basha ▌

Serbia .... **(0) 1-2 (1)**........ **Portugal**
HOME 6-4   DRAW 9-4   AWAY 9-4
POS   60/40
SH ON   4/4
SH OFF   9/2
CRN   4/0
SCORERS **Serbia:** Tosic (65) **Portugal:**
Nani (5) Moutinho (78)
CARDS **Serbia:** Mitrovic ▌ Kolarov ▌▌
Tosic ▌ Matic ▌ **Portugal:**
Nelsinho ▌ Danny ▌ Nani ▌ Pereira ▌
Andre Andre ▌

GROUP I TOP SCORERS

	P	Goals	
C Ronaldo (Portugal)	6	5	●●●●●
Z Tosic (Serbia)	8	3	●●●

Players scoring three goals or more in this group

WORLD CUP 2018 EUROPEAN QUALIFYING DRAW

Group B Portugal, Switzerland, Hungary, Faroe Islands, Latvia, Andorra **Group D** Wales, Austria, Serbia, Ireland, Moldova, Georgia **Group E** Romania, Denmark, Poland, Montenegro, Armenia, Kazakhstan **Group G** Spain, Italy, Albania, Israel, Macedonia, Liechtenstein

Hosts Russia and nine group winners qualify. Eight best runners-up go to playoffs

PLAYOFFS

Norway......... **(0) 0-1 (1)**........ **Hungary**
HOME 20-21   DRAW 12-5   AWAY 15-4
POS   63/37
SH ON   5/4
SH OFF   10/2
CRN   16/0
SCORERS **Hungary:** Kleinheisler (26)
CARDS **Norway:** Tettey ▌ Elabdellaoui ▌
Hungary: Gera ▌ Kadar ▌ Guzmics ▌

November 13, 2015

Bosnia-Hz. ..... **(0) 1-1 (0)**........... **Ireland**
HOME 21-20   DRAW 12-5   AWAY 10-3
POS   62/38
SH ON   3/2
SH OFF   5/2
CRN   3/2
SCORERS **Bosnia-Hz.:** Dzeko (85)
Ireland: Brady (82)
CARDS **Ireland:** Ward ▌

November 14, 2015

Sweden......... **(1) 2-1 (0)**........ **Denmark**
HOME 7-5   DRAW 9-4   AWAY 5-2
POS   37/63
SH ON   4/2
SH OFF   6/7
CRN   5/5
SCORERS **Sweden:** Forsberg (45)
Ibrahimovic (pen 50) **Denmark:**
Jorgensen (80)
CARDS **Sweden:** Forsberg ▌
Denmark: Agger ▌

Ukraine......... **(1) 2-0 (0)**........ **Slovenia**
HOME 8-13   DRAW 11-4   AWAY 6-1
POS   55/45
SH ON   6/0
SH OFF   5/3
CRN   10/1
SCORERS **Ukraine:** Yarmolenko (22)
Seleznev (54)

TOP SCORERS IN THE PLAYOFFS

	P	Goals	
Z Ibrahimovic (Sweden)	2	3	●●●
J Walters (Ireland)	1	2	●●
A Yarmolenko (Ukraine)	2	2	●●

Players scoring two goals or more in the playoffs

THIRD-PLACED TEAMS

	Group	P	W	D	L	F	A	GD	Pts
Turkey	A	8	5	1	2	12	7	+5	16
Hungary	F	8	4	3	1	8	5	+3	15
Ukraine	C	8	4	1	3	11	4	+7	13
Norway	H	8	4	1	3	8	10	-2	13
Denmark	I	8	3	3	2	8	5	+3	12
Sweden	G	8	3	3	2	11	9	+2	12
Ireland	D	8	3	3	2	8	7	+1	12
Bosnia-Hz.	B	8	3	2	3	11	12	-1	11
Slovenia	E	8	3	1	4	10	11	-1	10

Results against sixth-placed teams in Groups A-H not included

CARDS **Ukraine:** Seleznev ▌
Khacheridi ▌ Rakitskiy ▌
Slovenia: Novakovic ▌ Krhin ▌

Hungary .... **(1) 2-1 (0)**........ **Norway**
Hungary won 3-1 on aggregate
HOME 9-5   DRAW 11-5   AWAY 15-8
POS   33/67
SH ON   5/5
SH OFF   4/5
CRN   4/9
SCORERS **Hungary:** Priskin (14)
Henriksen (83 og) **Norway:** Henriksen
(87)

CARDS **Hungary:** Nagy ▌ Bode ▌
Norway: Johansen ▌ Forren ▌

November 16, 2015

Ireland......... **(1) 2-0 (0)**.... **Bosnia-Hz.**
Ireland won 3-1 on aggregate
HOME 6-4   DRAW 11-5   AWAY 23-10
POS   31/69
SH ON   2/1
SH OFF   4/4
CRN   3/5
SCORERS **Ireland:** Walters (pen 24, 70)
CARDS **Ireland:** McClean ▌
Bosnia-Hz.: Spahic ▌ Lulic ▌
Zukanovic ▌ Dzeko ▌ Djuric ▌

November 17,2015

Denmark....... (0) 2-2 (1)..........Sweden
Sweden won 4-3 on aggregate

HOME 6-5   DRAW 5-2   AWAY 11-4
POS   61/39 ▰▰▰▰▰▰▰▰
SH ON   5/4 ▰▰▰▰▰▰
SH OFF   8/2 ▰▰▰▰▰▰
CRN   11/5 ▰▰▰▰▰▰▰

SCORERS **Denmark:** Poulsen (81)
Vestergaard (90) **Sweden:** Ibrahimovic
(19, 76)

CARDS **Denmark:** Durmisi ▮ Poulsen
▮ Hojbjerg ▮ **Sweden:** Bengtsson ▮
Larsson ▮

Slovenia....... (1) 1-1 (0)..........Ukraine
Ukraine won 3-1 on aggregate

POS   54/46 ▰▰▰▰▰▰▰▰
SH ON   5/7 ▰▰▰▰▰▰
SH OFF   2/4 ▰▰▰▰
CRN   6/3 ▰▰▰▰▰▰

SCORERS **Slovenia:** Cesar (10)
Ukraine: Yarmolenko (90)

CARDS **Slovenia:** Cesar ▮ Jokic ▮
Pecnik ▮ Lazarevic ▮ Brecko ▮
Ukraine: Konoplyanka ▮ Rybalka ▮

Ireland's players celebrate after booking their place in France

RECENT & SCHEDULED FRIENDLIES

November 13, 2015
Belgium......... (1) 3-1 (1).............. Italy
Czech Rep..... (1) 4-1 (0)........... Serbia
France........... (1) 2-0 (0)........ Germany
N Ireland ...... (0) 1-0 (0)............Latvia
Poland .... (0) 4-2 (1)............Iceland
Qatar .... (1) 1-2 (0)........... Turkey
Slovakia....... (1) 3-2 (0)... Switzerland
Spain .... (0) 2-0 (0)........ England
Wales........... (1) 2-3 (1).......... Holland
November 14, 2015
Russia.......... (0) 1-0 (0)........Portugal
November 17, 2015
Albania........ (0) 2-2 (1)........Georgia
Austria......... (1) 1-2 (2)... Switzerland
England .... (1) 2-0 (0)........ France
Italy .... (0) 2-2 (1)....... Romania
Luxembourg . (0) 0-2 (1)........Portugal
Poland .... (2) 3-1 (1).....Czech Rep
Russia.......... (1) 1-3 (0)..........Croatia
Slovakia....... (0) 3-1 (1)..........Iceland
Turkey.......... (1) 0-0 (0).......... Greece
January 6, 2016
Sweden......... (0) 1-1 (0)..........Estonia
January 10, 2016
Sweden......... (1) 3-0 (0)..........Finland
January 13, 2016
Iceland .... (1) 1-0 (0)..........Finland
January 16, 2016
UAE............... (0) 2-1 (0)..........Iceland
January 31, 2016
USA............... (1) 3-2 (1)..........Iceland
March 23, 2016
Croatia.......... (2) 2-0 (0)............Israel
Poland .... (1) 1-0 (0)........... Serbia
Romania........ (0) 1-0 (0)....... Lithuania
March 24, 2016
Czech Rep..... (0) 0-1 (1)....... Scotland
Denmark....... (0) 2-1 (0)..........Iceland

Italy .... (0) 1-1 (0)..............Spain
Turkey.......... (1) 2-1 (0)..........Sweden
Ukraine......... (1) 1-0 (0)............Cyprus
Wales........... (0) 1-1 (0).......N Ireland
March 25, 2016
Holland......... (0) 2-3 (2)........France
Ireland.......... (1) 1-0 (0)... Switzerland
Portugal .... (0) 0-1 (1).........Bulgaria
Slovakia........ (0) 0-0 (0)............Latvia
March 26, 2016
Austria.......... (2) 2-1 (0)........ Albania
Germany....... (1) 2-3 (0)........ England
Hungary........ (0) 1-1 (1)..........Croatia
Poland .... (3) 5-0 (0)............Finland
Russia........... (1) 3-0 (0)....... Lithuania
March 27, 2016
Romania........ (0) 0-0 (0)............Spain
March 28, 2016
N Ireland .... (1) 1-0 (0)........Slovenia
Ukraine......... (1) 1-0 (0)...........Wales
March 29, 2016
Austria.......... (1) 1-2 (1)........ Turkey
England .... (1) 1-2 (1).......... Holland
France............ (2) 4-2 (0)........ Russia
Germany....... (2) 4-1 (0)............ Italy
Greece .... (2) 2-3 (1).........Iceland
Ireland........... (2) 2-2 (2)........Slovakia
Luxembourg . (0) 0-2 (0).......... Albania
Portugal .... (2) 2-1 (0)........ Belgium
Sweden......... (1) 1-1 (1).....Czech Rep
Switzerland .. (0) 0-2 (1)..... Bosnia-Hz.
May 22, 2016
England ....v .... Turkey
May 26, 2016
Czech Rep............v .... Malta
May 27, 2016
N Ireland ....v ....Belarus
England...............v ....Australia
Ireland................v ....Holland

Slovakia...............v ....Georgia
May 28, 2016
Switzerland..........v .... Belgium
May 29, 2016
Germany...............v ....Slovakia
Spain ....v .... Bosnia-Hz.
Italy ....v .... Scotland
Portugal ....v ....Norway
May 30, 2016
Sweden...................v ....Slovenia
France.....................v ....Cameroon
May 31, 2016
Austria....................v .... Malta
Norway...................v ....Iceland
June 1, 2016
Belgium ....v ....Finland
Czech Rep.............v .... Russia
Poland ....v ....Holland
Spain ....v .... S Korea
June 2, 2016
England ....v ....Portugal
Romania ....v ....Georgia
June 3, 2016
Switzerland..........v .... Moldova
June 4, 2016
Germany...............v ....Hungary
Slovakia..................v ....N Ireland
Austria....................v ....Holland
France......................v .... Scotland
Serbia......................v .... Russia
June 5, 2016
Czech Rep..............v .... S Korea
Sweden....................v ....Wales
Belgium...................v ....Norway
June 6, 2016
Poland ....v .... Lithuania
Italy ....v ....Finland
June 7, 2016
Spain ....v ....Georgia
June 8, 2016
Portugal ....v ....Estonia

2015 EUROPEAN UNDER-21 CHAMPIONSHIP RESULTS

Group A	P	W	D	L	F	A	GD	Pts	Group B	P	W	D	L	F	A	GD	Pts
Denmark	3	2	0	1	4	4	0	6	Portugal	3	1	2	0	2	1	1	5
Germany	3	1	2	0	5	2	3	5	Sweden	3	1	1	1	3	3	0	4
Czech Rep	3	1	1	1	6	3	3	4	Italy	3	1	1	1	4	3	1	4
Serbia	3	0	1	2	1	7	-6	1	England	3	1	0	2	2	4	-2	3

Group A

June 17, 2015

Czech Rep..... (1) 1-2 (0)........Denmark
Germany....... (1) 1-1 (1)............Serbia

June 20, 2015

Czech Rep.... (2) 4-0 (0)............Serbia
Germany....... (1) 3-0 (0).......Denmark

June 23, 2015

Czech Rep..... (0) 1-1 (0).......Germany
Denmark....... (1) 2-0 (0)............Serbia

Group B

June 18, 2015

Italy.............. (1) 1-2 (0).........Sweden
England........ (0) 0-1 (0).........Portugal

June 21, 2015

Sweden........ (0) 0-0 (1)......... England
Italy.............. (0) 0-0 (0).......Portugal

June 24, 2015

England........ (0) 1-3 (2)............... Italy
Portugal .... (0) 1-1 (0).........Sweden

Semi-finals

June 27, 2015

Portugal .... (3) 5-0 (0).......Germany
Denmark....... (0) 1-4 (2).........Sweden

Final

June 30, 2015

Sweden........ (0) 0-0 (0).........Portugal
AET. Sweden won 4-3 on penalties

John Guidetti revels in Sweden's Under-21 Championship win

UNDER-21 CHAMPIONSHIP FINALS

	Hosts	Final
2013	Israel	Spain ....4-2 .... Italy
2011	Denmark	Spain ....2-0 . Switzerland
2009	Sweden	Germany.....4-0 ...... England
2007	Holland	Holland.......4-1 .... Serbia

UNDER-19 CHAMPIONSHIP FINALS

2015	Greece	Spain ....2-0 .... Russia
2014	Hungary	Germany.....1-0 ...... Portugal
2013	Lithuania	Serbia ....1-0 ....France
2012	Estonia	Spain ....1-0 .... Greece
2011	Romania	Spain ....3-2 ... Czech Rep
		AET. 1-1 after 90 minutes
2010	France	France.........2-1 .... Spain
2009	Ukraine	Ukraine.......2-0 ...... England
2008	Czech Rep	Germany.....3-1 .... Italy
2007	Austria	Spain ....1-0 .... Greece

UNDER-17 CHAMPIONSHIP FINALS

2015	Bulgaria	France.........4-1 .....Germany
2014	Malta	England ......1-1 ....Holland
		AET. England won 4-1 on penalties
2013	Slovakia	Russia ....0-0 .... Italy
		AET. Russia won 5-4 on penalties
2012	Slovenia	Holland.......1-1 .....Germany
		AET. Holland won 5-4 on penalties
2011	Serbia	Holland.......5-2 .....Germany
2010	Liechtenstein	England ......2-1 .... Spain
2009	Germany	Germany.....2-1 .aet Holland
		AET. 1-1 after 90 minutes
2008	Turkey	Spain ....4-0 ....France
2007	Belgium	Spain ....1-0 ...... England

CHAMPIONSHIP RECORDS BY TEAM

	Qualified	Wins	Runners-up
Albania	-		
Austria	1		
Belgium	4		●
Croatia	4		
Czech Rep	8	●	●
England	8		
France	9	●●	
Germany	11	●●●	●●●
Hungary	2		
Iceland	-		
Ireland	2		
Italy	8	●	●●
N Ireland	-		
Poland	2		
Portugal	6		●
Romania	4		
Russia	10	●	●●●
Slovakia	-		
Spain	9	●●●	●
Sweden	5		
Switzerland	3		
Turkey	3		
Ukraine	1		
Wales	-		

Championship records do not include Slovakia, Ukraine or Croatia competing as part of other nations

CORRECT SCORES & TOTAL GOALS

Scores	Groups	Quarters	Semis	Finals
1-0	23	3	-	2
2-0	18	3	-	-
2-1	23	2	2	-
3-0	10	1	1	-
3-1	4	-	-	-
3-2	7	1	1	-
4-0	1	-	-	1
4-1	4	-	-	-
4-2	1	1	-	-
4-3	1	-	-	-
0-0	8	6	4	-
1-1	15	2	2	2
2-2	2	-	-	-
3-3	2	-	-	-
4-4	-	-	-	-
Other	1	1	-	-

Goals	Groups	Quarters	Semis	Finals
<1.5	26%	45%	40%	40%
>1.5	74%	55%	60%	60%
<2.5	53%	70%	60%	80%
>2.5	47%	30%	40%	20%
<3.5	81%	85%	90%	80%
>3.5	19%	15%	10%	20%
<4.5	87%	85%	90%	100%
>4.5	13%	15%	10%	0%

Final tournaments since Euro 96. 90 minutes only

PENALTY SHOOTOUT RECORDS

	W	L		Win %
Czech Rep	3	0	███████████████████	100%
Belgium	1	0	███████████████████	100%
Turkey	1	0	███████████████████	100%
Ukraine	1	0	███████████████████	100%
Germany	5	1	████████████████	83%
Portugal	2	1	█████████████	67%
Spain	4	3	███████████	57%
France	3	3	██████████	50%
Ireland	1	1	██████████	50%
Sweden	1	1	██████████	50%
Italy	3	5	███████	38%
England	1	6	███	14%
Croatia	0	1		0%
Switzerland	0	1		0%
Romania	0	2		0%

All-time records. Table includes countries playing at Euro 2016 who have contested at least one penalty shootout at a previous European Championship or World Cup. Czech Republic's record includes matches played as Czechoslovakia, Germany's includes West Germany

TOP SCORERS IN QUALIFYING BY TEAM

	Goals	Player(s)
Albania	1	Balaj, Gashi, Lenjani, Mavraj, Sadiku, Xhimshiti
Austria	7	Janko
Belgium	5	De Bruyne, Hazard
Croatia	6	Perisic
Czech Rep	4	Dockal
England	7	Rooney
France	3	Benzema, Giroud, Griezmann
Germany	9	Muller
Hungary	2	Bode, Nemeth, Priskin
Iceland	6	Sigurdsson
Ireland	5	Keane, Walters
Italy	3	Pelle
N Ireland	7	Lafferty
Poland	13	Lewandowski
Portugal	5	Ronaldo
Romania	2	Budescu, Papp, Stancu
Russia	8	Dzyuba
Slovakia	5	Hamsik
Spain	5	Alcacer
Sweden	11	Ibrahimovic
Switzerland	4	Shaqiri
Turkey	4	Yilmaz
Ukraine	6	Yarmolenko
Wales	7	Bale

Includes France's record in centralised friendlies against teams in qualifying Group I and playoff games for Hungary, Ireland, Sweden and Ukraine